Chaucer's *Troilus*

Chaucer's *Troilus*

Essays in Criticism

edited by

STEPHEN A. BARNEY

Scolar Press: London

First published in the United States of America in 1980 by
The Shoe String Press, Inc.

This edition first published in Great Britain in 1980 by Scolar
Press, 90/91 Great Russell Street, London WC1B 3PY
Scolar Press is an imprint of Bemrose UK Limited

British Library Cataloguing in Publication Data

Chaucer's Troilus
  1. Chaucer, Geoffrey.   Troilus and Criseyde.
  —Addresses, essays, lectures
  I.   Barney, Stephen A.
  821'.1   PR1896
ISBN 0 85967 607 2

to
Marshall Hobart Barney
and
Mary Swett Barney

Contents

Preface

Gathering these articles I made no effort to span a period of years, to insure a variety of approach, or to represent a spectrum of opinion. Out of respect for Chaucer and concern for his students I have admitted only one principle of selection: to present the best essays on the *Troilus*. These are the essays I would urge the serious student to read first. The exceptions are of two kinds: each author is represented by one essay alone (Lewis or Bloomfield or Donaldson could have provided more), and selected pages on *Troilus* from longer works of sustained argument are not included here (I think of the books on Chaucer by Muscatine and Payne; Empson's essay is an exception to the exception). From the great volume of very good work done on Chaucer's masterpiece, these essays are remarkable, to me, for their particular intelligence and seriousness and care.

The essays are all printed in their entirety. The original pagination of reprinted essays is noted; the page number, between slashes, precedes the page it indicates. Several of the writers have provided for this anthology and "Afterward" which follows their essays. As indicated in the footnote on the first page of their articles, some authors have lightly revised their work; otherwise I have reproduced the originals even in matters of editorial form. Three of the essays—those by Barbara Newman, Karla Taylor, and Winthrop Wetherbee—are printed here for the first time.

"I n'am but a lewd compilator," and my own labor is almost completely absorbed in the labors I must acknowledge: I am very grateful to all the authors for their generosity in letting me publish these essays. Two of the authors are dead: George Lyman Kittredge and

C. S. Lewis. I think being joined in their great company can partly repay the kindness shown me by the living Chaucerians, whose work I am proud to display.

The little residue of my own labor I dedicate to my parents, wishing it were more, and happy knowing it doesn't matter how much.

New Haven
July, 1979

S.A.B.

Troilus
by George Lyman Kittredge

Chaucer is known to everybody as the prince of story-tellers, as incomparably the greatest of our narrative poets. Indeed, if we disregard the epic, which stands in a class by itself, I do not see why we should hesitate to call him the greatest of all narrative poets whatsoever, making no reservation of era or of language. His fame began in his own lifetime, and was not confined, even then, to the limits of his native country. It has constantly increased, both in area and in brilliancy, and was never so widespread or so splendid as at the present day. Besides, he is a popular poet, and this popularity—more significant than mere reputation—has grown steadily with the gradual extension of the reading habit to all sorts and conditions of men.

To most readers, however, Chaucer means only the Canterbury Tales; and even so, it is with but half-a-dozen of the pilgrims that they are intimately acquainted. This is manifest destiny, which it would be ridiculous to deplore: "What wol nat be, mot nede be left." Nor should we lament what Sir Thomas Browne calls /109/ "the iniquity of oblivion"; for oblivion has treated Chaucer generously. She has exempted enough of the poet's achievement to bring him popularity, which the conditions of his own time could neither afford nor promise, and she has spared besides, for such of us as care to read it, that masterpiece of psychological fiction

Reprinted from George Lyman Kittredge, *Chaucer and His Poetry* (Cambridge: Harvard University Press, 1915). The text here is drawn from the reissue (fifteenth printing), edited with an excellent account of Kittredge by B.J. Whiting, 1970. Reprinted by permission of the publishers. Copyright 1915 by George Lyman Kittredge; Copyright 1970 by the President and Fellows of Harvard College. The pagination of the chapter, pages 108 to 145 of the 1970 printing, is indicated between slashes.

1

> In which ye may the double sorwes here
> Of Troilus in lovynge of Criseyde,
> And how that she forsook hym er she deyde.

The Troilus is not merely, as William Rossetti styles it, the most beautiful long narrative poem in the English language: it is the first novel, in the modern sense, that ever was written in the world, and one of the best. Authorship is a strange art: it is nearest akin to magic, which deals with the incalculable. Chaucer sat down to compose a romance, as many a poet had done before him. The subject was to be love; the ethical and social system was to be that of chivalry; the source was the matter of Troy; the material was Italian and French and Latin. His readers were to be the knights and ladies of the court, to whom the fame of the hero as a lover and a warrior was already familiar. Psychology it was to contain, or what passed for psychology in the mediæval love-poets, the analysis of emotion in terms of Chrétien de Troyes and the Roman de la Rose. Yet the work was not, in /110/ Chaucer's intention, to be a romance precisely. He conceived it as what scholars then called a "tragedy,"—though with a somewhat peculiar modification of the standard term. Tragedies described the malice of Fortune when she casts down men of high estate and brings them to a miserable end. This was to be a tragedy of love, and the fall of the hero was to be from happy union with his lady to the woe and ruin of her unfaithfulness. And so Chaucer took his pen in hand, and drew his quire of paper to him, and wrote a prologue.

The magician has marked out his circle, and pronounced his spells, and summoned his spirits. He knows their names, and the formulas that will evoke them, and the task that he shall require them to perform. And lo! they come, and there are strange demons among them, and when the vision is finished and the enchanter lays down his wand, he finds on his desk—a romance, to be sure, which his pen has written; a tragedy, in the sense in which he knew the word; a love-tragedy, with a background of the matter of Troy, and thousands of lines from Boccaccio, with bits of Benoit and Guido delle Colonne, and a sonnet of Petrarch's, and a section out of Boethius, and a closing prayer to the Christian God. Everything is as he had planned it. But, when he reads it over, he finds that he has produced a /111/ new thing. Nothing like it was ever in the world before.

The Troilus is a long poem, extending to more than eight thousand verses, but the plot is so simple that it may be set forth in a dozen sentences.

Troilus, Priam's son, and second in valor to Hector only, is a scoffer at love and lovers. On a high holiday, as he strolls idly about the temple of Pallas, heart-free and glorying in his freedom, his eye falls upon Cressida, daughter of Calchas. Her father has fled to the Greeks, to escape the doom of Troy; but Cressida remains in the city. She is a widow, young, rich, and of surpassing beauty. Troilus falls madly in love, but fears to reveal his passion. Pandarus, Cressida's uncle and Troilus' friend, coaxes the secret from him, and helps him with all his might. Cressida yields, after long wooing, and the lovers see naught but happiness before them.

One day, however, during an exchange of prisoners, Calchas persuades the Greeks to offer Antenor for Cressida, whom he fears to leave in the city of destruction. To resist is impossible. The lovers are parted; but Cressida promises to return in ten days, feeling sure that she can cajole her aged father. Her woman's wiles are fruitless: she must remain in the Grecian camp, where Diomede pays court to her assiduously. /112/ He wins her at length, though not without her bitter grief at the thought of her unfaithfulness. Troilus is slain by Achilles.

This is the barest outline, but it suffices to show the simplicity of the story. The interest lies in the details, which are told with much particularity, and in the characterization, which is complex and subtle in a high degree. Readers who look for rapid movement and quick succession of incident, are puzzled and thwarted by the deliberation, the leisureliness, of the Troilus. The conversations are too long for them; they find the soliloquies languid; the analysis of sentiment and emotion and passion fails to keep their minds awake. But the Troilus is not a tale for a spare hour: it is an elaborate psychological novel, instinct with humor, and pathos, and passion, and human nature. Condensation would spoil it. Once yield to its charm, and you wish that it might go on forever.

Fate dominates in the Troilus. The suspense consists not in waiting for the unexpected, but in looking forward with a kind of terror for the moment of predicted doom. The catastrophe is announced at the outset: we are to hear of "the double sorrow of Troilus in loving Cressida, and how she forsook him at the last." Neither Troilus nor Cressida suspects what is to come; but we know all about it from the beginning. /113/ There is no escape for anybody. We are looking on at a tragedy that we are powerless to check or to avert.

Chaucer himself conveys the impression of telling the tale under a kind of duress. Not, of course, that there is any literal compulsion. It is rather that he is entangled, somehow, in the subject, and that, since he has begun, he is in duty bound to finish his task.

> Syn I have bigonne,
> Myn auctour shal I folwen, if I konne.*

There is no weariness, as in some of the tales in the Legend of Good Women. His interest in the matter is intense, and it never falters. But he feels the burden of the ruin that is to come. At times he even seems to struggle against the fate which has allotted him so sad a duty. He would change the tale if he could, but he must tell the truth, though it is almost more than he can bear. He would actually impugn the evidence if that were possible: —

> For how Criseyde Troilus forsook,
> Or at the leeste, how that she was unkynde,
> Moot hennesforth ben matere of my book,
> As writen folk thorugh which it is in mynde.
> Allas! that they sholde evere cause fynde
> To speke hire harm, and if they on hire lye,
> Iwis, hemself sholde han the vilanye.
>
> (iv. 15–26)

/114/ So mightily is he stirred by Cressida's grief that he would extenuate her guilt, or even excuse it altogether, for sheer pity. She has been punished enough; and, after all, she was only a weak woman, "tendre-herted, slydynge of corage."

> Ne me ne list this sely womman chyde
> Forther than the storye wol devyse.
> Hire name, allas! is punysshed so wide,
> That for hire gilt it oughte ynough suffise.
> And if I myghte excuse hire any wise,
> For she so sory was for hire untrouthe,
> Iwis, *I wolde excuse hire yet for routhe.*
>
> (v.1093–99)

*ii., 48–49; cf. i. 265–66, v. 1765–69.

This extraordinary outburst works powerfully upon our feelings. The case is hopeless. There is no excuse but destiny, and destiny, though irresistible, cannot be pleaded even in extenuation. Such is the law, and Chaucer bows to its everlasting antinomy, which, like Œdipus before him, he does not pretend to reconcile.

Everywhere in the poem we find this idea of a compelling destiny. It was Troilus' fate to love (i. 520); he rode by Cressida's palace on "his happy day," —

> For which, men seyn, may nought destourbed be
> That shal bityden of necessitee.
>
> (ii. 622-23)

"Swich is love," so Cressida moralizes, "and ek myn aventure" (ii. 742). The oak topples over when it /115/ receives "the fallyng strook" (ii. 1382). Troilus apostrophizes the Parcæ, who settled his life for him before he was born:—

> "O fatal sustren, which, er any cloth
> Me shapen was, my destine me sponne."
>
> (iii. 733-34)

"Pleasure comes and goes in love," says Pandarus, "as the chances fall in the dice" (iv. 1098-99). It was Fortune that cast Troilus down, "and on her wheel she set up Diomede," but Fortune is only the "executrix of weirds," and the influences of the stars govern us mortals as the herdsman drives his cattle: —

> But O Fortune, executrice of wyrdes,
> O influences of thise hevenes hye!
> Soth is, that under God ye ben oure hierdes,
> Though to us bestes ben the causes wrie.
>
> (iii. 617-20)

Most significant of all is the long meditation of Troilus on foreknowledge and freedom of the will in the Fourth Book (iv. 958ff.). This is from Boethius, and Chaucer has been as much blamed for inserting it as Shakspere for making Hector quote Aristotle. Doubtless the passage is inartistic and maladjusted; but it is certainly not, as some have called it, a digression. On the contrary, it is, in substance, as pertinent and opportune as any of Hamlet's soliloquies. The situation /116/ is well-imagined. Cressida is to be sent to the Grecian camp. Parliament has so decided, and resistance would be vain. Troilus, in despair, seeks the solitude of a temple, and prays to almighty and omniscient Jove either to help him or to let him die. Destiny, he feels, has overtaken him, for there seems to be no likelihood that Cressida, if once she joins her father, will ever return to Troy. What can he do but pray? Perhaps Jove will work a miracle to save him. And as he meditates, in perplexity and distress, his mind travels the weary maze of fate and free will, and finds no issue, unless in the god's omnipotence.

All this, no doubt, is un-Trojan; but that is a futile objection. We have already accepted Troilus as a mediæval knight and a mediæval lover, and we cannot take umbrage at his praying like a man of the middle ages, or arguing with himself in the mediæval manner. In details, to be sure, the passage is open to criticism, and it is undoubtedly too long; but in substance it is dramatically appropriate, and it is highly significant as a piece of exposition. For Troilus finds no comfort in his meditation. Whatever clerks may say, the upshot of the matter is that "al that comth, comth by necessitee." Whatever is foreknown, must come to pass, and cannot be avoided. /117/

> "And thus the bifallyng
> Of thynges that ben wist bifore the tyde,
> They mowe nat ben eschued on no syde."

The fate which darkens the loves of Troilus and Cressida is strangely intensified (in our apprehension of it) by the impending doom of Troy. This is no mere rhetorical analogue — no trick of symbolism. Their drama is an integral part of the great Trojan tragedy. They are caught in the wheels of that resistless mechanism which the gods have set in motion for the ruin of the Trojan race. This is a vital, determining fact in their history, as Chaucer understands it, and he leaves us in no doubt as to its intense significance. Calchas, we are told at the outset, deserted Priam because Apollo had revealed the doom of Troy: —

> For wel wiste he by sort that Troye sholde
> Destroyed ben, ye, wolde whoso nolde.

And again and again we are reminded, as the tale proceeds, of the inevitable outcome of the ten years' war. Troilus is smitten with love when he sees Cressida in the temple. It is the great festival of Palladion, a relic, Chaucer calls it, in Christian phrase, in which the Trojans put their trust above everything. They were celebrating "Palladion's feast," for they would not intermit their devout observances, although /118/ the Greeks had shut them in, "and hir cite biseged al aboute." When Pandarus finds his friend plunged in a lover's grief, despairing of ever winning the least favor from the lady he has seen in the temple, the gibe that he casts at him, — for the nonce, to anger him and arouse him from his stupor — is an accusation of cowardice: — "Fear, perhaps, has prompted you to pray and repent, as at the approach of death.

> "God save hem that biseged han oure town,
> That so kan leye oure jolite on presse,
> And bringe oure lusty folk to holynesse!"

When Pandarus first reveals to Cressida the secret of Troilus' love, he approaches the subject carefully, so as not to startle her. "I could tell you something," he cries, "that would make you lay aside your mourning." "Now, uncle dear," she answers, "tell it us, for love of God! Is the siege over, then? I am frightened to death of these Greeks."

> "As evere thrive I," quod this Pandarus,
> "Yet koude I telle a thyng to doon yow pleye."
> "Now, uncle deere," quod she, "telle it us
> For Goddes love; is than th'assege aweye?
> I am of Grekes so fered that I deye."

(ii. 120–24)

Cressida felt the first thrill in her heart when she saw Troilus riding through the street on his return /119/ from battle — his helm hewn to pieces, his shield pierced with Grecian arrows and cut and broken with the blows of swords and maces, — and the people were all shouting in triumph as he passed.

Always and everywhere we are oppressed by the coming doom of the city. This it is that prompts Calchas to beg the Greeks to give up their prisoner Antenor in exchange for Cressida. They need not hesitate, he argues; one Trojan captive more or less is nothing to them, — the whole city will soon be theirs. The time is near at hand

"That fire and flaumbe on al the town shal sprede,
And thus shal Troie torne to asshen dede."

(iv. 118–19)

And, when Hector opposes the exchange, the Trojan people, in a riotous parliament, shout out their unanimous vote in its favor, and carry the day. Hector was right, though he did not know it for he was acting, not from policy or superior foresight, but from an honorable scruple: Cressida was not a prisoner, he contended; and Trojans did not use to sell women. And the people were fatally wrong. The "cloud of error" hid their best interests from their discernment; for it was the treason of Antenor that brought about the final catastrophe. It is, then, /120/ the impendent doom of Troy that parts the lovers; and from this time forward, there is no separating their fate from the fate of the town.

When Cressida joins Calchas in the Grecian camp, she means to return in a few days. She has no doubt whatever that she can trick her father, and she has won Troilus over to her scheme. But she soon discovers that she has matched her woman's wit, not against her dotard father merely, but against the doom of Troy. No pretexts avail, not because Calchas suspects her plot, but because he knows that the city is destined to destruction. Nor does she dare to steal away by night, lest she fall into the hands of the savage soldiery. And finally, when Diomede wooes her, and gets a hearing, though little favor at first, his most powerful argument is the certain and speedy fate of Troy. He does not know that Cressida loves Troilus, — she tells him that she is heart-whole, but for her memory of her dead husband, — yet he cannot believe that so fair a lady has left no lover behind her, and he has seen her ever in sorrow. "Do not," he urges her, "spill a quarter of a tear for any Trojan; for, truly, it is not worth while. The folk of Troy are all in prison, as you may see for yourself, and not one of them shall come out alive for all the gold betwixen sun and sea!"

Thus, from first to last, the loves of Troilus /121/ and Cressida are bound up with the inexorable doom that hangs over the city. The fate of Troy is their fate. Their story begins in the temple of the Palladium; it is Calchas' foreknowledge and the people's infatuation that tear them asunder; it is the peril of the town that thwarts woman's wit, until Diomede subdues the inconstant heart. The tragedy of character grows out of the tragedy of situation.

Yet, after all, the Troilus is a tragedy of character—profoundly moving and profoundly ethical. We must study the characters, therefore,—

Troilus, Cressida, Pandarus.

There is little to be said of Boccaccio's Pandaro, and almost as little of his Griseida. Both are vivid and lifelike, but neither shows any subtlety in the delineation. Pandaro is young, careless, and loose in his morals. He appeals for his justification to the code of love, but only in a perfunctory way. Griseida is frankly amorous, and her procrastination is quite *pro forma:* it does not even amount to coquetry. Pandaro sees through her pretences, and has slight reason for treating them with respect. Troilo is hardly distinguishable from Pandaro, except in his misfortunes. Both are simply young men about town, with the easy principles of their class. If they changed places, we should not know the difference. The winning of Griseida /122/ takes time, but requires slight craft or cleverness. No man in his senses could expect her to be faithful.

Let us not minimize Chaucer's indebtedness to Boccaccio. It is very great, in gross and in detail. Without the Filostrato, the Troilus would never have existed. But the characterization is Chaucer's own.

Nothing can be more absurd than to describe Chaucer's Troilus as a "lovesick boy." On the contrary, he is a gallant warrior, second only to the unmatchable Hector in prowess. And he is wise withal, except in scoffing at the god of love. To have brought down such a victim with a single shaft is convincing evidence of the might of the god. "Take warning, all ye haughty gentlemen who think you are your own masters. Love can subdue you when he will. Wisdom is no protection against his assaults. History is full of examples":—

> Men reden nat that folk han gretter wit
> Than they that han be most with love ynome.

Troilus is jeering at lovers at the very moment when the god smites him: —

> "I have herd told, pardieux, of youre lyvynge,
> Ye loveres, and youre lewed observaunces,
> And which a labour folk han in wynnynge
> Of love, and in the kepyng which doutaunces;
> And whan youre prey is lost, woo and penaunces. /123/
> O veray fooles, nyce and blynde be ye!
> Ther nys nat oon kan war by other be."

> And with that word he gan caste up the browe,

Ascaunces, "Loo! is this naught wisely spoken?"
At which the God of Love gan loken rowe
Right for despit, and shop for to ben wroken.
He kidde anon his bowe nas naught broken;
For sodeynly he hitte hym atte fulle;
And yet as proud a pekok kan he pulle.

(i. 197–210)

Here Chaucer is in full conformity with the doctrines of the chivalric system, and we must accept the convention before we try to interpret the character of his hero. Nothing is more axiomatic, in this system, than the irresistible nature of love. The god is perfectly arbitrary. The will of a man has nothing to do with the matter. You can no more explain why one person falls in love with another than why this fish comes into the weir rather than that. Such is Chaucer's own expressive comparison (iii. 33–35).

The sufferings of Troilus are in complete accord with the mediæval system. Lovers were expected to weep and wail, and to take to their beds in despair. It was likewise an article of the code that they should be afraid to declare their passion. Humility was one of the cardinal virtues of the chivalric system. The lover must feel convinced of his unworthiness; he must regard /124/ it as inconceivable that his lady should stoop to such as he.

Now all these dogmas are merely expressions, in language different from ours, of facts that no one challenges when couched in modern terms. To ignore them is impossible; to translate them into our conventions would be unendurably prosaic. We must understand them in their fourteenth-century attire, or refrain from judging the words or the actions of Chaucer's *dramatis personae*. The convention is only the costume in which emotion attires itself, and fashions change. If Garrick were to come back, and play Macbeth once more in knee-breeches and a tie-wig, should we take the clothes for the character? We are preposterous when we laugh at a mediæval hero for his love-madness. One would fancy that we never read the newspapers, or that (like Chaucer in the House of Fame) we had no tidings from our very neighbors. Give me forty-eight hours, and I will translate every mediæval symptom into modern journalese, and my version shall keep step with the daily records.

Such madness, indeed, makes a definite category among the kinds of insanity described by the old physicians whom Chaucer specifies as the masters of his Doctor in the Canterbury Tales. It is what Burton calls "heroical love." /125/ The history of the term has very recently been traced by Professor Lowes in a masterly essay. It is the "lover's malady of Hereos" which the Knight mentions in his tale. There are two points at issue, the medical and the chivalric. What to the physician were symptoms—grief, pallor, sleeplessness, incessant unmotivated activity— became, in the chivalric system, duties—ideals of emotion which the true lover must live up to, and which the hypocrite takes pains to counterfeit.

Chaucer's mental attitude toward the whole phenomenon is at once sympathetic and ironical. He understood, for he was human, and human nature was, to him, the most interesting and moving subject in the world,—the only tangible thing, indeed, in a universe of mystery and thwarted endeavor. There is a God, who governs us, and to whom we must submit; but he is an object of faith. Human nature is the one thing that we can comprehend; and to comprehend, with Chaucer, was to sympathize, for he felt himself a part of all he saw. But Chaucer was also the supreme ironist, the kindly man of humor, with a touch of subtle melancholy which is essential in such a temperament. If we could imagine a being whose nature should be pure reason, how absurd we should all appear to him! "He that sitteth in the heavens shall laugh: /126/ the Lord shall have them in derision." But, even to a mortal with keen perceptions, the everlasting tangle of humanity, in its frenzied pursuit of the unattainable, its undying hope, uninstructed by experience, is a fit subject for humorous contemplation. Otherwise, what shall one do but despair and die?

Cressida is as lifelike as Boccaccio's heroine, but far more complex. Griseida is elemental: her emotions are simple and straightforward, and involve no problems. But Cressida is marvellously subtilized, baffling alike to us and to herself. Quite as amorous as her prototype, she is of a finer nature, and has depths of tender affection that no Griseida could fathom. Her love for Troilus begins in that vague feeling of interest, with a touch of sentiment, which is the natural reflex of his love for her. Then, at the moment of destiny, he rides by her window, returning from battle, with the scars of conflict on his shield and helmet, amid the shouts of the exultant throng:—

> His helm tohewen was in twenty places,
> That by a tyssew heng his bak byhynde;
> His sheeld todasshed was with swerdes and maces,
> In which men myght many an arwe fynde
> That thirled hadde horn and nerf and rynde;

> And ay the peple cryde, "Here cometh oure joye,
> And, next his brother, holder up of Troye!"
>
> (ii. 638–44)

/127/ Something stirs in her soul,—too indistinct for expression, even in thought. It is still sentiment, not passion; but it affects her strangely, so that she asks herself in gentle wonder, "Am I under a spell?"

> That to hireself she seyde, "Who yaf me drynke?"

Here Chaucer is very explicit, for he is determined not to be misunderstood. "This was no sudden passion," he protests. "I do not mean that she fell in love with Troilus all in a moment. What I say is, that she began to like him, and I have told you why; and thus, in time, and by faithful service, he won her love, but in no sudden way."

> Now myghte som envious jangle thus:
> "This was a sodeyn love; how myght it be
> That she so lightly loved Troilus,
> Right for the firste syghte, ye, parde?"
> Now whoso seith so, mote he nevere ythe!
> For every thyng, a gynnyng hath it nede
> Er al be wrought, withowten any drede.
>
> For I sey nought that she so sodeynly
> Yaf hym hire love, but that she gan enclyne
> To like hym first, and I have told yow whi;
> And after that, his manhood and his pyne
> Made love withinne hire herte for to myne,
> For which, by proces and by good servyse,
> He gat hire love, and in no sodeyn wyse.

Slowly, almost insensibly, under the sweet influences /128/ of the stars in their courses, sentiment develops into tender and passionate love. The passion is inconstant; it shifts from Troilus to Diomede: but the tenderness knows neither chance nor change.

This softness of affection is, in truth, the secret of Cressida's enduring charm. Troilus was never so dear as when she forsook him. "Men say," writes Chaucer, "that she gave her heart to Diomede, but I cannot tell. She was false, no doubt, for thus the record stands; but she grieved so piteously that I would excuse her sin, for very ruth, if that were possible!" She makes no defence at the bar of her conscience,—offers no plea in extenuation. Troilus is the truest lover woman ever had, and, in the very agony of her self-pity, looking forward to everlasting shame, she lauds his faithfulness, and vows to cherish his memory as long as she lives. Infinite is the pathos of her valediction:—

> But trewely, the storie telleth us,
> Ther made nevere woman moore wo
> Than she, whan that she falsed Troilus.
> She seyde, "Allas! for now is clene ago
> My name of trouthe in love, for everemo!
> For I have falsed oon the gentileste
> That evere was, and oon the worthieste!
>
> "Allas! of me, unto the worldes ende,
> Shal neyther ben ywriten nor ysonge /129/
> No good word, for thise bokes wol me shende.
> O, rolled shal I ben on many a tonge!
> Thorughout the world my belle shal be ronge!
> And wommen moost wol haten me of alle.
> Allas, that swich a cas me sholde falle!
>
> "Thei wol seyn, in as muche as in me is,
> I have hem don dishonour, weylayay!
> Al be I nat the first that dide amys,
> What helpeth that to don my blame awey?
> But syn I se ther is no bettre way,
> And that to late is now for me to rewe,
> To Diomede algate I wol be trewe.
>
> "But, Troilus, syn I no bettre may,
> And syn that thus departen ye and I,
> Yet prey I God, so yeve yow right good day,
> As for the gentileste, trewely,
> That evere I say, to serven feythfully,
> And best kan ay his lady honour kepe";—
> And with that word she brast anon to wepe.
>
> "And certes, yow ne haten shal I nevere;

And frendes love, that shal ye han of me,
And my good word, al sholde I lyven evere.
And, trewely, I wolde sory be
For to seen yow in adversitee;
And gilteles, I woot wel, I yow leve.
But *al shal passe;* and thus take I my leve."

                                                    (v. 1051–85)

Everything passes, mutability is the order of the world; and what is so deceitful as her own heart? Yet she cannot quite despair. She has youth and beauty, and Diomede is a gallant knight. To him, at all events, she will be constant! /130/

"But syn I se ther is no bettre way,
And that to late is now for me to rewe,
To Diomede algate I wol be trewe."

Critics are strangely at variance in their judgment of Cressida. The confusion results from a failure to grasp, or to remember, the principles of courtly love. Under this code, there was nothing wrong in Cressida's yielding to Troilus. That, indeed, was a meritorious action. Her sin consisted solely in her unfaithfulness, in forsaking him for Diomede. On this point there cannot be the slightest doubt. Courtly love, however it may be adorned with flowers of rhetoric, was not platonic. Its doctrines were never thought to be reconcilable with Christian ethics. It had its own morality, in which fidelity was the highest virtue, infidelity the most heinous of crimes. How far this code was a mere convention, and how far it was reduced to practice by the ladies and gentlemen of the middle ages, is a long and troublous debate, into which we need not enter. The system was, at the very least, sufficient basis for a novel; for it commanded a theoretical acceptance and was closely connected with habits of conversation and various social amusements. The moral Gower, who was undeniably religious, adopted the code for literary purposes in his Confessio Amantis, with no thought of incongruity. /131/

The theories of the chivalric code were known to Chaucer's readers, and they were immediately taken for granted on his announcement, in the proem to the First Book, that the Troilus is dedicated to love's servants. However correct their personal code of morals, they accepted the ethics of chivalric love for the purposes of this poem without demur, precisely as we in modern times accept the barbarous and outworn code of revenge when we read Hamlet. The lover must be violently affected by his passion. He must suffer torments and give way to bitter grief. Yet he should not utterly despair, for that would show lack of faith in the god. As for the lady, she should not scorn her suitor, but should regard his passion as entitling him to consideration. Her self-respect requires her to be distant, cold, and even cruel. She must not yield too easily; but if she finds her lover courteous, faithful, and discreet, she may properly return his love when he has proved his fitness for so great a reward.

These considerations clear up many difficulties. Chaucer's Cressida belonged to a social system which accepted the chivalric code. She knew its precepts well, and this knowledge is, so to speak, the background on which her thoughts and words and actions are all projected. She is not easily won, but her surrender is conscious /132/ and voluntary; for she is neither ignorant nor unsophisticated. The dialect of chivalric love is as familiar to her as it is to Pandarus, and she is never cajoled by her uncle's high-flying phrases. To regard her as an innocent girl, basely tricked by a perfidious go-between, is to misconceive both the situation and the *dramatis personae*. Pandarus uses plain language more than once, and even his wiles are transparent enough to one who understands the courtly doctrines. Cressida, though soft-hearted and of a pliant disposition, is an uncommonly clever woman, and she is mistress of her own actions. Certainly she is in no sense the victim of a plot. When Pandarus invites her to pay him a visit, she asks, in a whisper, "if Troilus is there" (iii. 569). Pandar lies, of course, but it is perfectly clear that she does not believe his protestations. And later, to clinch the matter, we have her answer to Troilus: "Dear heart, if I had not yielded long ago, I should not now be here."

> "Ne hadde I er now, my swete herte deere,
> Ben yold, ywis, I were now nought heere!"
>
> (iii. 1210–11)

She glories in her love, and her happiness is unclouded by regret. Shame and repentance would have been unintelligible terms. She has acted in obedience to her own code, and our ethical system has no status in the case. /133/

Cressida, then, is not a victim, as some have thought. Just as little is she, as others hold, a scheming adventuress. This view of her character is, indeed, so patently erroneous as to need no refutation. True, she keeps her eyes open, and takes no leaps in the dark. She has also the excellent mental habit of looking at a subject or a proposition from several points of view. Finally, she is a lively conversationalist, the best company in the world. These are good traits, however, and, combined as they are with a tender and affectionate heart, an emotional nature, and a certain timidity in the face of possible danger, they vastly increase her feminine charm. It is ridiculous to accuse her of insincerity in her love for Troilus. To be sincere, it is not necessary to be either solemn or stupid. The allegation that she encourages Troilus because he is a prince, and with a view to securing his protection,—in a word, from selfish regard to her personal interests—rests upon a strange misunderstanding. When she turns her mind to these conditions of his rank and her own precarious position as the daughter of a traitor, she is merely seeking to justify to her reason the interest she is beginning to feel in her gallant lover,—for she knows full well that it may ripen into love. The subterfuges by which, at a later time, she expects to /134/ induce her father to assent to her return, are simply pathetic in their futility. They serve the double purpose of proving her love for Troilus, since Chaucer says they were well meant, and of displaying the weakness of a woman's wit (or a man's either, for that matter) when it sets itself up in opposition to the decree of the gods.

Still another interpretation of Cressida's character finds that it deteriorates suddenly in the latter part of the poem, and explains this change either as the logical result of sin, or as the unsteadiness of Chaucer's portraying hand.

To all this, the answer is a flat denial, both general and specific. First, there has been no sin—that is, no sin against the god of love, whose commandments alone are the ethics here applicable. Let us test this judgment by an hypothetical case. Suppose Cressida had assented to Troilus' plan to resist the parliament's decree and had been slain in the insurrection. Why she would have been love's martyr,—she would have won a place in the Legend of Cupid's Saints! Sin begins when she wavers in fidelity, when she lends an ear to the wooing of "this sudden Diomede." And secondly, there is no deterioration; or, to take the other point of view, there is neither inconsistency nor unsteadiness in Chaucer's portrayal of his /135/ heroine. As Cressida is at the beginning, such is she to the end; amorous, gentle, affectionate, and charming altogether, but fatally impressionable and yielding. Her strength of will is no match for her inconstant heart. "Tendre-herted," Chaucer calls her, "slydynge of corage." The Filostrato is the tragedy of Troilus; Chaucer has made it the tragedy of Cressida also—this "sely woman," who could not withstand her nature, but who was so sorry for her untruth that he would forgive her if he could. The record stands, punishment must follow; but there shall be no rebuking words from the judge who passes sentence.

> Ne me ne list this sely womman chyde
> Forther than the storye wol devyse.

Cressida is not a simple character, like the elemental Griseida of Boccaccio; but her inconsistencies are those of human nature. There is one Cressida, not two; or rather, there are two in one,—not a type, but an individual, unified by the interplay of her very contradictions.

This effect of complex unity in Cressida's character is heightened, with extraordinary subtlety, by a trait which I almost fear to touch, lest I blur its delicate clearness with a critic's clumsy finger. It is the trait of religious skepticism. Her father is Apollo's priest, but she has scant reverence for his sacred office, and little faith /136/in the revelations that the deity vouchsafes. Oracles, she protests, are ambiguous always; the gods speak ever in crafty double meanings, telling twenty lies for one truth. Perhaps, indeed, there are no gods at all, save those that shape themselves in the dark corners of man's timid soul. "Primus in orbe deos fecit timor."

> "Eke drede fond first goddes, I suppose."
>
> (iv. 1408)

I am very anxious not to be misunderstood. This is doubt, not dogma. Cressida is fighting with fate, not laying down the law. Torn from her lover by external forces that she cannot resist, she swears to return, in vows that "shake the throned gods," but it is not to the gods that she trusts in her exigency. A woman's wit is to be wiser than the powers that govern the world.

It is a very pregnant manifestation of Chaucer's feeling for the irony of life and circumstance when he makes Pandarus the exponent of chivalric love. Here we must walk circumspectly. Before attempting analysis of character, we should determine externals; for it is as easy to get Pandarus wrong as to misconceive the position of Polonius in the Danish state.

Pandarus is a Trojan nobleman, next in rank, it appears, to princes of the blood and on intimate terms with the whole royal family. He /137/ is the head of a powerful clan, which he offers to rally to Troilus' assistance in preventing the exchange of Cressida for Antenor.

Boccaccio's Pandaro is a young gallant, and a cousin of Cressida's; Chaucer's Pandarus is her uncle, and considerably older than Troilus. The change is, of course, deliberate, and by its means Chaucer is enabled to raise his Pandar from a typical, though lifelike, figure to one of the most remarkable of all comedy characters. We must take care, however, not to exaggerate the difference in age between the friends; for Troilus is not a boy, and middle age in the fourteenth century was ten years younger than it is to-day. It will never do, with William Rossetti, to call Pandar a "battered man of the world." He likes to talk, and with good reason, for he is the very demon of expressiveness. He has wit at will and humor inextinguishable. Mankind has been his study; life is his delightful privilege. His conversation is full of point and spirit, shifting continually from grave to gay, from game to earnest, easy, graceful, alert, never flagging, always at the highest tension, but with no sense of strain. Man of the world he is, assuredly, but the world has not "battered" him. He is gallant and high-spirited, himself a lover and a servant of the god with all his heart. He might even be a sentimentalist, if he were not /138/ a humorist and a man of action. He is never more sincere than when he jests most recklessly. There is nothing cynical about him, except at times the turn of his epigrams.

This Pandarus, the arch-humorist, who preaches of the duties and the rewards of lovers like a devotee, has had no luck in his own affair. He has paid court for years to an obdurate lady, and his notorious sufferings have made him the laughingstock of his friends. Yet, depite his own miserable failure, he is radiant with optimism. "Many a man has served his lady for twenty years without so much as a kiss. Ought he, therefore, to fall into despair, or to abandon his allegiance to the god? No, no! He should rejoice that he can serve the dear queen of his heart, and he should count it a guerdon merely to serve her, a thousandfold greater than he deserves!"

> "Thow mayst allone here wepe and crye and knele,—
> But love a womman that she woot it nought,
> And she wol quyte it that thow shalt nat fele;
> Unknowe, unkist, and lost, that is unsought.
> What! many a man hath love ful deere ybought
> Twenty wynter that his lady wiste,
> That nevere yet his lady mouth he kiste.
>
> "What? sholde he therefore fallen in dispayr,
> Or be recreant for his owne tene,

Or slen hymself, al be his lady fair?
Nay, nay, but evere in oon be fressh and grene /139/
To serve and love his deere hertes queene,
And thynk it is a guerdon, hire to serve,
A thousand fold moore than he kan deserve."

(i. 806–19)

Pandarus bears his affliction with a jaunty air; "a jolly woe" he calls it, "a pleasant sorrow"; and he never takes offence at jests. "Good morning, uncle," says Cressida roguishly, "how far have you come forward in the dance of love?" "By Jove!" he cries, catching up the trope, "I always go hopping along in the rear; I cannot keep up with the other dancers!" We must not refuse, however, to take his passion seriously. Chaucer saw the danger, and he has put the facts beyond the reach of doubt (ii. 50–70).

Pandarus has the distinctive quality of the pure humorist: he perceives the true comic element in himself, that is, in his own standing toward his character and environment, his theories and his acts. He has the gift to see himself, not, perhaps, as others see him, but as they might see him if they were Pandarus; and he is, therefore, the object of his own sympathetic amusement. Thus he is a rare but perfectly human compound of enthusiasm and critical acumen. To take him for a cynic is a pretty flagrant piece of critical aberration.

Pandarus is Troilus' friend and Cressida's uncle. This double relation is the sum and substance /140/ of his tragedy, for it involves him in an action that sullies his honor to no purpose. Since Cressida is faithless, he not only labors in vain, but ruins his friend by the very success that his plans achieve. This humorous worldly enthusiast has two ideals, friendship and faith in love. To friendship he sacrifices his honor, only, it seems, to make possible the tragic infidelity of Cressida, which destroys his friend. The system of courtly love had neither comfort nor excuse for Pandarus. Though Cressida's love for Troilus was blameless, or even meritorious, under the code, yet that same code, in its inconsistency, held no justification for the go-between. And, after all, Cressida is not persuaded by Pandarus, but by her own temperament. She reads her uncle easily, and acts as she will, no matter what he may say. Herein consists the subtlest of all the ironies in this amazing document. "The fly sat on the chariot wheel, and cried, 'What a dust do I raise!' "

Pandarus is Troilus' friend. The middle ages liked to exemplify virtues and vices to the last gasp, as in the case of Griselda's patience, even if the conflict of duties was ignored. Pandarus, however, is too individual and

lifelike to take sanctuary in a parable, though his conduct might well
entitle him to some such refuge. It was an old theory, which Lælius
repudiated /141/ with horror, that friendly devotion should know
neither limit nor scruple:—*si voluisset, paruissem*. There was some excuse
for this view in the middle ages, when men changed sides with a light
heart and personal loyalty was much needed as a steadying element in
politics and society. In Pandarus, no doubt, the ideal has gone astray in
the application, but there is something pathetic in the intensity with
which he errs. It is, in truth, the monomania of personal devotion, and
that too on the part of a humorous ironist, who cherishes few illusions. "I
have," he declares, "in true or false report, in wrong and right, loved thee
all my life." One should remember, too, that he feared Troilus would die
or go mad, and that the experience of every day proves that his fear,
though we scoff at it as a literary convention, was by no means
unreasonable. In his desperate fidelity to his passion of friendship,
Pandarus cares nothing for himself. "Resist the king and the
parliament," he cries, "and carry Cressida off in spite of their teeth. I will
stand by you, though I and all my kindred shall be slain and lie dead, like
dogs, in the street!"

> "I wol myself ben with the at this dede,
> Theigh ich and al my kyn, upon a stownde,
> Shulle in a strete as dogges liggen dede,
> Thorugh-girt with many a wid and blody wownde."
>
> (iv. 624–27)

/142/ This is not rhetoric; it is stark realism. Chaucer and all of his
readers had seen slain men lying in the street like dead dogs.

From the beginning, the Troilus professes to be a poem in praise of the
God of Love and in celebration of his wondrous powers. Chaucer is, so he
avers, a mere outsider in such things; but he is the *servus servorum* of the
divinity, and he hopes that his work may be of some use to Love's faithful
disciples.

Troilus is a scoffer at first. He calls the devotees of the courtly system
"fools," and the god of love "St. Idiot, the lord of fools." "Your order is
well-ruled;" he cries in contempt, "you get not good for good; but scorn
for faithful service." Later he becomes a convert to love's religion, and
the great exemplar to all who worship the god. Cressida, at the very
moment of renouncing him, calls him the most faithful of lovers; and "as
true as Troilus" was a proverb for hundreds of years.

But, as we read on, we become aware that something is amiss. For there are no happy lovers in the story. Pandarus himself is a sufferer from unrequited affection ; Œnone has been abandoned by Paris; Helen has brought the city to the edge of the abyss; Cressida is false to Troilus, and Diomede, we forsee, will scarcely be true to her. /143/

The tone does not change. The faithful devotion of Troilus is represented as the highest of virtues, and the treason of Cressida as the most heinous of crimes, still from the point of view of the chivalric code. Yet we come more and more to suspect that Troilus was right in his first opinion; that the principles of the code are somehow unsound; that the god of love is not a master whom his servants can trust. And then, suddenly, at the end of the poem, when the death of Troilus has been chronicled, and his soul has taken its flight to the seventh sphere, the great sympathetic ironist drops his mask, and we find that he has once more been studying human life from the point of view of a ruling passion, and that he has no solution except to repudiate the unmoral and unsocial system which he has pretended to uphold.

"Such was the end of Troilus, despite his honor and his royal estate. Thus began his loving of Cressida, and in this wise he died at the hands of Achilles. O ye young men and maidens, in whom love grows with your growth, and strengthens with your strength, leave the vanity of the world and cast up the visage of your hearts to God! Set your love upon Christ, who died for love of you, for I dare well assure you that he will never betray the heart that trusts him." /144/

> Swich fyn hath, lo, this Troilus for love!
> Swich fyn hath al his grete worthynesse!
> Swich fyn hath his estat real above,
> Swich fyn his lust, swich fyn hath his noblesse!
> Swich fyn hath false worldes brotelnesse!
> And thus bigan his lovyng of Criseyde,
> As I have told, and in this wise he deyde.
>
> O yonge, fresshe folkes, he or she,
> In which that love up groweth with youre age,
> Repeyreth hom fro worldly vanyte,
> And of youre herte up casteth the visage
> To thilke God that after his ymage
> Yow made, and thynketh al nys but a faire
> This world, that passeth soone as floures faire.

And loveth hym, the which that right for love
Upon a crois, oure soules for to beye,
First starf, and roos, and sit in heven above;
For he nyl falsen no wight, dar I seye,
That wol his herte al holly on hym leye.
And syn he best to love is, and most meke,
What nedeth feynede loves for to seke?

(v. 1828–48)

This manifestly involves an utter abandonment of the attitude so long
sustained, and therein lies its irresistible appeal. The Troilus is not milk
for babes; but it is a great work of art, and as such, I believe, inevitably
ethical. It is our own fault, not Chaucer's, if we miss the application.

Yet, even after this parting, moving as it is, and sincerely expressive of
the poet's nature, /145/ Chaucer cannot say farewell without turning his
irony upon himself.

Lo here, of payens corsed olde rites,
Lo here, what alle hire goddes may availle;
Lo here, thise wrecched worldes appetites;
Lo here, the fyn and guerdoun for travaille
Of Jove, Appollo, of Mars, of swich rascaille!
Lo here, the forme of olde clerkis speche
In poetrie, if ye hire bokes seche.

Who am I, that I should exhort you to turn aside from the follies of love
and the vanities of human endeavor? A mere student, poring over my
ancient books and repeating, as so many have done before me, the
wonderful and transitory things that they record; a versifier, humbly
tracing the footsteps of Virgil, and Ovid, and Homer, and Lucan, and
Statius:—

Lo here, the forme of olde clerkis speche
In poetrie, if ye hire bokes seche.

And so the Troilus closes, with a dedication to Strode and Gower and a
prayer to the Triune God: —

Thow oon, and two, and thre, eterne on lyve,
That regnest ay in thre, and two, and oon,

Uncircumscript, and al maist circumscrive,
Us from visible and invisible foon
Defende, and to thy mercy, everichon,
So make us, Jesus, for thi mercy digne,
For love of mayde and moder thyn benigne.

(On the "Troilus") From "Seven Types of Ambiguity"
by William Empson

One is tempted to think of these effects as belonging to the later stages of Renaissance refinement, as something oversophisticated in the manner of Caroline shape–poems, and due to a peculiar clotting of the imagination. It is worth while then to /58/ produce examples from *Troilus and Criseyde*, as one of the most leisurely, simplest as to imagery, and earliest poems in English literature. In the first love scene between the two, Criseyde says petulantly she doesn't know what she's expected to say; what does he mean, now, in plain words?

> What that I mene, O swete herte dere?
> Quod Troilus. O goodly fresshe free,
> That with the stremes of your eyen clere
> You wolde frendly sometimes on me see;
> And then agreen that I may be he. . . .
>
> (iii. 128.)

and so on for three verses, an enthusiastic and moving statement of the chivalric evasion of the point at issue. *Stremes* has the straightforward meaning of 'beams of light' *(Compleynte unto Pite, line 94)*. The N.E.D. does not give this meaning, but shows *stremes* as already a hyperbolical commonplace use for blood and tears, or 'beams of sweet influence,' like

From Chapter II ("second-type ambiguities") of William Empson, *Seven Types of Ambiguity* (London: Chatto and Windus, 1930). All British Commonwealth and Canadian rights reserved to Chatto and Windus Ltd; all U.S. rights reserved to New Directions Publishing Corporation, New York. Reprinted from pages 57–68 of the New Directions edition (1966) by permission of New Directions, Chatto and Windus, and the author. Footnotes are renumbered in one series. The pagination of the New Directions edition is noted between slashes.

those of the Pleiades. Thus after *fresh* and *free*, there is some implication
of a stream (Naiads) that he can drink of and wash in, cleansing and
refreshing, so that one glance of her eyes recovers him as by crossing a
stream you break the spells of black magic, or the scent by which the
hounds of your enemies are tracking you down; and the ready tears of her
sympathy are implied faintly, as in the background.

At the climax of the great scene in the second book, when Pandarus has
got his ward alone to talk to her about her money affairs, mysteriously
congratulated her on her good luck, and gradually led her through the
merits of Troilus to an appeal to her pity for his unhappiness, Cressida
seems suddenly to guess his meaning and makes a great display of
outraged virtue. One must not suppose, of course, because Chaucer
shows us her machinery — 'I shal fele what he meneth, I-wis'—'It nedeth
me ful sleyly for to pleye'—that we are not to believe in the reality of the
virtue, or that it is not the modest and proper machinery.

> What? Is this al the joye and al the feste?
> Is this your reed, is this my blisful cas?
> Is this the verray mede of your biheste?
> Is al this peynted proces seyd, alas,
> Right for this fyn?

> (ii. 421.)

/59/ The last three lines, I submit, are extremely Shakespearean; they
have all the concentrated imagery, the bright central metaphor steeped
and thickened in irrelevant incidental metaphors, of his mature style. I
thought at first the meanings might have been quite simple in Chaucer's
English, and have acquired a patina of subtlety in the course of time; it
would have been fun to maintain that Shakespeare learnt his style from a
misunderstanding of Chaucer; but the N.E.D. leaves no doubt that
(whether Shakespeare was influenced by it or not) time has faded rather
than enriched the original ambiguity.

Reed, of course, is advice; he had told her her *cas* was *blisful*, to have
caught the eye of the prince; *mede* meant at that time wages, a bribe,
merit, a meadow and a drink made with honey; *biheste* meant a vow, a
promise, and a command; *proces* meant a series of actions, the course of a
narrative, proceedings in an action at law, and a procession; and *fyn*
meant generally 'end,' with accepted derivatives like the object of an
action, death, and a contract; by itself it would not suggest a money
penalty before 1500, but it might suggest 'money offered in the hope of

exemption.' Thus the materials are ample enough, but this is not to say they were all used.

I shall pause to illustrate the force of *beheste* and the harangue of Pandarus that has gone before:

> Now understand, that I yow nought requere
> To binde ye to him thorough no beheste,
> But only that yew make him bettre chere,
> Than ye had don er this, and more feste,
> So that his life be saved, at the leste.

Either 'I do not ask it, as a *command* from your guardian, that you should bind yourself to him (permanently or sinfully),' or 'I do not ask you to bind yourself to him with anything so definite as a *vow*.'

> Think eke, how elde wasteth every houre
> In eche of yow a party of beautee;
> And therefore, er that age thee devoure,
> Go love, for olde, ther wol no wight of thee.
> Lat this proverbe a lore unto yow be;
> 'To late y-war, quod Beautee, whan it paste';
> And elde daunteth daunger at the laste.

/60/ It is not at first plain why there is so much power of song in the poetical commonplace of the first four lines; why its plainest statement seems to imply a lyric; so that the modern reader feels the pre-Raphaelites in it, and Chaucer felt in it his Italians (*Filostrato*, ii. 54). A statement of the limitations of human life is a sort of recipe for producing humility, concentration, and sincerity in the reader; it soothes, for instance, jealousy, makes the labours of the practical world less pressing because less likely to make any real difference (games have the same mode of approach); sets the mind free, therefore, to be operated on by the beauty of the verse without distraction; and makes you willing to adopt, perhaps to some slight extent permanently, the point of view of the poet or of the character described, because, having viewed your limits, marked your boat's position with regard to distant objects on the shore, you are able without losing your bearings to be turned round or moved to another part of the bay.

Further, to think of human life in terms of its lowest factors, considered as in themselves dignified, has a curious effect in dignifying the individual concerned; makes him a type, and so something larger and more significant than before; makes his dignity feel safer, since he is sure he has at least these qualifications for it; makes him feel accepted and approved of by his herd, in that he is being humble and understanding their situation (poor creatures); makes it seem likely, since he understands their situation, because he feels it in himself, that they will return to him also this reserved and detached sympathy; makes him, indeed, feel grander than the rest of his herd, for a new series of reasons; because by thinking of them he has got outside them; because by forming a concept of them he has made them seem limited; because he has thereby come to seem less subject to the melancholy truths he is recognising; because to recognise melancholy truths is itself, if you can be protected somehow, an invigorating activity; and (so that we complete the circle back to humility) because to think about these common factors has a certain solidity and safety in that it is itself, after all, one of the relevant common factors of the human mind.

However, it is the mode of action of the last two lines which is my immediate business. *Y-war* may mean prudent or experienced; /61/ *too late,* 'Then first when too late,' or 'going on until too late.' 'First prudent when too late'—I have found that one should be careful to avoid risks, perhaps such as that of never getting a lover, but, more strongly, such as are involved in unlawful satisfactions. 'First conscious when too late'—I have found too late that one should be determined to obtain satisfaction. 'Having been prudent until too late'—I have found that one can wait too long for the safest moment for one's pleasures. 'Having been conscious till too late'—I have found that one can seek one's pleasure once too often. Pandarus, of course, only meant the second and third; Chaucer (it is shown not as irony but as a grand overtone of melancholy) meant all four. (This, by the way, is the fourth type of ambiguity, but I am taking the whole passage together.)[1]

And elde daunteth daunger at the last.

Daunt means subdue or frighten; *daunger* at this time had a wealth of meaning that it has since lost, such as disdain, imperiousness, liability, miserliness, and power. 'Old age will break your pride, will make you afraid of the independence you are now prizing; the coming of old age is stronger than the greatness of kings, stronger than all the brutal powers that you are now afraid of, stronger even than the stubborn passion of misers that defeat it for so long; you must act now because when you are old you will be afraid to take risks, and you may take heart because, however badly you are caught, it will be all the same after another century; even in your own lifetime, by the time you are an old woman you will have lived down scandal.' Or taking *elde* as an old woman, not as the age that defeats her, the phrase interacts with the passing of beauty, whether after a life of sin or of seclusion (there appear to have been no alternatives) in the preceding line, and the old hag is finally so ugly that all the powers in *daunger* shrink away from the gloom of her grandeur, are either lost to her or subdued to her, and the amorous risks and adventures will be at last afraid to come near. /62/

The line is a straightforward ambiguity of the second type, and I hope the reader will not object that I have been making up a poem of my own. Mr. Eliot somewhere says that is always done by bad critics who have failed to be poets; this is a valuable weapon but a dangerously superficial maxim, because it obscures the main crux about poetry, that being an essentially suggestive act it can only take effect if the impulses (and to some extent the experiences) are already there to be called forth; that the process of getting to understand a poet is precisely that of constructing his poems in one's own mind. Of course, it is wrong to construct the wrong poem, and I have no doubt Mr. Eliot was right in his particular accusations.

> Is this the verray mede of youre beheste?
> Is this your reed, is this my blisful cas?

replies Cressida, to these ambiguities of Pandarus: 'Is this the wage that is offered to me in return for obeying your commands? Is this my inducement to be a good ward, that I must continually have the trouble, and pain to think you so wicked, of repelling solicitations? Is this what your advice is worth? Is this what your promise to look after me is worth?' The honest meaning (wage) carries contempt; the dishonest meaning (bribe) an accusation. 'Is this why the prince has been so friendly with you? Is this what you stand to make out of being my guardian?' And if *mede* carries any echo of meaning (it is impossible at this distance of time to say) from the natural freedom of the open meadow, or the simple delightfulness of that form of beer, we have, 'Is this the meadow, or the beer, you had promised me, or proposed for yourself? Is this my blissful case you have described?' It is the two meanings of *beheste* which give her so powerful a weapon against Pandarus, in his double position of guardian and go-between.

> Is al this peynted proces seyd, alas,
> Right for this fyn?

These two lines have a lesser but a more beautiful complexity; Pandarus' great harangue is seen, by using the puns on *fyn* and *process,* as a brightly coloured procession (*peynted* would suggest frescoes in churches) moving on, leading her on, to dusty death /63/ and the everlasting bonfire; and behind this simple framework, that gives the movement, the immediate point, of the phrase, *process* hints at a parallel with legal proceedings, ending where none of the parties wanted, when at last the lawyers, like Pandarus, stop talking and demand to be paid; and rising behind that again, heard in the indignation of the phrase, is a threat that she may expose him, and *peyn*-ted and *fyn* suggest legal pains and penalties.

'To whom do they suggest these things?' the reader may ask; and there is no obvious reply. It depends how carefully the passage is supposed to be read; in a long narrative poem the stress on particular phrases must be slight, most of the lines do not expect more attention than you would give to phrases of a novel when reading it aloud; you would not look for the same concentration of imagery as in a lyric. On the other hand, a long poem accumulates imagery; I am dealing with a particularly dramatic point where the meaning needs to be concentrated; and Chaucer had abandoned his original for a moment to write on his own.

It is a more crucial question how far *peynted,* in a proper setting, can suggest 'pains'; how far we ought to leave the comparatively safe ground of ambiguity to examine latent puns. The rule in general, I believe, is that a mere similarity of sound will not take effect unless it is consciously noticed, and will then give an impression of oddity. For it is the essential discipline of language that our elaborate reactions to a word are called out only by the word itself, or what is guessed to be the word itself; they are trained to be very completely inhibited by anything near the word but not quite right. It is only when a word has been passed in, accepted as sensible, that it is allowed to echo about in the mind. On the other hand, this very inhibition (the *effort* of distinction, in cases where it would have been natural to have taken the other word) may call forth effects of its own; that, for instance, is why puns are funny; may make one, perhaps, more ready, or for all I know rhythmically more and less ready, to react to the word when it comes. I have sometimes wondered whether Swinburne's *Dolores* gets any of its energy from the way the word Spain, suggested by the title and by various things in the course of the poem, although one is forced to wonder what /64/ the next rhyme is going to be, never appears among the dozen that are paired off with *Our Lady of Pain*. But so little is known about these matters that it is rather unwise to talk about them; one goes off into Pure Sound and entirely private associations; for instance, I want to back up my 'pains' from *peynted* by calling in 'weighted' and 'fainted,' and the suggestion of labour in *all that painted*. The study of subdued bad puns may be very important, but it is less hopeful than the study of more rational ambiguities, because you can rely on most word associations being called out (if one's mind does not in *some* way run through the various meanings of a word, how can it arrive at the right one?), whereas the puns, in a sense, ought not to be there at all.

A good illustration of this point, not that most people will require to be convinced of it, is given by the words 'rows' and 'rose.' 'Rows' suggests regimentation, order, a card index system, and the sciences; 'rose' suggests a sort of grandeur in the state of culture, something with all the definiteness and independence of Nature that has been produced within the systems of mankind (giving a sort of proof of our stability), some of the overtones of richness, delicacy, and power of varying such as are carried by 'wine'; various sexual associations from its appearance and the *Romaunt of the Roos;* and notions of race, dignity, and fine clothes as if from the Wars of the Roses. These two words never get in each other's way; it is hard to believe they are pronounced the same. Homonyms with less powerful systems of association, like the verb 'rows' and the 'roes' of fishes, lend themselves easily to puns and seem in some degree attracted towards the two more powerful systems; but to insist that the first two are the same sound, to pass suddenly from one to the other, destroys both of them, and leaves a sort of bewilderment in the mind.[2]

On the other hand, there was a poem about strawberries in *Punch* a year or two ago, which I caught myself liking because of /65/ a subdued pun; here what was suggested was a powerful word, what was meant was a mere grammatical convenience:

> Queenlily June with a rose in her hair
> Moves to her prime with a langorous air.
> What in her kingdom's most comely? By far
> Strawberries, strawberries, strawberries are.

I was puzzled to know why the first line seemed beautiful till I found I was reading *Queenlily* as 'Queen Lily,' which in a child's poetry-book style is charming; 'the lily with a rose in her hair,' used of a ripening virgin and hence of early summer, in which the absolute banality of roses and lilies is employed as it were heraldically, as a symbol intended not to be visualised but at once interpreted, is a fine Gongorism, and the alternative adverb sets the whole thing in motion by its insistence on the verb. It is curious how if you think of the word only as an adverb all this playful dignity, indeed the whole rhythm of the line, ebbs away into complacence and monotony.

It is a little unfair, perhaps, to use Chaucer for my purpose; I have used him because it is important if true that these effects are somehow part of the character of the language, since they were so much in evidence so early, and in a writer apparently so derivative from the French and Italian literatures, which don't seem ambiguous in the same way. I admit it is much easier to muddle one's readers when using the unfamiliar stresses of fourteenth-century speech, and when dealing with unfamiliar uses of words. This, for instance, I thought at first was an ambiguity, when Troilus' sickness, caused by love of Criseyde, and used to arrange a meeting with her, is announced to the assembled company:

> Compleyned eke Eleyne of his sycknesse
> So feithfully, that pitee was to here,
> And every wight gan waxen for accesse
> A leech anon, and seyde, 'in this manere
> Men curen folk; this charm I wol yow lere.'
> But there sat oon, al list hir nought to teche.
> That thoughte, beste coude I yet been his leche.

> (ii. 1576.)

Access in the fourteenth century meant some kind of feverish attack, and I believe is not used in any other sense by Chaucer; /66/ but it was used by Wyclif to mean the act of coming near, or the right of coming near, and acquired later the meaning of accession to an office of dignity. So that it might mean that everybody said they knew how to cure fevers so as to seem dignified at the party, so as to put themselves forward, and perhaps so as to be allowed to visit the prince on his sick-bed. The break of the line which separates *accesse* from *leech* and connects it with *gan* helps this overtone of ironical meaning, which is just what the social comedy of the passage requires; and if you wish to stress the influence of Chaucer as a stylist, it is these later meanings, and not the medical meaning, which were most prominent by the sixteenth century; this, for instance, is just the suggestive way Shakespeare would use a Latinised word. But to

Chaucer at any rate, I believe, the joke was strong enough to stand by itself, and too pointed to call up overtones; I have put it in to show a case where a plausible ambiguity may be unprofitable, and the sort of reasons that may make one refuse to accept it.

Rather a pretty example turns up when Criseyde is reflecting it would be unwise to fall in love (ii. 752). I am, she says,

> Right yong, and stand unteyed in lusty lese
> Withouten jalousye or swich debaat.

Lese, among the absurd variety of its meaning, includes lies, a snare for rabbits, a quantity of thread, a net, a noose, a whip-lash, and the thong holding hunting dogs; one would take with these *lusty* in the sense of amorous. Or *lese* may mean a contract giving lands or tenements for life, a term of years, or at will (hence guaranteed permanence and safety), open pasture-land (as in leas), picking fruit, the act of coursing (she is her own mistress), or a set of three (the symbol of companionship as opposed to passion); one would take with these *lusty* in the sense of hearty and delightful, its more usual meaning at the time. Thus, while the intended meaning is not in doubt, to be *in lusty lese* may be part of the condition of being *unteyed* or of being *teyed.* I have put down most of the meanings for fun; the only ones I feel sure of are: 'I am not entangled in the net of desire,' and 'I am disentangled like a colt in a meadow'; these are quite enough for the ambiguity of syntax.

You may say that these meanings should be permuted to convey /67/ doubt: 'I am sprawling without foothold in the net of desire,' and 'I have *not* been turned out to grass in the wide meadow of freedom.' But in paraphrasing these meanings I have had to look for an idiom that will hide the main fact of the situation, that she is *unteyed.* Or you might say that *stand* attracts *in,* so that *lese* must be taken only with *unteyed.* But *withouten* suggests a parallel with *unteyed,* which would make *lese* go with *teyed.* It would have been consistent enough with Criseyde's character to have been expressing doubt, but about this line, whatever its meaning, there is a sort of complacency and decision which convince me it is only of the second type.

At the same time, I admit that this is a monstrously clotted piece of language; not at all, for instance, a thing it would be wise to imitate, and it would be unfair to leave Chaucer without reminding the reader of something more beautiful. It is during the scene, then, leading to the actual seduction of Criseyde, when she has no doubt what she wants but is determined to behave like a lady, when Troilus is swooning about the place, always in despair, and Pandarus sees no immediate prospect of pushing them into bed together, that this sheer song of ironical happiness pours forth from the lips of their creator.

> But now pray God to quenchen al this sorwe.
> So hope I that he shall, for he best may.
> For I have seen of a full misty morwe
> Folwe ful ofte a merie somer's day,
> And after winter folweth grene May.
> Men sen alday, and reden eke in stories,
> That after sharpe shoures ben victories.

It is the open and easy grandeur, moving with the whole earth, of the middle lines, that made me quote them; my immediate point is *shoures*. It meant charge, or onslaught of battle, or pang, such as Troilus' fainting-fits, or the pains of childbirth; if you take it as showers of rain (I. iv. 251), the two metaphors, from man and the sky, melt into each other; there is another connection with warriors, in that the word is used for showers of arrows; there is another connection with lovers in that it is used for showers of tears.

I hope I have made out a fair case for a poetical use of ambiguity, in one form or another, as already in full swing in the English /68/ of Chaucer; so that it has some claim to be considered native to the language. I really do not know what importance it has in other European languages; the practice of looking for it rapidly leads to hallucinations, as you can train yourself always to hear a clock ticking: and my impression is that while it is frequent in French and Italian, the subsidiary meanings are nearly always bad idiom, so that the inhabitants of those countries would have too much conscience to attend to them. At any rate it is not true, obviously enough, that Chaucer's ambiguities are copied from Boccaccio; I found it very exciting to go through my list in a parallel text and see how, even where great sections of the stuff were being translated directly, there would be a small patch of invention at the point I had marked down.[3]

Notes

1. A dramatic irony as such need not be called fourth-type, but this one, I think, marks a complexity of feeling in Chaucer (that is, he half agreed with Pandarus and half not). I don't think there are other examples in this chapter which properly belong in later chapters.

2. What you normally get from a likeness of sound is an added force to the Paget effect (p. 14) in cases where there is a clear group of words with similar sound and meaning (*e.g.* skate, skid, skee, scrape). But this makes you feel the meaning of the one word more vividly, not confuse it with the meanings of the others. On the other hand, it might be argued that a controlled partial confusion of this sort is the only real point of using alliteration and rhyme.

3. I do not know that any critic has either refuted or defended this treatment of Chaucer. I still believe in it myself.

What Chaucer Really Did to "Il Filostrato"
by C. S. Lewis

A great deal of attention has deservedly been given to the relation
between the *Book of Troilus* and its original, *Il Filostrato*, and Rossetti's
collation placed a knowledge of the subject within the reach even of
undergraduate inquirers. It is, of course, entirely right and proper that
the greater part of this attention has been devoted to such points as
specially illustrate the individual genius of Chaucer as a dramatist and a
psychologist. But such studies, without any disgrace to themselves, often
leave singularly undefined the historical position and affinities of a book;
and if pursued intemperately they may leave us with a preposterous
picture of the author as that abstraction, a *pure* individual, bound to no
time nor place, or even obeying in the fourteenth century the aesthetics
of the twentieth. It is possible that a good deal of misunderstanding still
exists, even among instructed people, as to the real significance of the
liberties that Chaucer took with his source. M. Legouis, in his study of
Chaucer to which we all owe so much, remarks that Chaucer's additions
'implied a wider and more varied conception' than those of Boccaccio;
and again 'Chaucer's aim was not like Boccaccio's to paint sentimentality
alone, but to reflect life'. I do not wish to contradict either statement, but
I am convinced that both are capable of conveying a false impression.
What follows may be regarded as a cautionary gloss on M. Legouis's text.
I shall endeavour to show that the process which *Il Filostrato* underwent
at Chaucer's hands was first and foremost a process of *medievalization*.
One aspect of this process has received some attention from scholars,[1]

Reprinted from *Essays and Studies* 17 (1932): 56–75 with the kind permission of the
publishers, The English Association. Footnotes are renumbered in one series. The
original pagination is noted between slashes.

but its importance appears to me to be still insufficiently stressed. In what follows I shall, therefore, restate this aspect in my own terms while endeavouring to replace it in its context. /57/

Chaucer had never heard of a renaissance; and I think it would be difficult to translate either into the English or the Latin of his day our distinction between sentimental or conventional art on the one hand, and art which paints 'Life'—whatever this means—on the other. When first a manuscript beginning with the words *Alcun di giove sogliono il favore* came into his hands, he was, no doubt, aware of a difference between its contents and those of certain English and French manuscripts which he had read before. That some of the differences did not please him is apparent from his treatment. We may be sure, however, that he noticed and approved the new use of stanzas, instead of octosyllabic couplets, for narrative. He certainly thought the story a good story; he may even have thought it a story better told than any that he had yet read. But there was also, for Chaucer, a special reason why he should choose this story for his own retelling; and that reason largely determined the alterations that he made.

He was not yet the Chaucer of the *Canterbury Tales*: he was the *grant translateur* of the *Roman de la Rose*, the author of the *Book of the Duchesse*, and probably of 'many a song and many a lecherous lay'.[2] In other words he was the great living interpreter in English of *l'amour courtois*. Even in 1390, when Gower produced the first version of his *Confessio Amantis*, such faithful interpretation of the love tradition was still regarded as the typical and essential function of Chaucer: he is Venus' 'disciple' and 'poete', with whose 'ditees and songes glade . . . the lond fulfild is overal'. And Gower still has hopes that Chaucer's existing treatments of *Frauendienst* are only the preludes to some great 'testament' which will 'sette an ende of alle his werk'.[3] These expectations were, of course, disappointed; and it is possibly to that disappointment, rather than to a hypothetical quarrel (for which only the most ridiculous grounds have been assigned), that we should attribute Gower's removal of this passage from the second text of the *Confessio Amantis*. It had become apparent that Chaucer was following a different /58/ line of development, and the reference made to him by Venus had ceased to be appropriate.

It was, then, as a poet of courtly love that Chaucer approached *Il Filostrato*. There is no sign as yet that he wished to desert the courtly tradition; on the contrary, there is ample evidence that he still regarded himself as its exponent. But the narrative bent of his genius was already urging him, not to desert this tradition, but to pass from its doctrinal treatment (as in the *Romance of the Rose*) to its narrative treatment. Having preached it, and sung it, he would now exemplify it: he would show the code put into action in the course of a story—without prejudice (as we shall see) to a good deal of doctrine and pointing of the amorous moral by the way. The thing represents a curious return upon itself of literary history. If Chaucer had lived earlier he would, we may be sure, have found just the model that he desired in Chrestien de Troyes. But by Chaucer's time certain elements, which Chrestien had held together in unity, had come apart and taken an independent life. Chrestien had combined, magnificiently, the interest of the story, and the interest of erotic doctrine and psychology. His successors had been unable or unwilling to achieve this union. Perhaps, indeed, the two things had to separate in order that each might grow to maturity; and in many of Chrestien's psychological passages one sees the embryonic allegory struggling to be born.[4] Whatever the reason may be, such a separation took place. The story sets up on its own in the prose romances—the 'French book' of Malory: the doctrine and psychology set up on their own in the *Romance of the Rose*. In this situation if a poet arose who accepted the doctrines and also had a narrative genius, then *a priori* such a poet might be expected to combine again the two elements—now fully grown—which, in their rudimentary form, had lain together in Chrestien. But this is exactly the sort of poet that Chaucer was; and this (as we shall see) is what Chaucer did. The *Book of Troilus* shows, in fact, the /59/ very peculiar literary phenomenon of Chaucer groping back, unknowingly, through the very slightly medieval work of Boccaccio, to the genuinely medieval formula of Chrestien. We may be thankful that Chaucer did not live in the high noon of Chrestien's celebrity; for, if he had, we should probably have lost much of the originality of Troilus. He would had less motive for altering Chrestien than for altering Boccaccio, and probably would have altered him less.

Approaching *Il Filostrato* from this angle, Chaucer, we may be sure, while feeling the charm of its narrative power, would have found himself, at many passages, uttering the Middle English equivalent of 'This will never do!' In such places he did not hesitate, as he might have said, to *amenden* and to *reducen* what was *amis* in his author. The majority of his modifications are corrections of errors which Boccaccio had committed against the code of courtly love; and modifications of this kind have not been entirely neglected by criticism. It has not, however, been sufficiently observed that these are only part and parcel of a general process of medievalization. They are, indeed, the most instructive part of that process, and even in the present discussion must claim the chief place; but in order to restore them to their proper setting it will be convenient to make a division of the different capacities in which Chaucer approached his original. These will, of course, be found to overlap in the concrete; but that is no reason for not plucking them ideally apart in the interests of clarity.

✓   I. Chaucer approached his work as an 'Historical' poet contributing to the story of Troy. I do not mean that he necessarily believed his tale to be wholly or partly a record of fact, but his attitude towards it in this respect is different from Boccaccio's. Boccaccio, we may surmise, wrote for an audience who were beginning to look at poetry in our own way. For them *Il Filostrato* was mainly, though not entirely, 'a new poem by Boccaccio'. Chaucer wrote for an audience who still looked at poetry in the medieval fashion—a fashion for which the real literary units were 'matters', 'stories', and the like, rather than individual authors. For them the /60/ *Book of Troilus* was partly, though of course only partly, 'a new bit of the Troy story', or even 'a new bit of the matter of Rome'. Hence Chaucer expects them to be interested not only in the personal drama between his little group of characters but in that whole world of story which makes this drama's context: like children looking at a landscape picture and wanting to know what happens to the road after it disappears into the frame. For the same reason they will want to know his authorities. Passages in which Chaucer has departed from his original to meet this demand will easily occur to the memory. Thus, in i. 141 et seq., he excuses himself for not telling us more about the military history of the Trojan war, and adds what is almost a footnote to tell his audience where they can find that missing part of the story—'in Omer, or in Dares, or in Dyte'. Boccaccio had merely sketched in, in the preceding stanza, a general picture of war sufficient to provide the background for his own story—much as a dramatist might put *Alarums within* in a stage direction: he has in view an audience fully conscious that all this is mere necessary 'setting' or hypothesis. Thus again, in iv. 120 et seq., Chaucer inserts into the speech of *Calkas* an account of the quarrel between *Phebus* and *Neptunus* and *Lameadoun*. This is not dramatically necessary. All that was needed for *Calkas's* argument has already been given in lines 111 and 112 (cf. *Filostrato*, iv. xi). The Greek leaders did not need to be told about Laomedon; but Chaucer is not thinking of the Greek leaders; he is thinking of his audience who will gladly learn, or be reminded, of that part of the cycle. At lines 204 et seq. he inserts a note on the later history of *Antenor* for the same reason. In the fifth book he inserts unnecessarily

lines 1464–1510 from the story of Thebes. The spirit in which this is done
is aptly expressed in his own words:

> And so descendeth down from gestes olde
> To Diomede.
>
> (v. 1511, 1512)

The whole 'matter of Rome' is still a unity, with a structure and life of its
own. That part of it which the poem in hand /61/ is treating, which is, so
to speak, in focus, must be seen fading gradually away into its 'historial'
surroundings. The method is the antithesis of that which produces the
'framed' story of a modern writer: it is a method which romance largely
took over from the epic.

II. Chaucer approached his work as a pupil of the rhetoricians and a
firm believer in the good, old, and now neglected maxim of Dante: *omnis
qui versificatur suos versus exornare debet in quantum potest.* This side of
Chaucer's poetry has been illustrated by Mr. Manly[5] so well that most
readers will not now be in danger of neglecting it. A detailed application of
this new study to the *Book of Troilus* would here detain us too long, but a
cursory glance shows that Chaucer found his original too short and
proceeded in many places to 'amplify' it. He began by abandoning the
device—that of invoking his lady instead of the Muses—whereby
Boccaccio had given a lyrical instead of a rhetorical turn to the
invocation, and substituted an address to *Thesiphone* (*Filostrato,* I. i–v, cf.
Troilus, i. 1–14). He added at the beginning of his second book an
invocation of *Cleo* and an apology of the usual medieval type, for the
defects of his work (ii. 15–21). Almost immediately afterwards he
inserted a *descriptio* of the month of a May (an innovation which
concerned him as poet of courtly love no less than as rhetorician) which
is extremely beautiful and appropriate, but which follows, none the less,
conventional lines. The season is fixed by astronomical references, and
Proigne and *Tereus* appear just where we should expect them (ii. 50–6,
64–70). In the third book the scene of the morning parting between the
two lovers affords a complicated example of Chaucer's medievalization.
In his original (III. xlii) Chaucer read

> Ma poich' e galli presso al giorno udiro
> Cantar per l'aurora che surgea.

He proceeded to amplify this, first by the device of *Circuitio* or

Circumlocutio; galli, with the aid of Alanus de Insulis, became 'the cok, comune astrologer'. Not content with this, /62/ he then repeated the sense of that whole phrase by the device *Expolitio,* of which the formula is *Multiplice forma Dissimuletur idem: varius sis et tamen idem,*[6] and the theme 'Dawn came' is varied with *Lucifer* and *Fortuna Minor,* till it fills a whole stanza (iii. 1415-21). In the next stanza of Boccaccio he found a short speech by *Griseida,* expressing her sorrow at the parting which dawn necessitated: but this was not enough for him. As poet of love he wanted his *alba;* as rhetorician he wanted his *apostropha.* He therefore inserted sixteen lines of address to Night (1427-42), during which he secured the additional advantage, from the medieval point of view, of 'som doctryne' (1429-32). In lines 1452-70 he inserted antiphonally Troilus's *alba,* for which the only basis in Boccaccio was the line *Il giorno che venia maledicendo* (III. x liv). The passage is an object lesson for those who tend to identify the traditional with the dull. Its matter goes back to the ancient sources of medieval love poetry, notably to Ovid, *Amores,* i. 13, and it has been handled often before, and better handled, by the Provençals. Yet it is responsible for one of the most vivid and beautiful expressions that Chaucer ever used.

> Accursed be thy coming into Troye
> For every bore hath oon of thy bright eyen.

A detailed study of the *Book of Troilus* would reveal this 'rhetoricization', if I may coin an ugly word, as the common quality of many of Chaucer's additions. As examples of *Apostropha* alone I may mention, before leaving this part of the subject, iii. 301 et seq. (*O tonge*), 617 et seq. (*But o Fortune*), 715 et seq. (*O Venus*), and 813 et seq. where Chaucer is following Boethius.

III. Chaucer approached his work as a poet of *doctryne* and sentence. This is a side of his literary character which twentieth-century fashions encourage us to overlook, but, of course, no honest historian can deny it. His contemporaries and immediate successors did not. His own creatures, the pilgrims, regarded *mirthe* and *doctryne,*[7] or, as it is elsewhere /63/ expressed, *sentence* and *solas,*[8] as the two alternative, and equally welcome, excellences of a story. In the same spirit Hoccleve praises Chaucer as the *mirour of fructuous entendement* and the universal *fadir in science*[9]—a passage, by the by, to be recommended to those who are astonished that the fifteenth century should imitate those elements of Chaucer's genius which it enjoyed instead of those which we enjoy. In respect of *doctryne,* then, Chaucer found his original deficient, and *amended* it. The example which will leap to every one's mind is the Boethian discussion on free will (iv. 946–1078). To Boccaccio, I suspect, this would have seemed as much an excrescence as it does to the modern reader; to the unjaded appetites of Chaucer's audience mere thickness in a wad of manuscript was a merit. If the author was so 'courteous beyond covenant' as to give you an extra bit of *doctryne* (or of story), who would be so churlish as to refuse it on the pedantic ground of irrelevance? But this passage is only one of many in which Chaucer departs from his original for the sake of giving his readers interesting general knowledge or philosophical doctrine. In iii. 1387 et seq., finding Boccaccio's attack upon *gli avari* a little bare and unsupported, he throws out, as a species of buttress, the *exempla* of *Myda* and *Crassus.*[10] In the same book he has to deal with the second assignation of Troilus and Cressida. Boccaccio gave him three stanzas of dialogue (*Filostrato,* III. lxvi–lxviii), but Chaucer rejected them and preferred—in curious anticipation of Falstaff's thesis about pitch—to assure his readers, on the authority of *thise clerkes wyse* (iii. 1691) that *felicitee* is felicitous, though *Troilus* and *Criseyde* enjoyed something better than *felicitee.* In the same stanza he also intends, I think, an allusion to the *sententia* that occurs elsewhere in the Franklin's Tale.[11] In iv. 197–203, immediately before his *historical* insertion about Antenor, he introduces a *sentence* from Juvenal, partly /64/ for its own sake, partly in order that the story of Antenor may thus acquire an exemplary, as well as a *historial* value. In iv. 323–8 he inserts a passage on the great *locus communis* of Fortune and her wheel.

In the light of this sententious bias, Chaucer's treatment of Pandarus should be reconsidered, and it is here that a somewhat subtle exercise of the historical imagination becomes necessary. On the one hand, he would be a dull reader, and the victim rather than the pupil of history, who would take all the doctrinal passages in Chaucer seriously: that the speeches of Chauntecleer and Pertelote and of the Wyf of Bath not only *are* funny by reason of their sententiousness and learning, but are intended to be funny, and funny by that reason, is indisputable. On the other hand, to assume that sententiousness became funny for Chaucer's readers as easily as it becomes funny for us, is to misunderstand the fourteenth century: such an assumption will lead us to the preposterous view that *Melibee* (or even the Parson's Tale) is a comic work—a view not much mended by Mr. Mackail's suggestion that there are some jokes *too* funny to excite laughter and that *Melibee* is one of these. A clear recognition that our own age is quite abnormally sensitive to the funny

side of sententiousness, to possible hypocrisy, and to dulness, is
absolutely necessary for any one who wishes to understand the past. We
must face the fact that Chaucer's audience could listen with gravity and
interest to edifying matter which would set a modern audience sleeping or
sniggering. The application of this to Pandarus is a delicate business.
Every reader must interpret Pandarus for himself, and I can only put
forward my own interpretation very tentatively. I believe that Pandarus
is meant to be a comic character, but not, by many degrees, so broadly
comic as he appears to some modern readers. There is, for me, no doubt
that Chaucer intended us to smile when he made Troilus exclaim

> What knowe I of the queene Niobe?
> Lat be thyne olde ensaumples, I thee preye.
>
> (I. 759)

But I question if he intended just that sort of smile which we actually give
him. For me the fun lies in the fact that /65/ poor Troilus says what I
have been wishing to say for some time. For Chaucer's hearers the point
was a little different. The suddenness of the gap thus revealed between
Troilus's state of mind and Pandarus's words cast a faintly ludicrous air
on what had gone before: it made the theorizing and the *exempla* a little
funny in retrospect. But it is quite probable that they had not been funny
till then: the discourse on contraries (i. 631–44), the *exemplum* of Paris
and Oenone, leading up to the theme 'Physician heal thyself' (652–72),
the doctrine of the Mean applied to secrecy in love (687–93), the *sentences*
from Solomon (695) and elsewhere (708), are all of them the sort of thing
that can be found in admittedly serious passages,[12] and it may well be that
Chaucer 'had it both ways'. His readers were to be, first of all, edified by
the doctrine for its own sake, and then (slightly) amused by the contrast
between this edification and Troilus's obstinate attitude of the plain man.
If this view be accepted it will have the consequence that Chaucer
intended an effect of more subtility than that which we ordinarily
receive. We get the broadly comic effect — a loquacious and
unscrupulous old uncle talks solemn platitude at interminable length.
For Chaucer, a *textuel* man talked excellent doctrine which we enjoy and
by which we are edified: but at the same time we see that this 'has its
funny side'. Ours is the crude joke of laughing at admitted rubbish:
Chaucer's the much more lasting joke of laughing at 'the funny side' of
that which, even while we laugh, we admire. To the present writer this
reading of Pandarus does not appear doubtful; but it depends, to some

extent, on a mere 'impression' about the quality of the Middle Ages, an
impression hard to correct, if it is an error, and hard to teach, if it is a
truth. For this reason I do not insist on my interpretation. If, however, it
is accepted, many of the speeches of Pandarus which are commonly
regarded as having a purely dramatic significance will have to be classed
among the examples of Chaucer's doctrinal or sententious insertions.[13]
/66/

IV. Finally, Chaucer approached his work as the poet of courtly love.
He not only modified his story so as to make it a more accurate
representation in action of the orthodox erotic code, but he also went out
of his way to emphasize its didactic element. Andreas Capellanus had
given instructions to lovers; Guillaume de Lorris had given instructions
veiled and decorated by allegory; Chaucer carries the process a stage
further and gives instruction by example in the course of a concrete
story. But he does not forget the instructional side of his work. In the
following paragraphs I shall sometimes quote parallels to Chaucer's
innovations from the earlier love literature, but it must not be thought
that I suppose my quotations to represent Chaucer's immediate source.

1. Boccaccio in his induction, after invoking his mistress instead of the
Muses, inserts (I. vi) a short request for lovers in general that they will
pray for him. The prayer itself is disposed of in a single line.

Per me vi prego ch'amore preghiate.

This is little more than a conceit, abandoned as soon as it is used: a
modern poet could almost do the like. Chaucer devotes four stanzas (i.
22–49) to this prayer. If we make an abstract of both passages, Boccaccio
will run 'Pray for me to Love', while Chaucer will run 'Remember, all
lovers, your old unhappiness, and pray, for the unsuccessful, that they
may come to solace; for me, that I may be enabled to tell this story; for
those in despair, that they may die; for the fortunate, that they may
persevere, and please their ladies in such manner as may advance the
glory of Love'. The important point here is not so much that Chaucer
expands his original, as that he renders it more liturgical: his prayer, with
its careful discriminations in intercession for the various recognized
stages of the amorous life, and its final reference *ad Amoris majorem
gloriam,* is a collect. Chaucer is emphasizing that parody, or imitation, or
rivalry—I know not which to call it—of the Christian religion which was
inherent in traditional *Frauendienst.* The thing can be traced back /67/ to
Ovid's purely ironical worship of Venus and Amor in the *De Arte*

Amatoria. The idea of a love religion is taken up and worked out, though still with equal flippancy, in terms of medieval Christianity, by the twelfth-century poet of the *Concilium Romaricimontis*,[14] where Love is given Cardinals (female), the power of visitation, and the power of cursing. Andreas Capellanus carried the process a stage further and gave Love the power of distributing reward and punishment after death. But while his hell of cruel beauties (*Siccitas*), his purgatory of beauties promiscuously kind (*Humiditas*), and his heaven of true lovers (*Amoenitas*)[15] can hardly be other than playful, Andreas deals with the love religion much more seriously than the author of the *Concilium*. The lover's qualification is *morum probitas*: he must be truthful and modest, a good Catholic, clean in his speech, hospitable, and ready to return good for evil. There is nothing in *saeculo bonum* which is not derived from love:[16] it may even be said in virtue of its severe standard of constancy, to be 'a kind of chastity'—*reddit hominem castitatis quasi virtute decoratum*.[17]

In all this we are far removed from the tittering nuns and *clerici* of the *Concilium*. In Chrestien, the scene in which Lancelot kneels and adores the bed of Guinevere (as if before a *corseynt*)[18] is, I think, certainly intended to be read seriously: what mental reservations the poet himself had on the whole business is another question. In Dante the love religion has become wholly and unequivocably serious by fusing with the real religion: the distance between the *Amor deus omnium quotquot sunt amantium* of the *Concilium*, and the *segnore di pauroso aspetto* of the *Vita Nuova*,[19] is the measure of the tradition's real flexibility and universality. It is this quasi-religious element in the content, and this liturgical element in the diction, which Chaucer found lacking /68/ in his original at the very opening of the book, and which he supplied. The line

> That Love hem bringe in hevene to solas

is particularly instructive.

2. In the Temple scene (Chaucer, i. 155–315. *Filostrato*, I. xix–xxxii) Chaucer found a stanza which it was very necessary to *reducen*. It was Boccaccio's twenty-third, in which Troilus, after indulging in his 'cooling card for lovers', mentions that he has himself been singed with that fire, and even hints that he has had his successes; but the pleasures were not worth the pains. The whole passage is a typical example of that Latin spirit, which in all ages (except perhaps our own) has made Englishmen a little uncomfortable; the hero must be a lady-killer from the very beginning, or the audience will think him a milksop and a booby. To have

abashed, however temporarily, these strutting Latinisms, is not least among the virtues of medieval *Frauendienst*: and for Chaucer as its poet, this stanza was emphatically one of those that 'would never do'. He drops it quietly out of its place, and thus brings the course of his story nearer to that of the *Romance of the Rose*. The parallelism is so far intact. Troilus, an unattached young member of the courtly world, wandering idly about the Temple, is smitten with Love. In the same way the Dreamer having been admitted by Ydelnesse into the garden goes 'pleying along ful merily'[20] until he looks in the fatal well. If he had already met Love outside the garden the whole allegory would have to be reconstructed.

3. A few lines lower Chaucer found in his original the words

> il quale amor trafisse
> Più ch'alcun altro, pria del tempio uscisse.
>
> (I. xxv)

Amor trafisse in Boccaccio is hardly more than a literary variant for 'he fell in love': the allegory has shrunk into a metaphor and even that metaphor is almost unconscious and fossilized. Over such a passage one can imagine Chaucer /69/ exclaiming, *tantamne rem tam negligenter?* He at once goes back through the metaphor to the allegory that begot it, and gives us his own thirtieth stanza (I. 204-10) on the god of Love in anger bending his bow. The image is very ancient and goes back at least as far as Apollonius Rhodius.[21] Ovid was probably the intermediary who conveyed it to the Middle Ages. Chrestien uses it, with particular emphasis on Love as the avenger of contempt.[22] But Chaucer need not have gone further to find it than to the *Romance of the Rose*,[23] with which, here again, he brings his story into line.

4. But even this was not enough. Boccaccio's *Amor trafisse* had occurred in a stanza where the author apostrophizes the *Cecità delle mondane menti,* and reflects on the familiar contrast between human expectations and the actual course of events. But this general contrast seemed weak to the poet of courtly love: what he wanted was the explicit erotic *moral* based on the special contrast between the ὕβρις of the young scoffer and the complete surrender which the offended deity soon afterwards extracted from him. This conception, again, owes much to Ovid; but between Ovid and the Middle Ages comes the later practice of the ancient Epithalamium during the decline of antiquity and the Dark Ages: to which, as I hope to show elsewhere, the system of courtly love as a whole is heavily indebted. Thus in the fifth century Sidonius

Apollinarus, in an Epithalamium, makes the bridegroom just such another as Troilus: a proud scoffer humbled by Love. Amor brings to Venus the triumphant news

> Nova gaudia porta
> Felicis praedae, genetrix. Calet ille *superbus*
> Ruricius.[24]

Venus replies

> gaudemus nate, *rebellem*
> *Quod vincis.*

In a much stranger poem, by the Bishop Ennodius, it is not the ὕβρις of a single youth, but of the world, that has stung /70/ the deities of love into retributive action. Cupid and Venus are introduced deploring the present state of Europe.

> Frigida consumens multorum possidet artus
> Virginitas.[25]

and Venus meets the situation by a threat that she'll 'larn 'em':

> Discant populi tunc crescere divam
> Cum neglecta iacet.[26]

They conclude by attacking one Maximus and thus bringing about the marriage which the poem was written to celebrate. Venantius Fortunatus, in his Epithalamium for Brunchild, reproduces, together with Ennodius's spring morning, Ennodius's boastful Cupid, and makes the god, after an exhibition of his archery, announce to his mother, *mihi vincitur alter Achilles*.[27] In Chrestien the role of tamed rebel is transferred to the woman. In *Cligès* Soredamours confesses that Love has humbled her pride by force, and doubts whether such extorted service will find favour.[28] In strict obedience to this tradition Chaucer inserts his lines 214–31, emphasizing the dangers of ὕβρις against Love and the certainty of its ultimate failure; and we may be thankful that he did, since it gives us the lively and touching simile of *proude Bayard*. Then, mindful of his instructional purpose, he adds four stanzas more (239–66), in which he directly exhorts his readers to avoid the error of Troilus, and that for two reasons: firstly, because Love *cannot* be resisted (this is the policeman's argument—we may as well 'come quiet'); and secondly because Love is a thing 'so vertuous in kinde'. The second argument, of course, follows traditional lines, and recalls Andreas's theory of Love as the source of all secular virtue.

5. In lines 330–50 Chaucer again returns to Troilus's scoffing—a scoffing this time assumed as a disguise. I do not wish to press the possibility that Chaucer in this passage is attempting, in virtue of his instructional purpose, to stress /71/ the lover's virtue of secrecy more than he found it stressed in his original; for Boccaccio, probably for different reasons, does not leave that side of the subject untouched. But it is interesting to note a difference in the content between this scoffing and that of Boccaccio (*Filostrato* I. xxi, xxii). Boccaccio's is based on contempt for women, fickle as wind, and heartless. Chaucer's is based on the hardships of love's *lay* or religion: hardships arising from the uncertainty of the most orthodox *observances*, which may lead to various kinds of harm and may be taken amiss by the lady. Boccaccio dethrones the deity: Chaucer complains of the severity of the cult. It is the difference between an atheist and a man who humorously insists that he 'is not of religioun'.

6. In the first dialogue between Troilus and Pandarus the difference between Chaucer and his original can best be shown by an abstract. Boccaccio (II. vi–xxviii) would run roughly as follows:

T. Well, if you must know, I am in love. But don't ask me with whom (vi–viii).

P. Why did you not tell me long ago? I could have helped you (ix).

T. What use would *you* be? Your own suit never succeeded (ix).

P. A man can often guide others better than himself (x).

T. I can't tell you, because it is a relation of yours (xv).

P. A fig for relations! Who is it? (xvi).

T. (after a pause) Griseida.

P. Splendid! Love has fixed your heart in a good place. She is an admirable person. The only trouble is that she is rather *pie (onesta)*: but I'll soon see to that (xxiii). Every woman is amorous at heart: they are only anxious to save their reputations (xxvii). I'll do all I can for you (xxviii).

Chaucer (I. 603–1008) would be more like this:

T. Well, if you must know, I am in love. But don't ask me with
    whom (603-16).

P. Why did you not tell me long ago? I could have helped you
    (617-20).

T. What use would *you* be? Your own suit never succeeded
    (621-3). /72/

P. A man can often guide others better than himself, as we see
    from the analogy of the whetstone. Remember the
    doctrine of contraries, and what Oenone said. As regards
    secrecy, remember that all virtue is a mean between two
    extremes (624-700).

T. Do leave me alone (760).

P. If you die, how will she interpret it? Many lovers have
    served for twenty years without a single kiss. But should
    they despair? No, they should think it a guerdon even to
    serve (761-819).

T. (much moved by this argument, 820-6) What shall I do?
    Fortune is my foe (827-40).

P. Her wheel is always turning. Tell me who your mistress is. If
    it were my sister, you should have her (841-61).

T. (after a pause)—My sweet foe is Criseyde (870-5).

P. Splendid: Love has fixed your heart in a good place. This
    ought to gladden you, firstly, because to love such a lady
    is nothing but good: secondly, because if she has all these
    virtues, she must have Pity too. You are very fortunate
    that Love has treated you so well, considering your
    previous scorn of him. You must repent at once (874-
    935).

T. (kneeling) Mea Culpa! (936-8).

P. Good. All will now come right. Govern yourself properly:
    you know that a divided heart can have no grace. I have
    reasons for being hopeful. No man or woman was ever
    born who was not apt for love, either natural or celestial:
    and celestial love is not fitted to Criseyde's years. I will do
    all I can for you. Love converted you of his goodness.
    Now that you are converted, you will be as conspicuous
    among his saints as you formerly were among the sinners
    against him (939-1008).

In this passage it is safe to say that every single alteration by Chaucer is an alteration in the direction of medievalism. The Whetstone, Oenone, Fortune, and the like we have already discussed: the significance of the remaining innovations may now be briefly indicated. In Boccaccio the reason for Troilus's hesitation in giving the name is Criseida's relationship to Pandaro: and like a flash comes back Pandaro's startling answer. In Chaucer his hesitation is due to the courtly /73/ lover's certainty that 'she nil to noon suich wrecche as I be wonne' (778) and that 'full harde it wer to helpen in this cas' (836). Pandaro's original

> Se quella ch'ami fosse mia sorella
> A mio potere avrai tuo piacer d'ella
>
> (xvi)

is reproduced in the English, but by removing the words that provoked it in the Italian (E tua parenta, xv) Chaucer makes it merely a general protestation of boundless friendship in love, instead of a cynical defiance of scruples already raised (Chaucer 861). Boccaccio had delighted to bring the purities of family life and the profligacy of his young man about town into collision, and to show the triumph of the latter. Chaucer keeps all the time within the charmed circle of *Frauendienst* and allows no conflict but that of the lover's hopes and fears. Again, Boccaccio's Pandaro has no argument to use against Troilo's silence, but the argument 'I may help you'. Chaucer's Pandarus, on finding that this argument fails, proceeds to expound the code. The fear of dishonour in the lady's eyes, the duty of humble but not despairing service in the face of all discouragement, and the acceptance of this service as its own reward, form the substance of six stanzas in the English text (lines 768–819): at least, if we accept four lines very characteristically devoted to 'Ticius' and what 'bokes telle' of him. Even more remarkable is the difference between the behaviour of the two Pandars after the lady's name has been disclosed. Boccaccio's, cynical as ever, encourages Troilo by the reflection that female virtue is not really a serious obstacle: Chaucer's makes the virtue of the lady itself the ground for hope— arguing scholastically that the *genus* of virtue implies that *species* thereof which is *Pitee* (897-900). In what follows, Pandarus, while continuing to advise, becomes an adviser of a slightly different sort. He instructs Troilus not so much on his relationship to the Lady as on his relationship to Love. He endeavours to awaken in Troilus a devout sense of his previous sins against that deity (904-30) and is not satisfied without confession (931-8), briefly enumerates the commandments /74/

(953–9), and warns his penitent of the dangers of a divided heart.

In establishing such a case as mine, the author who tranfers relentlessly to his article all the passages listed in his private notes can expect nothing but weariness from the reader. If I am criticized, I am prepared to produce for my contention many more evidential passages of the same kind. I am prepared to show how many of the beauties introduced by Chaucer, such as the song of Antigone or the riding past of Troilus, are introduced to explain and mitigate and delay the surrender of the heroine, who showed in Boccaccio a facility condemned by the courtly code.[29] I am prepared to show how Chaucer never forgets his erotically didactic purpose; and how, anticipating criticism as a teacher of love, he guards himself by reminding us that

> For to winne love in sondry ages
> In sondry londes, sondry ben usages.[30]
>
> (ii, 27)

But the reader whose stomach is limited would be tired, and he who is interested may safely be left to follow the clue for himself. Only one point, and that a point of principle, remains to be treated in full. Do I, or do I not, lie open to the criticism of Professor Abercrombie's 'Liberty of Interpreting'?[31]

The Professor *quem honoris causa nomino* urges us not to turn from the known effect which an ancient poem has upon us to speculation about the effect which the poet intended it to have. The application of this criticism which may be directed against me would run as follows: 'If Chaucer's *Troilus* actually produces on us an effect of greater realism and nature and freedom than its original, why should we assume that this effect was accidentally produced in the attempt to conform to an outworn convention?' If the charge is grounded, it is, to my mind, a very grave one. My reply /75/ is that such a charge begs the very question which I have most at heart in this paper, and but for which I should regard my analysis as the aimless burrowings of a thesismonger. I would retort upon my imagined critic with another question. This poem is more lively and of deeper human appeal than its original. I grant it. This poem conforms more closely than its original to the system of courtly love. I claim to prove it. What then is the natural conclusion to draw? Surely, that courtly love itself, in spite of all its shabby origins and pedantic rules, is at bottom more agreeable to those elements in human, or at least in European, nature, which last longest, than the cynical Latin gallantries of

Boccaccio? The world of Chrestien, of Guillaume de Lorris, and of Chaucer, is nearer to the world universal, is less of a closed system, than the world of Ovid, of Congreve, of Anatole France.

This is doctrine little palatable to the age in which we live: and it carries with it another doctrine that may seem no less paradoxical—namely, that certain medieval things are more universal, in that sense more classical, can claim more confidently a *securus judicat,* than certain things of the, Renaissance. To make Herod your villain is more human than to make Tamburlaine your hero. The politics of Machiavelli are provincial and temporary beside the doctrine of the *jus gentium.* The love-lore of Andreas, though a narrow stream, is a stream tending to the universal sea. Its waters move. For real stagnancy and isolation we must turn to the decorative lakes dug out far inland at such a mighty cost by Mr. George Moore; to the more popular corporation swimming-baths of Dr. Marie Stopes; or to the teeming marshlands of the late D. H. Lawrence, whose depth the wisest knows not and on whose bank the hart gives up his life rather than plunge in:

>   þær mæg nihta gehwæm niðwundor seon
>   Fyr on flode!

Notes

1. *v.* Dodd, *Courtly Love in Chaucer and Gower,* 1913.

2. *C.T.,* I 1086.

3. *Conf. Am.* viii. 2941–58.

4. v. *Lancelot,* 369–81, 2844–61; *Yvain,* 6001 et seq., 2639 et seq.; *Cligès,* 5855 et seq.

5. *Chaucer and the Rhetoricians,* Warton Lecture XVII, 1926.

6. Geoffroi de Vinsauf, *Poetr. Nov.* 220–5.

7. *Canterbury Tales,* B 2125.

8. Ibid., A 798.

9. *Regement,* 1963 et seq.

10. This might equally well have been treated above in our rhetorical section. The instructed reader will recognize that a final distinction between *doctrinal* and *rhetorical* aspects, is not possible in the Middle Ages.

11. *C.T.,* F 762.

12. Cf. *C.T.*, I 140–155.

13. From another point of view Pandarus can be regarded as the *Vekke* of the *R. R.* (cf. Thessala in *Cligès*) taken out of allegory into drama and changed in sex so as to 'double' the roles of *Vekke* and *Frend*.

14. *Zeitschrift für Deutsches Alterthum*, vii, pp. 160 et seq.

15. Andreas Capellanus, *De Arte Honeste Amandi*, ed. Troejel, i. 6 D^2 (pp. 91–108).

16. Ibid., i. 6 A (p. 28).

17. Ibid., i. 4 (p. 10).

18. *Lancelot*, 4670, 4734 et seq.

19. *Vit. Nuov.* iii.

20. *R. R.* 1329 (English Version).

21. *Argonaut*, iii. 275 et seq.

22. *Cligès*, 460; cf. 770.

23. *R. R.* 1330 et seq.; 1715 et seq.

24. *Sid. Apoll.* Carm. xi. 61.

25. Ennodius Carm. I, iv. 57.

26. Ibid. 84.

27. Venant. Fort. VI, i.

28. *Cligès*, 682, 241.

29. A particularly instructive comparison could be drawn between the Chaucerian Cresseide's determination to yield, yet to seem to yield by force and deception, and Bialacoil's behaviour. *R. R.* 12607–88: specially 12682, 3.

30. Cf. ii. 1023 et seq.

31. *Proceedings of Brit. Acad.*, vol. xvi, Shakespeare Lecture, 1930.

Character and Action in the Case of Criseyde
by Arthur Mizener

A good deal of attention has been devoted to the question of Chaucer's intention when he created the character of Criseyde.[1] Almost all answers have as their starting point a common assumption: that Chaucer was doing his best to create a unified character in the modern sense of the phrase. They start, that is, from the assumption that Chaucer meant Criseyde's character and actions to appear all of a piece and from the fact that he made her false to Troilus in the end. Only two conclusions are possible on the basis of these premises: either Chaucer intended Criseyde's character to appear compatible with her betrayal of Troilus from the first, or he intended it to appear to change during the course of the narrative in response to the events. The first of these conclusions, with its assumptions as to Chaucer's conception of things, is the one most frequently encountered.

Professor Root, for example, concludes that Criseyde was intended to appear calculating, emotionally shallow, and a drifter from the first. Concrete evidence for hypotheses of this general type can be provided only by making very subtle psychological analyses of carefully selected details of the poem, on the tacit assumptions that Chaucer (1) thought of Criseyde as living a very complex inner life and (2) deliberately chose to reveal the nature of that inner life clearly only by the most indirect hints. Professor Root speaks of the line "Tendre herted, slydynge of corage"[2]— which Chaucer took over from Benoit—as if this were the key to Criseyde's character.[3] It is difficult enough to believe that Chaucer would

Reprinted by permission of the author and the Modern Language Association of America from *PMLA* 54 (1939): 65–81. The original pagination is indicated between slashes in the text.

put the whole burden of clarifying Criseyde's motive for betraying Troilus on a half line near the end of the poem, and even more difficult to believe that he could have meant it to outweigh the import of the preceding five and one half lines, even if it be assumed that this passage /66/ is intended as an explanation of Criseyde's motives rather than a simple listing of the general qualities of her character.[4]

But the main difficulty with this type of explanation is not the doubtfulness of these interpretations of details. It must be shown either (1) that Chaucer meant them as the essence of his intention, the rest of the poem to the contrary notwithstanding, or (2) that the hypothesis which is in accord with these interpretations fits the implications of the rest of the poem. The first of these alternatives is manifestly impossible. And it is impossible, too, to show in detail that the calm, essentially innocent but prudent, and finally deeply moved woman[5] of the early part of the poem was intended to appear so morally instable that her betrayal of Troilus is a natural consequence of her character.

Professor Kittredge's more convincing explanation also suffers from the fact that he tries to find in Criseyde's character the cause of her unfaithfulness: "As Cressida is at the beginning, such is she to the end; amorous, gentle, affectionate, and charming altogether, but fatally impressionable and yielding."[6] Is it possible to believe that Chaucer intended to convey such an impression when he lengthened Boccaccio's period of wooing, when he was so careful to point out that Criseyde did not fall in love suddenly and to describe her admirable conduct in her difficult situation in Troy?[7] Are not all these changes made so that Criseyde shall not appear "impressionable and yielding" at the beginning? Yet only by believing that she is meant to appear some such thing as this can we explain her unfaithfulness on the assumption Professors Root and Kittredge make.[8] /67/

It may appear gratuitous to say that Criseyde is unfaithful because the story makes her so, but it is just the insufficient attention given to this possibility which has made it seem necessary to prove that there was from the start some tragic flaw in her character which motivated her betrayal of Troilus.[9] The purpose of this essay is to suggest a different hypothesis of Chaucer's conception of character and its relation to events from the one which previous critics have used, and to test that hypothesis by analyzing Criseyde. This hypothesis is that for Chaucer a character consisted in a group of unchanging fundamental qualities, and that the relation between such a character and the events of the narrative was one of congruence rather than of cause and effect. This hypothesis is the outgrowth of a conviction that Chaucer's chief interest was in the action rather than in the characters.[10] If this conviction be valid, the arrangement of his narrative was determined primarily by a desire to develop fully the dramatic possibilities of the action, not by a desire to reveal the characters of the personages in the narrative by making motivation the significant aspect of it. The subtlety and richness of such a narrative, in so far as it is a matter of character alone, will be, not in the reader's sense that each episode is a further revelation of profoundly /68/ analyzed motives, but in his sense of how perfectly Chaucer has visualized a character of unchanging fundamental qualities in a series of situations which are there because they are necessary to the action. Certainly everyone will agree that Chaucer knew, and knew how to show the reader, precisely how a character of a certain kind would respond in a given situation. The point in question, therefore, is not the subtlety of Chaucer's observation of humanity but only whether he intended us to take each observation as a hint toward the efficient causes of the successive situations of the narrative or as part of the adequate realization of the character in a situation the efficient cause of which lay elsewhere. It is a question of whether Chaucer does not, for the sake of the action, sometimes omit what is necessary for a complete explanation of events in terms of characters, sometimes distort what needs to be clear for that purpose, and even put into the mouths of various characters remarks which are appropriate to them on no theory of character.[11]

Chaucer's method of characterization is, in this view, essentially static: a character is presented, that is, shown as made up of certain characteristics such as pity or generosity; and then, by the events of the story, it is placed in various circumstances in which it always acts in accord with these characteristics. Chaucer's characters do not change or develop under the impact of experience; they display various aspects of an established set of characteristics as the progress of the narrative places them in varying circumstances.[12] Conversely, the events of the narrative are not determined by the particular moral qualities ascribed to the characters. It would not occur to a mind which conceived of the relationship of character and event in this fashion to ask how a person who exhibited a certain character in one set of circumstances could possibly have acted so as to get himself into certain other circumstances; because in this conception the personages of the narrative do not get themselves into circumstances; the circumstances are primarily determined by the necessities of the action.

Whatever the advantages of the modern method, devised for a

narrative in which the primary interest is the revealing of character, there can be no question that it involves the sacrifice of many of the dramatic effects which were possible with Chaucer's method. One such effect of major importance is the tragic emphasis Chaucer is able to manage in /69/ the Fifth Book;[13] but on a smaller scale such effects are to be found everywhere in the poem.[14]

Our conviction that in real life or in a psychological novel the Criseyde of the Fifth Book must have been different from the Criseyde of the early books to act as she did is no doubt true. And that Chaucer should have intended to imply no causal interaction between what Criseyde does and what she is therefore runs counter to all our habits of thought on this subject. Yet Chaucer's poem, looked at without prejudice, offers, I believe, no evidence that he intended Criseyde's unfaithfulness to appear either the cause of a change, or the consequence of an established vice, in the character he presents to us. In fact, there are grounds for an initial presumption to the contrary, for it is only if there is a contrast between what she is and what she does that Criseyde's fate is tragic. A Criseyde whose fall is the product either of an inherent vice or of a change for the worse in her character is at best an object of pathos. The argument here is, then, that from the beginning to the end of the poem Criseyde, whenever described or shown in action,

> sobre was, ek symple, and wys withal,
> The best ynorisshed ek that myghte be,
> And goodly of hire speche in general,
> Charitable, estatlich, lusty, and fre;
> Ne nevere mo ne lakkede hire pite;
> Tendre herted, slydynge of corage; . . .[15]

Criseyde's first prolonged appearance in the narrative is the interview with Pandar in the Second Book. Before that her beauty is described and a brief account is given of her conduct at the time Calchas left Troy. Chaucer departs radically from Boccaccio in this scene when he introduces the long preliminary skirmish between Pandar and Criseyde. This addition permits him, among other things, to present at leisure Criseyde's character: her charm, intelligence, feminine simplicity, and sensitiveness. Having established the character, Chaucer then returns to Boccaccio for the main outline of the action. /70/

In the matter of character, as in so many other matters,[16] an adequate explanation of Boccaccio's poem is not necessarily an adequate

explanation of Chaucer's. By this time Chaucer has created a fixed
character and, even when he translates directly, the effect against such a
background is very different from that in Boccaccio, for what Chaucer
borrows operates in a different context. This different effect is no
accident, but the deliberately planned consequence of Chaucer's art. In
the scene where Pandar reveals Troilus's love, for example, Chaucer's
Criseyde senses that Pandar is about to say something important and
lowers her eyes just before he tells of Troilus's love,[17] in Boccaccio the
revelation is made before Criseyde exhibits any signs of embarrassment.[18]
By this slight change Chaucer makes his heroine appear, unlike
Boccaccio's, both modest and sensitive to the implications of a social
situation. In Chaucer's account, too, Criseyde's subsequent question as
to how Pandar discovered Troilus's love impresses the reader as a typical
example of the innocent curiosity which is generally believed to be
characteristic of women under these circumstances.[19] But in Boccaccio
Criseyde, having just subscribed heartily to Pandar's gather ye rosebuds'
speech, then adds:

> But let us now stop thinking of this, and tell me whether I may
> still have solace and joy [giuoco] of love, and in what way thou
> didst first take note of Troilus.[20]

Boccaccio's Criseyde is a practical young lady arranging an affair.
Chaucer, using much the same material, so arranges it as to convey a very
different impression of his heroine. The delicacy and complexity of this
scene can hardly be exaggerated, and it is difficult to see how anyone can
find evidence in the character presented for Criseyde's later action. Only
the supposed necessity for finding weaknesses in her can have led people
to read them into this fine rendering of an admirable woman.

The implications of the next scene are not so obvious and will probably
be determined ultimately on the basis of the reader's conception of
Chaucer's main intentions. A great deal has been made of it as evidence
for Criseyde's cold-blooded, calculating nature.[21] But to call Criseyde's
consideration of all the factors involved in her acceptance or refusal of
Troilus calculating seems to me possibly only if one fails to recognize the
difficulty and complexity of her situation.[22] She would not appear either
/71/ sober or prudent if she were to rush into the affair without
considering that in her precarious situation in Troy, Troilus might easily
have her "in despit,"[23] or without thinking over carefully the
disadvantages of the change.

A more significant point about this scene, however, is the fact that Chaucer does not motivate Criseyde's falling in love. In Boccaccio Troilus does not go by her house until after her meditation and only then Criseyde "praised to herself his manner, his pleasing actions, and his courtesy, and so suddenly was she captivated that she desired him above every other good."[24] This apparently struck Chaucer as producing an undesirable effect, for he shifted this scene so that it comes before Criseyde's meditation. It was not that Chaucer saw any psychological inadequacy in love-at-first-sight, for he used it without hesitation in the case of Troilus. Nor does he, in Criseyde's case any more than in Troilus's, describe a gradual change in her psychological attitude leading eventually to her being in love. He simply states, quite flatly, that the process was gradual.[25] This change was not made, then, so that Chaucer might describe Criseyde's development from one state of mind to another.

Chaucer is anxious, however, that Criseyde's attitude in this scene should appear congruous with her established character, and that is the positive consequence of his shifting the location of Troilus's ride past Criseyde's house in the sequence of the narrative. In Boccaccio[26] Criseyde's meditation follows immediately upon Pandar's revelation that some one, not known to her personally, is in love with her. She thus appears to be weighing the joys of love (of a sort) against its risks, and the reader gains the impression that she is a shrewd and sensual young lady for whom the sight of Troilus's elegant person in the end turns the scales. In Chaucer's poem, on the other hand, despite his protest that Criseyde's glimpse of Troilus was only the beginning of love,[27] we come to her soliloquy with a vivid memory of Criseyde gazing out the window at Troilus and wondering "who yaf me drynke?"[28] This soliloquy, as a result of Chaucer's change in the narrative sequence, is bound to be read as the thoughts of a person already in love with Troilus. If Chaucer's purpose was to reveal the development of Criseyde's character, then he /72/ has either deliberately and unaccountably tried to confuse the reader at this point or he has without deliberation blundered into doing so. For he has created an impression of Criseyde's feelings the existence of which he himself denies. If on the other hand his purpose was to make us read Criseyde's soliloquy, not as "cool calculation" but as the meditation of a prudent but tender-hearted woman in love, and at the same time to make us remember her as having fallen in love slowly, then this shift in the sequence of the narrative is masterly.[29]

The first exchange of letters between Troilus and Criseyde also raises the question of how Chaucer intended the reader to interpret Criseyde's attitude. Critics have believed that this scene was intended by Chaucer to illustrate Criseyde's tendency to drift into things.[30] There is no drifting earlier in the poem, for no one with a knowledge of courtly love can doubt Criseyde's sincere belief in Pandar's threat that unless she yields a little both he and Troilus will die. Criseyde yields there quite deliberately to what appears to her serious necessity; she does not drift. And in this scene she conducts herself as any intelligent but modest lady would. When she accepts Troilus's letter she consciously takes the first step on the long road to the goal of courtly love; the way in which she at first refuses this letter shows she is perfectly aware of what it means to accept it.[31] And when she writes Troilus she takes quite consciously again (as Chaucer himself tells us) another.[32]

In both Chaucer and Boccaccio Troilus's letter is given, and then Criseyde laughs; in Boccaccio she laughs at this speech of Pandar's:

> A strange thing is this to consider that at what is most desired
> by her sex each lady should, in the presence of others, show
> herself annoyed and vexed. I have spoken to thee so much of
> this matter that thenceforth thou shouldst not play the prude
> with me.[33]

No such speech is the cause of Criseyde's laughter in Chaucer; given her established and now familiar character in this situation it is very evident that she is incapable of the light-hearted cynicism of Boccaccio's heroine. At the same time she must act deliberately. Chaucer's task is to make her appear definite but neither cynical nor immodest. The definiteness is /73/ there, for not only the embarrassment at the moment when Pandar gives her the letter, but the tacit assumption on his part after dinner that she has read it are evidence that they both clearly understood the implications of Criseyde's taking the letter. Yet even in Chaucer's times those implications had their embarrassing side for such a genteel if unhypocritical lady as Criseyde. She therefore attempts to prevent their appearing as it were naked between Pandar and herself by smiling and remarking

em, I preye,
Swich answere as yow list youre self purveye;
For, trewely, I nyl no lettre write.

And Pandar, realizing that this is not really a refusal at all but an exhibition of tact, accepts the turn Criseyde is trying to give the conversation and replies in kind with an equally tactful little joke. "Therwith she lough, and seyde: 'go we dyne.' "[34] The subtlety with which Chaucer visualizes and communicates the attitude of his character in this situation can probably not be exaggerated. But there is nothing in that attitude which suggests a character capable of the ultimate betrayal of Troilus, and nothing in Chaucer's narrative which justifies the assumption that he intended it to suggest such a character.

The decorous slowness with which Criseyde falls in love is further emphasized by Chaucer's introducing a second scene in which Troilus passes by her house and by his carefully pointing out that it is far too soon for Criseyde to consider yielding to Troilus, a thing she does not do for a considerable time. Criseyde, when she sees Troilus pass by for the second time, definitely becomes very much in love,[35] and from this point on Chaucer assumes that we understand that fact.

When Criseyde encounters Troilus at Deiphebus's house she acts exactly as we should expect, calmly and with a complete understanding of the situation and the meaning of all that is said.[36] She loves Troilus and she is perfectly clear as to what that involves. It is difficult to imagine how Chaucer, short of showing her making the advances, could have done more to prevent her appearing to "drift genially with circumstance," for the progress in the relations of the two lovers made at Deiphebus's house is almost entirely due to her. Her acceptance of Troilus is characteristically deliberate and unambiguous, for all its delicacy. Certainly there was no question in the minds of Pandar and Troilus of Criseyde's meaning or of the magnitude of her decision.[37] /74/

As a question of character there is no necessity for Pandar's elaborate scheme for bringing Troilus and Criseyde together. But by inventing this scene Chaucer adds a tensely dramatic situation to the action. The introduction of this material is justified on these grounds; it cannot be justified on the grounds that the development of the character demanded it. For if Chaucer had been interested in the changes in Criseyde's mind which led up to her attitude at the moment Pandar came in with his cock and bull story about Orestes,[38] he would have centered his attention in that. But he does not, and the result for the reader who does is unhappy. Chaucer, so the explanation runs, makes it clear that Criseyde sees through Pandar when, while inviting her to his house for supper, he implies that Troilus is out of town.[39] But if Criseyde's action through the events of the night at Pandar's house must be explained in terms of a

Criseyde who knew all along that Pandar was manoeuvering her into Troilus's arms, then her attitude, when Pandar comes in with his tale of Troilus's jealousy, must be put down as pure hypocrisy.[40] Can any one read this last passage and believe that Chaucer meant Criseyde to appear hypocritical in her protestations?[41]

If, however, we assume that this scene was introduced primarily because it is necessary to the complete development of the action, and not because it plots a point on the curve of Criseyde's gradual demoralization, and look at Chaucer's portrayal of Criseyde in this scene, not as his attempt to reveal what characteristic in her caused the scene to occur, but as his attempt to visualize how a woman of the type he has shown Criseyde to be all along would act if placed in this situation, then, it seems to me, the full subtlety of Chaucer's portrayal becomes clear. Every single word and gesture fits Chaucer's fixed character perfectly, reasserts with apparently inexhaustible variety of detail one or another of the qualities which he has already ascribed to her. She is seriously concerned at Troilus's jealously and eager to explain to him. For, believing Pandar's tale, she assumes that an explanation is what is required.[42] It is her affection for Troilus which finally makes her do what Pandar /75/ says will satisfy Troilus, however foolish it may seem to her.[43] Her eagerness to help Troilus when he faints is again not the acting of hypocrisy but the result of sincere and affectionate anxiety.[44] And at last there is her famous flash of humor when Troilus takes her in his arms.

Every word of Criseyde's in the scene is just what would be expected from the woman Chaucer has described, were she placed in the situation of the story. In that sense, psychology of the subtlest kind abounds, but in the sense that what she says is an explanation of her past or future behavior it does not. If an attempt, for example, is made to consider Criseyde's statement that she would not be there had she not yielded long before[45] as an explanation of her state of mind during what has preceded, rather than as a reassertion of her sense of humor, there is again the necessity of explaining her attitude when Pandar tells of Troilus's jealousy. Once again only the assumption that she was playing the hypocrite will serve, and Chaucer has given us every reason to suppose Criseyde is quite sincere when she offers to see Troilus the next day and explain everything.[46] There is not an ounce of hypocrisy in Criseyde up to this point; what reason could there be for Chaucer's making her suddenly acquire it? And yet there is no escaping a belief in her hypocrisy unless it is accepted that Chaucer had no intention of revealing Criseyde's motives here, but only of keeping her attitude consonant with her established character.

Somewhat similar motives have been read into the scene the next morning when Pandar comes to Criseyde's room and asks with assumed anxiety if the rain has disturbed her sleep. This beautiful presentation of two witty but tactful people has been considered as evidence that Criseyde was not much in love with Troilus,[47] since she can joke about it. But to this Professor Kittredge's answer is sufficiently devastating: "It is ridiculous to accuse her of insincerity in her love for Troilus. To be sincere, it is not necessary to be either solemn or stupid."[48]

The ending of the poem, especially the Fifth Book, shows most clearly Chaucer's method and its purpose. It is Criseyde who, true to her character, offers most of the practical suggestions when it comes to making plans for her return, it is she who brings hope and wisdom and a plan to the final meeting of the lovers; while Troilus, true to his character also, does little except tell of his love and sorrow. That Criseyde is to be /76/ thought of not as a deliberate hypocrite or facile optimist, but as perfectly sincere and determined to return soon cannot be questioned, for Chaucer is careful to tell us these things in his own words.[49] That is, the woman in this scene is exactly the same as she is in every other place in the poem, just as the man is. Yet in the face of Chaucer's word that Criseyde means all she says, she says a great many things which, while they are exactly what we expect from the character, cannot be brought into accord with her later conduct.[50] They are true to her character in the circumstances in which they are spoken, and they both heighten the tragic effect of the parting and emphasize by their very sincerity the tragic irony of the scene.

But if Criseyde's words here are not meant as hypocrisy or the self-deception of a weak and shallow nature, perhaps the discrepancy between her professions and subsequent actions may be reconciled (and the tragic irony removed) by arguing that she encountered overwhelming obstacles to her plans when she got to the Greek camp and that it was impossible for her to return to Troy:

> . . . she soon discovers that she has matched her woman's wit, not against her dotard father merely, but against the doom of Troy. No pretexts avail, not because Calchas suspects her plot, but because he knows that the city is destined to destruction.[51]

This line of reasoning, unfortunately, ignores Chaucer's poem. For it is after Criseyde has realized the hopelessness of persuading her father that she finally determines to return to Troy in spite of all the difficulties she has been running over in her mind.[52]

Mr. Graydon has worked out with great ingenuity the most probable chronology of the Fifth Book; Chaucer (for good reasons) deliberately obscures the evidence for it and once even professes ignorance of it.[53] But if Chaucer had any chronology in mind at all, it must have been some such one as Mr. Graydon suggests.[54] As nearly as can be determined /77/ Criseyde's second letter, which practically states she will return, is written more than two months after her departure,[55] and her yielding to Diomede comes about two years after her departure.

But all through the Fifth Book Chaucer avoids this chronological sequence. His purpose is to describe the sorrow of Troilus, and to heighten the tragic appearance of that sorrow, and the arrangement of the narrative for that purpose inevitably involves what seems to the reader, who is looking for an orderly development and explanation of character, an unaccountable confusion of the chronology of events. The whole story of Criseyde is presented at the beginning of the Fifth Book down to the time she gives herself to Diomede, a period of about two years.[56] Chaucer then goes back to the ninth day after her departure from Troy and takes up his description of Troilus's sorrow.[57] By concealing such chronological references as he gives and by telling of Criseyde's fall in comparatively few words, Chaucer gives the impression that that fall is very rapid. With this defection and its apparent undignified haste fresh in the reader's mind, he describes Troilus on the Trojan walls sighing his soul towards the Grecian tents, pathetically confident that each approaching figure is Criseyde. Chaucer has arranged the sequence of the events in the narrative in the order which will give the maximum effectiveness to the tragic scene. This arrangement hopelessly muddles in the reader's mind any possible chronology, so necessary if we are to follow the development of Criseyde's character. Yet Troilus's sorrow would be infinitely less pathetic if Chaucer were to say: "And as a matter of fact, just about this time Criseyde was courageously determining to return to Troy."[58] If Chaucer had centered his purpose in the development of the characters, something like that would have been necessary, but since his purpose was to create a tragic action, it was not only unnecessary but highly undesirable.

All through these final scenes this purpose is apparent. Criseyde, rather surprisingly, has by far the larger number of protestations of love and loyalty.[59] They were not meant to prove her either a hypocrite or a moral weakling. Each of them is true to Chaucer's static characterization of her, and each of them, against the background of the reader's knowledge of the future, has an ironic effect in terms of the action. Troilus accuses Criseyde of disloyalty long before she has actually contemplated /78/ any such thing.[60] This accusation was certainly not intended by Chaucer to prove Troilus's unreasoning jealousy, as Mr. Graydon argues, but merely to give the impression that the fatal conclusion of the action was rapidly and irresistibly approaching. As soon as Criseyde is out of Troy, Pandar suddenly becomes certain she will never return.[61] No reason for this opinion is given, and it utterly contradicts his previous serious and considered praise of Criseyde's integrity.[62] This change of front is unmotivated. It serves the purpose of heightening by contrast the tragic irony of Troilus's confidence that Criseyde will return; it is not a hint of Criseyde's motive for not returning.

There is, finally, the crux of the poem so far as this question of Criseyde's character is concerned, that is, her unfaithfulness. Her soliloquy on the ninth night in the Greek camp[63] is so similar to her earlier meditation on whether she ought to yield to Troilus or not[64] that it is difficult to avoid comparing them. In each she considers carefully all the facts involved and in each reaches a definite decision; in the latter soliloquy her decision is that she will go to Troy in spite of all the difficulties.[65] It is not easy to see how the woman presented in this soliloquy differs in any fundamental respect from the woman of the earlier parts of the poem. And the difficulty of believing Chaucer meant this speech to be taken as an indication that Criseyde was "calculating" is as great as the difficulty of believing that that was his intention in writing her soliloquy on love in Book Two. Furthermore, instead of describing a change in her attitude subsequent to this soliloquy which we are to take as the cause of her staying with the Greeks, Chaucer merely states in five brief lines that she did stay, that two months later she was still in the Greek camp.[66] Criseyde's failure to return to Troy is one of the necessary events in the story Chaucer is telling. The whole structure of the poem at this point shows that he did not think of it as determined by Criseyde's character.

Nor does Chaucer, in any serious psychological sense, motivate Criseyde's physical betrayal of Troilus. She betrays Troilus because the action requires it, because she had to if the tragic possibilities of the main action, "the double sorwe of Troilus," were to be worked out completely, and not because of anything in her character which made that betrayal inevitable. Chaucer says she is guilty, but he never shows us a woman whose state of mind is such as to make the reader believe /79/ her capable of betraying Troilus.[67] In fact, Chaucer carefully avoids showing the reader Criseyde at all from the time when she makes her last statement of loyalty to Troilus to the time when she expresses her grief at her betrayal of him.[68] He even refuses to say that "she yaf hym [i.e., Diomede] hire herte, "[69] and there is what appears to be a conscious effort on Chaucer's part to blur Criseyde's inconstancy in the reader's mind as much as he can without destroying belief in it altogether.[70] The nearest Chaucer comes to offering on his own account (as apart from dramatically presenting) a reason for Criseyde's betrayal of Troilus is to hint at one in the stanza in which he explains why she did not return to Troy.[71] But this reason is not psychologically reconcilable with the character displayed by Criseyde. No conceivable character capable of acting as Criseyde did for this reason can be brought into accord with the woman presented in the first four and one half books of the poem or with the woman who was grief-stricken "whan that she falsed Troilus."

The Criseyde we are shown, both before and after the event of her yielding to Diomede, displays exactly the same characteristics we have associated with Criseyde since the beginning of the narrative. It is difficult to believe that Chaucer was not conscious of the consequences of this arrangement of the narrative. It leaves us knowing that Criseyde has betrayed Troilus and yet visualizing her, as we have from the start, as gentle, tender-hearted, loving and honorable. In other words, Chaucer's arrangement is calculated to leave our sense of Criseyde's character as little affected as possible by our knowledge of her act; it does the best it can to prevent our substituting for the Criseyde we have known all along the character we must invent if we are successfully to imagine Criseyde's yielding to Diomede.[72] /80/

The hypothesis that Chaucer meant to ascribe to Criseyde a character calculated to explain her betrayal of Troilus seems to me to break down most completely at this most crucial point. For one thing, it is so incompatible with Chaucer's treatment of this part of the narrative that in order to set it up in the first place the critic must rewrite the poem in his imagination, at least to the extent of adding a new scene. For another, it requires proof that Chaucer has shown Criseyde as consistently "impressionable and yielding" or psychopathically terrified from the first, and it seems to me impossible to present this proof without distorting the implications of the first four books of the poem. Finally, such an explanation prevents the reader from seeing Criseyde as a tragic figure. If Criseyde's character is such as to be a complete explanation of her betrayal of Troilus then she is at best merely pathetic; it is only if there is a contrast between what she seems to the reader to be and what he knows her to have done that she becomes tragic. It may be argued, of course, that Chaucer invented her only as an instrument for producing the tragedy of Troilus, but if he intended Criseyde, in addition, to be tragic in her own right, then he must have aimed at this contrast between what she is and what she does, a contrast which we destroy if we insist on seeing her as no better than she should be.

In real life as we believe it to be or in a psychological novel that contrast would be impossible. For in these worlds deeds are the outward manifestations of a process of which the inward manifestations are congruous thoughts and feelings. In them, therefore, people cannot approach and look back upon an act of inconstancy rebelling against it with their whole natures, any more than they can take this attitude while committing murder.[73] But Chaucer's Criseyde, not living in such a world, can and does rebel against her own act, Chaucer shows her as horrified at her disloyalty, regretful of the loss of her good name and greatly admiring Troilus. Is not this precisely the attitude to be expected from the woman portrayed in the first four books of the poem had she to face the situation in which Criseyde finds herself? Chaucer could scarcely have portrayed her in this fashion had he meant us to think of her character as now degenerated to the point where her betrayal of Troilus is the perfect manifestation of it, and he certainly would not have so portrayed her, here or elsewhere, had he meant us to think of her as capable of that betrayal from the start.

From this point forward Chaucer's arrangement of the narrative is governed by his wish to emphasize the sorrow of Troilus. Criseyde's /81/ suffering and her hope that she may yet return to Troy, even though she has overstayed her ten days,[74] are presented just before Chaucer describes her thoughts as she decides — Troilus and Troy being forgotten — to remain in the Greek camp.[75] This sequence is incongruous, so far as any explanation of her character goes, but it strengthens the pathos of her peroration on Troilus which follows and so heightens the tragedy.

When Criseyde's first letter from the Greek camp is summarized, Chaucer very definitely gives the impression that the letter is not quite honest, and advises Troilus to give up any hope of Criseyde.[76] This impression is contrary to what we can, if we wish, prove to be the "facts," for Chaucer tells us elsewhere that the letter was written about two months after Criseyde's departure,[77] and on Chaucer's own say-so she was at that period not at all entangled with Diomede and probably had not

yet ceased to hope she might return to Troy.[78] But these "facts" must not
be allowed to obtrude here, for they would interrupt the steady and fatal
progression of Troilus's tragedy. The "false" impression that Chaucer
gives furthers that tragedy; it makes us sympathize with Troilus's
growing belief that Criseyde has been unfaithful to him, and that is
Chaucer's purpose.

The same method is followed with Criseyde's second letter.[79] There is
no way of knowing exactly when it was written[80] or whether Criseyde is
lying. Chaucer does not even bother to provide this information so vital
to a complete understanding of Criseyde's character. The letter is part of
Troilus's fate; it completes his tragedy.[81]

So, it seems to me, Criseyde is meant to be taken. Her character is a
combination of subtly observed characteristics, and the illusion of reality
that character leaves on a reader's mind is the result, not of Chaucer's
painstaking motivation of every event from within the character, but
rather of the variety and concreteness with which he puts these
characteristics on display in any scene in which the character is
presented. The character of Criseyde is primarily an instrument for, and a
unit in, a tragic action; it is therefore statically conceived and is related to
the action by congruence rather than by cause and effect. For both
Troilus and Criseyde are the victims of an act determined, not by
Criseyde's character, but by the dramatic necessities of the action.

Notes

1. "The author's intention" is of course a fiction; his actual intention is something one
can never, in any exact sense, know, and is perhaps not really relevant to the meaning of
the poem. But it is a convenient fiction, not simply because the nature of language makes
it difficult to avoid, but because it indicates that the purpose of this analysis is to suggest
the response which the structure of the poem seems to require. Analysis may have other
purposes, and in so far as the analyses discussed below do have other purposes, justice is
not done them in this essay.

2. v, 825. — All references are to *Chaucer's Troilus and Criseyde*, ed. R. K. Root
(Princeton, 1926).

3. *The Poetry of Chaucer* (Cambridge, 1922), p. 114. "Slydynge of corage" is interpreted
as meaning emotionally shallow and inclined to be fickle (see Professor Root's note to this
line in his edition of the poem).

4. The passage in question is quoted on page 58. Nor does it seem probable that anyone
reading Criseyde's remark in her first soliloquy, "It nedeth me ful sleighly for to pleie"
(II, 462), in its context would interpret it as evidence that she was calculating in the

pejorative sense. *Sleighly* may mean "guilefully" or "wisely." But in this instance the context as a whole and two of the texts (which read *wisly*) show that the meaning was "wisely." Her later words, plainly an elaboration of this line, clinch the matter:

> But natheles, with goddes governaunce,
> I shal so doon, myn honour shal I kepe,
> And ek his [i.e., Pandar's] lif.

As Mr. C.S. Lewis has said, "If we are determined to criticize her behaviour in the first part of the poem from any standpoint save that of Christian chastity, it would be more rational to say that she is not wanton enough, not calculating enough." *The Allegory of Love* (Oxford, 1936), p. 183.

5. Or if one wants Chaucer's own adjectives, *sobre, symple, wys, tendre herted.* (V, 820–825; the passage is quoted on p. 58).

6. *Chaucer and his Poetry* (Cambridge, 1915), p. 135. "Baffling alike to us and to herself" (*ibid.*, p. 126) [above, pp. 16, 11], he adds elsewhere, as if Chaucer intended us not to be able to understand her.

7. II, 673–679.

8. Mr. C.S. Lewis's more recent analysis of the meaning of Criseyde (*The Allegory of Love*, pp. 179–190) is of this general type. According to Mr. Lewis we are meant to see Criseyde as from beginning to end governed by an almost pathological fear ("a dash of what is now called mazochism"); this theory leads him to argue that Chaucer meant the reader to see Criseyde's remarks at the last meeting of the lovers as "desperate speeches in which Creseide, with pitiful ignorance of her self, attempts to assume the role of comforter . . ." and that he meant her resolutions to return to Troy after she had reached the Greek camp to be seen by the reader as "desperate efforts to rise above herself."

9. "Emphasis cannot be too strong when placed upon the fact that in *Troilus and Criseyde* an absolutely inescapable necessity governs the progress of the story." W. C. Curry, "Destiny in Chaucer's *Troilus*," *PMLA*, XLV (1930), 152.

10. The allied problem of the connection between Chaucer's conception of character on the one hand and of Fortune and Destiny on the other is far too complex to be taken up here. But see W.C. Curry, "Destiny in Chaucer's *Troilus*," *PMLA*, XLV (1930), 129–168; H. R. Patch, "Troilus on Determinism," *Speculum*, VI (1931), 225–243; and William Farnham, *The Medieval Heritage of Elizabethan Tragedy* (Berkeley, 1936), especially pp. 155–157. Professor Patch, if I understand him correctly, argues that any narrative in which there is not "the interplay of free motivation" is "the spectacle of the action of irresponsible puppets." If this line of reasoning be valid, then it must follow from the argument of this essay that Chaucer was a complete determinist, a conclusion which is certainly open to question. But Professor Patch's line of reasoning seems to me not only to involve a confusion of literal and metaphorical statements (it is only by metaphor that one can speak meaningfully of any characters as "irresponsible puppets" since literally speaking all characters are just that) but also to over-simplify the problem by assuming that there must be a direct connection between an author's narrative method and his philosophic opinions. Some kind of connection no doubt always exists, but surely it is not such that one can conclude that all narratives except those which provide a tight cause-and-effect relationship between the characters and the events are evidence of their author's disbelief in the freedom of the human will and the responsibility of human beings for their own acts.

11. I cannot, for example, believe that we are intended to draw any conclusions as to character from the fact that Chaucer puts into Criseyde's mouth learned arguments borrowed from Boethius (e.g., III, 813-826).

12. This is not to say, of course, that they do not fall in love, become unhappy, or change their opinions from time to time as the story may demand. It is to say that the basic set of characteristics given them at the beginning remains unchanged through these varying circumstances of the story to the end.

13. The point is discussed below.

14. Consider, for example, the splendid tragic irony of Criseyde's anxious apology for what she says at the lovers' last meeting in Troy (IV,1282-95. That Chaucer did not intend Criseyde to appear hypocritical here is evident from IV, 1415-21). The speech is completely in character in Chaucer's sense of the word; that is, it fits precisely Criseyde's already established characteristics of reasonableness and patient affection. According to the modern conception of character, however, the speech is impossible. Criseyde has no motive whatsoever, either in Troilus's character or in her own so far as Chaucer has presented them to us, for expecting Troilus to object to plans which will bring them new hope.

15. V, 820-825.

16. See Karl Young, "Chaucer's 'Troilus and Criseyde' as Romance," *PMLA*, LIII (1938), p. 39.

17. II, 253-254.

18. II, 38. The references to Boccaccio are to *The Filostrato of Giovanni Boccaccio*, trans. N.E. Griffin and A. B. Myrick (Philadelphia, 1929).

19. II, 499-502. Note, further, the implications of line 505.

20. II, 55.

21. See note 4. Professor Root, indeed, takes it as evidence of both "cool calculation" and a tendency to drift into things. *Op. cit.*, p. 108.

22. And only, too, if one ignores the convention whereby the soliloquy is used to convey information which the character could not or ought not to be aware of. *Cp.* Pandar's thoughts (II, 267-273), which are certainly not intended to make us think him "calculating."

23. II, 711.

24. II, 83.

25. II, 666-679, 1265-74.

26. II, 65 ff.

27. II, 673-675. For Criseyde to fall deeply in love with Troilus immediately would be shockingly indecorous according to the courtly love code. In other words, if she is to appear an admirable person, the reader must be made to believe she fell in love slowly.

28. II, 651.

29. Professor Kittredge has described perfectly the effect Chaucer was aiming at. *Op cit.*, p. 133 [above, pp. 15-16].

30. "For the character of Criseyde as Chaucer has conceived it, such a course of action [i.e., yielding at once] would have been much too direct. It would have required a definite decision instead of a genial drifting with circumstance." R.K. Root, *op. cit.*, p. 109.

31. II, 1128-41.

32.   She wente allone, and gan hire herte unfettre
       Out of the desdaynes prison but a lite (II, 1216-17).

33. II, 113.

34. II, 1159-63.

35. II, 1265-74. Note that it is here Chaucer translates the phrases Boccaccio used to describe Criseyde's first sight of Troilus (Boccaccio's words are quoted on p. 60).

36. III, 85-86.

37. III, 155-182. "Her surrender is conscious and voluntary; for she is neither ignorant nor unsophisticated." G.L. Kittredge, *op. cit.*, pp. 131-132. [above, p. 15].

38. III, 750 ff.

39. III, 568-581. This theory is based on the assumption that II, 575-581, are ironic (G. L. Kittredge, *op. cit.*, p. 132 [above, p. 15]; R.K. Root, *op. cit.*, p. 111). But *cp.*, II, 640-644.

40. III, 799-945.

41. In addition, the reader has Chaucer's own word for it that Criseyde was not playing at being anxious — for example, in III, 799-801, and particularly in III, 918-924. "The belief that she saw through the wiles of Pandarus, and only appeared to be led by circumstances while in fact she went the way she had intended from the beginning, can be held only in defiance of the text." C.S. Lewis, *op. cit.*, p. 182.

42.   Now certes, em, tomorwe, and I hym se,
       I shal of that as ful excusen me, etc. (III, 809-810).

43. Her hesitancy is not, of course, on the grounds that she considers surrender immoral, but, in accordance with courtly love doctrines, on the grounds of some lingering doubt as to Troilus's trustworthiness (III, 1226-39).

44. III, 1107-13.

45. III, 1210-11.

46. III, 848-849.

47. Joseph M. Beatty, Jr., "Mr. Graydon's 'Defense of Criseyde'," *SP*, XXVI (1929), 472.

48. G.L. Kittredge, *op. cit.*, p. 133 [above, p. 16].

49. IV, 1415-21, V, 19-21. "If any grief that poetry tells of was ever sincere, then so was Criseyde's grief at leaving Troilus." C.S. Lewis, *op.cit.*, pp. 184-185.

50. V, 771-784 and 897-903.

51. G.L. Kittredge, *op. cit.*, p. 120 [above, p. 8].

52. V, 694-700 and 764-765. If Professor Kittredge means here, not that Criseyde failed to return because she could not talk Calchas around, but that her failure was the

consequence rather of a Destiny beyond her control than her will (that however strongly she willed her return it would not take place), then this statement is not reconcilable with a theory which makes Criseyde's character the explanation of her actions. See W.C. Curry, *op. cit.*, p. 149, where Professor Kittredge's statement is taken to mean that the decrees of Destiny are stronger than Criseyde's will.

53. V, 1086-92.

54. Joseph S. Graydon, "Defense of Criseyde," *PMLA* (1929), 141-177. Two possibilities are of course present: (1) Chaucer had a chronology in mind and deliberately blurred it to achieve purposes which a clear account of the chronology would have made impossible; or (2) he never worked out a chronology, simply using time references, as Shakespeare sometimes did, for their immediate effect, without worrying if one time reference contradicted another.

55. V, 1348-51.

56. V, 687-1099.

57. V, 1100 ff. That Chaucer is picking up the account at about the ninth day is indicated by V, 680-681.

58. Which, if there is any chronology at all, she was. V, 764-765.

59. IV, 757-798 and 1681-87.

60. Graydon, *op. cit.*, p. 170.

61. V, 505-511.

62. III, 253-259 and 267-273.

> For never was ther wight, I dar wel swere,
> That evere wiste that she dide amys (III, 269-270).

63. V, 689-765.

64. II, 703-812.

65. This decision is stated twice in the soliloquy. V, 750-754 and 764-765.

66. V, 766-770.

67. The situation is parallel to that in Book Two where Chaucer says Criseyde is not in love with Troilus but shows us a woman who is. See above.

68. V, 1005-08, 1054-85.

69. V, 1050.

70. This apparently carefully calculated treatment is pervasive (e.g., IV, 15-21; V, 768-769; V, 1093-99); Chaucer suddenly ceases not only to present Criseyde to us but, ostensibly, to know what she thought or felt. "I fynde ek in stories elleswhere" or "Men seyn" replaces "And thus she to hym seyde as ye may here, / As she that hadde hir herte on Troilus, etc." We are made to feel, in Professor Root's words, that "with utmost reluctance, and of sheer compulsion, [Chaucer] narrates the shame of Criseyde as it stands recorded in his old books" (*op. cit.*, p. 114).

71. V, 1023-29.

72. All explanations of Criseyde which assume that Chaucer was primarily interested in character must start by imagining a woman capable of yielding to Diomede and must then attempt to reconcile that woman with the Criseyde portrayed in the poem. They must, since Chaucer failed to do so, invent an episode in which Criseyde yields to Diomede and portray the woman who participated in that episode (see, for example, C.S. Lewis, *op cit.*, p. 189); they are then committed to interpreting the rest of the poem in terms of this woman; the Criseyde of their explanation originally derives from a scene Chaucer omitted from the poem.

73. *Macbeth*, II, i, ii.—For like Criseyde's, Macbeth's tragedy, as distinguished from the tragic effect of the play as a whole, depends on the contrast between the essential nobility of his character and the wickedness of his deeds.

74. V, 862-868, 953-959 and 1002-08.

75. V, 1023-29.

76. V, 1429-35.

77. V, 1348-51.

78. See passages referred to in note 74.

79. V, 1590 ff.

80. The first letter was written something over two months after Criseyde's departure (V, 1348-49); the second letter some time later.

81. V, 1639-45.

Distance and Predestination in "Troilus and Criseyde"
by Morton W. Bloomfield

For we are but of yesterday. — Job viii.9

In *Troilus and Criseyde* Chaucer as commentator occupies an unusual role. It is indeed common for authors to enter their own works in many ways. Writers as diverse as Homer, Virgil, Dante, Cervantes, Fielding, Thackeray, and George Eliot all do so. Sometimes, as with Fielding, the author may keep a distance between himself and his story; sometimes, as with Dante, he may penetrate into his story as a major or the major character; and sometimes, as with Homer, he may both enter and withdraw at will. When Homer directly addresses one of his characters, he is deliberately breaking down, for artistic reasons, the aloofness to which he generally holds.

Chaucer also frequently appears in his own works, usually as one of his dramatis personae, and participates in the action.[1] Although he is not always an important or major character, his actions or dreams within the work frequently provide the occasion for, or give a supposed rationale to, his literary creations. Chaucer the character's decision to go on a pilgrimage to Canterbury provides the ostensible justification for the *Canterbury Tales*. His dreams as a character, following a great medieval literary convention, give rise to the *Parlement of Foules* and the *Hous of Fame*.

In *Troilus and Criseyde* Chaucer plays his artistic role with a striking difference. Here he conceives of himself as the narrator of a history, of a true event as the Middle Ages conceived it, which happened in the past;

Reprinted by permission of the author and the Modern Language Association of America from *PMLA* 72 (1957): 14–26. The original pagination is indicated between slashes in the text. The Afterword was written for this anthology.

and as historian he meticulously maintains a distance between himself and the events in the story. His aloofness is similar to and yet different from Fielding's in *Tom Jones* or Thackeray's in *Vanity Fair*. In these works the authors look upon their puppets from their omniscient, ironical, humorous, and at times melancholy point of view and make comments on them or their predicaments, using them as excuses for brief essays or paragraphs on different subjects. In *Troilus* Chaucer does not look upon his characters as his creations. His assumed role is primarily descriptive and expository. Though we are continually reminded of the presence of Chaucer the historian, narrator, and commentator, at /15/ the same time we are never allowed to forget that he is separate from the events he is recording.

Troilus is not a dream vision nor is it a contemporary event. It is the past made extremely vivid by the extensive use of dialogue, but still the past. Chaucer cannot change the elements of his story. As God cannot violate His own rationality, Chaucer cannot violate his data. Bound by his self-imposed task of historian, he both implies and says directly that he cannot do other than report his tale.

If we assume that Chaucer is a painstaking artist — and it is impossible not to — it is clear that the nature of the role he assumes has an extremely important meaning in the economy and plan of the poem. Why, we must ask, does Chaucer as character-narrator continually remind us of his aloofness from and impotence in the face of the events he is narrating? An historian takes for granted what Chaucer does not take for granted. A Gibbon does not tell us constantly that the events of the decline and fall of the Roman Empire are beyond his control. That is an assumption that anyone reading a true history makes at the outset. Chaucer introduces just this assumption into his body of his work, continually reminding us of what seems, in the context of a supposed history, most obvious. What is normally outside the historical work, a presupposition of it, is in the history of Troilus and Criseyde brought into the poem and made much of. This unusual creative act calls for examination.

We must also wonder at the quantitative bulk of Chaucer's comments on the story. Frequently, even in the midst of the action of the inner story, we are reminded of the presence of the narrator — sometimes, it is true, by only a word or two. We cannot dismiss these numerous comments merely as remarks necessary to establish rapport with the audience under conditions of oral delivery. The few remarks of this nature are easy to pick out. If we compare the simple comments made by the narrator in, say *Havelock the Dane* or any other medieval romance with those made by the *Troilus* narrator, I think the difference is plain.

Although many stanzas belong completely to the commentator *in propria persona* and others pertain to the events of the tale, so many are partly one or the other, or merely suggest the presence of a narrator, that a mathematical table which could reveal the actual percentage of commentator stanzas or lines would be misleading and inaccurate.[2] Anyone /16/ who has read the poem must be aware of the presence of the commentator most of the time; one is rarely allowed to forget it for long. And even more impressive than the number of comments are the times and nature of the author's intervention. At all the great moments he is there directing us, speaking in his own person close to us and far from the events of the tragedy which he is presenting to us within the bounds of historical fact.

This sense of distance between Chaucer as character and his story is conveyed to us in what may be designated as temporal, spatial, aesthetic, and religious ways, each reinforcing the other and overlapping. For the sake of clarity, however, we may examine each in turn as a separate kind of aloofness.

The aspect of temporal distance is the one most constantly emphasized throughout the poem. Chaucer again and again tells us that the events he is recording are historical and past. He lets us know that customs have changed since the time when Pandarus, Troilus, and Criseyde lived. The characters are pagans who go to temples to worship strange gods and are caught up in one of the great cataclysms of history. Their ways of living are different from ours. Their love-making varies from the modern style. They lived a long time ago, and Chaucer, to tell their story, is forced to rely on the historians. In order to understand their actions, we must make an effort in comprehension. Yet, says Chaucer, diversity of custom is natural. At times, it is true, Chaucer is very anachronistic, but he still succeeds in giving his readers (or listeners) a feeling for the pastness of his characters and their sad story and for what we today call cultural relativity.[3]

Throughout, Chaucer tries to give us a sense of the great sweep of time which moves down to the present and into the future and back beyond Troy, deepening our sense of the temporal dimension. He tells us that speech and customs change within a thousand years (II.22 ff.) and that this work he is writing is also subject to linguistic variability (V.1793 ff.). Kingdoms and power pass away too; the *translatio regni* (or *imperii*) is inexorable — "regnes shal be flitted/Fro folk in folk" (v. 1544–45). The characters themselves reach even farther backward in time. Criseyde and her ladies read of another siege, the fall of Thebes, which took place long before the siege of Troy (II.81 ff.). Cassandra, in /17/ her interpretation of Troilus' dream (V. 1450–1519), goes into ancient history to explain Diomede's lineage. We are all part of time's kingdom, and we are never allowed to forget it.

Yet, as I have already mentioned, Chaucer vividly reconstructs, especially in his use of dialogue, the day-by-day living of his chief characters. This precision of detail and liveliness of conversation only serve to weight the contrast between himself in the present and his story in the past, to make the present even more evanescent in the sweep of inexorable change. It is the other side of the coin. These inner events are in the past and in a sense dead, but when they occurred they were just as vivid as the events that are happening now. The strong reality and, in a sense, nearness of the past makes meaningful its disappearance and emphasizes paradoxically its distance. If there are no strong unique facts, there is nothing to lament. We cannot escape into the web of myth and cycle; the uniqueness of the past is the guarantee of its own transience. This is the true historical view and this is Chaucer's view. For him, however, even unique events have meaning, but only in the framework of a world view which can put history into its proper place.

Not frequently used, yet most important when it is, is the sense of spatial distance which Chaucer arouses in his readers. The events of the poem take place in faraway Asia Minor. Chaucer creates a sense of spatial distance by giving us a shifting sense of nearness and farness. At times we seem to be seeing the Trojan events as if from a great distance and at others we seem to be set down among the characters. This sense of varying distance is most subtly illustrated in the fifth book when Chaucer, after creating a most vivid sense of intimacy and closeness in describing the wooing of Criseyde by Diomede, suddenly moves to objectivity and distance in introducing the portraits of the two lovers and his heroine (799 ff.) — a device taken from Dares. With the approach of the hour of betrayal, as we become emotionally wrought up and closely involved, Chaucer the narrator brings us sharply back to his all-seeing eye and to a distance. The same technique may also be seen elsewhere in the poem. This continual inversion of the telescope increases our sense of space and gives us a kind of literary equivalent to the perspective of depth in painting.

Chaucer, in his insistence on cultural relativity, not only emphasizes chronological but also geographic variability. "Ek for to wynnen love in sondry ages,/In sondry londes, sondry been usages" (II.27–28). Above all we get this sense of spatial distance in the final ascent of Troilus to the ogdoad, the eighth sphere,[4] where in a sense he joins /18/ Chaucer in looking down on this "litel spot of erthe" and can even contemplate his own death with equanimity.

The sense of aesthetic distance[5] is evoked by the continual distinction Chaucer makes between the story and the commentator, between the framework and the inner events. Although his basic "facts" are given, Chaucer never lets the reader doubt for long that he is the narrator and interpreter of the story. Once, at least, he adopts a humorous attitude towards his dilemma. He insists that he is giving his readers Troilus' song of love (I.400 ff.), "Naught only the sentence" as reported by Lollius but "save oure tonges difference" "every word right thus." This attitude is, however, rare. But it is not unusual for Chaucer to insist upon his bondage to the facts. Yet he strains against the snare of true events in which he is caught. Indeed Chaucer tries again and again, especially where the betrayal of Criseyde is involved, to fight against the truth of the events he is "recording." He never hides his partiality for that "hevennysh perfit creature" (I.104), and in this attitude as in others he notifies us of the narrow latitude which is allowed him. As he approaches the actual betrayal, he slows down; and with evident reluctance, as his reiterated, "the storie telleth us" (V.1037), "I fynde ek in the stories elleswhere" (V. 1044), "men seyn—I not" (V.1050) show, he struggles against the predestined climax. The piling up of these phrases here emphasizes the struggle of the artist-narrator against the brutality of the facts to which he cannot give a good turn. As a faithful historian, he cannot evade the rigidity of decisive events — the given. Criseyde's reception /19/ of Diomede cannot be glossed over.[6] All this makes us more aware of Chaucer the narrator than ordinarily and increases our sense of aesthetic distance between the reporter and what is reported, between the frame and what is framed.

Finally we may call certain aspects of Chaucerian distance religious. Troilus, Pandarus, and Criseyde are pagans who lived "while men loved the lawe of kinde" (*Book of the Duchess*, l. 56) — under natural law. The great barrier of God's revelation at Sinai and in Christ separates Chaucer and us from them. Chaucer portrays them consciously as pagans, for he never puts Christian sentiments into their mouths.[7] He may violate our historic sense by making the lovers act according to the medieval courtly love code, but not by making them worship Christ. They are reasonable pagans who can attain to the truths of natural law — to the concept of a God, a creator, and to the rational moral law but never to the truths of

revealed Christian religion. Chaucer is very clear on this point and in the
great peroration to the poem he expressly says

> Lo here, of payens corsed olde rites,
> Lo here, what alle hire goddes may availle;
> Lo here, thise wrecched worldes appetites;
> Lo here, the fyn and guerdoun for travaille
> Of Jove, Appollo, of Mars, of swich rascaille! (V. 1849-53)

In general, until the end of the poem, Chaucer, as we shall see, plays
down his own Christianity for good reason. He even, at times and in
consonance with the epic tradition which came down to him, calls upon
the pagan Muses and Furies, but he does not avoid the Christian point of
view when he feels it necessary to be expressed. Although the religious
barrier is not emphasized until the conclusion, we are left in no doubt
/20/ throughout as to its separating Chaucer from his characters. This
sense of religious distance becomes at the end a vital part of the author's
interpretation of his story.

A close study of Chaucer's proems written as prefaces to the first four
books bears out the analysis offered here. In these Chaucer speaks out,
and from his emphases and invocations we may gain some clues as to his
intentions. At the beginning of the first proem, we are told of the subject of
the work and of its unhappy fatal end. Chaucer does not allow us to
remain in suspense at all. He exercises his role as historical commentator
immediately at the outset. Tesiphone, one of the Furies, is invoked as an
aid. She is a sorrowing Fury, as Dante had taught Chaucer to view her.
She is responsible for the torment of humans, but she weeps for her
actions. She is also in a sense the invoker himself who puts himself in his
poem in a similar role. Chaucer is also a sorrowing tormenter who is
retelling a true tale, the predestined end of which he cannot alter. Though
ultimately he is to conquer it through religion, Chaucer the commentator
is throughout most of the poem a victim of the historical determinism of
his own poem. Although it is set down in the introduction to the poem, we
may not understand the full meaning of Chaucer's entanglement and the
escape provided by Christianity until we reach its end. There the
Christian solution to the dilemma of the first proem is again presented but
deepened by our knowledge of Troilus' fate and by a greater emphasis.
Then, we shall have followed through the sad story under Chaucer the
commentator's guidance and the answer is plain. In the proem, on the
first reading, however, the problem and the solution cannot be clear in

spite of Chaucer's open words. We too must discover the answer.

On the other hand, in the first prologue, he does tell us, so that we may understand, that he the conductor and recorder of his story is like Troilus after the betrayal, unhappy in love. In the *Book of the Duchess*, the dreamer's unhappiness in love is assuaged within the dream and inner story by the grief of the man in black, whose loss of his beloved foreshadows what would have happened to the dreamer's love in one form or another, for all earthly love is transitory. Death is worse than unhappiness in love. Chaucer the *Troilus* narrator who dares not pray to love "for myn unliklynesse" is also going to learn in his tale that the love of the Eternal is the only true love. Actually Chaucer, because he conceives of himself as historian, has already learned before he begins. Hence, it is not quite accurate to say as above that he is going to learn, for he already knows. The reader, however, unless he is extraordinarily acute, remains in ignorance until he finishes the whole work. He discovers in the course of the experience of the history what Chaucer already knows and has really told him in the beginning, for Chaucer concludes his first proem by calling on all lovers both successful and unsuccessful /21/ to join him in prayer for Troilus. It is, he says, only in heaven, in the *patria* of medieval theology, that we can find lasting happiness. Troilus will find a pagan equivalent for this in his pagan heaven at the end. One cannot, however, quite believe Chaucer here until one reads the poem and finds that he is deadly serious when he prays that God "graunte" unhappy lovers "soone owt of this world to pace" (I.41). It is the love of God which is the answer to the love of woman and of all earthly things.

In other words, Chaucer in his introduction to the poem indicates his bondage to historical fact, his own grief at his position, the problem of the unhappiness in this world which he, like Troilus and all unhappy lovers, must face, and the only true solution for all the lovers of this world.

The second proem appeals to Clio, the Muse of history, and alludes to the diversity of human custom and language. The sense of history and cultural relativity manifested here emphasizes the distance in time which temporal barriers impose. "For every wight which that to Rome went/Halt not o path, or alwey o manere" (II.36-37).

The opening of Book III calls upon Venus, goddess of love, and, although it makes other points as well, underlines again the pagan quality of the history. Venus in her symbolic, astrological, and divine role conquers the whole world and binds its dissonances and discords together. It is she who understands the mysteries of love and who

explains the apparent irrationality of love. The proem closes with a brief
reference to Calliope, Muse of epic poetry, as Chaucer wishes to be
worthy, as an artist, of his great theme of love.

Finally, in the last proem, we have an appeal to Fortune the great
presiding deity of the sublunar world. Here as always she suggests
instability and transience. Chaucer then alludes to the binding power of
his sources. He closes his prologue with an invocation to all the Furies
and to Mars with overtones suggesting his unhappy role as commentator
and the paganness of the story he is unfolding.

These proems cannot be completely explained in terms of my
interpretation, for they are also, especially the third and fourth,
appropriate artistically to the theme of the books they serve to introduce
and the various stages of the narrative. In general they emphasize the
tragic end of the tale, the unwilling Fury-like role Chaucer has to play, the
historical bonds which shackle him, the pity of it all, the aloofness and
distance between the Chaucer of the poem and the history itself he is
telling, and the one possible solution to the unhappiness of the world. Nor
are these sentiments confined to the prefaces. They occur again and again
throughout the body of the poem.[8] Chaucer takes pains to create /22/
himself as a character in his poem and also to dissociate this character
continually from his story.

The attitude of Chaucer the character throughout makes it possible for
us to understand the crucial importance of the concept of predestination
in the poem. In the past there has been much debate in Chaucerian
criticism over the question of predestination in *Troilus*. We know that
Chaucer was profoundly interested in this question and that it was a
preoccupation of his age. It seems to me that, if we regard the framework
of the poem — the role that Chaucer sets himself as commentator — as a
meaningful part of the poem and if we consider the various references to
fate and destiny in the text, we can only come to the conclusion that the
Chaucerian sense of distance and aloofness is the artistic correlative to
the concept of predestination. *Troilus and Criseyde* is a medieval tragedy
of predestination because the reader is continually forced by the
commentator to look upon the story from the point of view of its end and
from a distance. The crux of the problem of predestination is knowledge.
So long as the future is not known to the participants in action, they can
act as if they were free. But once a position of distance from the action is
taken, then all can be seen as inevitable. And it is just this position which
Chaucer the commentator takes and forces upon us from the very
beginning. As John of Salisbury writes, "however, when you have

entered a place, it is impossible that you have not entered it; when a thing has been done it is impossible that it be classed with things not done; and there is no recalling to non-existence a thing of the past."[9] All this presupposes knowledge which is impossible *in media re*. It is just this knowledge that Chaucer the commentator-historian gives us as he reconstructs the past. Hence we are forced into an awareness of the inevitability of the tragedy and get our future and our present at the same time, as it were.

Bound by the distance of time and space, of art and religion, Chaucer sits above his creation and foresees, even as God foresees, the doom of his own creatures: God, the *Deus artifex* who is in medieval philosophy the supreme artist and whose masterpiece is the created world.[10] But Chaucer is like God only insofar as he can know the outcome, not as creator. Analogically, because he is dealing with history, and, we must remember, to the medieval Englishman his own history, he can parallel somewhat his Maker. He is not the creator of the events and personages he is presenting to us; hence he cannot change the results. On the other /23/ hand God is the creator of His creatures; but He is bound by His own rationality and His foreknowledge. The sense of distance that Chaucer enforces on us accentuates the parallel with God and His providential predestination. We cannot leap the barriers which life imposes on us, but in the companionship of an historian we can imitate God *in parvo*. As God with His complete knowledge of future contingents sees the world laid out before Him all in the twinkling of an eye, so, in the case of history, with a guide, we share in small measure a similar experience. The guide is with us all the way, pointing to the end and to the pity of it. We must take our history from his point of view.

It is, of course, as hazardous to attribute opinions to Chaucer as it is to Shakespeare. Yet I suspect both were predestinarians—insofar as Christianity allows one to be. It is curious that all the great speeches on freedom of the will in Shakespeare's plays are put into the mouths of his villains — Edmund in *Lear*, Iago in *Othello*, and Cassius in *Julius Caesar*. This is not the place to discuss the relation of Chaucer to fourteenth-century thinking or to predestination, but I think he stands with Bishop Bradwardine who, when Chaucer was still very young, thundered against the libertarians and voluntarists because they depreciated God at the expense of His creatures and elevated man almost to the level of his Creator. Even the title of his masterpiece *De causa Dei* reveals clearly his bias. God's ways are not our ways and His grace must not be denied. His power (i.e., manifest in predestination) must be defended. Chaucer is

probably with him and others on this issue and in the quarrel over future
contingents which became the chief issue[11] — a reduction of the problem
to logic and epistemology as befitted a century fascinated by logic and its
problems. Regardless of Chaucer's personal opinion, however, I think I
have shown that one of the main sources of the inner tensions of *Troilus* is
this sense of necessity of an historian who knows the outcome in conflict
with his sympathies as an artist and man, a conflict which gives rise to a
futile struggle until the final leap which elevates the issue into a new and
satisfactory context. This conflict causes the pity, the grief, the tears —
and in a sense the ridiculousness and even the humor of it all.

Yet, throughout, the maturity of Chaucer's attitude is especially
noteworthy. Predestination which envelops natural man implicates us
all. Only from a Christian point of view can we be superior to Troilus and
Criseyde and that is not due to any merit of our own, but to grace. As
natural men and women we too are subject to our destiny whatever it may
be. Chaucer links himself (and us) with his far-off characters, thereby
strengthening the human bond over the centuries and increasing the
/24/ objectivity and irony of his vision. We are made to feel that this is
reality, that we are looking at it as it is and even from our distance
participate in it.

There is no escape from the past if one chooses to reconstruct
artistically, as Chaucer does, the past from the vantage ground of the
present. Chaucer's creation of himself in *Troilus* as historian-narrator and
his emphasis on the distance between him and his characters repeat, in
the wider frame of the present and in the panorama of complete
knowledge, the helplessness and turmoil of the lovers in the inner story.
The fact that Chaucer regards his story as true history does not, of course,
make his point of view predestinarian; in that case all historians would be
committed to a philosophy of predestination. The point is that the author
creates a character — himself — to guide us through his historical
narrative, to emphasize the pitiful end throughout, to keep a deliberate
distance suggested and stated in various ways between him and us and the
characters of the inner story. He makes his chief character awake to the
fact of predestination towards the end of the story and at the conclusion
has this character join, as it were, us and Chaucer the character — in
space instead of time — in seeing his own story through the perspective of
distance. It is all this which gives us the clue. The outer frame is not
merely a perspective of omniscience but also of impotence and is in fact
another level of the story. It serves as the realm of Mount Ida in the *Iliad*
— a wider cadre which enables us to put the humans involved into their

proper place.

Every age has its polarities and dichotomies, some more basic than others. To believing medieval man, the fundamental division is between the created and the uncreated. God as the uncreated Creator is the unchanging norm against which all His creatures must be set and the norm which gives the created world its true objectivity. The true Christian was bound to keep the universe in perspective: it was only one · of the poles of this fundamental polarity. The city of God gives meanings to the city of the world.

The impasse of the characters can only be solved on this other level and in this wider cadre. Actually for Troilus and Criseyde there is no final but merely a temporary solution — the consolation of philosophy — from which only the betrayed lover can benefit. Troilus begins to approach his narrator's viewpoint as he struggles against his fate beginning in the fourth book. The political events have taken a turn against him, and he tries to extricate himself and his beloved. But he is trapped and, what is even worse, long before Criseyde leaves he becomes aware of his mistake in consenting to let her go. In spite of her optimistic chatter, he predicts almost exactly what will happen when she joins her father. And he tells her so (IV.1450 ff.) Yet like one fascinated by his own /25/ doom he lets her go. He struggles but, in spite of his premonitions, seems unable to do anything about it.

It has long been recognized that Troilus' speech in favor of predestination (IV.958 ff.) is an important element in the poem.[12] It certainly indicates that Troilus believes in predestination, and I think in the light of what we have been saying here represents a stage in Troilus' approach to Chaucer. When, in the pagan temple, he finally becomes aware of destiny,[13] he is making an attempt to look at his own fate as Chaucer the commentator all along has been looking at it. The outer and inner stories are beginning to join each other. This movement of narrator and character towards each other in the last two books culminates in the ascent through the spheres at the end where Troilus gets as close to Chaucer (and us) as is possible in observing events in their proper perspective — *sub specie aeternitatis*. As Boethius writes in the *Consolation of Philosophy*

> Huc [Nunc] omnes pariter uenite capti
> Quos fallax ligat improbis catenis
> Terrenas habitans libido mentes
> Haec erit uobis requies laborum,

Hic portus placida manens quiete,
Hoc patens unum miseris asylum. (III, metrum x)

Or as Chaucer himself translates these lines

Cometh alle to gidre now, ye that ben ykaught and ybounde
with wikkide cheynes by the desceyvable delyt of erthly
thynges enhabitynge in your thought! Her schal ben the
reste of your labours, her is the havene stable in pesible
quiete; this allone is the open refut to wreches.

From this vantage point all falls into its place and proper proportion. /26/
Troilus now has Chaucer's sense of distance and joins with his author in
finding what peace can be found in a pagan heaven.

Just before this soul journey, Chaucer has even consigned his very
poem to time and put it in its place along with all terrestrial things (V.
1793 ff.) in the kingdom of mutability and change. As Chaucer can slough
off his earthly attachments and prides, even the very poem in which he is
aware of their transitory nature, Troilus his hero can also do so.

Thus towards the end, in the last two books, we see the hero beginning
to imitate his narrator and the narrator, his hero, and the distance set up
between the two begins to lessen and almost disappear. A dialectic of
distance and closeness which has been from the beginning more than
implicit in the poem between God, Chaucer the commentator-narrator,
and the characters—notably Troilus—of the inner story, becomes
sharply poised, with the triangle shrinking as the three approach each
other.[14] A final shift of depth and distance, however, takes place at the
end. The poem does not come to a close with Troilus joining Chaucer. A
further last leap is to establish again, even as at the beginning, a new
distance. Beyond the consolation of philosophy, the only consolation
open to Troilus is the consolation of Christianity. In the last stanzas,
Chaucer the narrator escapes from Troilus to where the pagan cannot
follow him; he escapes into the contemplation of the mysteries of the
Passion and of the Trinity, the supreme paradox of all truth, which is the
only possible way for a believing Christian to face the facts of his story.
The artist and the historian who have been struggling in the breast of
Chaucer can finally be reconciled. Here free will and predestination,
human dignity and human pettiness, joy and sorrow, in short all human
and terrestrial contradictions, are reconciled in the pattern of all
reconciliation: the God who becomes man and whose trinity is unity and

whose unity is trinity. Here the author-historian can finally find his peace at another distance and leave behind forever the unhappy and importunate Troilus, the unbearable grief of Criseyde's betrayal, the perplexities of time and space, and the tyranny of history and predestination.

Notes

1. On this point in connection with the *Canterbury Tales* see Donaldson's stimulating "Chaucer the Pilgrim," *PMLA*, LXIX (1954), 928–936. I am indebted to Professor Donaldson for several suggestions made orally to me which I have woven into this article — notably the root idea of n. 14 below.

2. For what they are worth, I give the following statistics on the first book. All Chaucer quotations are from the edn. of F. N. Robinson, Boston, 1933. The following passages seem to me to belong wholly or partially to the narrator as commentator: ll. 1 56 (proem), 57–63, 100, 133, 141–147, 159, 211–217, 232–266, 377–378, 393–399, 450–451 (a direct rapport remark), 492–497, 737–749 (doubtful), 1086–92. Excluding ll. 737–749, we find that 141 lines out of 1092 may be said to be comments by the author as commentator. Roughly 12% of the lines of the first book (one line in 8 1/3 lines) belong to the commentator. Even allowing for subjective impressions, 10% would certainly be fair. This is a remarkably high percentage I should say. The proem I shall analyze below. The other remarks bear on his sources, moralize, establish a mood of acceptance, indicate distance and pastness and refer to fate and destiny. For overt references to fate and providence in the poem, see the list in Eugene E. Slaughter, "Love and Grace in Chaucer's *Troilus*," *Essays in Honor of Walter Clyde Curry* (Nashville, 1955), p. 63, n. 8.

3. See Morton W. Bloomfield, "Chaucer's Sense of History," *JEGP*, LI (1952), 301–313.

4. Although irrelevant to the point I am making about the sense of distance in the journey to or through the spheres, there is some question as to the reading and meaning here (V. 1809). I follow Robinson and Root who take the reading "eighth" rather than "seventh" as in most manuscripts. Boccaccio uses "eighth," and there is a long tradition extending back to classical antiquity which makes the ogdoad the resting place of souls (see Morton W. Bloomfield, *The Seven Deadly Sins*, East Lansing, 1952, pp. 16–17 ff.). Cf., however, Jackson I. Cope, "Chaucer, Venus and the 'Seventhe Spere'," *MLN*, LXVII (1952), 245–246. (Cope is unaware of the ogdoad tradition and also assumes that Troilus is a Christian.) There is also the problem of the order in which the spheres are numbered. If the highest is the first then the eighth sphere is that of the moon, the one nearest the earth. Root believes Chaucer is following this arrangement. However, as Cope points out, Chaucer in the opening stanza of Bk. III names "Venus as the informing power of the third sphere" and therefore must be using the opposite numbering system. Troilus then goes to the highest sphere, that of the fixed stars.

E. J. Dobson ("Some Notes on Middle English Texts," *Eng. and Ger. Stud.*, Univ. of Birmingham, I [1947–48], 61–62) points out that Dante, *Paradiso* XXII, 100–154, which is Boccaccio's (and hence Chaucer's) source for this passage in the *Teseide*, makes clear that the emendation to "eighth" is justified.

5. Needless to say I am not using this phrase in the sense given it by Edward Bullough in his "'Psychical Distance' as a Factor in Art and an Aesthetic Principle," *Brit. Jour. of Psychol.*, V (1913), reprinted in *A Modern Book of Esthetics, An Anthology*, ed. Melvin Rader, rev. ed. (New York, 1952) pp. 401–428, He refers to "distance" between the art object on the one hand and the artist or audience in the other. The distance here referred to is within the poem, between the character-narrator Chaucer and the events.

6. Chaucer sets himself the problem of interpreting Criseyde's action here by his sympathetic portrayal of her character and by his unblinking acceptance of the "facts" of his history. Boccaccio evades it by his pre-eminent interest in Troilus. Henryson gives Troilus an "unhistorical" revenge. Shakespeare has blackened Cressida's character throughout. Christopher Hassall, in his libretto for William Walton's recent opera on the subject, makes Criseyde a victim of a mechanical circumstance and completely blameless. Only Chaucer, by a strict allegiance to the "historical" point of view, poses the almost unbearable dilemma of the betrayal of Troilus by a charming and essentially sympathetic Criseyde.

7. The only exception is to be found in the Robinson text where at III. 1165 we find the reading in a speech by Criseyde "by that God that bought us both two." I am convinced that the Root reading "wrought" for "bought" is correct. It would be perfectly possible for pagans to use "wrought" but not "bought." If we admit "bought" it would be the only Christian allusion put into the mouths of the Trojan characters and would conflict with the expressedly pagan attitude of these figures. I now take a stronger position on the matter than I allowed myself to express in "Chaucer's Sense of History," *JEGP*, LI (1952), 308, n. 17. Various references to grace, the devil (I.805), a bishop (II. 104), saints' lives (II.. 118) and celestial love (I. 979) need not, from Chaucer's point of view of antiquity, be taken as Christian.

8. See n. 2 above.

9. *Policraticus*, II, 22, ed. C. C. I. Webb (Oxford, 1909), I, 126. The translation is by Joseph B. Pike, *Frivolities of Courtiers* (Minneapolis, 1938), p. 111. Incidentally it should be noted that Calchas' foreknowledge through divination is on a basic level the cause of the tragedy.

10. "We are looking on at a tragedy that we are powerless to check or avert. Chaucer himself conveys the impression of telling the tale under a kind of duress" (G. L. Kittredge, *Chaucer and his Poetry*, Cambridge, 1915, p. 113) [above, pp.3–4].

11. On this dispute in the 14th century, see L. Baudry, *La querelle des futurs contingents* (Paris, 1950), and Paul Vignaux, *Justification et prédestination au XIVe siécle* (Paris, 1934).

12. I am aware, of course, that this famous speech was added only in the second or final version of the poem as Root has clearly shown. I do not think that this point is much relevance to my argument one way or another. Inasmuch as we can probably never know why Chaucer added the passage, one explanation is as good as another. We must take the poem in its final form as our object for analysis. My case, which is admittedly subjective, does not rest on this passage. It may be that Chaucer felt that by adding this speech he was making clearer a point he already had in mind. Or it is possible that it was only on his second revision that he saw the full implications of his argument. Or finally it may have occurred to him that by bringing Troilus closer to his own position before the end, he would deepen the significance of what he wished to say. These explanations for the addition are at least as plausible and possible as any other.

13. The location of this speech is not, I think, without significance. The end of pagan or

purely natural religion is blind necessity, and in its "church" this truth can best be seen.

14. Another triangle has its apex in Pandarus who is, of course, the artist of the inner story as Chaucer is of the outer one and as God is of the created world. Pandarus works on his material — Troilus and especially Criseyde — as his "opposite numbers" do with their materials. All are to some extent limited — Pandarus by the characters of his friend and niece and by political events; Chaucer by his knowledge and by history; God by His rationality. All this is another story, however; my interest here is primarily in the triangle with Troilus as apex.

Afterword: 1979

Any return to a creation written more than twenty years before is bound to raise doubts and questions in the author's mind even if as with Swift (and certainly not with me) one can admire his past genius. Yet I think if I were offered the chance to do the *Troilus* essay over again, I would refuse, although I am still not satisfied with it. Like the Chaucer persona in the poem, I too am bound by my history and sense of the past and must let what has been fated to take its course, take its course, even if I have no ogdoad to escape to (at least for the moment).

The article has been much quoted and referred to, as well as much criticized. A recent article on the poem announces that I am "absolutely incorrect." I have never regarded my article as the final word on the poem or even on its point of view, let alone as beyond error. It does not cover all aspects of the poem, neither its techniques nor its themes, and above all not the external social and literary influences on it. The article has found some friends and has influenced both positively and negatively some remarkably fine articles and approaches to the poem. I am grateful that it has been useful or at least stimulating to some writers and students.

The essay is an early example of formalistic "New Criticism" as applied to *Troilus and Criseyde*. My never total adherence to New Criticism was perhaps at its height in 1955–56 when I was writing this essay.

In spite of Bloom and Derrida, I think that the creator of a literary work does more for the world than a critic or scholar. Yet I do think literary criticism and scholarship inevitable because we cannot but be curious about what we admire and what is potentially enriching, and because great literature needs to be explored and understood in its many aspects even if, to refer to Swift once again, "learned commentators view / In Homer more than Homer knew."

M. W. B.

Chaucer's Nightingales
by Marvin Mudrick

Sweeney's nightingales which

> *. . . sang within the bloody wood*
> *When Agamemnon cried aloud,*
> *And let their liquid siftings fall*
> *To stain the stiff dishonoured shroud . . .*

can prove their independent animal nature only by performing, at a tragic crisis of the human spirit, the least dignifiable of animal acts: so Mr. Eliot succeeds, by this suavely sonorous shock of justaposition, in reclaiming for poets what for Chaucer is as natural as seeing:

> *A nyghtyngale, upon a cedir grene,*
> *Under the chambre wal ther as she lay,*
> *Ful loude song ayein the moone shene,*
> *Peraunter, in his briddes wise, a lay*
> *Of love, that made hire herte fressh and gay.*

Chaucer's nightingale happens to be decoratively placed, assisting with its song in Criseyde's first revery of love; but it is a bird to begin with and by no means merely decorative, it sings (we may matter-of-factly suppose: "Peraunter, in his briddes wise") for itself or for a prospective mate, it is true to its own /70/ nature and indifferent to man, it can never

From the *Hudson Review* 10 (1957): 88–95, reprinted here from Marvin Mudrick, *On Culture and Literature* (New York: Horizon Press, 1970), pp. 69–77, by the kind permission of the author. The pagination of the Horizon collection is here indicated between slashes.

be absorbed by an anthropocentrism that obsequiously elevates animal nature in order to degrade the human —

> *Hail to thee, blithe Spirit!*
>   *Bird thou never wert . . .*

or grants it a sardonic equality —

> *The coxcomb bird, so talkative and grave,*
> *That from his cage cries Cuckold, Whore, and Knave,*
> *Tho' many a passenger he rightly call,*
> *You hold him no philosopher at all . . .*

or dissolves it into a nostalgic symbol of the humanly unachievable —

> *Thou wast not born for death, immortal Bird!*

or regards it as another emblem and incarnation of man's idea of indivisible deity —

> *I caught this morning morning's minion, king-*
>   *dom of daylight's dauphin, dapple-dawn-drawn Falcon . . .*

or even limits it to a lover's serviceable ornament —

> *Wilt thou be gone? it is not yet near day:*
> *It was the nightingale, and not the lark,*
> *That pierc'd the fearful hollow of thine ear;*
> *Nightly she sings on yon pomegranate tree:*
> *Believe me, love, it was the nightingale.*

These are all of them ways of dealing with the enigma of animal nature (and of the non-human generally). Chaucer's way, which may be more precisely identified as a way of *seeing*, is not, then, the only way; but at least it differs, and deserves special scrutiny.

Chaucer is likely to start with discrimination and outline, with what can be detached and observed. Criseyde's nightingale, for example, is one of a distinct and specifiable kind, like the singing birds in the spring scene that opens the *Canterbury Tales*: /71/

And smale foweles maken melodye,
That slepen al the nyght with open ye
(So priketh hem nature in hir corages) . . .

— three lines of description that set apart the kind, note its habits and
impulses, and establish its remoteness from the purposes of man, while
the weightless fluidity of the first line affirms without taking into custody
the beauty (free, alien, uncoerced) of birdsong.

Not that a bird is ever merely a bird: like Mr. Eliot's nightingales,
Chaucer's birds may have a history and a symbolic value, as when
Criseyde, falling asleep to the song of the nightingale, dreams

How that an egle, feathered whit as bon,
Under hire brest his longe clawes sette,
And out hire brest he rente, and that anon,
And dide his herte into hire brest to gon,
Of which she nought agroos, ne nothyng smerte;
And forth he fleigh, with herte left for herte.

The Promethean eagle of course symbolizes, in Criseyde's dream, her
complex attitude toward the impending aggressions of love, but what
sharpens and steadies this symbolism is the poet's attention to the
identity of the bird itself: the lordliness — *darkened* by the disquieting
simile "whit as bon" — inherent (and unembellished except by the one
simile) in its very name and appearance; its own characteristic abrupt
predatory violence as Criseyde's dread and anticipation direct it. The
eagle is an eagle still, drawn out of its natural setting and the old cruel
myth by the force of Criseyde's egoistic passionate anxiety (which
protects itself by symbol), but in all that clarity of image reserving its
mystery and uncompromised separateness.

Criseyde, borrowing from its public myth the pitiless bird of prey,
invents in her need an *ad hoc* private myth, and by the details tells us
more about her motives than she herself knows. So myth — the ready-
made variety too — may serve the character as a screen against his
anxieties and the reader as an index to them. On a spring morning the
myth of Philomela and Procne invades Pandarus's dream to protect him,
while he prepares to /72/ launch his energy on Troilus's business of love,
with the generalization that love — not only for himself — is cruel and
ruinous:

> *. . . Pandarus, for al his wise speche,*
> *Felt ek his part of loves shotes keene,*
> *That, koude he never so wel of lovyng preche,*
> *It made his hewe a-day ful ofte greene.*
> *So shop it that hym fil that day a teene*
> *In love, for which in wo to bedde he wente,*
> *And made, er it was day, ful many a wente.*
>
> *The swalowe Proigne, with a sorowful lay,*
> *When morwen com, gan make hire waymentynge,*
> *Whi she forshapen was; and ever lay*
> *Pandare abedde, half in a slomberynge,*
> *Til she so neigh hym made hire cheterynge*
> *How Tereus gan forth hire suster take,*
> *That with the noyse of hire he gan awake,*
>
> *And gan to calle, and dresse hym up to ryse,*
> *Remembryng hym his erand was to doone*
> *From Troilus, and ek his grete emprise. . . .*

Man universalizes the human and domesticates the non-human; so that even a bird may be the victim of a tragic passion. In the myth, as Pandarus's dream recalls it, Procne is metamorphosed in consequence of a terrible disloyalty and failure of passion. The myth is necessary to Pandarus. In the moment of his own despair, when this newly self-appointed manager of lovers and pledged betrayer of a blood-relative is faced by the solitary shape of failure (the recognized true image of himself), he might, if there were no such myth, have to invent one; for the myth allows Pandarus to escape, from his private failure and his abandonment of honor, into familiarly desperate emotions to whose persons and circumstances he is committed only by the illusion of universal sympathy.

Criseyde, while she is accompanied in her first freely amorous imaginings by the voice of the nightingale, needs no escape or protection, she is only *lulled*: her particular bird, singing with its customary loveliness impervious to human crises, comes to her not out of the myth it shares with its sister the swallow (where, in a less comfortable mood of Criseyde's, it /73/ might belong) but out of the deferential orchestra that nature provides for lovers. Pandarus's bird is a different sort of accompanist. Since Pandarus — the resourceful but luckless lover, in an

embattled city the presumptive guardian of his otherwise friendless niece
— comes fresh from promising with brisk daylight confidence to win his
niece to the uses of his unresourceful passionate friend, he has good
reason to languish, in wakeful night, for want of the sympathy and aid he
offers others and to seek the protection of myth and self-forgetfulness.
The eventual half-sleep into which he drifts after many a turn in bed (as
the poet reports with unsentimental precision) is troubled, then, not by
the savage family-myth which the swallow's song evokes and from which
it at length disengages itself, but by the lonely recognition of his own
failure and of his looming treachery to Criseyde which, in a dream, the
universal poignance of the myth dims somewhat and makes more
endurable. When "hire cheterynge," too close to be taken for anything
but the "noyse" of a bird, dissipates the myth's grandiose pattern (and
Pandarus's personal incubus) of betrayal and doom, the swallow
withdraws — only a bird — into the featureless background of
Pandarus's morning; and Pandarus, his shattered self remagnetized into
the legwork-and-stratagem persona by which he holds off the waking
world, resumes his name and business. The briskly colloquial diction —
interrupted only during Procne's lament — slips back into place as if
nothing has happened. The nightingale and the swallow, cut off from
Criseyde's yearning and from Pandarus's premonition of ruin and
dishonor, go on singing somewhere nevertheless, intact and unheard.

   To demonstrate that animal nature is at many points indifferent and
inaccessible to man is not to ignore, but rather to lead us toward
identifying more carefully, its areas of contact with human nature. When
Troilus, ramping in complacent unattached maleness before the lovelorn
knights and squires of his company, is suddenly struck down by love,
Chaucer's comment takes the form of a condensed beast-fable:

> As proude Bayard gynneth for to skippe
> Out of the weye, so pryketh hym his corn, /74/
> Til he a lasshe have of the longe whippe;
> Than thynketh he, "Though I praunce al byforn
> First in the trays, ful fat and newe shorn,
> Yet am I but an hors, and horses lawe
> I moot endure, and with my feres drawe." . . .

The fable is apt not merely because Bayard (the knightly horse), "feeling
his oats" too, behaves very much as Troilus does and so serves the
ironist's purpose of diminishing Troilus to his animal aspect, nor because

here Troilus's awakened appetite is in fact far more "animal" than Bayard's urge "to skippe/Out of the weye," but, perhaps chiefly, because in the comic balance between Bayard as Troilus and Bayard as horse the passing resemblance between man and animal becomes their irrepressible common fate: to keep imagining (though not all animals are so articulate as Bayard) freedom where there is none, or very little ("Yet am I but an hors"); to act incorrigibly as if the energetic and the beautiful ("ful fat and newe shorn") are curbless and exempt from any law (but "horses lawe/ I moot endure, and with my feres drawe"). Chaucer's respect for distinctions is also a respect for significant likenesses.

Criseyde, too, has her time of identification with the mystery of impulse and of animal nature. Having recalled to us Criseyde's dream of the rending eagle by this image — as she yields at last to Troilus — of another resistless predatory bird:

> *What myghte or may the sely larke seye,*
> *Whan that the sperhauk hath it in his foot?*

Chaucer shows us now another view of the bird whose music casually presided over Criseyde's earliest acceptance of the possiblility of love:

> *And as the newe abaysed nyghtyngale,*
> *That stynteth first when she bygynneth to synge,*
> *Whan that she hereth any herde tale,*
> *Or in the hegges any wyght stirynge,*
> *And after siker doth hire vois out rynge,*
> *Right so Criseyde, whan hire drede stente,*
> *Opned hire herte, and tolde hym hire entente.*

/75/ From her briefly revived fear of surrender and outrage (like the lark's "fear" of the sparrowhawk), so that

> *Right as an aspes leef she gan to quake,*
> *Whan she hym felte hire in his arms folde . . .*

Criseyde moves into the diminished placid reassuring world of a country night: the timid nightingale, needlessly "abashed" by the harmless usual sounds of the night but recovering its confidence to sing out, is in this aspect and at this moment Criseyde herself, throwing off at last her fear of love and opening her heart to her lover. If this imagery is more than

shimmering and Shelleyan, it is because we have learned, during the
preceding four thousand lines of the poem, just how different Criseyde
has always been — in the prudence, calculatedness, sophistication,
vanity, cynicism, and appealing naïveté of her temperament — from any
ascertainable animal nature, and by just how distressful, tortuous,
steady, and Pandarus-plotted a route she has arrived at a moment when
she recedes from all she is in order to become, for the moment, another
sister of the nightingale and the instinctive simple celebrant of love.

In the tenderness and immediate pathos of this comparison (as
everywhere else), Chaucer will not blur an outline, sacrifice anything
marginal or past to the reader's vicarious absorption in the human center
and present of the poem. The reader, like Criseyde, is not catapulted into
an exaltation, he arrives at it; and what does the guiding is Chaucer's
concern with the history as well as the local commotion of things, his
acceptance of irreducible plurality, his acknowledgment of separate
orders of existence each of them at some points contiguous and analogous
to the others but each reserving an uninvadable self-sufficiency, his
respect for a diversity of appearances: that perpetual grace of judgment
which will not take a likeness or one aspect for the thing itself, or ignore
the final isolation — even from its most reasonable linkages with the non-
human world — of the human spirit.

There is ultimately a pathos beyond the reach of metaphor, a pathos
attainable only when the human spirit has penetrated and lost all illusion
of support outside itself, even the support /76/ of metaphor. Lear,
exhausted after a lifetime of imperial rhetoric, says to his daughter:

> *I know you do not love me, for your sisters*
> *Have (as I do remember) done me wrong.*
> *You have some cause, they have not. . . .*

and Cordelia replies, "No cause, no cause." This earned simplicity of
pathos is very rare in Shakespeare: his heroes and heroines live and die,
characteristically, within Lear's lost illusion regarding the magical
powers of rhetoric.

In Chaucer's world, however, whose disparate phenomena rhetoric can
set in some order but has no power to alter or commingle, such nakedness
of spirit is commoner and more likely. Rhetoric persists, of course
(though with characteristic Chaucerian fineness of distinction), as long
as there are illusions. At a moment when Troilus glories and can still take
comfort in his princeliness and Criseyde's love, the poet himself suggests

that we see Criseyde as, returning from the hunt, Troilus may see her:

> . . . whan that he com ridyng into town,
> Ful ofte his lady from hire wyndow down,
> As fressh as faukoun comen out of muwe,
> Ful redy was hym goodly to saluwe.

Thus Criseyde appears as the noble and beautiful hunting-bird of her worshipful falconer (while the poet may be implying, in this metaphor which not only identifies an instant of the lovers' relationship but catches up its history, that Criseyde has been and remains dangerous, possibly inconstant, not quite subduable). On the other hand, the Troilus who has accepted at last the fact of Criseyde's betrayal is beyond the self-indulgences, however reasonable, of rhetoric:

> "And certeynly, withouten moore speche,
> From hennesforth, as ferforth as I may,
> Myn owen deth in armes wol I seche.
> I recche nat how soone be the day!
> But trewely, Criseyde, swete may,
> Whom I have ay with al my myght yserved,
> That ye thus doon, I have it nat deserved."

/77/ Troilus has reached a summit of awareness from which he shares at last with his author a view of the futility, at such levels, of rhetoric. If Troilus's statement seems understatement, it is because the lover has lost his illusions regarding the efficacy, and perhaps the truth, of those partially enlightening lovers' metaphors that may seem, in retrospect, lovers' lies: Criseyde as lark, as nightingale, as falcon, as saint and love-goddess, as almost anything except the intolerably perplexed, timorous, untrustworthy, endearing woman she is.

Lear arrives at his clarity of awareness only through the most terrible wrenchings of spirit and language (as if the poet too must work his way through these). Troilus's ordeal may not be so terrible as Lear's; but Chaucer, scrupulously defining every counter of rhetoric his characters use or are used by, keeps us clear enough of the ordeal to leave it Troilus's only, and to grant to himself and the reader an inviolable and uninterrupted design. What Lear discovers after catastrophe and madness, Chaucer has been continously instructing us in by an unillusioned examination of image and metaphor from the beginning:

that nothing — no power or vanity of language or of temporary human
comfort — can save man from the recognition of his own solitude and
eventual powerlessness. Tragedy is beyond sulphurous and thought-
executing fires, as it is also beyond larks and nightingales.

The Trojan Scene In Chaucer's "Troilus"
by John P. McCall

For many years critics have accepted Kittredge's view on the role of the Trojan setting in Chaucer's *Troilus*, namely, that an atmosphere of doom pervades the Troy scene and is a fitting backdrop for the story of the doomed love of Troilus and Criseyde.[1] Still, two serious objections have been leveled against this interpretation. Patch has criticized it for being fatalistic and Mayo has contended that it is impressionistic.[2] My present aim is to re-examine the problem for the purpose of showing that Chaucer adapted the tragedy of Troy as a suitable background for the tragedy of Troilus, and that he made the characters, careers and fortunes of the two parallel and even analogous.

At the outset, a few things should be noted. First, according to classical and medieval traditons the fall of Troy was ascribed not simply to blind destiny, but to foolish pride and criminal lust.[3] The city freely and mistakenly had followed a course of action which not only brought it great prosperity, but ruin and /264/ destruction as well. The history of Troy was accordingly looked upon as a civic or corporate tragedy, and in particular a tragedy of love or lust.[4] The rape of Helen and the subsequent determination of the city to defend the crime had provoked the subjection of Troy to a woman and to the caprice of Fortune. That Chaucer himself was acquainted with the tradition of the tragedy of Troy is clear.[5] It is also likely that he was aware of identifications between the city and his protagonist: by "medieval etymology" Troilus literally means "little Troy";[6] and Chaucer's principal source told him that Troilo was afflicted

Reprinted from *ELH* 29 (1962): 263–75, by permission of the author and the John Hopkins University Press. The original pagination is indicated between slashes in the text. The essay also appears in John P. McCall, *Chaucer Among the Gods: The Poetics of Classical Myth* (Pennsylvania State University Press, 1979), pp. 93–104.

by the same love that doomed all Troy to destruction.[7]

But let us turn to the *Troilus* itself to see what Chaucer has done. In Book One, like Boccaccio, he begins by immediately setting the scene. A thousand Greek ships have come to Troy /265/ to avenge the rape of Helen, and Calchas, learning that the city will be destroyed, flees and leaves behind his widowed daughter, Criseyde. Of the war between the Trojans and the Greeks, Chaucer remarks only in passing what was commonplace—Fortune is in control.

> The thynges fellen, as they don of werre,
> Bitwixen hem of Troie and Grekes ofte;
> For som day boughten they of Troie it derre,
> And eft the Grekes founden nothing softe
> The folk of Troie; and thus Fortune on lofte,
> And under eft, gan hem to whielen bothe
> Aftir hir course, ay whil that thei were wrothe. (I 134–40)[8]

But with the "gestes" and how Troy fell, the poet will not concern himself. He will concentrate, instead, on the story of Troilus, and advises those who are interested in the long history of the city and its battles to read "In Omer, or in Dares, or in Dite." Although Chaucer's initial outline of the Trojan scene is brief, and drawn largely from the *Filostrato*, it is still significant. In a few stanzas he has given a threefold picture of the Troy story — the rape, the rule of Fortune in the ensuing war, and the destruction to come — a picture which is comparable to the initial three-part outline of Troilus' story in the Proem to Book One, "Fro wo to wele, and after out of joie."

From the twenty-first stanza of Book One until the beginning of Book Four, no mention in made of the destiny of Troy or of its fall.[9] With perhaps one exception,[10] everything that we read about Troy is favorable. At the feast of the Palladion we see the gaiety of Spring, and a crowd of Trojan knights and maidens at ease and well arrayed (I 155ff). Later we hear two brief allusions to women of Troy, Helen and Polyxena (I 454–55, 676–79), /266/ who are renowned for their beauty. In addition, Pandare quotes a portion of Oenone's letter to Paris (I 652–65), a good example for his argument, but also a reminder of the concern for love in Troy. Moreover, there are suggestions of victories by Troy and Troilus (I 470–83); we hear Pandare joke about the siege (I 558–60), and finally, we learn that Troilus is playing the lion amid the Greek host after Pandare has promised to help him in his cause (I 1072–75).

Before this relaxed and prosperous setting, we find that Troilus, like Troy, has become devoted to a woman and subject to the whims of Fortune. "Ful unavysed of his woo comynge," he determines with full assent, "Criseyde for to love, and nought repente." He is willing to offer full service to his love and even to deny his royal lineage; no longer will he fight for the city, or his family, or his own self-respect, but rather "To liken hire the bet for his renoun." Also, with this new devotion comes all the uncertainty of a love dependent upon Fortune (I 330-50). Even the bright future that Pandare sees is closely tied to the movement of the goddess' turning wheel; if you are now in sorrow, he tells Troilus, take comfort in the fact that Fortune changes.

> "Woost thow nat wel that Fortune is comune
> To everi manere wight in som degree?
> And yet thow hast this comfort, lo, parde,
> That, as hire joies moten overgon,
> So mote hire sorwes passen everechon." (I 843-47)

Such comfort will be small when we hear it again under different circumstances (IV 384-99). But at this point there are no worries about the war, nor will Troilus need to worry about his love. All is well as Pandare leads the way: "Tho Troilus gan doun on knees to falle, / And Pandare in his armes hente faste, / And seyde, 'Now, fy on the Grekes alle! / Yet, pardee, God shal helpe us atte laste.'" (I 1044-47)

But if the pleasant Troy setting is significant at this early stage of the narrative, it becomes even more important in Books Two and Three. First we encounter the gay, mannered scene at Criseyde's house where the women listen to the romance of Thebes, and where Pandare urges Criseyde to forget her status as a widow and go out and enjoy the usual "Trojan" May games (II 78ff). There is also the garden scene in which Antigone /267/ sings of love (II 813ff), and there are the parties, first at Deiphebus' house and then later, in Book Three, at Pandare's. But the Trojans are not only happy at home; they continue to be fortunate in battle. We learn of Troilus' victories from Pandare (II 190-203), and also that he and Troilus spent half a day in the palace garden discussing a plan for defeating the Greeks (II 505-11). We hear of another victory when Criseyde watches Troilus return triumphant from putting the Greeks to flight (II 610-44); and later, in Book Three, part of the plan for deceiving everyone on Troilus' night of bliss is the fabricated story that he is waiting at the temple of Apollo for an omen, "To telle hym next whan

Grekes sholde flee." (III 544)

But let us go back a moment to Chaucer's most colorful addition to the bright picture of Troy, the party at Deiphebus' house where we meet Helen. There is nothing of this in Chaucer's sources,[11] and its effect is to enhance the joy, beauty, and easy pleasures that we have already seen in the city. Helen is invited by Deiphebus to attend a dinner for those who want to "protect" Criseyde, but the reason for her being asked is independently interesting since it provides a background of male subservience at a particularly crucial time: "'What wiltow seyn, if I for Eleyne sente / To speke of this? I trowe it be the beste, / For she may leden Paris as hire leste.'" (II 1447-49) At the gathering that takes place Helen holds the social center of attention and, along with Pandare, dominates the conversation. After Troilus' illness is mentioned, she complains so "that pite was to here," and when Pandare explains Criseyde's problem, Helen rises to the occasion with a speech that echoes with ironic associations between the two women:

> Eleyne, which that by the hond hire [Criseyde] held,
> Took first the tale, and seyde, "Go we blyve";
> And goodly on Criseyde she biheld,
> And seyde: "Joves lat hym nevere thryve,
> That doth yow harm, and brynge hym soone of lyve,
> And yeve me sorwe, but he shal it rewe,
> If that I may, and alle folk be trewe!" (II 1604-10)

Everyone at the dinner then determines to be Criseyde's friend in the suit brought against her by the traitorous straw-man, Poliphete. /268/ But before the matter is dropped Helen and Deiphebus invade Troilus' sickroom to elicit his aid and to give us a glimpse of the gracious allurements of Menelaus' wife, whose actions are a prologue to Criseyde's.

> Eleyne, in al hire goodly softe wyse,
> Gan hym salue, and wommanly to pleye,
> And seyde, "Iwys, ye moste alweies arise!
> Now, faire brother, beth al hool, I preye!"
> And gan hire arm right over his shulder leye,
> And hym with al hire wit to reconforte;
> As she best koude, she gan hym to disporte.
>   (II 1667-73; cf. III 168; 1128-34)

Without much prodding Troilus consents to help defend Criseyde, much to Helen's gratification. Troilus next deceives his brother and sister-in-law with a letter and a document which they take to the nearby garden. Finally, after the secret meeting of the lovers and the miracle of Criseyde's first kiss, they return, and "Eleyne hym kiste, and took hire leve blyve, / Deiphebus ek, and hom wente every wight."

As Mayo has already noted, the references to the Trojan scene through most of Book One, and all of Books Two and Three, show that Chaucer made no effort to direct attention to the final destruction of the city. And yet the picture of Troy is still important as a scene of prosperity. No mention is made of the fall of the city because Chaucer is describing Troy in good fortune, and this background suits the growing prosperity and good fortune of Troilus in love. With "wordes white" Pandare is hard at work undermining Criseyde's status, arranging for the exchange of letters, the meetings of the lovers, and the night of joy. And like Troy, Troilus is playing a game of chance for worldly bliss in which all depends on the roll of the dice (II 1347-49). Lucky occasions and the properly calculated time mean everything in this game for, as Pandare says, "wordly joie halt nought but by a wir . . . Forthi nede is to werken with it softe." (III 1636-38) Thus, as the exaggerated paradisiacal imagery accumulates in the last part of Book Three, we are often reminded of the inconstancy of earthly love.[12]

Then at the beginning of Book Four we learn that fickle Fortune is about to overturn Troilus and take away his joy. /269/

> But al to litel, weylaway the whyle,
> Lasteth swich joie, ythonked be Fortune,
> That semeth trewest whan she wol bygyle,
> And kan to fooles so hire song entune,
> That she hem hent and blent, traitour comune!
> And whan a wight is from hire whiel ythrowe,
> Than laugheth she, and maketh hym the mowe. (IV 1-7)

Immediately after the proem, as a prelude and backdrop for Troilus' misfortune, we find that Troy, too, has come upon bad days. For the first time we hear of a serious set-back to the Trojan forces: "Ector and many a worthi wight" go out to battle and, after the long day's struggle,

> . . . in the laste shour, soth for to telle,
> The folk of Troie hemselven so mysledden

That with the worse at nyght homward they fledden.

At which day was taken Antenore . . .
So that, for harm, that day the folk of Troie
Dredden to lese a gret part of hire joie. (IV 47–56)

In the Greek camp Calchas is soon pleading that Antenor be exchanged
for Criseyde, and he reiterates at length the prophecy we heard at the
outset: Troy shall be "ybrend, and beten down to grownde."

A parliament is then held in Troy to decide whether the Greek terms of
exchange should be accepted. Here Chaucer alters and expands
Boccaccio's account, and ironically describes the foolish self–betrayal of
the people, who "sholden hire confusioun desire" by seeking the
deliverance of Antenor, "that brought hem to meschaunce": "For he was
after traitour to the town / Of Troye; allas, they quytte him out to rathe! /
O nyce world, lo, thy discrecioun!" (IV 204–6) With this mistake, on top
of the defeat in battle, the atmosphere of Chaucer's Troy scene becomes
dark and foreboding, and treachery lurks in the background.

Faced with the dilemma of disclosing his love for Criseyde or losing
her, Troilus abandons all self–control. He batters himself about and roars
useless complaints against Fortune and Cupid (IV 260–94). But even
now, when all our attention seems fixed on the internal struggles of
Troilus, we do not lose sight of the city. In his lament Troilus wonders
why Fortune has not slain him, or his brothers, or his "fader, kyng of
Troye" (IV 274–78) /270/ — eventualities which will come soon
enough. Moreover, after Troilus cries against the trick that Fortune has
played on him, Pandare offers several cures. He suggests a different gift
from Fortune, another woman; and failing that, he recalls the cause of
Troy's predicament and advises that Troilus follow suit.

"Go ravisshe here ne kanstow nat for shame!
And other lat here out of towne fare,
Or hold here stille, and leve thi nyce fare.

"Artow in Troie, and hast non hardyment
To take a womman which that loveth the,
And wolde hireselven ben of thyn assent?
Now is nat this a nyce vanitee?" (IV 530–36)

But for Troilus this will not do; another rape would be intolerable during the present misfortunes: "'First, syn thow woost this town hath al this werre / For ravysshyng of wommen so by myght, / It sholde nought be suffred me to erre, / As it stant now, ne don so gret unright.'" (IV 547–50) Besides, Criseyde's "name" is at stake. Still Pandare goes right on, recalling how Paris solaced himself and asking why Troilus should not do the same. (V 608–9).

Later, when the lovers are together for the last time, Criseyde frenetically lists a number of ways by which they may be reunited. Among other things she mentions a current peace rumor: if Helen, the cause of the war, were restored to her rightful husband, then their situation — as well as Troy's — would improve.

> "Ye sen that every day ek, more and more,
> Men trete of pees; and it supposid is
> That men the queene Eleyne shal restore,
> And Grekis us restoren that is mys.
> So, though ther nere comfort non but this,
> That men purposen pees on every syde,
> Ye may the bettre at ese of herte abyde." (IV 1345–51)

Then toward the end of her exhortation Criseyde implies, as Troilus did before, that Troy has not been faring well of late; she urges Troilus to forget about fleeing the city with her, "'syn Troie hath now swich nede / Of help'." (IV 1558–59)

In Book Five Chaucer not only continues to paint the decline of Troy with an eye on his failing hero, but he comes close to identifying the two. The week-long feast at Sarpedoun's (V 428–501), /271/ with its wine, women, and song, pathetically recalls the bright and gay parties in the Troy of Books Two and Three, and the letters which Troilus reads in seclusion recall the happier days when they were written. The vanity of past joys for Troy and Troilus is becoming ever more apparent. After his return home Troilus refers to the Trojan scene again when he links himself with the city: "'Now blisful lord [Cupide], so cruel thow ne be / Unto the blood of Troie, I preye the, / As Juno was unto the blood Thebane, / For which the folk of Thebes caughte hire bane.'" (V 599–602) Cupid, like Fortune, is cruel and blind,[13] and will — so to speak — destroy not only Troilus, but all the "blood of Troie."

But even more pointed are the comments of Diomede and Criseyde in the Greek camp. Diomede's persuasive love talk, for example, is shot through with an insistent dual purpose: Greeks are stronger than Trojans

— he will be a better lover than any Trojan; the Greeks will destroy Troy
and everyone in the city — including Criseyde's lover.[14] The high point of
his argument is reached when he declares that those imprisoned in Troy
will suffer unmercifully for the rape of Helen:

> "Swiche wreche on hem, for fecchynge of Eleyne.
> Ther shal ben take, er that we hennes wende,
> That Manes, which that goddes ben of peyne,
> Shal ben agast that Grekes wol hem shende.
> And men shul drede, unto the worldes ende,
> From hennesforth to ravysshen any queene,
> So cruel shal oure wreche on hem be seene."
>
> . . . .
>
> "What wol ye more, lufsom lady deere?
> Lat Troie and Troian fro youre herte pace!" (V 890-96, 911-12)

/272/ Diomede has tied the failing fortunes of the city to those of Troilus
with unerring insight into Criseyde's heart. For she herself, we may
remember, had reminisced on the past joys of Troy and Troilus (V
729-35), and, in anticipation of Diomede's success, the narrator had
commented that, "bothe Troilus and Troie town / Shal knotteles
thorughout hire herte slide; / For she wol take a purpos for t'abyde." (V
768-70) For Diomede, Criseyde and the narrator, Troy and Troilus are
one.

Meanwhile, waiting in vain for Criseyde's return, Troilus dreams that
his love is taken by a boar. In the *Filostrato* Troilo understands that
Diomede is the boar and that he has lost Criseyde, but Chaucer's Troilus
knows nothing of the kind. Instead he asks the advice of his sister,
Cassandra, who tells him that to understand the dream — and, by
implication, his own tragic condition — he must learn its background:
"'Thow most a fewe of olde stories heere, / To purpos, how that Fortune
overthrowe / Hath lordes olde . . . '" (V 1459-61) The sketch of Theban
history that follows is primarily a list of tragedies, and the conclusion is
that Diomede is the boar and Troilus' lady — whom Cassandra by a smile
suggests she knows — is gone: "'This Diomede is inne, and thow art
oute.'" The immediate effect of the introduction of Cassandra from the
framework of the Trojan scene is to have her provide, in panoramic
fashion, some concrete analogies to the condition of Troilus as a tragic
victim of Fortune. Her speech is an historic or mythic counterpart of the
Boethian philosophic discourse in Book Four. The latter deepens our

insight into Troilus' psychic failure, but this extends the implications of
his trust in Fortune beyond even the immediate Trojan setting and
prepares for the ultimate vision of the closing stanzas of the poem.

   We are now near the end, and in anticipation of Troilus' death Chaucer
turns to the city which is on the verge of suffering its worst misfortune.

> Fortune, which that permutacioun
> Of thynges hath, as it is hire comitted
> Thorugh purveyance and disposicioun
> Of heighe Jove, as regnes shal be flitted
> Fro folk in folk, or when they shal be smytted,
> Gan pulle awey the fetheres brighte of Troie
> Fro day to day, til they ben bare of joie. (V 1541–47)

/273/ The brightest feather of Troy is plucked when Hector is slain. Now
the handwriting is clearly on the wall for Troy — and Troilus too, for
soon after Hector's death Troilus sees the captured "cote-armure" of
Diomede and on it finds the brooch he gave Criseyde. Fortune has played
a game with him as well: "Gret was the sorwe and pleynte of Troilus; /
But forth hire cours Fortune ay gan to holde. / Criseyde loveth the sone
of Tideüs, / And Troilus moot wepe in cares colde. / Swich is this world,
whoso it kan byholde." (V 1744–48) Again, foreground and background
are closely knit: the imperial dominion will pass from Troy to Greece, as
Criseyde passes from Troilus to Diomede; and as Fortune's tragic
movement is completed for Troilus, Chaucer anticipates the fall of the
city in the background.

   Thus, in the last two Books of the *Troilus*, the initial analogies between
the loves and fortunes of Troy and Troilus reach a classically symmetrical
resolution. The change of the city's fortune, which comes with the
capture and exchange of the traitorous Antenor, is simultaneously the
occasion for the change of Troilus' fortune and an anticipation of
Criseyde's betrayal.[15] In addition, the disenchantment regarding the war
and the rape that caused it become minor motifs during the complaints of
the lovers. In the thoughts of Criseyde and in the persuasive speeches of
Diomede we find an insistent identification between Troy and Troilus. At
the end there are the last explicit analogies between Fortune's shift from
Troilus to Diomede, from Troy to Greece. Troy and Troilus, then, have
become one in misfortune, just as they had been one in prosperity.

                    *   *   *   *   *

The similarities between the foreground and background of Fortune's activities in the *Troilus* lead to a conclusion, somewhat different from Kittredge's, that the tragedy of Troy is akin to the tragedy of Troilus in substance and contour. Moreover, these similarities disclose in Chaucer's poem an "intrahistorical" movement such as Auerbach has found generally lacking in antique literature. In the *Troilus* the fortunes of an individual are set against the background of a whole society enmeshed in similar fortunes, so that what happens to Troilus seems in no way /274/ extraordinary, "especially arranged," or "outside the usual course of events." Thus the instability of Fortune in the case of Troilus "results from the inner processes of the real historical world" in which Chaucer portrays him as a real historical figure.[16] On one hand, then, Chaucer has portrayed a psychological tragedy in which the scene constantly enriches and enlightens his principal subject: it provides an additional dimension to the tragedy of Troilus. On the other hand, the tragedy of Troilus is a particular and concrete source of poignancy for the corporate tragedy of the city.

As Bloomfield has shown, despite all sorts of anachronisms, Chaucer displays a sense of history in the *Troilus*.[17] One aesthetic effect is that the narrative becomes more realistically and completely dramatic. The setting is an integral part of the main action, and not simply suited to it in a naive or rigidly rhetorical way; nor is Chaucer floundering about, as though only dimly aware of a basic tool of his art. But the fact that this background is first historical and dramatic in no way detracts from the fact that it is also symbolic. What we have in the Trojan scene is a social, civic, or what some medieval critics might call an allegorical level of meaning, founded in the realities of history and appearing from time to time as an analogue of the moral — or trolopogical — development of Troilus' particular tragedy. At one point in the *Troilus*, and perhaps only at this point, these three levels of significance — historical, moral, and social — converge with a transcendental or analogical vision of reality.[18] /275/

Finally, throughout the poem, wherever the Troy scene is mentioned, it is carefully under Chaucer's control. It is so unobtrusively shaded and colored by the hues of the foreground that it fails to call special attention to itself as something separate and distinct — as it might have if Chaucer has clumsily pointed out bold historical and moral parallels between Troy and Troilus. The analogies, then, are implicit and vital: felt or sensed, but not directly stated. Moreover, they are all real and historical, not arbitrary or manipulated. Thus we find something that critics are becoming more aware of: the subtle and skillful hand of Chaucer the artist.

Notes

1. G. L. Kittredge, *Chaucer and His Poetry* (Cambridge, Mass., 1915), pp. 117–21 [above, pp. 6–8]. See also W.C. Curry, "Destiny in Chaucer's *Troilus*," PMLA XLV (1930). 135; G. Dempster, *Dramatic Irony in Chaucer* (Stanford, 1932), pp. 12–13; J.L. Lowes, *Geoffrey Chaucer and the Development of His Genius* (Boston, 1934), p. 180; T. A. Stroud, "Boethius' Influence on Chaucer's *Troilus*," *MP*, XLIX (1951), 9; and D. Everett, *Essays on Middle English Literature* (Oxford, 1955), p. 133.

2. H.R. Patch, "Troilus on Determinism," *Speculum*, VI (1931), 225–43; R. D. Mayo, "The Trojan Background of the *Troilus*," *ELH*, IX (1942), 245–56.

3. In general, see Horace's *Epistle to Maximus Lollius* in the Loeb *Horace* (London, 1926), p. 263; and for Chaucer's knowledge of the pertinent passage, R. A. Pratt's, "A Note on Chaucer's Lollius," *MLN*, LXV (1950), 183–7. References to the pride of Troy ("superbum Ilium" from *Aeneid* III 2–3) are numerous: see Seneca, n. 4 below; *Troilus*, ed. T. Merzdorf (Lipsiae, 1875), pp. 37, 187; *Inferno* I 75, XXX 13–15; and Salutati's *De Laboribus Herculis*, ed. B.L. Ullman (Zurich, 1951), I 348. In *Adversus Jovinianum* (*PL* XXIII 292), Jerome blames the Trojan War on the rape of a single *respecteuse* ("muliercula"); and in the popular medieval *Pergama flere volo* . . . the blame is more bluntly ascribed to the "fatal whore": Carmina 101, ll. 43–45 in *Carmina Burana*, ed. W. Meyers, A. Hilka and O. Schumann (Heidelberg, 1930–1941), 2 vols. The criminal lust of Troy was simply an extension of Paris' crime to the whole city: see n. 4 below.

4. In *The Goddess Fortuna in Medieval Literature* (Cambridge, Mass., 1927), p. 114, Patch notes that Troy was a familiar civic example of Fortune's infidelity. For a classical example, see Seneca's *Troades* in the Loeb *Tragedies* (London, 1917), I 125. For the medieval encyclopedic tradition that Troy was an exemplar of tragic lust, wantonness and foolish love, see A. Neckam's *De Naturis Rerum*, ed. T. Wright (London, 1863), p. 350; Brunetto Latini's *Li Livres dou Tresour*, ed. F.J. Carmody (Berkeley, 1948), p. 290; and Salutati's *De Laboribus Herculis*, I 252. In a poem by Godefroid de Reims, Achilles harangues the Trojans for being effeminate and sluggish devotees of Venus: A. Boutemy, "Trois oeuvres inédites de Godefroid de Reims," *Revue du Moyen Age Latin*, III (1947), 304. It would seem that the traditional interpretation of the judgment of Paris — and later the judgment of all Troy — has some bearing on the foolish love ascribed to the city. Paris was reputed to have preferred fleshly delight (Venus) to wealth (Juno) and wisdom (Pallas): Fulgentius, *Mitologia* II 1; Boccaccio, *Genealogie Deorum*, VI xxii; J. Seznec, *The Survival of the Pagan Gods* (New York, 1953), pp. 107ff.

5. When Chaucer's Aeneas speaks of Troy's fall he echoes the commonplace medieval definition of tragedy: "'Allas, that I was born' quod Eneas; / Thourghout the world oure shame is kid so wyde, / Now it is peynted upon every syde. / We, that weren in prosperite, / Been now desclandred, and in swich degre, / No lenger for to lyven I ne kepe.'" (*LGW* 1027–32). Compare the phraseology in the definitions of tragedy in Monk's Tale, 1973–77, and the translation of the *Consolations*, II, pr. 2. For these, and subsequent references I have used the edition of F.N. Robinson, *The Works of Geoffrey Chaucer*

(Cambridge, Mass., 1957).

6. This would be not the Greek, but the Latin diminutive in -lus,-la, -lum: *Priciani Grammatici Caesariensis Libri Omnes* (Venice, 1527), pp. 28b-32a, and W. M. Lindsay, *The Latin Language* (Oxford, 1894), pp. 331-33. For suggesting the role of a character *by name*, see the comment on Boccaccio's use of *Pandaro*, "to signify one who 'gives all' for his friend" in N. E. Griffin and A. B. Myrick's translation of *The Filostrato* (Philadelphia, 1929), pp. 41-42; also, Chaucer's word-play on *Calchas* (I 71) and on the frequent epithet *queene Eleyne* (II 1556, 1687, 1703, 1714).

7. *Filostrato*, Bk. VII, st. 86. Casandra tells Troilo that he has "suffered from the accursed love by which we all must be undone, as we can see if we but wish" (my translation).

8. The reference to Fortune is Chaucer's own, although it was easily suggested by *Filostrato*, I, st. 16.

9. Mayo, *ELH*, IX, 250.

10. One passage (II 1111-13) may suggest that Sinon is within the walls of Troy. When Pandare meets Criseyde for the second time in his "paynted proces" of bringing her to love, he takes her aside to deliver Troilus' letter; as an excuse for speaking alone with her, he says he has just heard new tidings from the Greek spy who is a guest in the city: " 'Ther is right now come into town a gest, / A Greek espie, and telleth newe thinges, / For which I come to telle yow tydynges,' " Although the activities of Sinon, or any spy, provide an analogy for the deceptions of Pandare (e. g., II 409-20; III 267-80, 1564-68), still the news is announced as another sign of Troy's good fortunes.

11. The incident may have been suggested by *Filostrato* VII, st. 84-85, but this is very different from Chaucer's scene.

12. *Troilus* III 813-36, 1527-47, 1618-38.

13. The close kinship between blind Cupid, or lust (*Troilus* I 202; III 1808; V 1824), and blind or blinding Fortune (IV 5) is clear throughout the poem — e. g., IV 260-94 — and Chaucer's knowledge of it doubtless dates back to his reading of the *Roman de la Rose* (*The Works of Geoffrey Chaucer*, pp. 605-6, lines 4353ff.). See also Pierre Bersuire's *Metamorphosis Ovidiana Moraliter . . .* (Paris 1515), fo. viiiᵛ-ix; in his *Studies in Iconology* (New York, 1939), p. 112, Panofsky notes the association between blind Cupid, Night, Synagogue, Infidelity, Death and Fortune, but makes a distinction, which is generally unnecessary, between Cupid in mythographical works and Cupid in literary works. For the kinship of Venus and Fortune, see Patch's *The Goddess Fortuna*, pp. 90-98, and M. W. Stearns, *Robert Henryson* (New York, 1949), p. 89ff.

14. *Troilus* V 118-26, 141-43, 876-96, 904-24.

15. The connection between Fortune's change and treachery is proverbial, but see especially *Troilus* IV 1-5.

16. See E. Auerbach, *Mimesis*, trans. by W. Trask (Princeton, 1953), pp. 28-29. Perhaps Unamuno's treatment of the individual as an epitome of his society comes close to illustrating what Chaucer has done.

17. "Chaucer's Sense of History," *JEGP*, LI (1952), 301-13.

18. In the closing stanzas Chaucer directs our attention not only to Troilus, now departed, and to Troy, now in grief, but also to the relationship of both the the awesome facts of the after-life and the redemptive love of Christ.

And down from thennes faste he gan avyse
This litel spot of erthe, that with the se
Embraced is, and fully gan despise
This wrecched world, and held al vanite
To respect of the pleyn felicite
That is in hevene above; and at the laste,
Ther he was slayn, his lokyng down he caste.

And in hymself he lough right at the wo
Of hem that wepten for his deth so faste;
And dampned al oure work that foloweth so
The blynde lust, the which that may nat laste . . . (V 1814ff)

Afterword: 1979

This essay is an old friend. It was drawn from the last, and I think best, chapter of a dissertation written for D. W. Robertson, Jr., and it recently became part of a book on Chaucer's classical mythology. I like to hope this essay, besides helping the reader a bit, might imply something useful for our understanding of Chaucer's development, for in writing the *Troilus* he found a way to turn ancient history and a perennial theme into a continuous, single story. He had apparently taken a step in this direction with the early version of the Knight's Tale, but here he has the full form. Then, having put together a complete work, coherent and balanced, Chaucer sets out to find something new. He "goes back" to a separation of past and present in the *Legend of Good Women*, and then on to the amalgam of Canterbury genres where past, present, and future flow together in an uninterrupted drama of England Now. Among other things, we see a very adventurous poet.

J. P. M.

The Ending of "Troilus"
by E. Talbot Donaldson

One of Chaucer's familiar pretenses is that he is a versifier utterly devoted to simplicity of meaning — for the reason that he considers himself, apparently, utterly incapable of complexity. He defines his poetic mission as the reporting of facts in tolerable verse, and he implies that that's hard enough to do. True poetry may, for all of him, do something much better but it is not clear to Chaucer exactly what it is or how it does it. He and *ars poetica* are, to be sure, on parallel roads, moving in the same direction; but the roads are a long way apart and are destined to meet, perhaps, not even in infinity. On the one hand, Chaucer, reciting his simple stories 'in swich Englissh as he can'; on the other, poetry, penetrating regions of complex significance far beyond the grasp of a simple straightforward versifier.

Chaucer's pretended inferiority complex on the subject of poetry must have stemmed from something real in his own life probably connected with his being a bourgeois writing for highborn members of the royal court. What interests me now however, is not the origin of the pose, but its literary value. For I think that Chaucer discovered in the medieval modesty convention a way of poetic life: that, by constantly assuring us, both through direct statement and through implication, of his inability to write anything but the simplest kind of verse, Chaucer creates just that poetry of complex significance that he disclaims striving for. In this paper I shall focus attention on the last stanzas of *Troilus*, where it seems to me that a kind of dramatization of his poetic ineptitude achieves for him a

First published in *Early English and Norse Studies, presented to Hugh Smith* . . . , ed. Arthur Brown and Peter Foote (London: Methuen, 1963) and reprinted by permission of the author and Associated Book Publishers Ltd., and Methuen & Co. Ltd. The text here is taken from the slightly revised version printed in E. Talbot Donaldson, *Speaking of Chaucer* (New York: Norton, 1970; London: Athlone, 1970), pp. 84–101. Footnotes from the Norton edition are renumbered in one series. The pagination of the Norton edition is here indicated between slashes in the text.

115

poetic success that not many poets in any language have attained. But I shall first /85/ consider briefly some characteristic Chaucerian 'ineptitudes' in his other works.

Modesty is endemic both with Chaucer in his own first person — whoever that is — and with his dramatic creations: none of them can do much in the way of poetry. Like the Squire, they cannot climb over so high a stile, or, like his father, they set out to plough, God wot, a large field with weak oxen; or, if they are not ploughing a field, they're gleaning it, like the author of the Prologue to the *Legend of Good Women*, and are full glad of any kernel that their talented predecessors have missed. Or else, like the Prioress, they are so afflicted by infantilism that they speak no better than a child of twelvemonth old, or less. Like the Merchant and the Franklin, they are rude men, 'burel' men, they cannot glose, they have no rhetoric, they call a spade a spade; they come after even such second-rate poets as that fellow Chaucer, bearing only *hawe bake* — pig food — and are reduced to prose, like the Man of Law in his Prologue. They can't even get the data down in the right order, like the Monk or like the narrator of the Prologue to the *Canterbury Tales*. Or, worst of all, as in the case of the pilgrim who recites the romance of Sir Thopas, their inability to frame a story of their own makes them resort to 'a rim I lerned longe agoon', and when that is shot down in mid-flight, they have to take refuge in one of the most anaesthetic sermons that ever mortified a reader. If it is dramatically appropriate that they be capable rhetoricians, like the Clerk, they comply at once with a decree that declares high style to be inappropriate to their audience. In short, they seldom admit to more than a nodding acquaintance with the Muse.

The normal function of the modesty convention is, I suppose, to prepare a pleasant surprise for the reader when the poem turns out better than he has been led to expect, or, at worst, to save him disappointment when the implied warning is fulfilled. This latter alternative is perhaps valid in some of Chaucer's tales, notably the Monk's. But the really important function of the modesty convention in Chaucer is to prepare a soil in which complexity of meaning may grow most fruitfully. That is, the narrator's assertion, implicit or explicit, of his devotion to the principle of simplicity, his denial of regard for possible /86/ complexity, results, by a curious paradox, *in* complexity; for the harder he tries to simplify issues, the less amenable to simplification they become, and, in artistic terms, the more complex and suggestive the poem becomes. To epitomize, the typical Chaucerian narrator begins by assuring you, either by a modesty prologue or by the notable simplicity of his manner —

sometimes by both — that in what you are about to hear there will be nothing but the most straightforward presentation of reality: the narrator's feet are firmly on the ground, but he is no poet, and his control of anything but fact is weak. Subsequently the poet Chaucer, working from behind the narrator, causes to arise from this hard ground a complex of possible meanings, endlessly dynamic and interactive, amplifying, qualifying, even denying the simple statement: these draw much of their vitality from the fact that they exist — or seem to exist — either, unknown to or in spite of the narrator; indeed, the latter sometimes betrays an uneasy awareness that the poem has got out of hand and is saying something he doesn't approve of or at least didn't intend, and his resistance to this meaning may well become an important part of it. That is, the ultimate significance of the poem derives much from the tension between the narrator's simple statement and the complex of implications that have arisen to qualify it.

The Chaucer who tells of the pilgrimage to Canterbury provides an obvious example of this tension between the simple and the complex. At the very beginning of the Prologue he lets us know exactly what we may expect of his narrative — namely what he saw with his own two eyes, and not an adverb more. And, as I have tried to show elsewhere,[1] his prospectus itself is a miracle of stylistic simplicity, its pedestrian matter-of-factness supporting by example the limited poetic ideal that it is expressing. Yet it is because he has succeeded in persuading the reader to expect no more than meets the eye that, when he comes to the portrait of the Prioress,[2] the poet is able to reveal to us the profoundest depths of that rather shallow lady. The narrator, to be sure, describes her flatly as he saw her, and what he saw was attractive, and it attracted the warm fervour of his /87/ love; but what he did not see was that everything he did see amounted to a well-indexed catalogue of the Prioress's shortcomings, which seen coldly would produce a kind of travesty of a Prioress. But because of his love for the woman, he is unaware of the satirical potential of his portrait, so that this potential, while always imminent, is never actually realized. One feels that if any one had pointed it out to the narrator, he would have been horrified, as, indeed, the Prioress would have been horrified if any one had pointed it out to her — and as even today certain readers are horrified when one points it out to them. And quite rightly, too, because of the great love that permeates the simple description. But the effect achieved by means of a narrator who resists complexity is of a highly complex strife between love and satire, between wholehearted approval and heartless criticism. These are factors

which in logic would cancel one another, as a negative cancels a positive;
but in poetry they exist forever side by side — as they also do in reality
wherever there are ladies at once so attractive and so fallible as the
Prioress. Indeed, the two factors, love and satire, unite with one another
to form a third meaning — one which both qualifies and enhances the
Prioress's own motto, *amor vincit omnia*, by suggesting something of the
complex way in which love does conquer all. This occurs because the
narrator, incapable of complexity, adheres rigorously to the presentation
of simple fact.

The ways in which Chaucerian narrators enhance the meaning of their
stories by missing the point of them are various. Occasionally, indeed, a
narrator will rise up in the pulpit sententiously to point *out* or at least to
point *to* what he takes to be his real meaning. The only trouble is that his
aim is likely to be poor: he will suggest a meaning which, while it bears
some logical relation to the ultimate significance, is at best no more than
gross over-simplification. For instance, the Nun's Priest, at the end of his
remarkably verbose epic of Chauntecleer, solemnly addresses his
audience:

> Lo, swich it is for to be recchelees
> And necligent, and truste on flaterye.
> But ye that holden this tale a folye,
> As of a fox, or of a cok and hen,
> Taketh the moralitee, goode men. (B²3736-40)

/88/ He then goes on to quote St Paul in a way that suggests that doctrine
is produced every time a pen inscribes words on paper — a thought most
comforting to an author hard put to determine his own meaning. With
Pauline authority on his side, the Nun's Priest exhorts us:

> Taketh the fruit, and lat the chaf be stille. (B²3443)

Now all this certainly bids us find a simple moral in the story; but, so far
as I know, no two critics have ever found the same moral: most agree only
in rejecting the Nun's Priest's stated moral about negligence and flattery.
The reason for this disagreement is, as I have tried to suggest elsewhere,[3]
that the real moral of the Tale is in the chaff — the rhetorical
amplifications which make of Chauntecleer a good representative of
western man trying to maintain his precarious dignity in the face of a
universe and of a basic avian (or human) nature which fail to co-operate

with him. But the Nun's Priest, characteristically, suggests this moral
only by pointing towards another which satisfies nobody.

Another Canterbury narrator, the Knight, similarly asks us to take a
simple view of a story which is really very complex. After describing the
languishing of Arcite in Theban exile and of Palamon in Athenian prison,
both of them quite out of the running in their race for Emily, the narrator
finishes off the first part of his poem with a *demande d'amour*:

> You loveres axe I now this questioun:
> Who hath the worse, Arcite or Palamoun? (A1347-8)

With this tidy rhetorical flourish the Knight suggests that his story is a
simple one about a rivalry in love. The question invites the reader to take
sides in this rivalry, to feel sorrier for one youth than the other, and
hence to choose a favourite for the contest that is to come. He appeals,
that is, to our sense of justice. Until recently, the majority of Chaucerian
critics put their money on Palamon; and since at the end of the story
Providence accords him Emily and lets him live happily ever after, while
it buries Arcite, this majority have naturally felt /89/ that justice has
operated in an exemplary manner, and nothing is pleasanter than to see
justice behave itself. Yet there has always been a noisy group — with
whom I deeply sympathize — who feel that Arcite is very badly treated by
the story. This disagreement represents a kind of protracted response to
the Knight's rhetorical question.

The lack of critical agreement, however, once again suggests that there
is something wrong both about the question and about the debate. If
intelligent readers cannot agree on which of the two young men is the
more deserving, then there is probably not much difference between
them. And indeed, the way the poem carefully balances their claims bears
this out. On temperamental grounds you may prefer a man who mistakes
his lady for Venus to a man who knows a woman when he sees one, or you
may not; but such preference has no moral validity. The poem concerns
something larger than the young men's relative deserts, though it is
something closely related to that question. Recognition of their equality
leads to the conclusion that the poem does not assert the simple triumph
of justice when Palamon ends up with Emily, nor the triumph of a
malignant anti-justice when Arcite ends up in his cold grave, alone. What
is does suggest — and I think with every syllable of its being — is that
Providence is not working justly, so far as we can see, when it kills Arcite,
nor, so far as we can see, unjustly when it lets Palamon live happily ever

after. For no matter how hard we look, we cannot hope to see why Providence behaves as it does; all we can do is our best, making a virtue of necessity, enjoying what is good, and remaining cheerful.

But to most of us this is an unpalatable moral, far less appealing than the one which will result if only we can promote Palamon into an unchallenged position of deserving; and it is a very stale bit of cold cabbage indeed unless it is as hard-won as the Knight's own battles. The experience by which the individual attains the Knight's tempered view of life is an important part of that view, and renders it, if not palatable, digestible and nourishing. This experience must include our questioning of relative values, our desire to discover that even-handed justice does prevail in the universe, and our resistance to the conclusion that justice, so far as we can see, operates at best with only /90/ one hand. The emotional history of the ultimate conclusion makes it valid; and the way the Knight's question is framed, pointing at what we should like to believe, and through that at what we shall have to believe, causes us to share in that experience — leads us through the simple to the complex.

It is at the end of *Troilus* that Chaucer, employing the kind of devices I have been discussing, achieves his most complex poetic effect. His narrator has worked hard, from the very beginning, to persuade us of his simplicity, though from the very beginning his simplicity has been compromised by the fact that, apparently unknown to himself, he wavers between two quite different — though equally simple — attitudes towards his story. It is the saddest story in the world, and it is the gladdest story in the world. This double attitude appears strongly in the opening stanzas, when he tells us that his motive for writing is, paradoxically, to bring honour to Love and gladden lovers with a love story so sad that his verses shed tears while he writes them and that Tisiphone is his only appropriate Muse. Yet though he starts out firmly resolved to relate the double sorrow of Troilus

> . . . in loving of Criseide,
> And how that she forsook him er she deide, (*TC* I. 55-6)

as the story progresses he seems to forget all about the second sorrow. The historical perspective, which sees before and after and knows the sad ending, gives way to the limited, immediate view of one who loves the actors in the story, and in his love pines for what is not so desperately that he almost brings it into being. The scholar's motive for telling a sad story simply because it is true finds itself at war with the sentimentalist's

motive of telling a love story simply because it is happy and beautiful. The
optimism that one acquires when one lives with people so attractive
makes a gay future for all seem inevitable. Once launched upon the love
story, the narrator refuses to look forward to a future that the scholar in
him knows to be already sadly past; at moments when the memory of that
sad future breaks in on him, he is likely to deny his own sources, and to
suggest that, despite the historical evidence to the contrary, /91/
Criseide was, perhaps, not unfaithful at all — men have been lying about
her.[4]

For the greater part of the poem the intimately concerned, optimistic
narrator is in full control of the story — or rather, the story is in full
control of him, and persuades him that a world that has such people in it is
not only the best of all possible worlds, but the most possible. When in
the fifth book the facts of history force him back towards the historical
perspective, which has always known that his happiness and that of the
lovers were transitory, illusory, he does his best to resist the implications
arising from his ruined story — tries to circumvent them, denies them,
slides off them. Thus an extraordinary feeling of tension, even of
dislocation, develops from the strife in the narrator's mind between what
should be and what was — and hence what is. This tension is the
emotional storm-centre which causes the narrator's various shifts and
turns in his handling of the ending, and which also determines the great
complexity of the poem's ultimate meaning.

So skilfully has Chaucer mirrored his narrator's internal warfare — a
kind of nervous breakdown in poetry — that many a critic has concluded
that Chaucer himself was bewildered by his poem. One, indeed, roundly
condemns the whole fifth book, saying that it reads like 'an earlier draft
... which its author lacked sufficient interest to revise'. According to this
critic, Chaucer 'cannot bring himself to any real enthusiasm for a plot
from which the bright lady of his own creation has vanished'. And,
elsewhere, 'What had happened to the unhappy Criseyde and to her
equally unhappy creator was that the story in which they were involved
had betrayed them both'.[5] Now this is, in a rather sad way, the ultimate
triumph of Chaucer's method. The critic responds with perfect sympathy
to the narrator's bewilderment, even to the extent of seeming to suggest
that the poet had written four-fifths of his story before he discovered how
it came out. But in fact Chaucer's warmly sympathetic narrator has
blinded the critic's eyes as effectively as he had blinded his own. It is not
true that the bright lady of Chaucer's /92/ creation has vanished —
Criseide is still very much present in book five. What has vanished is the

bright dream of the enduring power of human love, and in a burst of creative power that it is not easy to match elsewhere.

For the *moralitee* of *Troilus and Criseide* (and by morality I do not mean 'ultimate meaning') is simply this: that human love, and by a sorry corollary everything human, is unstable and illusory. I give the moral so flatly now because in the remainder of this paper I shall be following the narrator in his endeavour to avoid it, and indeed shall be eagerly abetting him in trying to avoid it, and even pushing him away when he finally accepts it. I hope in this way to suggest how Chaucer, by manipulating his narrator, achieves an objective image of the poem's significance that at once greatly qualifies and enhances this moral, and one that is, of course, far more profound and less absolute than my flat-footed statement. The meaning of the poem is not the moral, but a complex qualification of the moral.

Let us turn now to that part of the poem, containing the last eighteen stanzas, which is often referred to by modern scholars, though not by the manuscripts, as the Epilogue. I object to the term because it implies that this passage was tacked on to the poem after the poet had really finished his work, so that it is critically if not physically detachable from what has gone before.[6] And while I must admit that the nature of this passage, its curious twists and turns, its occasional air of fecklessness, set it off from what has gone before, it also seems to me to be the head of the whole body of the poem.[7]

The last intimately observed scene of the action is the final, anticlimactic interview between Troilus and Pandarus, wherein the latter is driven by the sad logic of his loyalty and of his pragmatism to express hatred of his niece, and to wish her dead. Pandarus's last words are, 'I can namore saye', and it is now up to the narrator, who is as heart-broken as Troilus and Pandarus, /93/ to express the significance of his story. His first reaction is to take the epic high road; by means of the exalted style to reinvest Troilus with the human dignity that his unhappy love has taken from him. The narrator starts off boldly enough:

> Greet was the sorwe and plainte of Troilus;
> But forth hire cours Fortune ay gan to holde.
> Criseide loveth the sone of Tydeüs,
> And Troilus moot weepe in cares colde. (TC V. 1744–7)

But though the manner is epic, the subject is not: an Aeneas in Dido's pathetic plight is no fit subject for Virgilian style. And the narrator, overcome by the pathos of his story, takes refuge in moralization:

> Swich is this world, whoso it can biholde:
> In eech estaat is litel hertes reste—
> God leve us for to take it for the beste!

How true! And how supremely, brilliantly, inadeqate! It has been said
that all experience does no more than prove some platitude or other, but
one hopes that poetic experience will do more, or in any case that poetry
will not go from pathos to bathos. This moral, the trite moral of the
Monk's Tale — Isn't life awful? — which the Monk arrives at — again
and again — *a priori* would be accepted by many a medieval man as a
worthy moral for the *Troilus*, and the narrator is a medieval man. But the
poet behind the narrator is aware that an experience that has been
intimately shared — not merely viewed historically, as are the Monk's
tragedies — requires not a moral, but a meaning arrived at *a posteriori*,
something earned, and in a sense new. Moreover, the narrator seems still
to be asking the question, Can nothing be salvaged from the wreck of the
story? For he goes on once more to have recourse to epic enhancement of
his hero, more successfully this time, since it is the martial heroism of
Troilus, rather than his unhappy love, that is the subject: there follow
two militant stanzas recounting his prowess and his encounters with
Diomede. But again the epic impulse fails, for the narrator's real subject
is not war but unhappy love, for which epic values will still do nothing —
will neither salvage the dignity of Troilus nor endow his experience with
meaning. In /94/ a wistful stanza, the narrator faces his failure to do by
epic style what he desires to have done:

> And if I hadde ytaken for to write
> The armes of this ilke worthy man, [But, unfortunately, *arma
> virumque non cano*]
> Than wolde ich of his batailes endite;
> But for that I to writen first bigan
> Of his love, I have said as I can—
> His worthy deedes whoso list hem heere,
> Rede Dares — he can telle hem alle yfere. (1765-71)

This sudden turn from objective description to introspection mirrors the
narrator's quandary. Unable to get out of his hopeless predicament, he
does what we all tend to do when we are similarly placed: he begins to
wonder why he ever got himself into it. The sequel of this unprofitable

speculation is likely to be panic, and the narrator very nearly panics when he sees staring him in the face another possible moral for the love poem he has somehow been unwise enough to recite. The moral that is staring him in the face is written in the faces of the ladies of his audience, the anti-feminist moral which is at once obvious and, from a court poet, unacceptable:

> Biseeching every lady bright of hewe,
> And every gentil womman what she be,
> That al be that Criseide was untrewe,
> That for that gilt she nat be wroth with me.
> Ye may hir giltes in othere bookes see;
> And gladlier I wol write, if you leste,
> Penelopeës trouthe and good Alceste.

While anticipating the ladies' objections, the narrator has, with that relief only a true coward can appreciate, glimpsed a possible way out: denial of responsibility for what the poem says. He didn't write it in the first place, it has nothing to do with him, and anyhow he would much rather have written about faithful women. These excuses are, of course, very much in the comic mood of the Prologue to the *Legend of Good Women* where Alceste, about whom he would prefer to have written, defends him from Love's wrath on the grounds that, being no more than a translator, he wrote about Criseide 'from innocence, /95/ and knew not what he said'. And if he can acquit himself of responsibility for Criseide by pleading permanent inanity, there is no reason why he cannot get rid of all his present tensions by funneling them into a joke against himself. This he tries to do by turning upside down the anti-feminist moral of the story:

> N'I saye nat this al only for thise men,
> But most for wommen that bitraised be . . .

And I haven't recited this exclusively for men, but also, or rather but mostly, for women who are betrayed

> Thrugh false folk — God yive hem sorwe, amen! —
> That with hir grete wit and subtiltee
> Bitraise you; and this commeveth me
> To speke, and in effect you alle I praye,

Beeth war of men, and herkneth what I saye.

The last excursion into farce — in a poem that contains a good deal of farce — is this outrageous inversion of morals, which even so has a grotesque relevance if all human love, both male and female, is in the end to be adjudged unstable. With the narrator's recourse to comedy the poem threatens to end. At any rate, he asks it to go away:

> Go, litel book, go, litel myn tragedye,
> Ther God thy makere yit, er that he die,
> So sende might to make in som comedye. . . .

(Presumably a comedy will not blow up in his face as this story has, and will let him end on a note like the one he has just sounded.) There follows the celebrated injunction of the poet to his book not to vie with other poetry, but humbly to kiss the steps of Virgil, Ovid, Homer, Lucan, and Statius. This is the modesty convention again, but transmuted, I believe, into something close to arrogance. Perhaps the poem is not to be classed with the works of these great poets, but I do not feel that the narrator succeeds in belittling his work by mentioning it in connection with them; there is such a thing as inviting comparison by eschewing comparison. It seems that the narrator has abandoned his joke, and is taking his 'little book' — of /96/ more than 8,000 lines — seriously. Increasing gravity characterizes the next stanza, which begins with the hope that the text will not be miswritten nor mismetred by scribes and lesser breeds without the law of final *-e*. Then come two lines of emphatic prayer:

> And red wherso thou be, or elles songe,
> That thou be understonde, God I biseeche.

It is perhaps inconsiderate of the narrator to implore us to take his sense when he has been so irresolute about defining his sense. But the movement of the verse now becomes sure and strong, instead of uncertain and aimless, as the narrator moves confidently towards a meaning.

For in the next stanza, Troilus meets his death. This begins — once again — in the epic style, with perhaps a glance at the *Iliad:*

> The wratthe, as I bigan you for to saye,
> Of Troilus the Greekes boughten dere.

Such dignity as the high style can give is thus, for the last time, proffered Troilus. But for him there is to be no last great battle in the West, and both the stanza, and Troilus's life, end in pathos:

> But wailaway, save only Goddes wille:
> Despitously him slow the fierse Achille.

Troilus's spirit at once ascends into the upper spheres whence he looks down upon this little earth and holds all vanity as compared with the full felicity of heaven. The three stanzas describing Troilus's afterlife afford him that reward which medieval Christianity allowed to the righteous heathen. And in so doing, they salvage from the human wreck of the story the human qualities of Troilus that are of enduring value — most notably, his *trouthe*, the integrity for which he is distinguished. Moreover, this recognition by the plot that some human values transcend human life seems to enable the narrator to come to a definition of the poem's meaning which he has hitherto been unwilling to make. Still close to his characters, he witnesses Troilus's rejection of earthly values, and then, apparently satisfied, now that the mortal good in Troilus has been given immortal reward, he is willing to make that rejection of *all* mortal goods towards /97/ which the poem has, despite his resistance, been driving him. His rejection occurs — most unexpectedly — in the third of these stanzas. Troilus, gazing down at the earth and laughing within himself at those who mourn his death,

> . . . dampned al oure werk that folweth so
> The blinde lust, the which that may nat laste,
> And sholden al oure herte on hevene caste.

Up until the last line Troilus has been the subject of every main verb in the entire passage; but after he has damned all *our* work, by one of those syntactical ellipses that make Middle English so fluid a language, Troilus's thought is extended to include both narrator and reader: in the last line, *And sholden al oure herte on hevene caste*, the plural verb *sholden* requires the subject *we*; but this subject is omitted, because to the narrator the sequence of the sense is, at last, overpoweringly clear. When, after all his attempts not to have to reject the values inherent in his love story, he finally does reject them, he does so with breath-taking ease.

He does so, indeed, with dangerous ease. Having taken up arms against the world and the flesh, he lays on with a will:

> Swich fin hath, lo, this Troilus for love;
> Swich fin hath al his grete worthinesse;
> Swich fin hath his estaat real above;
> Swich fin his lust, swich fin hath his noblesse;
> Swich fin hath false worldes brotelnesse:
> And thus bigan his loving of Criseide,
> As I have told, and in this wise he deide.

But impressive as this stanza is, its movement is curious. The first five lines express, with increasing force, disgust for a world in which everything — not only what merely *seems* good, but also what really *is* good — comes to nothing in the end. Yet the last two lines,

> And thus bigan his loving of Criseide,
> As I have told, and in this wise he deide,

have, I think, a sweetness of tone that contrasts strangely with the emphatic disgust that precedes them. They seem to express a deep sadness for a doomed potential — as if the narrator, /98/ while forced by the evidence to condemn everything his poem has stood for, cannot really quite believe that it has come to nothing. The whole lovely aspiration of the previous action is momentarily recreated in the spare summary of this couplet.

The sweetness of tone carries over into the next two stanzas, the much-quoted ones beginning

> O yonge, freshe folkes, he or she,
> In which that love up groweth with youre age,
> Repaireth hoom fro worldly vanitee,
> And of youre herte up casteth the visage
> To thilke God that after his image
> You made; and thinketh al nis but a faire
> This world that passeth soone as flowres faire.

The sweetness here adheres not only to what is being rejected, but also to what is being sought in its stead, and this marks a development in the narrator. For he does not now seem so much to be fleeing away, in despair and disgust, from an ugly world — the world of the Monk's Tale — as he seems to be moving voluntarily through this world *towards* something infinitely better. And while this world is a wretched one — ultimately — in which all love is *feined,* 'pretended' and 'shirked', it is also a world full of the young potential of human love — 'In which that love up groweth with *oure* age'; a world which, while it passes soon, passes soon as flowers fair. All the illusory loveliness of a world which is man's only reality is expressed in the very lines that reject that loveliness.

In these stanzas the narrator has been brought to the most mature and complex expression of what is involved in the Christian rejection of the world that seems to be, and indeed is, man's home, even though he knows there is a better one. But the narrator himself remains dedicated to simplicity, and makes one last effort to resolve the tension in his mind between loving a world he ought to hate and hating a world he cannot help loving; he endeavors to root out the love:

> Lo, here of payens cursed olde rites;
> Lo, here what alle hir goddes may availe;
> Lo, here thise wrecched worldes appetites;
> Lo, here the fin and guerdon for travaile /99/
> Of Jove, Appollo, of Mars, of swich rascaile;
> Lo, here the forme of olde clerkes speeche
> In poetrye, if ye hir bookes seeche.

For the second time within a few stanzas a couplet has undone the work of the five lines preceding it. In them is harsh, excessively harsh, condemnation of the world of the poem, including gods and rites that have played no great part in it. In brilliant contrast to the tone of these lines is the exhausted calm of the last two:

> Lo, here the forme of olde clerkes speeche
> In poetrye, if ye hir bookes seeche.

There is a large imprecision about the point of reference of this couplet. I do not know whether its *Lo here* refers to the five preceding lines or to the poem as a whole, but I suppose it refers to the poem as a whole, as the other four *Lo here's* do. If this is so, then the form of *olde clerkes speeche* is being damned as well as the *payens cursed olde rites* — by parataxis, at least. Yet it is not, for the couplet lacks the heavy, fussy indignation of the earlier lines: instead of indignation there is, indeed, dignity. I suggest that the couplet once more reasserts, in its simplicity, all the implicit and explicit human values that the poem has dealt with, even though these are, to a medieval Christian, ultimately insignificant. The form of old clerks' speech in poetry is the sad story that human history tells. It is sad, it is true, it is lovely, and it is significant, for it is poetry.

This is the last but one of the narrator's searches for a resolution for his poem. I have tried to show how at the end of *Troilus* Chaucer has manipulated a narrator capable of only a simple view of reality in such a way as to achieve the poetic expression of an extraordinarily complex one. The narrator, moved by his simple devotion to Troilus, to Pandarus, above all to Criseide, has been vastly reluctant to find that their story, so full of the illusion of happiness, comes to nothing — that the potential of humanity comes to nothing. To avoid this — seemingly simple — conclusion he has done everything he could. He has tried the epic high road; he has tried the broad highway of trite moralization; he has tried to eschew responsibility; he /100/ has tried to turn it all into a joke; and all these devices have failed. Finally, with every other means of egress closed, he has subscribed to Troilus's rejection of his own story, though only when, like Gregory when he wept for Trajan, he has seen his desire for his hero's salvation confirmed. Once having made the rejection, he has thrown himself into world-hating with enthusiasm. But now the counterbalance asserts its power. For the same strong love of the world of his story that prevented him from reaching the Christian rejection permeates and qualifies his expression of the rejection. Having painfully climbed close to the top of the ridge he did not want to climb, he cannot help looking back with longing at the darkening but still fair valley in which he lived; and every resolute thrust forward ends with a glance backward. In having his narrator behave thus, Chaucer has achieved a meaning only great poetry can achieve. The world he knows and the heaven he believes in grow ever farther and farther apart as the woeful contrast between them is developed, and ever closer and closer together as the narrator blindly unites them in the common bond of his love. Every false start he has made has amounted, not to a negative, but to a positive; has been a necessary part of the experience without which the moral of the poem would be as meaningless and unprofitable as in the form I gave it a little while ago. The poem states, what much of Chaucer's poetry states, the necessity under which men lie of living in, making the best of, enjoying, and loving a world from which they must remain detached and which they must ultimately hate: a little spot of earth that with the sea embraced is, as in Book Three Criseide was embraced by Troilus.

For this paradox there is no logical resolution. In the last two stanzas of the poem Chaucer, after asking Gower and Strode for correction, invokes the power that, being supra-logical itself, can alone resolve paradox. He echoes Dante's mighty prayer to the Trinity, 'that al maist circumscrive', and concludes with the lines:

> So make us, Jesus, for thy mercy digne,
> For love of Maide and Moder thyn benigne.

The poem has concerned a mortal woman whose power to love /101/ failed, and it ends with the one mortal woman whose power to love is everlasting. I think it is significant that the prayer of the poem's ending leads up, not to Christ, son of God, but to his mother, daughter of Eve — towards heaven, indeed, but towards heaven through human experience.

Notes

1. See 'The Masculine Narrator and Four Women of Style,' in *Speaking of Chaucer* (New York, 1970), pp. 46–47.

2. For further discussion of this portrait, see *Speaking of Chaucer*, pp. 3–4 and 59–64.

3. See E. T. Donaldson, ed., *Chaucer's Poetry*, pp. 940–4; also 'Patristic Exegesis in the Criticism of Medieval Literature: The Opposition', *Selected Papers from the English Institute, 1958–1959*, repr. in *Speaking of Chaucer*, pp. 146–50.

4. TC IV. 20–1.

5. Marchette Chute, *Geoffrey Chaucer of England* (London, 1946), pp. 179, 180, and 178.

6. The extreme exponent of detachability is W. C. Curry in his well-known essay, 'Destiny in *Troilus and Criseyde*', *PMLA*, xlv (1930), 129 ff., reprinted in his *Chaucer and the Mediaeval Sciences* (second revised and enlarged ed., 1960): see especially pp. 294–8.

7. I believe that this is the opinion of many Chaucerians. See, e.g., Dorothy Everett, *Essays on Middle English Literature* (1955), pp. 134–8, and Dorothy Bethurum, 'Chaucer's Point of View as Narrator', *PMLA*, lxxiv (1959), 516–18.

Narrative Structure in Chaucer's "Troilus and Criseyde"

by Gerry Brenner

Speaking of Pandarus' scheming near the end of Book I, Chaucer's narrator comments,

> For everi wight that hath an hous to founde
> Ne renneth naught the werk for to bygynne
> With rakel hond, but he wol bide a stounde,
> And sende his hertes line out fro withinne
> Aldirfirst his purpose for to wynne. (I, 1065–69)

This architectural metaphor aptly suggests the careful deliberation that went into constructing Chaucer's *Troilus and Criseyde*. Critics, although observing the symmetry of the poem, have not tried to view the narrative construct as it functions. Instead they have only worked over particular areas, fragmenting the total structural meaning. I will try to rebuild the narrative paradigm of the poem by focusing on the overall structure, narrative methods, and the implications of the methods as they inform the structural meaning of the poem.

The overall narrative structure of *Troilus and Criseyde* is ostensibly classical since much of the poem displays a high degree of symmetry. From the opening lines of the poem that propose to tell of Troilus's "double sorwe" and his adventures "Fro wo to wele, and after out of

Reprinted from *Annuale Mediaevale* 6 (1965): 5–18, slightly revised by the author, with the kind permission of the author and Humanities Press, Inc., New Jersey. The original pagination is indicated between slashes in the text.

joie," Chaucer establishes a metaphor of pattern, of repetition, of balance. As Kemp Malone observes, the poem can be diagrammed as a *W*, the three high points being before Troilus falls in love, when Troilus and Criseyde consummate their love, and when Troilus is transported into the eighth sphere; the two low points occur when Troilus voices his lovesickness to Pandarus and when he sees his brooch on the captured coat-armor of Diomede.[1] However, the diagrammatic letter should probably be thin at the extremities and thick in the center since the first and third high points receive only sketchy treatment. Malone's *W* would perhaps see Troilus's joys progress from self-love to sexual love to divine love, a gradual shift from egocentricity to self-denial, just the reverse of Criseyde's development. /6/ And Troilus's woes move from mawkish self-indulgence to poignant lamentation. Malone's diagram is probably more accurate than Sister Gill's interpretation that the action is circular in structure, based on the recurring metaphor of the wheel of Fortune, since circularity implies repetition without development.[2] Troilus's somersaults from joy to woe defy any suggestion of static repetition. The only circularity in the poem resides in the accretion of unhappy lovers: the narrator's "unliklynesse" denies him love; Pandarus suffers from unrequited love; Oenone is abandoned by Paris; her song tells of Phebus' unrequited love for Admetus' daughter; the use of Procne and the nightingale alludes to their betrayal by Tereus; Helen falses Menelaus; and Venus (ironically invoked in the proem to III) cuckolds Vulcan.[3]

Although Malone's diagram is useful, it serves more to describe Troilus's love career than the structure of the poem. As several critics have noted, the poem divides into an ascending and a descending action.[4] The inverted *V* resembles the theoretical structure of medieval tragedy with the rising and falling of the hero. However, Chaucer only flirts with the convention. The rise of Troilus is rendered in comic terms, his effeminate courtship climaxing when Pandarus has to pitch him into bed with Criseyde. And since in the ascending action Chaucer has set Troilus's heroic stature partly in comic terms, his decline ultimately resists a tragic interpretation. That is, his poignant lamentations all too strongly echo his comic self-indulgence, thereby dissociating the reader from full participation in Troilus's decline.

Besides indicating the triangular love affair of Troilus, Criseyde and Diomede, the inverted *V* also provides a useful image for visualizing the convergence of action and character in space and time, since in Book Three Chaucer draws together the disparate bands of the poem. That is, before and after Book Three the action and characters are nicely separated, a continual shifting from Troilus to Criseyde, Pandarus now with one, next with another. And even though there may be a semblance of unity in the /7/ separation scene at the end of Book IV, Pandarus is absent. In contrast to this, Pandarus is present in both wooing scenes in III. Chaucer deliberately makes Pandarus' whereabouts equivocal in the consummation scene; he never explicitly indicates that Pandarus exists.[5] Thus Book III contains the only trio scenes. (Deiphebus' invitation to Criseyde occurs while Pandarus is still present, but the scene is tersely presented in a stanza of exposition.) The narrative function of having the two trio scenes take place in Book III could be seen as Chaucer's studied attempt to emphasize the central unity of that book. As Charles A. Owen observes, ". . . the consummation of love in the Third Book is framed by the two contrasting sorrows; those, in turn, by the two contrasting laughters; and those, in turn, by the two contrasting prayers."[6] Chaucer also deploys Troilus's two songs and the two exchanges of love letters strategically around the Third Book. Owens further comments upon the symmetry of the Third Book, noting how the Boethian stanzas on love at the end match those by Boccaccio in the proem, how Venus is invoked in the first and last stanzas, and how both enclose the meeting of the lovers at Deiphebus' house and their consummation at Pandarus' house.[7] The sexual bliss here purports to anticipate the spiritual bliss that awaits Troilus in the epilogue. Pandarus hints at this when he extracts Troilus from the "stewe" and bawdily tells him " 'Make the redy right anon / For thou shalt into hevene blisse wende —' " (III, 703-4). The unity of action and symmetry of technique in this book permits viewing it as the fulcrum for the rising and falling action.

The inverted V also comments obliquely upon space and time as narrative elements in the rising and falling action. Meech notes that the central location for the poem is Troilus's chamber, "where with the world locked out the exigencies of the heart seem all important."[8] That most of the action does take place in someone's chamber, bedroom, or closet (Criseyde writes to /8/ Troilus from her closet and Pandarus beds her down in his "litel closet") indicates not only the constricted world of romance, but also suggests the religious motif of Troilus's Solomonic meditations, a sexual image of the object of Troilus's desire, and also the appropriate image for the tomb Troilus so earnestly seeks throughout the poem. The little bedrooms of Book III structurally unify this spatial concern; after the Third Book, settings become more disparate.

This disparateness of setting is reiterated in Chaucer's use of time, especially the highly fragmented time patterns of Book Five. However,

Chaucer also maintains a relative simultaneity of time in the last two books as a mockery of the falling out of the once-unified lovers. That is, in the first two books, the time narration proceeds sequentially, Chaucer clearly indicating that episodes occur in a chronological sequence: on the morning of the fourth of May Pandarus argues Troilus's love; in the evening he instructs Troilus in letter writing; the following morning he thrusts the letter in Criseyde's bosom; that evening he brings her reply to Troilus. The two bedroom scenes of III unify time. But, in the Fourth and Fifth Books, instead of the narration wholly regressing to the earlier sequential relationship, Chaucer maintains a relatively confused overlapping of narrative sequence. Although he tells of Troilus's lamentations and Criseyde's self-flagellations, he refuses to attach a time sequence to their actions, and in the last bed scene, their rapport achieves a unity of time which only mocks their impending separation. In the Fifth Book the simultaneity of time becomes an ironic and dramatic agent: Chaucer skillfully superimposes a flashback of Troilus's tenth-day actions upon the earlier-related episode between Criseyde and Diomede on the same tenth day, suggesting again a hollow unity of the two original lovers. But this mocking unity of time is undercut by the preponderance of confused time. Action and time both run pell-mell in the last book, in concord with the disunity of the lovers.

The fragmentation of space and time in Book V assists in projecting a linear view of the poem's structure. In the first four books two lines of action, Troilus's and Criseyde's, make a unified pilgrimage, merge in Book III, and are tenuously sustained in the strained unity of IV. But in V the pilgrimage splinters. Francis Lee Utley's article, "Scene-division in Chaucer's Troilus /9/ and Criseyde," provides one way of seeing this fragmentation; Utley breaks the poem down into eighty-three episodes of dialogue or monologue and thirty-five digressions or transitions, the episode-digression relationship falling six and five in I, twenty-six and seven in II, thirteen and four in III, nine and two in IV, and twenty-seven and fourteen in V.[9] Although it would seem that Book II is as fragmented as V, Utley's breakdown fails to indicate that in II there are only three major settings for scene, Criseyde's, Troilus's, and Deiphebus' palaces, while in V, there are at least seven scene settings, and some scenes are given no spatial location. And IV, although it is the least episodic, has five scene settings compared to III's four and I's three. Since much of the action in the early books depends upon a unity of setting for the parallels of action, it might be inferred that the unity of setting would contribute to the narrative harmony found especially in those books (an idea I will develop later). This would contrast with the anarchy of setting in the Fifth Book.

This anarchy of setting in Book V is echoed in its anarchy of time. Although Meech's statement that Chaucer "establishes the chronology of sequences as if he were a meticulous historian"[10] can be applied to the first four books, the Fifth Book resists the judgment. Its chronology, appropriate to Troilus's grief, smacks of surrealistic chaos. The book erupts at a tumultuous pace: although the mocking unity of the tenth-day activities has been mentioned, any semblance of unity is fractured by the dissociated sequence of the ten days, by the narrator's mention of Criseyde's defection after two months, and by the complete dismissal of time, indicated by the silent tattoo of the undated latters, and the undated recognition of Troilus's death and translation. Time becomes blurred with the separation of the lovers just as it had been clarified with their union. The pell-mell pace of time is asserted in the second stanza of the Fifth Book which arrests attention by commenting that three years have lapsed since Troilus "Bigan to love hire first for whom his sorwe / Was al . . ." (V, 13-14). The fragmentation of time is also implied in "sudden" Diomede's courtship of Criseyde.

The anarchy of the fragmented Fifth Book is exhibited in various other ways. In contrast with the preceding books, V lacks /10/ the formalizing proem, lacks the narrator's insistent dependence upon "myn auctour" (here he comments on Criseyde's giving her heart to Diomede "Men seyn — I not" [1050]), and lacks the normal social estrangement of Troilus. These elements all contribute to a view of the splintering linear structure of the rising and falling actions.

Chaucer enlists several overlapping narrative methods to encompass this rising and falling action, inducing a classical symmetry. One of the most noticeable of these methods is parallelism. Chaucer unites the poem with occasional verbal echoes as one ramification of parallelism. Patch notes that Criseyde's pragmatic attitude toward her involvement with Troilus is echoed in Diomede's attitude toward courting Criseyde: in II, 807–8, Criseyde, resolving her conflicts says, " 'He which that nothing undertaketh / Nothyng n'acheveth'"; Diomede in V, 784 resolves also that "'For he that naught n'asaith, naught n'acheveth.'"[11] Again, in Book III Criseyde is brought to the bedside of "kankedorted" Troilus, of whom the narrator comments, "But, Lord, so he wex sodeynliche red" (82); when Troilus is brought to Criseyde's bedside in the second bed scene the narrator again comments, "But, Lord, so she wex sodeynliche red" (956). And in III again, Troilus unwittingly predicts his own slayer when, in vowing to Pandarus his secrecy to Criseyde, he says "'And, if I lye, Achilles with his spere / Myn herte cleve, al were my lif eterne'" (374–75).[12] Another interesting verbal parallel is in Pandarus' statement to Troilus near the end of Book I when he assigns himself to be Troilus's intercessor: "' Yef me this labour and this bisynesse, / And of my spede be thyn al that swetnesse!'" (1042–43). This recalls the narrator's proem to the same Book in which, admitting his "unliklynesse," he compensates by saying that " . . . if this may don gladnesse / To any lovere, and his cause availle, / Have he my thonk, and myn be this travaille!" (19–21). The parallel here transcends mere verbal parallelism. Just as the narrator structures his rendition of the material, as a conscious artist, so too does Pandarus see himself as a conscious artist taking delight in putting his machinery into operation. As /11/ the narrator intercedes for lovers in the opening prayer, Pandarus is a parodic version of intercessor in praying for Troilus and receiving his confession. Both, alas, are only servants of Love's servants. An outgrowth of these verbal parallels occurs in the constant search for a cure for dying victims of love, the words heal, cure, remedy and related synonyms recurring constantly.

Chaucer also unifies the poem most noticeably through parallels of action. One unifying action is, of course, the relationship of the doomed love story to its framework, the doomed city. This relationship is also emphasized by the references to the destruction of Thebes, mentioned in the Second Book as the story being read to Criseyde and her ladies, and again in the Fifth Book in Cassandra's revelation of Troilus's dream, telling him that Diomede is of Theban heritage.[13] Further parallels accrue with near-predictable symmetry: the falsity of Calkas is repeated by Criseyde; Hector comes to Criseyde's defense at the outset of the poem and when she is to be bartered for Antenor; Antenor is Criseyde's enemy twice, once for Pandarus' trumped-up fiction of Antenor's malice toward her, and once as the cause of her separation from Troilus; Troilus and Criseyde reject love initially; Criseyde is wooed by Troilus and Diomede; the bed scene at Deiphebus' house is reconstructed at Pandarus' house; in both bed scenes Criseyde is lured under false pretenses (and in both she may well know they are false pretenses!); Antigone's love song of harmony in the garden in II is replayed in III by Troilus in another garden; just as Pandarus thrusts Troilus's love letter into Criseyde's bosom in II, in III Pandarus has to thrust Troilus into her bed, also a repetition of Troilus's "illness" of the first bed scene; Criseyde's swoon in the fourth book recalls Troilus's "mannes herte" in his swoon at Criseyde's bedside; Criseyde's dream of Troilus is matched with his

dream of her; just as Pandarus pandars for Troilus, Troilus in gratitude
offers to pandar for Pandarus.[14]

These parallels of action, obvious as they are, are aided by the chess-
like moves of narrative presentation: Troilus sees Criseyde in Book I and
is struck with love, and then in Book II Criseyde is struck when she sees
Troilus ride by: "'Who yaf me drynke!'" Chaucer continually gives one
scene with Troilus and Pandarus, /12/ then one with Criseyde and
Pandarus, the shifts becoming almost predictable and leading critics to
such statements as: the symmetry has almost a "logical precision";[15] it
exhibits "consummate skill in dramatic construction" and deserves
praise for "the artistic calculation of proportions";[16] "his structural idea
. . . is artistic unity emergent from lifelike diversity."[17]

But Chaucer does more with structure than just arrange it in an orderly
sequence through verbal parallels, corresponding action or narrative
presentation. The careful structuring of the poem not only displays
Chaucer's control over the poem, but also functions as a metaphor of
harmony and order. In a sense, the symmetry of the narrative structure
can be seen as another ally for the Christian-otherworldly, deterministic,
and tragic view of the poem's ultimate meaning since the metaphor
prepares for the Christian morality of "herkenyng armonye / With
sownes ful of hevenyssh melodie"; since the metaphor suggests an almost
predetermined predictability of similar events; and since the metaphor
confirms that Troilus will be embraced by a greater harmony of tragic
justice.

However, it is interesting to look again at Pandarus' advice to Troilus
on writing his first love letter:

> "And if thow writ a goodly word al softe,
> Though it be good, reherse it nought to ofte.
>
> "For though the beste harpour upon lyve
> Wolde on the beste sowned joly harpe
> That evere was, with alle his fyngres fyve,
> Touche ay o streng, or ay o werbul harpe
> Were his nayles poynted nevere so sharpe,
> It sholde maken every wight to dulle,
> To here his glee, and of his strokes fulle. (II, 1028-36)

Pandarus is instructing Troilus not to be a Johny-one-note. Perhaps
Chaucer also heeds Pandarus' advice. And perhaps by using such a series

of parallel actions Chaucer is deliberately gulling us into seeing the metaphor of order merely to create an "amphibology." To be direct, in any parallel scene, the bed-scenes to cite a specific example, although the type of situation at Pandarus' /13/ resembles the earlier one at Deiphebus', the circumstances have altered enough to create a modification of the earlier scene. Instead of being identical to the earlier scene, which would confirm the harmony metaphor, the situation has changed enough to comment upon earthly mutability. Instead of a repetition of the earlier scene, Chaucer inverts the parallel. This use of inverted parallel continually teeters the seemingly balanced events.

It may certainly be argued that the changed circumstances of parallel scenes is only part of the storyteller's art and that the variation is necessary for artistic development. However, that Chaucer should deliberately attempt to repeat certain features with such a high degree of incidence would seem to indicate a conscious effort to use the repetitions functionally, transcending mere storytelling. The most noticeable thing about the repetitions is not their similarity, but rather their dissimilarity. For example, in the Second Book, Pandarus visits Criseyde to sell her on Troilus. This inverts the situation of Book I in which Pandarus had to sell his own trustworthiness to Troilus. And whereas in Book I Pandarus had to wheedle the cause of Troilus's woe from him, in Book II Chaucer inverts the episode so that Pandarus arouses Criseyde's curiosity and has Criseyde wheedle information from him. The episodes have a surface order to them since someone obtains information from someone else in both. But the easy parallel is undermined by the ironic inversion.

My point is this: just as Chaucer yokes together the unresolvable antinomies of fate and free will, Christian and pagan, classical and medieval, ideal and real, tragic and comic, and a plethora of lesser contrasts of style, character, and so on, so too does Chaucer yoke two types of narrative structure as dramatic devices to complement the unresolvable status of the poem's dialectic of dualities. One type of narrative structure, the surface harmony that narrative repetition creates, lends itself easily to a metaphor of harmony. The other type of narrative structure, the underlying chaos that inverted parallels, ironic foreshadowing, and multiple points of view wreak upon the surface harmony, lends itself to a metaphor of cacaphony and disorder. Although these three latter narrative techniques of inverted parallel, ironic foreshadowing and multiple points of view may also be viewed as forming a harmonizing pattern, they nonetheles form a negative kind of irony, a harmonic reminder only of earthly mutability, a negative way of bolstering a harmonic view of the poem. As a /14/ metaphor of disorder this second type of narrative structure (which I would broadly call irony, for want of a more inclusive term) would seem to ally it with the pagan-thisworldly, free-will, and comic view of the poem's ultimate meaning. The metaphor repeatedly prepares for Criseyde's thisworldly defection: it sounds moral caution not to repent this world, but to be prepared to expect fickleness since earthly participation necessitates contamination, a rejection of the Christian purity that requires cloistered passivity; the metaphor intimates a free-will unpredictability of events or an ironic reversal of seemingly similar events; the metaphor comically confirms that Troilus's proud idealism and ineffectuality deserve the comic justice of Criseyde's about-face. This view of the poem is dramatically suggested by the rupturing anarchy that an ironic narrative structure dictates.

One of the three narrative methods of this structural anarchy is a use of inverted parallels. Besides the inverted parallelism of Pandarus' wheedling-wheedled episodes, Chaucer also provides inverted parallelism in Criseyde's dream and in its counterpart, Troilus's dream. Although Chaucer hints at a degree of parallellism, since both have dreams, Criseyde's dream bodes love and Troilus's bodes betrayed love.[18] But Chaucer pushes the inversion even further. Criseyde dreams of having her heart rent by a white eagle, a symbol of the purity of Troilus; Troilus dreams of Criseyde kissing a sleeping boar, a symbol of Diomede. Yet when Chaucer dramatizes Troilus as such a timorous dove, the eagle image clashes; and when the narrator tells of the temerity of Diomede's courtship and when he comments that Criseyde gave Diomede her heart after he was wounded by Troilus, the eagle image more aptly suits Diomede. Moreover, the image of Criseyde kissing a sleeping boar fits the comic image of Criseyde lavishing her remedial kisses on the swooned Troilus of the consummation scene. Other inverted parallels can be seen in the simple contrast of Pandarus' fidelity and Criseyde's infidelity, the contrasting courtships of Troilus and Diomede, the contrasting entreaties of Pandarus to halt Troilus's two sorrows, the contrast of Troilus's imminent death in the first two books and the required counterfeiting in the bed scene at Deiphebus' house, and the contrast of Troilus's laugh at foolish lovers in Book I and his final laugh at worldly vanity in Book V. [19] The most developed /15/ inverted parallel revolves around the two bed scenes in III, finding a reversal of bedside wooers, a reversal of Troilus's sham illness for his genuine swoon, and a reversal of expected romantic ardor in Criseyde's reproach of Troilus's jealousy, to point out a few inversions. As obvious as these inverted parallels are, they combine to entreat a wary-eyed view of surface harmony.

But even more devasting to the apparent order of events is Chaucer's narrative use of ironic foreshadowing. This finds verbal demonstration when Pandarus sneaks in and tells Troilus, at the end of Book II, "'God have thy soule, ibrought have I thi *beere!*'" (1638), neither Pandarus nor Troilus realizing the pun, that Criseyde prompts the hastening of Troilus's death. The most obvious example of ironic foreshadowing occurs when Troilus haughtily scorns lovers:

> "Lord, so ye lyve al in lest,
> Ye loveres! for the konnyngeste of you,
> That serveth most ententiflich and best
> Hym tit as often harm therof as prow.
> Youre hire is quyt, ayeyn, ye, God woot how!" (I, 330–34)

Troilus's ironic taunt in the last line of this same speech becomes double-edged. "'Lord, wel is hym that may ben of you oon!'" (I, 350). Pandarus' urgings of Troilus realize a metaphorical ironic foreshadowing in Book II when Pandarus equates Criseyde with the oak rather than the reed:

> "Thenk here-ayeins: whan that the stordy ook,
> On which men hakketh ofte, for the nones,
> Receyved hath the happy fallyng strook,
> The greete sweigh doth it come al at ones,
> As don thise rokkes or thise milnestones;
> For swifter cours comth thyng that is of wighte,
> Whan it descendeth, than don thynges lighte.
>
> "And reed that boweth down for every blast,
> Ful lightly, cesse wynd, it wol aryse;
> But so nyl nought an ook, whan it is cast." (1380–89)

Again, Criseyde's excoriation of Troilus's fictitious jealousy ironically exonerates his later jealousy and anguish:

> "But certeyn is, some manere jalousie
> Is excusable more than some, iwys;   /16/
> As whan cause is, and som swich fantasie
> With piete so wel repressed is
> That it unnethe doth or seyth amys,

But goodly drynketh up al his distresse;
And that excuse I, for the gentilesse." (III, 1030–36)

Pandarus' assertion of Antenor's hostility toward Criseyde provides the
ruse for getting Criseyde to Deiphebus' house and ironically foreshadows
the fatal barter of Criseyde for Antenor, and that in turn foreshadows
Antenor's betrayal of the Trojan people who choose him over Criseyde.[20]
But Chaucer can massage this architectonic device of ironic fore-
shadowing too thoroughly, as in the long separation scene at the end of
Book IV in which Criseyde so vigorously argues her fidelity and in which
Troilus unwittingly prophesies her defection:

"Ye shal ek seen so many a lusty knyght
Among the Grekis, ful of worthynesse,
And ech of him with herte, wit, and myght
To plesen you don al his bisynesse,
That ye shul dullen of the rudenesse
Of us sely Troians . . . " (1485–90)

Like the use of inverted parallels and the foregoing ironic fore-
shadowings, Chaucer's use of point of view also reverberates narrative
meaning. It too fragments the contrasting structural harmony since the
multiplicity of views creates an irreconcilable final viewpoint, each
character presenting his own attitude toward the poem's meaning. And
the dramatic narration of the poem deters any single harmonious view of
any thematic issue. From Criseyde's point of view, her life-urge
repudiates the epilogue's rejection of worldly action; from Troilus's point
of view, his death-urge repuditates the vitality of the poem's subject
matter; from Pandarus' point of view, his duality accepts both views, but
not simultaneously. Further, the narrator vacillates too much in his
attitudes for an acceptance of any hasty epilogue of well-grounded
Christian sentiment. This vacillation toward the characters of the drama
is best shown in his attitudes toward Criseyde. In Book II /17/ after she
and Pandarus see Troilus ride by, the narrator comments, with bantering
hostility,

To God hope I, she hath now kaught a thorn,
She shal not pulle it out this nexte wyke.
God sende mo swich thornes on to pike! (II, 1272–74)

But following Criseyde's final scene, the narrator sympathizes with her:

> Ne me ne list this sely womman chyde
> Forther than the storye wol devyse.
> Hire name, allas! is punysshed so wide
> That for hire gilt it oughte ynough suffise.
> And if I myghte excuse hire any wise,
> For she so sory was for hire untrouthe,
> Iwis, I wolde excuse hire yet for routhe. (V, 1093–99)

In contrast to this, the narrator never makes evaluative comments about the other characters.

The multiple points of view deny resolution of total narrative effect since the variations lead to different interpretations of the poem. The realism of Criseyde's view grates against the idealism of Troilus's, the poem's paganism grating against the epilogue's Christianity. If a single-eyed interpretation of the poem is required, then only one point of view is regarded. But the intransigent points of view necessitate a two-eyed view of the poem. The point of view of either Troilus or Criseyde might provide an orderly view of the poem, but when the narrator adopts both of them and subordinates his to theirs, then only a multiple view of the poem emerges. Criseyde can be sympathized with as a victim of circumstances, almost forced into her affairs with both Troilus and Diomede: told her refusal will kill two men, constantly threatened by possible banishment because of her turncoat father, and told of the imminent razing of Troy. But if her viewpoint is accepted, then Troilus's death resulting from her betrayal must be partly ignored. The poem requires that both characters receive sympathy; yet if Troilus is to be sympathized with most, then Criseyde's impinging circumstances are overlooked and she whimsically makes her own choices. Our sympathies cannot be marshalled for a desired harmonious view of both. Hence, point of view becomes a narrative technique that also fragments the seeming structural order.
/18/

In contrast to the earlier balanced type of narrative structure the accretion of this ironic type of narrative structure, using inverted parallel, ironic foreshadowing, and point of view seems to imply that the poem is again caught between two antinomies, neither one necessarily pre-empting the other.

A final way of seeing this juxtaposition of orderly and disorderly structure may be presented by using Henry Sams' observations on the dual time-scheme in the poem. He notes the presence of "two concentric and contradictory time-schemes": one based on a series of seasonal images that develop from winter to spring to winter, and the other based on the formal dating of three years in the individual books.[21] The unity of imagery jars with the telescoped narrative sequence, providing a structural contrast of order and disorder.

In conclusion, the narrative structure of the poem, as technique, reflects the poem's dichotomy of issues, its meaning. The structure presents a clash of both a unifying symmetry of classical balance and a disunifying ironic anarchy, both of which can be seen in Malone's W, the inverted V, and in the linear fragmentation of both space and time in the poem. Moreover, the clash between these two types of structure also comments sanely upon Chaucer's ideas about and practice in relating the artist to literary conventions. The symmetrical structuring aligns him with those artists who create within conscious literary conventions, as is seen in his use of the broad outlines of the romance tradition. Yet, transcending the suffocation of the conventions, Chaucer treats them with individuality, with an independence that he achieves partly by manipulating them with irony and partly by refusing to submit to a formal structural configuration. The narrative structure exhibits the same moral and esthetic duality as the rest of the poem, a duality modestly sounded in the first line's declaration of its subject as Troilus's "double sorwe." Like Pandarus at the end of Book II when entreating Criseyde not to slay Troilus, perhaps Chaucer finds "vertu of corones tweyne," the two crowns possibly suggesting the not-too-distant Great Schism, an appropriate historical metaphor for the polyphonics of Chaucer's duality in *Troilus and Criseyde*. The polyphonics merge in a realistic view of human involvement.

Notes

1. Kemp Malone, *Chapters on Chaucer* (Baltimore, 1951), pp. 107–08.

2. Sister Anne Barbara Gill, *Paradoxical Patterns in Chaucer's "Troilus," An Explanation of the Palinode* (Washington: The Catholic University of America Press, 1960), xix.

3. Several of these are noted by George Lyman Kittredge, *Chaucer and His Poetry* (Cambridge, Mass. 1927), p. 142 [above, p. 21].

4. Gill, xx; Sanford B. Meech, *Design in Chaucer's Troilus* (Syracuse, N.Y., 1959), p. 5.

5. Francis Lee Utley, "Scene-Division in Chaucer's *Troilus and Criseyde*," in *Studies in*

Medieval Literature, ed. MacEdward Leach (Philadelphia, 1961), p.130.

6. Charles A. Owen, Jr., "The Significance of Chaucer's Revisions of *Troilus and Criseyde*," *MP*, LV (1957-58); reprinted in *Troilus and Criseyde and the Minor Poems*, ed. Richard J. Schoeck and Jerome Taylor, (Notre Dame, Ind., 1961) pp. 161-62.

7. Owen, p. 161.

8. Meech, p. 422.

9. Utley, pp. 131-38.

10. Meech, p. 10.

11. Howard Rollin Patch, *On Rereading Chaucer* (Cambridge, Mass., 1959), p. 76.

12. Meech, p. 44; also Germaine Dempster, *Dramatic Irony in Chaucer* (Palo Alto, Calif., 1932); reprinted (New York: The Humanties Press, 1959), p. 22.

13. Patch, p. 70; et al.

14. I fail to document particular sources for some of these parallels since several critics repeatedly note them: Meech, Patch, Dempster, et al.

15. Patch, p. 102.

16. Thomas R. Price, "*Troilus and Criseyde*, A Study in Chaucer's Method of Narrative Construction," *PMLA*, XI (1896), 310.

17. Meech, p. 15.

18. Patch, p. 70.

19. See footnote 14.

20. Meech, p. 425.

21. Henry W. Sams, "The Dual Time-Scheme in Chaucer's *Troilus*," *MLN*, LVI (1941), 94; reprinted in Schoeck and Taylor, p. 180.

The "Litera Troili" And English Letters
by Norman Davis

The letter from Troilus to Criseyde in Chaucer's *Troilus and Criseyde*, book v, lines 1317-1421, differs in both length and content from its exemplar in Boccaccio.[1] In contrast to his general expansion of Boccaccio's narrative, Chaucer here reduces it to little more than half the length — 105 lines in 15 stanzas against 192 lines in 24 stanzas — and alters much of its tone as well as the manner of its expression. The approximate relation, though not the precise correspondences of words and phrases, can be seen from W.M. Rossetti's edition with parallel translation of the Italian lines used by Chaucer.[2] In view of Professor R.A. Pratt's demonstration that Chaucer must have been influenced by Beauvau's French translation of *Il Filostrato*, it is necessary to take that into account as well.[3]

The only close agreement of any length between the letters of Troilus and Troilo is in Chaucer's fifth and sixth stanzas (ll. 1345–58) and Boccaccio's third and fourth (sts. 54–55), though there are many lesser links and paraphrases. For my present purpose four passages are especially to the point.

(a) Boccaccio begins the letter thus;

> Giovane donna, a cui Amor mi diede
> e tuo mi tiene, a mentre sarò 'n vita
> mi terrá sempre con intera fede,
> per ciò che tu nella tua dipartita

Reprinted from the *Review of English Studies*, n.s. 16 (1965): 233-44 by permission of the author and the Oxford University Press. The original pagination is indicated between slashes in the text. The Afterword was written for this anthology.

in miseria maggior ch'alcun non crede
qui mi lasciasti, l'anima smarrita
si raccomanda alla tua gran virtute,
e mandarti non può altra salute.

/234/ Beauvau renders this as follows:

La gente et belle damme à qui amour me donna, à qui
loyaulment me suis du tout tenu et tiendray tant que je seray
en vie, pour ce que a voustre partement vous me laissastes en
plus grant douleur que autre ne pence, mon pouvre cueur,
lequel est en tel estat que à paine se porroit il croire, se
recommande treshumblement à voustre grant vertu.

Chaucer begins:

Right fresshe flour, whos I ben have and shal,
Withouten part of elleswhere servyse,
With herte, body, lif, lust, thought, and al,
I, woful wyght, in everich humble wise
That tonge telle or herte may devyse,
As ofte as matere occupieth place,
Me recomaunde unto youre noble grace.

Thus Troilus opens with a complimentary phrase that is not in the Italian
or the French, makes his devotion a decision of his own rather than a
decree of Love, emphasizes here his humility rather than his
wretchedness (which comes in the next stanza), and commends himself
to 'his lady grace' in a direct personal way. The phrase of commendation
is the only verbal agreement between the English and the Italian; the
French, as Pratt notes (p. 535), has another in *treshumblement*, 'in everich
humble wise'.

   (b) Boccaccio in his fourth stanza (55) shows Troilo wishing to know
what Criseida's life among the Greeks was like:

ti scrivo . . .
                              . . . volenteroso
di saper qual la tua vita sia stata
poi che tra' Greci fosti permutata.

Beauvau does not translate *ti scrivo*; corresponding to the later lines he has:

> ... mon pouvre cueur, lequel est tant desirant et voluntarieux
> [*MS. Douce* volunteux] de savoir quelle a esté voustre vie
> depuis que fustes conduite et menée [*Douce* menee et
> conduite] en la main des Greux.

Chaucer's sixth stanza corresponds (1355-8):

> Yow write ich myn unresty sorwes soore,
> Fro day to day desiryng evere moore
> To knowen fully, if youre wille it weere,
> How ye han ferd and don whil ye be theere.

In sense this follows Boccaccio fairly closely, except that Troilus expresses greater concern for Criseyde's welfare. Yet there is no verbal agreement with the Italian; but in the French *desirant* (as Pratt again notes) corresponds to 'desiryng'. /235/

(c) After this Chaucer continues with two stanzas which have no counterpart at all in either Boccaccio or Beauvau (1359-72):

> The whos welfare and hele ek God encresse
> In honour swich that upward in degree
> It growe alwey, so that it nevere cesse.
> Right as youre herte ay kan, my lady free,
> Devyse, I prey to God so moot it be, . . .
>
> And if yow liketh knowen of the fare
> Of me, whos wo ther may no wit discryve,
> I kan namore, but, chiste of every care,
> At wrytyng of this lettre I was on lyve,
> Al redy out my woful gost to dryve. . . .

(d) Boccaccio concludes Troilo's letter with these words (st. 75):

> Nè più ti dico se non Dio sia teco
> e tosto faccia te esser con meco.

Beauvau enlarges this:

... et ne sçay à present autre chose que vou escripre, sinon
que je prie au puissant dieu d'amours qu'il donne à entendre à
voustre cueur la paine en quoy je suis.

Chaucer slightly expands Boccaccio in his penultimate stanza (1408-11):

I say namore, al have I for to seye
To yow wel more than I telle may.
But wheither that ye do me lyve or deye,
Yet praye I God so yeve yow right good day.

Pratt notes that the French *je prie*, not in the Italian, suggests
Chaucer's *praye I*; but he does not point out the more important fact that
in substance Chaucer's version is closer to Boccaccio — Beauvau,
altering *Dio* to the *dieu d'amours*, substitutes yet another complaint of the
lover's pain for the far more moving affectionate farewell.

Chaucer's editors and critics have not closely examined the changes he
made in Boccaccio's text of the letter. R. K. Root says simply: 'The letter
of Troilus is freely adapted from *Fil.* 7. 52-75'.[4] S.B. Meech says that 'he
edits the letter to perfect the hero in loverly decorum . . . '.[5] A. K. Moore
has referred briefly to it, and to Criseyde's reply (1590-1631), observing
with good reason that 'the Chaucerian epistles are written in the same
artificial style as many fifteenth-century letters, and were probably
known to /236/ most of those poets who attempted the form after 1400'.[6]
From the context 'letters' here evidently means literary 'epistles'. But
what gives Chaucer's version of Troilus's letter much of its shape and
point is his use, indeed exploitation, of the conventions of ordinary letter-
writing of the time in English. A few of these coincided with the forms of
expression used by Boccaccio and by Beauvau. Chaucer adopted these in
the same places, as I have set them out above; but he modified their
contexts, and added other familiar turns, with entirely original subtlety
and force.

Fifteenth-century letters in English of a formal, respectful kind very
often open with a long sequence of conventional phrases and sentences
constructed with minor variations upon a regular pattern.[7] Even when
some of the possible components are not present the same order of the
main items is observed. The full scale, seen best in letters from children to
parents, includes seven divisions, some with subdivisions, thus:[1] a
form of address most commonly beginning with the word 'Right' and an
adjective of respect ('worshipful', 'worthy', 'well-beloved', & c.) and the

appropriate noun ('sir', 'husband', 'father', & c.); [2] a formula
commending the writer to the recipient, often accompanied by [2a] an
expression of humility and, if the letter is to a parent, [2b] a request for a
blessing — this usually introduced by a present participle and
strengthened by an adverb or a phrase; [3] an expression of desire to hear
of the recipient's welfare — this again introduced by a participle; [4] a
prayer, introduced by a relative, for the continuation and increase of this
welfare 'to your heart's desire', or the like; [5] a conditional clause
deferentially offering news of the writer's welfare; [6] a report of the
writer's good health 'at the making of this letter'; [7] thanks to God for it.
(Items 3–7 might be colloquially summarized as the 'hoping this finds you
well as it leaves me at present' formula; for brevity I shall refer to them as
the 'health' formula.)

As a typical specimen embodying all these elements a letter written by
Elizabeth Poynings to her mother Agnes Paston early in 1459 may serve
as well as any.[8] '[1] Right worshipfull and my most entierly belovde
moder, [2a] in the most louly maner [2] I recommaund me unto youre
gode moderhode, [2b] besekeyng you dayly and nyghtly of your moderly
blissing; [3] evermore desiryng to here of your welfare and prosperite, [4]
the which I pray God to contynw and encresce to your hertes desyre. [5]
And yf it lyked youre moderhode to here of me and how I do, [6] at the
makyng of thys letter I was in gode hele of body, [7] t[h]anked be Jesu.'
Sir William Stonor's second wife wrote to him in 1480 in somewhat
different words but after the same pattern.[9] '[1] Right worshipfull
Maister, [2] y hertly comaund me unto you [2a] with alle suche servise as
y can or may, . . . [3] desyring to hire of youre welfare, [4] the which y
pray alle mighty Godde to preserve you to youre most pleasure and hertis
desire. [5] Please you to have enknowliche of my power welfare: [6] at
the /237/ making of this my letter y was in gode hele, and y trust in God
within short space to be beter.' Essentially the same conventions were
extremely widely used throughout the fifteenth century, and indeed
later, in many official as well as private letters. It is needless to multiply
quotations; examples from different social levels may be seen in an
amusingly inflated letter from the mayor, aldermen, and sheriffs of
London to the Duke of Clarence in 1419, and a letter from Richard Earl of
Warwick to Sir Thomas Tuddenham, perhaps in 1449.[10] Clearly this set of
formulas was well known to almost everybody who had letters to write,
and was preserved with remarkable firmness over a long time. So familiar
was it that Margery Brews, in one of her 'Valentine' letters to John Paston
III in 1477, was able to play upon the convention by denying the

customary good health: '[1] Ryght reverent and wurschypfull and my ryght welebeloved Voluntyne, [2] I recommande me unto yowe full hertely, [3] desyring to here of yowr welefare, [4] whech I beseche Almyghty God long for to preserve unto hys plesure and yowr hertys desyre. [5] And yf it please yowe to here of my welefare, [6] I am not in good heele of body ner of herte, nor schall be tyll I here from yowe.'[11] Indeed, in view especially of the poem by the Duke of Suffolk quoted on p. 152 below, this turn can hardly be credited to Margery Brews's own ingenuity (or that of someone who helped her to write the letter, which is in the hand of her father's clerk); it must have become a new convention in its own right.

The earliest English letters in which I have yet found some of these formulas are the two written by Sir John Hawkwood in 1392 and 1393, known from a copy of 1411.[12] The second of these begins, 'Dere, trusty, /238/ and welbeloved frend, hertliche I grete you wel, [3] desiryng to heren god tidynges of youre welfare'; the first is of more interest in its opening sentence, 'I grete you wel and do you to wytyn that [6] at the makyng of this lettre I was in god poynt, [7] I thank God'. There was no occasion here for a humble salutation, and Hawkwood chose to begin with 'Dear', which despite its modern predominance was rare until the seventeenth century: 'I greet you well' was an extremely common form from a superior or a parent.[13] But the other formulas are the familiar ones, essentially in the shapes in which they appear for the next century and more. This must mean that even at that date the conventions had become fully established in English, though we have no surviving letters to prove it.

Troilus and Criseyde seems most likely to have been written perhaps some seven years earlier than Hawkwood's letters. In Troilus's letter Chaucer deploys a notable range of formulas. [1] The opening word 'Right', corresponding to nothing in the Italian or the French, is overwhelmingly the commonest beginning to English letters for many years. [2] 'Me recomaunde' does echo *si raccomanda* and *se recommande*, but is in the English tradition as well. [2a] The expression of humility duly appears in 'in every humble wise'. Though, as I noted above, this corresponds to Beauvau's *treshumblement* its form is distinctive and is common in English letters — Chaucer's very rhyme here, between 'wise' and 'That tonge telle or herte may devyse', recurs in the London letter to Clarence to which I have referred, 'in as humble wyse as any poure men best can or may ymagine and devise', in several other letters of the same series,[14] and often elsewhere. Then Chaucer interrupts this sequence of formulas with another one of a different kind: he opens his second stanza with 'Liketh yow to witen' (1324), a very frequent transition (still commoner with 'Please . . .') from the *salutatio* and commendation to the *narratio*, which any of the fifteenth-century collections of letters will amply illustrate — but which is lacking in Boccaccio and Beauvau. The participial construction in l. 1334, 'I write . . . compleynyng', is another cliché of epistolary style. Then at the end of his rendering of Boccaccio's stanzas 54 and 55 (quoted in part above, p. 146) he introduces the form of words most commonly used in the inquiry after health — [3] 'desiryng evere moore [to knowen . . . how ye han ferd]'. The suggestion for this is ultimately Boccaccio's *volenteroso*, proximately Beauvau's *desirant*; but Chaucer adds the customary 'evermore' (the word /239/ used, for instance, by Elizabeth Poynings in the letter quoted on p. 149), and follows on with [4], the prayer, with its relative link, for increasing welfare to one's heart's desire:

> The whos welfare and hele ek God encresse . . .
> Right as youre herte ay kan, my lady free,
> Devyse.

He takes the convention further in the next stanza, for which there is no suggestion in the Italian or the French — [5] the deferential offer of news, 'And if yow liketh knowen of the fare Of me . . . '. Then he introduces 'I kan namore', yet another commonplace, though it usually comes nearer the end of a letter; it is used, for instance, by Griffith ap David ap Griffith in 1400, by Lady Zouche in 1402, and by Agnes Paston before 1450.[15] In the next line he gives a skilful and witty turn to the 'health' formula: [6] 'At wrytyng of this lettre I was on lyve' — Troilus is not 'in gode hele of body' or 'in god poynt'; he is only 'on lyve'. The point of this line can be seen only by a reader who knows the convention and expects the customary conclusion. (Margery Brews's distortion of the formula, noticed above, p. 150, is similar but cruder.) This is the culmination of Chaucer's use of these expressions, but a final touch appears near the end, where 'I say namore' is taken from the Italian. This too becomes a standard conclusion in English letters, as, for example, 'No more I wrighte to yow at this tyme, but Holy Gost have yow in kepyng' (Elisabeth Clere, before 1450), 'No more to yow at this tyme, but God hym save that mad this ryme' (John Paston I, 1465).[16] Chaucer expands this by a clause that is close to yet another later cliché, hardly regular enough to be called a formula: 'al have I for to seye To yow wel more than

I telle may'; which is recalled by such endings as the following, both by Margaret Paston: 'I may non leyser have to do wrytyn half a quarter so meche as I xulde seyn to yow yf I myth speke wyth yow' (probably 1443); 'I schuld wryth more, but I have no leysere at thys tyme'(1471).[17]

The letter of Troilus is thus much more than 'freely adapted' from *Il Filostrato*. Chaucer found suggestions in Boccaccio, and evidently in Beauvau as well, for a few of the simpler epistolary forms, and enriched them by adding more elaborate expressions regularly used along with them in English letters. The shape and development of the letter he did not devise simply 'for the nones', but based it on the familiar patterns of /240/ the kind of letter that his readers might have planned, or received, themselves.[18]

Many later poets used similar methods and, as Moore said, some of them must have known *Troilus and Criseyde*. R.H. Robbins observes that 'the love epistle is the main conventional form during the fifteenth century.[19] *The Index of Middle English Verse* lists eight poems beginning with 'Right' as part of an address — notably *Ryght goodly flour* and *Ryht godely fressh flour of womanhode*.[20] Others use the commonplaces of humble commendation and 'writing no more'; of these the aptest to this discussion is the three-stanza poem 'Myn hertys joy' attributed to the Duke of Suffolk, for it contains these lines:

> And yf ye lyst have knowlech of my qwert,
> I am in hele — God thankyd mot he be —
> As of body, but treuly not in hert,
> Nor nought shal be to tyme I may you se.[21]

It is clear that, though Chaucer's work may have encouraged the tradition of the verse epistle in the fifteenth century, and though no real letters in English from before his time survive, he did not invent the formulas. Before 1400, when English letters are extremely rare, there are many, from one Englishman to another, in French — in the Stonor collection alone there are 28.[22] The following is a typical extract from one of these, dated by Kingsford about 1380 (I number the formulas as above): '[1] Treshonore Sire et Meistre, [2] jeo me recomanke a vous si avaunt come soit ou plus puisse, . . . [3] desirant tout dys affectuelment bones novelles de vous oier et de vostre estate . . ., [4] le quele jeo pri le Dieu tout puissaunt qil voille maintenir en croissaunce et multepliaunce dez toutes honurs. [5] Et si de mon estat vous plese assavoir, [6] al departier du cestes jestoie en sancte du corps, [7] le mercie Dieu.'[23]

The appearance of all seven conventional formulas, in the same order as in the English letters, is no accident. No manuals of letter-writing in English from this period survive, though from the regularity of the practice /241/ it seems that some must have existed; but there are many manuscripts, written in England in the fourteenth and fifteenth centuries, which contain guides to the composition of letters in French. These offer model letters suitable for almost all manner of occasions (though not, as far as I know, for Troilus's particular case) — most of them no doubt invented but many evidently copied from genuine letters whether private or official. They are extensions into the vernacular of the study of the *ars dictaminis* which had been pursued widely in western Europe since the time of Alberic of Monte Cassino in the late eleventh century.[24] The best-known name today among English *dictatores* is that of Thomas Sampson of Oxford, whose earliest surviving work must date from about 1355, but was continually revised and augmented up to the end of the century.[25] Two examples, both 'De filio ad matrem' will suffice to show the value of the evidence of Sampson and his revisers about approved epistolary practice: *(a)* '[1] Treshonure et tresreverent dame et miere. [2] Jeo me recomanc a vous come je suffice, [2a, b] desirant de trestout mon coer et treshumblement vostre benisone [3] et que vous soiez en bone saintee, [4] qi prie al tresoveraigne Seignour Jesu Crist . . . que . . . bone saintee longement vous voille ottroier par sa grace. [5] Et treschere meire, pur ce que say de certeyn que semblables novelx desirez de moy oier, [6] ci face assavoir, ma trescher miere, q'a l'escrire d'ycestez fu en bone saintee de corps, [7] la merci nostre dit Seignour Jesu Crist.' *(b)* '[1] Tresreverente dame et miere. [2] Je me recomanc a vous, [2a] en tant come je suy digne, en totes reverences et honurs, [2b] vostre benisone [3] et qe vous soiez en saintee desirant d'entier coer. [6] Et moy, treschere dame, a la faisance du ceste lettre [5] vous pleise savoir en saintee de corps, [7] la mercy Dieu.'[26] Many similar sequences are to be found in these collections, and another rich source of them is Miss D. Legge's volume of *Anglo-Norman Letters and Petitions*.[27]

That the tradition is not only Anglo-Norman is proved by the appearance of the same forms in letters from the Continent. For example, Miss Legge's book furnishes specimens from Charles III of Navarre (no. 106, /242/ 1394): 'Et ce de vostre tresgrant honneur et curtoisie vous plaist savoir de mien, au partement de ces presentes j'estoie en bone santé de corps, graces a nostre Sire'; Charles VI of France (no. 172, 1395): 'Et se de nostre estat vous plaist savoir, quant ces lettres feurent escriptez, par la grace de Dieu nous estoions en bon point, la Dieu mercie'; Isabella of Bavaria (no. 177, *c.* 1397); the Duke of Milan (no. 217, undated).

The work of Sampson in particular takes the history of the French formulas back well before the date of *Troilus and Criseyde*. This is not the place to attempt to trace it further; but it may be worth while to note that some of the expressions can be found even in the thirteenth century. To cite a single example, a letter from Maurice de Craon to Edward I, evidently of 1282, has this: 'Sire, je vous merci moute de vos cortoises et amiables lettres que vous m'avez envoyées, èsqueles j'ai entendu vostre bon estat, que Dieu face touzjours bon, si cumme je le voudroie. Et d'entroit de mon estat que il vous plest à savoir, . . . je vous fais asavoir que j'estoie sain de corps, Dieu merci, quant ces lettres furent fetes.'[28]

Another question of great complexity, which I cannot pursue here, is the relation of French to Latin formulas. A few general points may be made. As Miss Legge has remarked, Latin and French were largely put to different uses, so that Latin formularies are mainly ecclesiastical in reference whereas French are governmental or private (which includes legal).[29] This generalization admits a good many exceptions. For instance, some collections of Latin model letters include love-letters,[30] though the Baumgartenberg formulary (*c.* 1300) says, 'Qualiter ad amasias sit scribendum, religionis causa pertranseo'.[31] But for the most part the greater formality of the relation between writer and reader of Latin letters no doubt goes far to account for the vigorous survival throughout the Middle Ages of the ancient form of address in the third person with *salutem*, much elaborated though it often is. A direct personal address is, nevertheless, common enough in Latin, but the formula of commendation, when it occurs, is more commonly expressed in a participial construction than by a personal verb as it is in French and English — a Paris manuscript quoted by Valois enjoins: 'Salutatio vero aliquando ponitur in ablativo absoluto, ut *Recommandatione premissa* . . .; item aliquando in aliis casibus, secundum voluntatem dictantis, ut *Recommandationem preponentes*, vel *Recommandationis titulum preponendo* . . .'.[32] But especially in the later manuals personal /243/ forms appear. Sometimes they are given in model letters offering both a Latin and a French text of the same matter, as in Sampson's alternative version of the second letter in French quoted on p. 153 above:

> Reuerendissima mater et domina. Vestre maternitati reuerende me vestrum filium humiliter recommendo, vestram benediccionem et quod votiua gaudeatis corporis sanitate totis desiderans affectibus mei cordis. Me vero, carissima mater,

scire dignemini in corporis sanitate ad presentis littere recessum, laudetur Omnipotens Ille Deus.[33]

But they are used independently of French as well;[34] and it is possible to find some of the other formulas at a much earlier date — Philip of France, writing to Henry III of England about 1267, said:

. . . serenitati vestræ significantes carissimum dominum et patrem nostrum, carissimamque matrem nostram, nos una cum ipsis, gaudere in confectione præsentium corporum sospitate, quod de vobis audire semper volumus et etiam exoptamus.[35]

It seems, however, that it was in French, and no doubt in France, that the various expressions of respect and politeness werc regularized into the system so generally observed in English letters of the fifteenth century. Some Chaucerian scribes, if not Chaucer himself, certainly associated the art of polite letter-writing with French, for three manuscripts and Thynne's edition subscribe Troilus's letter 'Le vostre T(roilus)', and four manuscripts (only one of them among the previous three) and Thynne similarly subscribe Criseyde's.[36] Chaucer's use of the plural pronoun *ye* throughout the letter, despite the example of Boccaccio's regular *tu*, also testifies to the force of French influence upon polite English usage. (Beauvau uses *vous* throughout, but there is no need to suppose that this influenced Chaucer directly.)[37]

That these epistolary conventions appear first in English in a fictional letter written by Chaucer is a strange accident of history. His delicate use of them is characteristic of his individual perception of matters of common experience.

Notes

1. I quote *Troilus and Criseyde* throughout from Robinson's second edition of the *Works* (1957), with minor changes of punctuation. The corresponding passage of *Il Filostrato* is part vii, sts. 52–75, which I quote from the edition of V. Pernicone (Bari, 1937).

2. Chaucer Society, 2nd series 9 (1873).

3. R. A. Pratt, 'Chaucer and *Le Roman de Troyle et de Criseida*', *S. P.*, liii (1956), 509–39. I quote the *Roman* from the edition by L. Moland and C. d'Héricault in *Nouvelles françoises en prose du XIV ͤ siècle* (Paris, 1858), pp. 117–304, used by Pratt. I have collated this with

the most easily accessible manuscript, Douce 331 in the Bodleian (ff. 68ʳ-70ʳ contain the letter), in case there should be relevant variants. There are some minor divergences, but nothing that affects the structure of the letter or the expressions with which I am here concerned.

4. Note on 5. 1317-1421 of his edition (Princeton, 1926), p. 551.

5. *Design in Chaucer's* Troilus (Syracuse, 1959), pp. 125-6.

6. 'Middle English Verse Epistles', *M.L.R.*, xliv (1949), 86-87.

7. These correspond to the *salutatio* and *benevolentia captatio* of the *dictatores;* see p. 153 below. Though the wording admits of a good deal of variety the sentiments are stereotyped and the phrases may fairly be called formulas.

8. Here and in later quotations I number the items as in the previous paragraph. The text is in *The Paston Letters*, ed. J. Gairdner (Westminster, 1900), no. 322 (1904 edn. no. 374), and in my *Paston Letters* (Clarendon series, Oxford, 1958), no. 22.

9. *Stonor Letters and Papers*, ed. C. L. Kingsford (Camden Soc., 3rd series 29, 30, 1919), no. 262.

10. *A Book of London English 1384-1425*, ed. R. W. Chambers and M. Daunt (Oxford, 1931), pp. 81-82; *Paston Letters*, ed. Gairdner, no. 73/98.

11. *Paston Letters*, ed. Gairdner, no. 783/897; Clarendon edn. no. 79.

12. A. H. Thomas, 'Notes on the History of the Leadenhall, A.D. 1195-1488', *London Topographical Record*, xiii (1923), pp. 1-22, esp. pp. 11 ff.; C. L. Kingsford, *Prejudice and Promise in XVth Century England* (Oxford, 1925), p. 23. Kingsford considered these to be the earliest known letters in English, but there are some which appear to be older in *The Correspondence . . . of the Priory of Coldingham*, ed. J. Raine (Surtees Soc., 1841), though they exist only in a later register (B.M. MS Cotton Faustina A VI). The earliest, from Robert II of Scotland, is dated by the editor 1390. But it does not use the formulas in question.

13. It goes back at least as far as the twelfth century. The so-called 'Letter of Edwin' begins: 'Ic Eadwine munuk, cilda mæstere an Niwan Mynstre, grete þe wel, Ælfsige biscop' (F. E. Harmer, *Anglo-Saxon Writs* (Manchester, 1952), pp. 387-95, 401-3). The letter purports to date from before 980, but Dr. Harmer shows that it is probably a twelfth-century forgery. For other formulas see also her 'The English Contribution to the Epistolary Usages of Early Scandinavian Kings', *Saga-Book of the Viking Society*, xiii (1949-50), 115-55.

14. *London English*, pp. 72, 79, 84.

15. *Original Letters*, ed. H. Ellis, iv (2nd series i) (London, 1827), p. 7; E. Rickert, 'Some English Personal Letters of 1402', *R.E.S.*, viii (1932), 257-63, esp. p. 262; *Paston Letters*, ed. Gairdner, no. 70/93.

16. *Paston Letters*, Gairdner nos. 71/94, 528/609, Clarendon edn. nos. 12, 40.

17. Gairdner nos. 36/47, 685/791; Clarendon edn. nos. 5, 65.

18. He did not do this in other letters in *Troilus and Criseyde*. Criseyde's reply has no formulas except the closing 'And fareth now wel, God have yow in his grace' (1631). In Troilus's earlier letter, which is reported indirectly (ii. 1065-84), 'in ful humble wise He gan hym recomaunde unto hire grace'; but that is all.

19. *Secular Lyrics of the XIVth and XVth Centuries* (Oxford, 2nd edn. 1955), p. 286, where many examples are noted.

20. *Index*, ed. C. Brown and R.H. Robbins (New York, 1943), nos. 2821-6, 2828. See also *Religious Lyrics of the XVth Century*, ed. C. Brown (Oxford, 1939), and Robbins, *Secular Lyrics*, p. xx.

21. Robbins, *Secular Lyrics*, no. 189 (spelling slightly modified to agree with other quotations).

22. See p. 149, n. 9 above, and the same editor's 'Supplementary Stonor Letters and Papers' in *Camden Miscellany XIII* (1924).

23. *Stonor Letters*, no. 28

24. For the early history see especially C.H. Haskins, 'The Early *artes dictandi* in Italy', in *Studies in Medieval Culture* (Oxford, 1929), pp. 170–92, and works named in the same volume, p. 2, n. 2. A recent bibliography is J.J. Murphy, 'The Medieval Arts of Discourse: an Introductory Bibliography', *Speech Monographs*, xxix (1962), 71–78, of which Part 3 section IV deals with *ars dictaminis* (but omits some important works, e.g. C.V. Langlois, 'Formulaires de lettres du XIIᵉ, du XIIIᵉ et du XIVᵉ siècle', *Notices et extraits*, xxxiv-v (1890-6), and *Oxford Formularies* noticed below).

25. Of the first importance is H.G. Richardson, 'Letters of the Oxford *Dictatores*', in *Formularies which bear on the History of Oxford c. 1204-1420*, ed. H.E. Salter, W.A. Pantin, H.G. Richardson (Oxford Hist. Soc., N.S., 4, 5, 1942), pp. 329–450. Earlier works are referred to in the notes, and the whole of these two volumes is relevant.

26. Richardson, pp. 374–5, 391.

27. Anglo-Norman Text Soc. 3 (Oxford, 1941). Particularly good examples are nos. 62 (1406), 89 (1386) — 'a la faisance de cestes en bon point', 297 (? c. 1399), 377 (undated).

28. *Lettres de rois, reines et autres personnages des cours de France et d'Angleterre*, ed. J.J. Champollion-Figeac (Paris, 1839), i. 298.

29. *Anglo-Norman Letters*, p. ix.

30. Haskins, *Studies*, p. 31.

31. L. Rockinger, *Briefsteller und Formelbücher des elften bis vierzehnten Jahrhunderts* (Munich, 1863), p. 743.

32. N. Valois, *De arte scribendi epistolas apud Gallicos medii ævi scriptores rhetoresve* (Paris, 1880), pp. 10–11.

33. Richardson, p. 390.

34. e.g. ibid., pp. 191, 311.

35. *Royal and other Historical Letters illustrative of the Reign of Henry III*, ed. W.W. Shirley (Rolls Series), ii (1866), 316.

36. The subscription is noticed by A. Mahr, *Formen and Formeln der Begrüssung in England von der normannischen Eroberung bis zur Mitte des 15. Jahrhunderts* (diss. Frankfurt a. M., 1911), p. 46; but of Troilus's letter itself he says only that the beginning is 'sehr geschraubt and charakteristisch für die stark französisch durchsetzte Hof- und Gesellschaftssprache der Chaucerschen Zeit'.

37. On this matter see most recently T. Finkenstaedt, *You und Thou. Studien zur Anrede im Englischen* (Berlin, 1963), of which pp. 77–87 deal with *Troilus and Criseyde*. Dr. Finkenstaedt rightly objects to Walcutt's conclusion ('The Pronoun of Address in *Troilus and Criseyde*', *P.Q.*, xiv (1935), 282–7) that 'the attitude of abject, patient adoration demanded of the courtly lover explains why Troilus consistently addresses Criseyde as *ye* and *you*'. He suggests rather that Troilus does not venture to depart from the conventions of his time [that is, no doubt, Chaucer's] and Criseyde, in also using *ye* almost always, does not give herself wholly to him. It seems to me that even this is reading too much into the use of the plural forms, which must by this time have been customary in good society even between husband and wife. The change from singular to plural, by both speakers, in the Wife of Bath's Tale, which has often been noticed (e.g. D. Everett, *Essays on Middle English Literature* (Oxford, 1955), p. 145, n. 2; N. Nathan, 'Pronouns of Address in the *Canterbury Tales*,' *Mediaeval Studies*, xxi (1959), 193–201; Finkenstaedt, p. 86) is surely not a matter of courtly love but of the knight's acceptance of the woman as a lady equal in *gentilesse* to himself — their first exchange (*C.T.*, D 1001–8) had also been in the polite form. Exactly the same change of pronoun appears in Gower's version of the story (*Confessio Amantis*, i. 1407–1861), still more sharply marked by the different distribution of the dialogue. Finkenstaedt is wrong in implying, by italicizing the pronouns, that the use of the plural in fifteenth-century letters from women to their husbands indicated 'eine gehorsame Liebe' (pp. 126–7). Expressions of obedience, of course, abound in such letters, but this is not part of them — the husbands used the same forms to their wives.

Afterword: 1979

This paper is reproduced exactly as it was printed in 1965. Since then Parts I and II of my edition of *Paston Letters and Papers of the Fifteenth Century (PLP)* have been published (Oxford, 1971, 1976), and the selection entitled *Paston Letters* in the Clarendon Medieval and Tudor Series (1958) has gone out of print. Quotations referred to by their numbers in the Clarendon edition, or in Gairdner's editions, may be found in the complete edition as follows:

n. 8	*PLP* no. 121
n. 11	415
n. 15	18
n. 16	446, 77
n. 17	126, 212

Since spelling in the Clarendon edition was slightly modernized, whereas that in *PLP* is not, there are minor differences; but they do not affect the substance.

N.D.

Experience, Language, and Consciousness: "Troilus and Criseyde," II, 596-931
by Donald R. Howard

In the *Legend of Good Women* Chaucer says he is writing about women who behaved nobly in love, as a penance for having written about Criseyde; there is a tradition going back to Lydgate that the penance might have been imposed by Queen Ann. Whether or not this is true, we can be pretty sure that his presentation of Criseyde did not go down entirely well with the ladies — Criseyde herself predicts that she will be rolled on many a tongue and that women will hate her most. The resentment against heroine and author is caused by the stark fact that she jilts Troilus. Everyone remembers how she must rejoin her father in the Greek camp: there is no decent alternative, so she goes, promising to return. Among the Greeks she meets Diomede, who escorts her out of Troy. At first cooly and then with cautious interest she agrees to be true "to him, anyway" (as she puts it); she does not return to Troy. In time she writes Troilus a letter, one of the worst of its kind on record.

How are we to react to this apparently treacherous woman? We can, as many do, hate her. The one alternative is to understand her motives, to forgive and pity her. Of course the same can be said of Iago or Milton's Satan; we live, it is true, in an age when sympathetic understanding of villains is spread around like antiseptic — if only Iago had got to an analyst, if only a social worker had found out Fagin in time. But this is not what I am saying. Criseyde does wrong and so is bad. Chaucer tells us so. He adds that *he* will forgive her out of pity. But does he mean for *us* to do

Reprinted with the kind permission of the author from *Medieval Literature and Folklore Studies: Essays in Honor of Francis Lee Utley*, ed. Jerome Mandel and Bruce A. Rosenberg (New Brunswick: Rutgers University Press, 1970). The text is very slightly revised, and the original pagination indicated between slashes. The Afterword was written for this anthology.

159

likewise? I say he does — not because he explains why she turns to Diomede (he leaves that for us to imagine), but because he makes us know what it feels like to *be* Criseyde, from the moment she first feels love for Troilus. /174/

That moment in her consciousness is what this paper is about. In Book II there is a scene — or a series of four scenes[1] — during which the reader is allowed to participate in Criseyde's mental life. Her uncle Pandarus has just persuaded her to take a favorable view of Troilus, and she has agreed, but with conditions — she cannot love him against her will but only please him from day to day, "mine honour sauf."[2] After this she asks Pandarus how he first learned of Troilus' love. Pandarus, seeing his threats and blandishments take root in her fancy, follows with a long, highly romanticized account of Troilus' recent conduct, ending with a hopeful reference to the time "when ye ben his al hool as he is youre" (587). Criseyde breaks in, "Nay, thereof spake I not, ha, ha!" He hastens to assure her that he "mente nought but well," she forgives him, and he takes his leave. Criseyde now rises and goes to her closet where she sits down "as still as any ston":

> And every word gan up and down to winde
> That he had said, as it came her to minde. (601–602)

From here until the end of the scene (596–931) we remain chiefly inside Criseyde's mind. Only about one-fifth of the scene is indebted to Boccaccio's *Filostrato*, and that chiefly barebones events; hence we can regard the passage as an original flight of Chaucer's imagination. At its beginning Criseyde is thinking over the conversation just finished; at its end she is asleep and dreaming. We are not told that she makes any decision during this scene, though we sense a drift and settling in her thoughts and feelings. Later (in III, 1210–1211) she will tell Troilus that she has long since yielded, and we are to know then that what we experienced in Book II was the moment of consciousness during which the balance was tipped.

The scene explores a problem often discussed in abstract terms — the relationship between experience (what we do) and consciousness (what we think). One ramification of this problem is the role language plays in the relationship; a second is the role of poetry. A further and perhaps more difficult problem is the place of decisions in this relationship: if every action has something in the way of a motive, experience and consciousness are the area of motives and so the provenance of action.

And if language reflects and in some degree shapes our experience, then language, including poetic language, must influence action. I am not sure the problem is much more difficult that this, though it could be made so by spinning out related problems. It can be /175/ and often is made a great deal more difficult by introducing an elaborate lexicon of abstractions like "mediation," "intersubjectivity," "vision," "objectification," and the like; but the poet's language, being concrete, has nothing to do with all that.

We honor poets because they are acute observers of human experience, because they have a heightened consciousness of their own experience, and because they have an extraordinary skill and subtlety of verbal expression. Here is a passage by a great poet where the pressures of experience, consciousness, and language interact to produce a determination or action. In it we can perhaps see before our eyes the thing as in itself it really happens — as much (say) as we can see "heredity" happen under a microscope or "phonology" on a sound-spectrograph. We are exploiting the poet as a sensitive instrument, I admit; but in doing so we shall see something no less worth while — Chaucer's skill in depicting Criseyde's mental state. It is hard to find a passage in early literature that equals the present one. It is one of the aspects of the poem which makes it seem, as Kittredge suggested, like a psychological novel. One could compare the great meditation scenes of nineteenth-century novels — those of Isabella in *Portrait of a Lady*, or Clara Middleton in *The Egoist*, or Dorothea in *Middlemarch*. Yet even in the novel, as much preoccupied as novelists are with the inner life of their characters, it is hard to find many passages which show so much instinctive understanding of human nature, so much empathy and dramatic flair. I have tried to show elsewhere how Chaucer succeeded in solving the difficult problem of depicting sexuality in such a way as to enlist rather than alienate the reader's involvement.[3] But his accomplishment in the present passage is greater. In it he does what few men have ever done in literature or life — he sees into the mind of a woman.

I

Experience itself, coming unpredictably from without, first breaks into Criseyde's thought. While she is sitting alone, a cry goes up in the streets, men call out "See, Troilus . . . ," and her ladies echo "Ah, go we see!" Troilus enters the city gate, triumphant, riding an easy pace with his soldiers. Chaucer gives three stanzas to his entrance through the gate of Dardanus; princely, armed save his head, his horse wounded, his helm

takes
as
narr

and shield damaged, "so fresh, so young, so weedly . . . It was an hevene upon him for to see." The people cry out, and Troilus "wex a litel red for shame": we are allowed to empathize with /176/ his modest reaction, then told it was a "noble game" to see how soberly he lowered his eyes. Given this tiny chance to see on our own his princely bearing and blushing modesty, we are then brought back to Criseyde's experience of it. She sees, she lets it sink softly in her heart, and, in an unforgettable moment, she says to herself "Who yaf me drinke?"

The line is so striking, and has so delighted all readers of the poem, that I shall try to say nothing about it. Normally glossed as a reference to a love-potion, it could as easily be strong wine which makes the head spin; and this ambiguity is perfect, for the metaphor suggests a feeling as yet undefined. In our pleasure over the exclamation we easily forget its aftermath: she blushes at the thought, remembers that this was he her uncle said loved her, and then, ashamed, pulls her head quickly inside the window! The conflict of impulse and restraint, a major theme in what follows, is here dramatically introduced, and we must pause to ask just what has happened.

Chaucer tells us she "said" the line "to herself," and in the next line calls it "her owne thought." We cannot understand from this that she murmured the words aloud or even formed them with her lips. Yet the thought is more than a mere impulse cloaked in words for the reader's benefit, for Chaucer could have described such an impulse had he chosen to.[4] It will not do to write it off as "literary convention," because no poet worth the name uses literary convention or tradition except as a means of understanding reality. And anyway the convention involved here, soliloquy, is straight realism: like the writer of any soliloquy, Chaucer is reporting, by imitation, the phenomenon of *inner speech*, the inward stream of language which bears our thoughts. He does not of course imitate it with much verisimilitude, for inner speech has, according to Vigotsky's famous description,[5] very special characteristics — it omits the subject of predications, agglutinates wordgroups, and combines senses. Inner speech is never articulated except perhaps by scarcely perceptible movements of the vocal cords, and in this it might be compared with the stream of language we experience in very rapid silent reading. We can distinguish the stream of inner speech from *thought*, and from what I shall call the stream of imagery. Our thinking really rides on these two inner streams, beneath which Vigotsky said lies the "affective and volitional tendency."[6] How do we know these streams exist? Because they are part of our own introspective experience of the mental life. They occur in our dreams and daydreams; but they are most dramatically present in those moments of /177/ semiconsciousness that we sometimes experience just as we drop off to sleep — what are now called hypnagogic phenomena, and were once called (by Macrobius) *fantasma*. In these moments we plunge sometimes very sharply into the stream of imagery, see one single and startling image, a face, perhaps, hovering close to us, a bird, an animal, an automobile hurtling forward. Or we may also be startled by our stream of inner speech — the voices we heard as a child[7] and sometimes strangely hear as adults, which speak some unattached assertion or greeting, or our names. "Inner speech," Vigotsky says, "is not the inner aspect of external speech. It is a function in itself. Inner speech still remains speech — it is thought connected with word. But while in external speech thought is embodied in words — in inner speech words perish and bring forth thought. . . . Inner speech is a dynamic process which moves between two stable poles of thinking-in-words; between words and thought."[8]

Criseyde's stream of inner speech weaves through the present scene. We encounter it first when we see her mulling over her conversation with her uncle. She experiences her own fear and calms herself by reciting inwardly the reassuring precept that a woman does not have to return anyone's love unless she wants to. Her unguarded attraction to Troilus takes shape in the words "Who yaf me drinke?" and then,

> "Lo, this is he
> Which that mine uncle swereth he mot be deed,
> But I on him have mercy and pitee." (653–655)

Then she begins to "cast and rollen up and down" all the good qualities of Troilus, and to think what a pity it was "to sleen swich oon, if that he mente trouthe." The narrator, after an interruption to remind us that she did not fall in love with wanton haste, announces that he will tell us "what she thoughte," and in a long passage (700–812) her inner speech is reported in direct discourse.

Her soliloquy is too familiar to need rehearsing. Its shape and structure are those of consciousness itself, not reasonable or logical in organization, but associative. Her conflict is between what she knows, which is abstract and proverbial, and what she feels, which is concrete and experiential. She can imagine what would happen if she returned Troilus' love, and her imagination of it is based on expediency and circumstance. An alliance with him would be an honor, beneficial to his welfare and her position; if she were to avoid him /178/ utterly he might have her in despite. He is her king's son, and his own good qualities are self-evident — he is handsome, has *gentilesse*, is not a boaster, is wise. Anyway, she cannot keep him from loving, and if people talk of that it cannot dishonor *her*; besides, she is "her own woman" — at ease in her position, young, and without a husband whose jealousy she must fear. "Shall I nat love," she argues to herself — "What, *pardieux*, I am not religious." Indeed (though she would prefer no one knew this thought), she realizes she is one of the fairest and goodliest ladies in Troy — "and so [she adds] men sayn."

In all this she is bolstering herself up, indulging in a fantasy, and rationalizing her desire to make the fantasy real. Then her fears take over — and like most fears they are spectral and abstract. But they come upon her with an overpowering reality — like a cloud covering the sun, Chaucer says, so that "for feer almost she gan to falle." She may, first, put her freedom in jeopardy. Then, too, love causes all kinds of trouble in people's lives — there are the wicked tongues of malicious and jealous persons and the proverbial fickleness of men.

We grasp Criseyde's thoughts and emotions intuitively throughout this passage. Soliloquy as a literary convention renders in dramatic form the phenomenon of inner speech and, especially in poetry, renders its emotional force; through rhythm, prosody, image, and metaphor it dramatizes the ineluctable fact that our thoughts and ideas are charged with feeling. In this, soliloquy relies upon and also dramatizes the fact that human beings are able to enter into the subjective emotional worlds of others. These two facts about human life can be labeled *affect* and *intersubjectivity*; but labeling them so makes them seem less like facts and more like abstractions. And we must keep our finger on the facts — that every sentence of Criseyde's inner speech is charged with the "affective and volitional tendency," with feeling, and that we are able to *feel* her feeling just as we are able to think her thoughts.

The passage therefore simply cannot be used to show that Criseyde is "self-centered" — that she is, as some think, vain and self-seeking. After all, everyone is self-centered in his inner speech, thought, and feeling[9] — the wonder is that we *can* empathize with others; when we condemn people for being "self-centered" we really mean that they cannot. Yet in Book III we are to see Criseyde open her heart to Troilus, empathize with his jealousy and sorrow, forgive him for not trusting her — all this, ironically, over a lie concocted by Pandarus with no protest from his lovesick protégé. Indecisive she may be, weak, /179/ frightened. She may indeed be vain (but women are permitted to be so). She may be looking out for herself, but circumstances have given her the best of causes. She may well be lacking in self-knowledge, a prey to her own feelings; and she is (or so Chaucer tells us) "sliding of corage." Yet Chaucer tells us too, "Ne nevermo ne lacked her pitee," calls her "tender herted" (V, 823–825). That she does wrong none can deny; Chaucer grants the point, adding only that he would excuse her "for routhe" (V, 1093–1099). In studies of the poem Criseyde has, as she herself predicted, been rolled on many a tongue. The justice of the charges against her is one issue, the spirit in which they are made is another. For however we may name her offense, we are meant to understand. Chaucer himself, as narrator, made the first effort to see her with charitable understanding, with *routhe*. As author he added to his source whatever could help us do likewise. So in the present scene he has made us participate in her conflicted emotions of attraction and fear, recognizing the conflict itself as a phase of human experience known through introspection and empathy.

II

To this inner conflict of attraction and fear Criseyde marshals up a certain kind of wisdom or lore. Ruminating on the question "what-would-happen-if," she can use this lore to rationalize both pro's and con's. On the positive side she exalts the aristocratic virtue *mesure*,[10] using as an example the time-honored case of a mean between drunkenness and total abstinence. On the negative side she can summon up a whole body of lore about men — they are jealous, overbearing, fickle, untrue.[11] This proverbial lore is different from other considerations she entertains, which are for the most part factual or concretely imagined from her own experience. Not that such lore is divorced from experience altogether, but it is based on others' experience, solidified and, as it were, fossilized — not merely expressed in sentences but preserved, transmitted, learned, and chiefly remembered in sentences. And with this body of lore, which itself makes up part of Criseyde's experience and is a notable feature of her mental life, we come into the realm of language, that is, the realm of *external* speech.

Language is articulate and communal, and inner speech could not exist without it. When Chaucer reaches the end of Criseyde's soliloquy he focuses upon this fact. Her last thought is the conventional anxiety of lovers about what people would say: Who, she asks herself, can stop every wicked tongue, or "soun of belles, while that they been runge?"

(805). /180/ The metaphor is doubly apt. She has been talking about *jangling*, which suggests pointless noise; and it is true that bells, once rung, do go on so. But the comparison, natural enough in itself, was already in Chaucer's time a commonplace,[12] so that his language reflects what it describes: Criseyde's anxiety about people's jangling is expressed with a touch of ordinary colloquial tongue-wagging. Then in the next line he tells us that "her thought gan for to cleere," and what strikes her in this moment of clarity is a proverb:

> "He which that nothing undertaketh
> Nothing n'acheveth, be him looth or deere." (807–808)[13]

It is the very sentiment Pandarus has tried to persuade her of. The notion — "nothing ventured, nothing gained" as we now phrase it — reflects his philosophy of life. We have seen him urge Troilus to "seeken boote" (I, 763), to "doon bisinesse" to his own help (795). We have seen him in his conversation with Criseyde argue that a good *aventure* is shaped for everyone at some point, but that it is up to us to take advantage of it and "cacch it anon" (II, 281–291). Pandarus has a consistently pagan view of life and a clear opinion about how others should behave. From such a view comes such a proverb.[14] To lovers of any era it is an appealing sentiment, and Pandarus with his charm and wit makes it seem a delight. But its philosophical underpinnings are in fact pessimistic. To Pandarus the world is in a state of flux, controlled by cheerless forces of destiny, capricious and inscrutable, which shape for everyone certain moments of "good aventure." Such moments, he explains, will always pass out of our lives as fleetingly as they entered, and it is up to us to seize the day "lest aventure slacke." At the end we are to learn that this way of thinking is wrong-headed; the "plain felicity that is in heaven above," of which Pandarus can know nothing, makes Christian *contemptus mundi* wiser than pagan *carpe diem*. And indeed this truth is implicit in their own lore if they could but see it.

I have been using the word *lore* to describe the proverbial wisdom which makes up a phase of Criseyde's consciousness. Etymologically, at least, lore is anything learned; but the term is usually associated with popular, anecdotal learning. All Criseyde's lore is unmistakably aristocratic — the notion of *mesure*, the traditional courtly notions about love's woes, her conceptions of jangling, jealousy, men's faithlessness, and her uncle's notion that nothing ventured is nothing gained. Such /181/ lore, like spoken language itself, reflects social class, and this raises the question whether we can call it folklore. If "folklore" does not simply mean *peasants'* lore — if, that is, the term is not specifically tied to a sociologist's view of class-stratification — is it feasible to restrict the term to oral tradition? In modern times almost any lore of interest quickly gets "frozen" in writing or through the mass media, and even in medieval times the lore of knights and troubadors came to be written down and then read aloud. It seems too rigid to put such bodies of lore beyond the reach of folklore study merely because they lose "pure" orality. And of course if we do so it means that we have *no* medieval folklore. So, at least, I used to believe and would probably believe still if I had not spent a pleasant evening in 1958 debating the point with Francis Lee Utley. As always in such conversations he damned up with patience his reservoir of scholarship, loosing on me instead a polite rivulet of ironic questions. But I know I came away convinced that the term folklore does have to be restricted to oral dissemination, that folklore is different in kind from what is frozen in writing or by the mass media — a special phenomenon of oral transmission having a character of its own and requiring a special method of study.[15]

Criseyde's lore is, from this point of view, not *necessarily* folklore. No doubt what these medieval Trojans think about love and life existed in medieval oral tradition; we see them singing songs and listening while someone *tells* the "tale of Wade" — but then we see them listening to a romance of Thebes being read aloud. Pandarus is full of wise saws, but he is not without learning and we cannot be certain he had his proverbs from oral tradition (though we can be fairly certain Chaucer did in many an instance). It is customary to talk about Pandarus' "proverbial wisdom" and be amused by his store of old saws, but this lore he possesses does not have to make him like Polonius or Uncle Wiggly. Chaucer's source for the proverbs was perhaps folklore, but in Pandarus' mouth they become part of a consistent view of life which he believes in and presents winningly and indeed learnedly. I have argued elsewhere that this was Chaucer's conception of paganism.[16] We see one phase of it here take root in Criseyde's thoughts. It combines with a body of lore and free-floating opinion which she already possesses. We might conceivably call such opinion *knightlore* — for we know that medieval aristocrats held certain values appropriate to their class, a "chivalric" and "courtly" ethos passed down among them in large part orally.[17] Still, they had /182/ the means and motive to patronize poets and to preserve on paper what they liked; they were reverent toward "olde bookes"; they were by no means universally illiterate; and they liked to be read to aloud. Criseyde's knightlore on such subjects as love could have been learned from oral tradition, but might as easily have been learned (allowing for the anachronism) from the *Roman de la Rose*. Hence what she thinks here may well be the product of an imagined literary tradition, the literature of Troy.

The same can be said of the "Trojan song" which Antigone sings (827–875). Criseyde, leaving her room, goes out into the garden, joining the ladies; they walk about arm in arm, they "playen that it joye was to see," and at last Antigone sings so clearly "that it an hevene was her voice to heere." The song, original with Chaucer,[18] is a characteristic courtly lyric. Antigone identifies its author as "the goodlieste maide/ Of greet estate in all the town of Troye" (880–881). She says the song was "made," and Criseyde speaks admiringly of how lovers can "fair endite" (886). There is enough suggestion of poetical composition so that one tends to see the piece rather as literature than as a folksong; we can be sure anyway that it is *not* an instance of *das Volk dichtet*. In content it is exceedingly literary — is almost a compendium of courtly love conventions, embodying the knightlore familiar to all readers of romances and courtly lyrics. But as it emphasizes one tenet or image over another, it chances to light upon the very aspects of courtly lore which most touch Criseyde's mental state. Addressed at first to the God of Love by one of his female servants, it extols love's joy, the virtues of her lover, and the power of love to banish "alle manner vice and sinne." In its two penultimate stanzas it dismisses the objections against love, in part those aspects of knightlore that have given Criseyde anxiety: whoever says love is vice or thralldom must be envious, foolish, or incapable of loving, for only those defame love who know it not. Then an analogy: the sun is none the worse because men's weak eyes cannot gaze on it direct, and so love none the worse because wretches cry out against it. Two proverbs in the song buttress the analogy: "He deserves no happiness who can endure no sorrow," and, "He who has a glass head should throw no stones in war." The last stanza is a profession of undying love, and it ends — for Criseyde the most telling line — with the couplet

> *Al dredde I first to love him to beginne,*
> *Now wot I well there is no peril inne.*

/183/ This spendid song brings to mind other songs in the *Troilus*. Against the background of a city about to fall, its doomed inhabitants are vibrant with lyricism in all its shades. Troilus himself, once in love, begins composing a song; there are the dawn-songs of the lovers in Book III and the plaintive *Canticus Troili* of Book V. At Pandarus' house they amuse themselves with both lyric and narrative: "He sang; she played; he tolde tale of Wade" (III, 614) — as earlier the ladies have been listening while one of them reads from the *Siege of Thebes* (II, 83–84).

So into Criseyde's mind at this point comes the unique quality of lyric poetry, particularly when sung. Lyric submerges the plain sense of language in song and image[19] — we can rarely repeat what a song "says" after hearing it sung; we remember "the words" as a disconnected jumble of image and phrase. Yet song endues words with a measure and intensity of its own which supplants what it takes away in syntax and logical flow. We never have trouble, with a good song, telling what it was *about*; and when we talk about the "haunting" and "moving" qualities of sung lyric we are talking in part of the power lyric has, by suspending normal syntactic and logical relations, to make outlandish notions seem compelling, to make sense out of non-sense. If anyone were to tell me I ought to wear a flower in my hair if I go to San Francisco I should think him mad, but the same sentiment, heard in the song popular a few years ago, managed to take on a pleasant fancy. So it is, I believe, that Antigone's song impresses Criseyde. What had frightened her before loses its terror, seems possible and appealing, takes on the "haunting" quality with which successful lyric cloaks any notion, and helps to convince her, in her feelings, that "ther is no peril inne."

We grasp her reaction to this lyric, and the lore it expresses, through a third aspect of language: conversation. Chaucer does tell us explicitly what her reaction to the song is, but not until he has let us see it for ourselves. The conversation (876–898) leaves much unsaid, and this we can see best in paraphrase:

"Now, niece," said Criseyde, "now who made up this nice song?"

Antigone answered, "Madame, I'll tell you — the most wonderful young lady of noble birth in the whole city of Troy, and led her life in the most joy and honor."

"Indeed, so it seems, to judge from her song," said Criseyde; and with that she sighed — "Lord! is there such bliss among lovers, that they can compose so gorgeously?" /184/

"Yes, for sure," said Antigone, "because not everybody that's ever lived could describe the bliss of love. Do you think just any wretch knows about love's perfect bliss? Why, not at

all! They think practically anything is love, just if they feel a
little glow. Go on, go on, they don't know anything about it.
You have to ask *saints* if it's nice in heaven — why? because
they can *tell* — and ask devils if hell's ugly."

  Criseyde answered nothing, but said "Sure it will be night
soon . . ."

Of course my paraphrase uses novelistic "dialogue," not really the
casual spoken style,[20] but what else? Play back a tape-recording of a lively
conversation in which you were a participant, and you see to your horror
that it was full of awkward pauses, crass interruptions, stammers,
repetitions, regrettable lapses. The novelist or romancer tries to capture
conversation as heard not by a detached observer but by an active
listener. What gives "life" to conversation is our emotional involvement
with it, the forward thrust of our expectations, our running efforts to
second-guess our interlocutors and frame what we are moved to say.
Conversation rides on an eager babble of inner speech, but an exact
transcript of a heard conversation monstrously abstracts the one from
the other; the artist simulates the experience as a whole. So in the present
scene we catch the force of Antigone's emotion in the jumble of her
discourse — it breaks out in rhetorical questions, repetitions, broken
sentences, little forward-rushing lapses of grammar; it is punctuated by
conversational ejaculations— "Why, nay, ywis!" "Do way, do way,"
"Why? For . . . ." And what this accomplishes is to suggest the flashing of
eye contact, the flickering of facial expressions in others, the tiny
movements of hand and eyebrow and shoulder that signal us our
listeners' comprehension and response. This non-verbal communication
which rides along with all intimate discourse is an acting-out of inner
speech — the listener *thinks* "Oh, but . . ." and a tiny furl flickers
between his brows. Feeling felt by feeling is the real event which happens
in this brief moment of conversation; hence Criseyde's silence speaks so
loud. When she answers nothing except "Ywis, it will be night as faste,"
we *feel* what she is thinking. Then, but only then, Chaucer tells us:

  But every word which that she of her herde,
  She gan to printen in her herte faste,
  And ay gan love less her for to aghaste
  Than it did erst, and sinken in her herte. . . . (899–902)

III

/185/ The greatest poetry is always a miracle, but the miracle here is that of evoking what is itself miraculous, the ability of one mind, closed within its little world of thought, to enter the mind of another. Chaucer makes us experience the reality Criseyde experienced — we see what she saw, hear what she heard. Chiefly he brings to us the experience as it existed for her in various aspects of language — inner speech, colloquialism, proverb and lore, song and poetry, conversation. Language in all these aspects is part of experience, but it is unique among phases of experience because it alone can name, interpret, and so influence those phases, itself among them. While we enter Criseyde's consciousness largely through its content of language, her language — and Chaucer's — brings with it the whole range of human experience from stated cultural values to non-verbal communication.

Language has therefore the *capacity* to become identical with consciousness, to encompass and express all consciousness; but in day-to-day reality, consciousness always races ahead of and runs circles about language. The "inadequacy" of language, about which tongues wag so much these days, is nothing more than the frustrating differential between language and consciousness; but the inadequacy is in us, not in language — the failure is our failure to use language well and to cultivate our gardens of consciousness. That is why it is so extraordinary in the present instance that Chaucer added to this scene a feature that pushes us into the realm of the non-verbal, as far indeed as the edges of consciousness. He makes us experience the *shape* of thought by imitating and rendering it in the scene itself. The structure of the scene, the arrangement and disposition of its parts, expresses the fluctuation and dialectic that we experience in those thoughts which deeply touch our actions. If we ask how the scene is organized, we have to say it has a simple episodic organization, event following event in quotidian fashion. Criseyde is alone thinking; she sees Troilus pass; she pops her head inside and thinks some more; she goes out in the garden, hears a song, and exchanges a few words with Antigone; she goes to bed, thinking more and finally dreaming. But these events are really arranged in alternation: three stretches of inner experience are twice interrupted by outer experiences, one visual and one auditory. This pattern repeats the fundamental alternation of our mental lives, that of stimulus and response. And it carries with it, as if in concentric circles, several other kinds of alternation, which we shall see best if we disentangle them:

/186/

(1) *Fear and attraction*. Criseyde is, we know, very much a worldling —
capable of vibrant emotions, sensitive to stimuli,

> Charitable, estatlich, lusty, free,
> Ne nevermo ne lacked her pitee,
> Tender herted, sliding of corage. (V, 823-825)

We know as well, and have witnessed from the start, that she is the
"feerfulleste wight / That mighte be" (II, 450–451). Fear alternates with
her open responsiveness to the world, her attraction to it. Thus when
Pandarus leaves her she is "somdeel astoned," but the sight of Troilus
trips off a violent reaction — "Who yaf me drinke?" — and sets her on a
train of thought in which she rehearses all that favors love. Yet
midstream in this "a cloudy thought" strikes her (768) "So that for feer
almost she gan to falle." This inner stimulus trips off an opposing train of
fears — for loss of her freedom, wicked tongues, betrayal; then she
reassures herself "He which that nothing undertaketh, / Nothing
n'acheveth"; then "with another thought her herte quaketh."

(2) *Insecurity and independence*. Against her vulnerability to fear and
attraction we find in her a feeling of self-contained invulnerability. When
she is alone with her thoughts, her associations and her stream of inner
speech make for her a kind of fortress against the world and foster a
conviction of her own independence. Pandarus leaves her and she is
"somdeel astoned in her thought," but presently she is telling herself that
a man can love a woman until his heart breaks "and she not love again,
but if her leste." She sees Troilus and is shaken, but presently she can
soliloquize the reasons why she is her "owne woman." She hears
Antigone's song and asks, sighing, if there is such bliss among these
lovers, but as every word is impressed in her heart "ay gan love less her
for to aghaste."

(3) *Emotion and reason*. Alternating with all these feelings — of fear
and insecurity, of attraction, of independence — is a strain of sweet
reasonableness, all the good sense and sound lore she possesses. Her
initial fear when Pandarus takes his leave is calmed with a generality —
that no woman must return a man's love "but if her leste." Her soliloquy
after seeing Troilus is full of logical and factual truth — is rationalization
in the fullest sense. The "cloudy thought" which makes her almost keel
over with fear is put into her mind by knightlore about the ills besetting
lovers — and is calmed by a proverb. Stimulus and impulse alternate with

common sense and knowledge, as always in /187/ decision-making — the id pushing forward lusts and fears, the superego parading solemn rationalizations and stern prohibitions; or, to put this in medieval terms, the movements of sense being mediated in the will against the moral truth of the higher and lower reason.[21]

This quality of alternation or fluctuation in the mental life, of which everyone has some personal experience, is bolstered by the imagery. Before Criseyde's soliloquy Chaucer tells us she "plited [turned back and forth] in many folde," adding "Now was hire herte warm, now was it colde" (697–698); at the end of it she is in the same case:

Then sleepeth hope, and after dreed awaketh —
Now hot, now cold. But thus betwixen twaye,
She rist her up. (810–812)

To this conventional image of hot and cold, which may be found in Boccaccio and almost anywhere in courtly writings, Chaucer adds a far more elaborate imagery of light and dark. Halfway through her soliloquy he introduces her sudden fear with a simile:

But right as when the sunne shineth brighte
In March, that changeth ofte time his face,
And that a cloud is put with wind to flighte,
Which oversprad the sun as for a space,
A cloudy thought gan through her soule passe,
That oversprad her brighte thoughtes alle. . . . (764–769)

In her thoughts as they follow fast upon, she reminds herself that love is the most stormy life, that always "some cloud is over that sunne." And in Antigone's song, about the bliss of love as opposed to its rumored peril, the image of the sun stands for love: is the sun any the worse, asks the song, because a man's weak eyes cannot gaze directly at its brightness? So things stand when at the end of the scene Chaucer devotes a full stanza to the waning sun, the dimming light, and the slow appearing stars:

The daye's honour and the hevene's eye,
The nighte's foe — all these clepe I the sunne —
Gan westren fast and downward for to wrye,
As he that had his daye's course y-runne,
And white thinges wexen dim and dunne

> For lack of light, and starres for to appere,
> That she and all her folk in went yfere. (904–910)

/188/ We are permitted to see the sun set and the light fade into ominous dark. In a moment, by a universal irony, she is to experience the clearest illumination of her thought in the darkest hours, and asleep.

The narrator's appearance here, as elsewhere, is one further way Chaucer dramatizes the alternating shape of Criseyde's thought.[22] Puffed with rhetorical phrases ("day's honor," "heaven's eye," "night's foe") he wheezes in — "all these clepe I the sunne." The narrator draws up close to us and joins us in thinking about her — just as before her soliloquy he had lectured us on the way she fell in love with no indecorous haste, adding "And what she thoughte somewhat shall I write" (699). Then he withdrew and we experienced her thoughts in direct discourse, Antigone's song, and the ladies' conversation. Only now does he pluck us away, just for a breath of fresh air out of sweet rhetoric's windbag. After that, the ladies retire, all is hushed, and Criseyde, lying still, thinks more; but, the narrator adds, he needn't rehearse this to us "for ye been wise." We the audience are suddenly and surprisingly pulled up to attention with the ironic jibe, and our alleged wisdom enlisted for the startling moment to come. Then, in what I have heard called the most beautiful lines in Chaucer, we hear "A nightingale, upon a cedir greene, / Under the chamber wall ther-as she lay. . . . " With that she sleeps and, sleeping, dreams.

The medievals were no less fascinated than we by dreams; but this is not because of their (or our) theories — rather the theories crop up again and again because dreams are and always were our most intense moments of consciousness. In them we grasp by night what we evade and cloak by day, recognizing with unwonted vividness images from a realm beyond our easy reach. The dream-visions of medieval literature may be stiffly conventional, but the successful ones — the *Roman, Piers Plowman, Pearl* — are powerfully dreamlike all the same. While Chaucer might make fun of dream *theory* in the Nun's Priest's Tale, no poet who had written *The Book of the Duchess* can have been insensitive to the wonder of dreams themselves. So, with Criseyde's dream of the white eagle, we must admit a degree of psychological realism. We can be aware that birds in medieval literature often suggest human propensities and impulses toward sin or virtue; it will do us no harm to be aware as well that birds, as they occur in the dream-world, often suggest fertility, birth, and rebirth.[23] In the fourteenth century eagles probably suggested gospel truth — for there were lecterns in churches fashioned in the shape of eagles. The eagle is uniformly considered a *noble* bird in Chaucer's works.[24] And his whiteness connotes /189/ purity (with perhaps some dread ambivalence at least for readers of Jung and *Moby Dick*). Because the eagle tears out her heart and replaces it with his own, it is easy to suppose he "represents Troilus." But Troilus so far has in no way pursued her or even spoken to her and has been the very reverse of a plundering eagle. Besides, the figures in our dreams are never the things themselves as they exist in the real world, but our inner imagination of them. The eagle is Troilus, but Troilus as he exists in Criseyde's inner thoughts, made white by hope and sentiment, made violent and rapacious by expectation and fear — noble, gorgeous, awesome, at once predatory and gentle. Perhaps indeed the eagle is love itself, Criseyde's hopeful and fearful image of it — sexual, lustrous, mystifying — revived in her now by Pandarus' urgings, by the glimpse of Troilus riding in triumph, by the song and talk of love's joy. Her dream can be a *somnium animale* tripped off by anxiety or a *somnium coeleste* foretelling what is to come. Like dreams themselves and the starkest facts, it is inscrutable and intense. The white eagle sets his claws under her breast, tears out her heart, and supplants it with his own, yet she feels no fear or pain. Beneath all the divagations of her thought, behind all the influences on it, is this *fact* — the gorgeous white eagle of her mind's eye, plunderer of hearts.

IV

What have we to learn from this scene about the poem as a whole? In recent years critics have centered attention upon the moral riddle of its ending: a poem which shows love in its highest and most tragic garb ends with the moving counsel against earthly love — "O younge freshe folkes, he or she . . . . " Their attention has thus shifted back to the Boethian element in the body of the poem itself, the slow process by which Fortune makes of the noblest human love another mundane vanity. But the Boethian element in the poem cannot *be* Boethian unless it encompasses what Boethius really said; and Boethius' notion was that while God's foreknowledge of our free choices does not *cause* us to make them, God *does* foreknow our choices and we *do* make them freely. Boethius leaves unanswered the question *how* we make our choices (he has some opinions about how we *should*); and Chaucer really picks up this aspect of the problem when he tries to see into Criseyde's mind.

He thus confronts the timeless riddle of human freedom. Our choices

seem to happen freely in our consciousness, but consciousness /190/ is a
hopeless swirl at the mercy of individual experience, of circumstance and
chance occurrence; of language itself and its heritage of cultural and
literary tradition, lore, precept; of reason's shaping dialectic. Our choices
can happen, as Criseyde's choice does, in the unfathomed reaches of
consciousness, beneath the stream of inner speech, in a realm clear to us
only through our stream of imagery. In Criseyde's choice there is thus a
subtle determinism and, as we are to learn in due course, a kind of
bondage. As much as she reasons and vacillates, the choice bursts upon
her in sleep, violent and lustrous, as a fact. It is not God who makes her
choice, yet something does — some determinism of this world which
makes us its slaves just as soon as we engage ourselves with it. Living
before the time of Christianity Criseyde lacks that great revealed lore
which could save her from the disappointing flux of her future life; yet as
a rational creature she knows it as through a glass darkly. While Troilus
waits outside her chamber she can say to Pandarus,

> "so wordly selinesse,
> Which clerkes callen false felicitee,
> Y-meddled is with many a bitternesse.
> Ful anguishous then is, God wot," quod she,
> "Condicioun of vain prosperitee;
> For either joyes comen not yfere,
> Or elles no wight hath hem alway here." (III, 813–819)

Yet a few moments later she is to say, embracing Troilus,

> "N' had I ere now, my sweete herte deere,
> Ben yold, ywis, I were now not here!" (1210–1211)

Later still she is to see with astonishing clarity how she will be "rolled on
many a tongue," how women will hate her most of all. But none of this
stops her — she proceeds with a kind of helpless, perhaps willful,
blindness. Though she has free will and tries to exercise it, she lapses
unconsciously into the decision. And Pandarus, glib proprietor of lore
and speech, encourages and misleads her. If we think she would proceed
otherwise were it not for the Fall, we are wrong — that did not, after all,
help Eve. She might proceed otherwise if she were a Christian, but
professing Christianity is not itself a guarantee of right moral choices.
Medieval moralists named rational consent as the test of sin; but the

subtler thinkers, St. Thomas among them, knew the cloudy /191/ area of unreasoning action.[25] Chaucer here explores this irrational element in our choices and finds that we are not free except in the most limited way.

This brings us to the reason why Criseyde stays with Diomede and does not return to Troilus. And the answer must be that it happens so. Chaucer does not give us a long immersion in her mental life as he had done before. He presents her regrettable choice with much tongue-clicking on the narrator's part and, so he tells us, feels pity for her. It would be possible to go through the final scenes and glean here and there a hint of her mental state or psychological fix: we are reminded of time's passing, her caution, Diomede's persuasive glibness, "His greet estate, and peril of the town, / And that she was alone, and hadde neede / Of freendes' help" (1025-1027). But what stands out is the rationalizing and perhaps self-destructive meditation (1054-1085) in which she castigates and excuses herself all at once — it is too late, she says; adds "To Diomede algate I will be trewe"; weeping, expresses what seems earnest praise of Troilus; and concludes that all will pass. Her two letters to Troilus, written after her decision is a *fait accompli*, both promise her return; the second, quoted in full, adds a lie about people's gossiping (1610), casts a subtle doubt on Troilus' good intention (1614-1617), and puts her return still more vaguely in the future. Troilus sees at once it is "straunge" and soon grasps the truth — "that she / Nas not so kind as that her oughte be" (1642-1643). I can explain no better than this why she prefers Diomede, whom I scorn, to Troilus, whom I like. All the same, I feel I do know why she forsook Troilus. I feel that she did it in the same way and for much the same reasons that she chose to love Troilus in the second book. I know, that is, *how* she made this final choice, which I deplore, because I know how she made her earlier one, which I applauded. And I know this because for a little while, for a space of some four hundred or more lines in Book II, I have *been* Criseyde, have experienced the world as she experienced it, have had my mind and being subsumed in hers. And having had that experience I can never shake it off. Chaucer thus gives his reader the ability to understand her falseness, but it is not the kind of understanding that results from distance. On the contrary, because we understand through empathy, through entering her mind, our understanding results from our closeness. We get not a clear overview of her conduct but the muddled sense we might have of such a choice if it had been our own. And, perhaps for that reason, her choice seems not at all free or rational; in such choices we /192/ are disposed to decision and action by tangled pressures of culture, lore, belief, habit. Our only freedom is in our conscious awareness of these pressures, in the possibility of doubting them or changing them — which means the possibility of knowing ourselves. Beyond that, our only choice is indifference — indifference to "this world, that passeth soon as flowers faire."

Notes

1. See Francis Lee Utley, "Scene-division in Chaucer's Troilus and Criseyde," in *Studies in Medieval Literature*, ed. MacEdward Leach (Philadelphia: University of Pennsylvania Press, 1961), pp. 109–138.

2. II, 470–489. *Troilus and Criseyde and Selected Short Poems*, ed. Donald R. Howard and James Dean (New York: New American Library, 1976).

3. "Literature and Sexuality: Book III of Chaucer's *Troilus*," *Massachusetts Review*, VIII (1967), 442–456.

4. Medieval literature had an elaborate iconography for suggesting nonverbal impulse, which Chaucer used in describing Troilus' first sight of Criseyde. In I, 206–210 Troilus is struck by Love's arrow; we are told "his herte wex a-feere" (229), and on seeing her that "he wex therewith astoned" (274). Only then do we get inner speech reported in direct discourse (276–277). On the passage see Robert M. Jordan, *Chaucer and the Shape of Creation* (Cambridge, Mass.: Harvard University Press, 1967), pp. 76–79.

5. L. S. Vigotsky, "Thought and Speech," in *Psycholinguistics*, ed. S. Saporta and J. R. Bastian (New York: Holt, Rinehart, Winston, 1961), pp. 509–535.

6. "Thought and Speech," p. 533.

7. On this phenomenon see the very interesting story or essay by Peter Taylor, "Demons," in *The New Yorker*, August 24, 1963, pp. 30–63.

8. "Thought and Speech," p. 532.

9. Indeed Vigotsky shows that inner speech develops from the "egocentric speech" of childhood: "Thought and Speech," pp. 514–524.

10. See lines 715–718. On moderation or *mesure* as an aristocratic virute, one can cite its frequent appearance in romances. Pandarus himself believes in it — see I, 687–689. See Lynn White, Jr., "The Iconography of *Temperantia* and the Virtuousness of Technology," in *Action and Conviction in Early Modern Europe*, ed. Theodore K. Rabb and Jerrold E. Siegel (Princeton: Princeton University Press, 1969), pp. 197–219.

11. Lines 755–756, 786–791. In earlier passage she is using it as encouragement — she has no husband who will be fickle and jealous.

12. OED and MED cite Gower, *Confessio Amantis* I, 2391 and V, 4640. *Jangle* and *clap* referred to any noise; but *clapper* was generally used to mean the "tongue" of a bell ("tongue" is not cited in this usage until the sixteenth century).

13. See F. N. Robinson's note for parallels in English proverbs: *The Works of Geoffrey*

Chaucer, 2nd. ed. (Boston: Houghton Mifflin, 1957).

14. Later, In V, 784, the opportunistic Diomede uses the same proverb.

15. His ideas on the subject appear in a later article, "Folk Literature: An Operational Definition," *Journal of American Folklore*, LXXIV (1961), 193–206.

16. *The Three Temptations: Medieval Man in Search of the World* (Princeton: Princeton University Press, 1966), pp. 135–138, and cf. 127–135. Pandarus twice mentions his reading, in I, 788 and II, 108; on his bookishness see also David I. Grossvogel, *Limits of the Novel* (Ithaca, New York: Cornell University Press, 1968), pp. 44–73.

17. See Ernst Robert Curtius, *European Literature and the Latin Middle Ages*, trans. Willard R. Trask, Bollingen Series No. 36 (New York: Pantheon Books, 1953), pp. 519–537.

18. But inspired, as Kittredge noted (*MLN*, *XXV* [1910], 158), by Machaut's "Paradis d'Amour."

19. Cf. Northrop Frye, *Anatomy of Criticism* (Princeton: Princeton University Press, 1957), pp. 270–281.

20. I have in mind here the detailed analysis of Martin Joos, *The Five Clocks*, Indiana University Research Center in Anthropology, Folklore, and Linguistics No. 22 (Bloomington, 1962), especially pp. 22–23. Joos shows that a characteristic of the casual style is the participation of the listener and the assumption of a common frame of reference. The ladies do *not* speak in the intimate style, where emotion is unexpressed because habitually felt; Antigone expresses enthusiasm openly while Criseyde tries to check and conceal her response.

21. On this phase of medieval psychology, see D. W. Robertson, Jr., *A Preface to Chaucer: Studies in Medieval Perspectives* (Princeton: Princeton University Press, 1962), pp. 71–76; and cf. Howard, *The Three Temptations*, pp. 56–65.

22. On this general function of the narrator, see Morton W. Bloomfield, "Distance and Predestination in *Troilus and Criseyde*," *PMLA*, LXXII (1957), 14–26 [above, pp. 75–90.]

23. Cf. for example C. G. Jung, *Symbols of Transformation*, Bollingen Series No. 20, 2nd ed. (Princeton, 1967), pp. 347–348.

24. So also in Thomas of Cantimpré, *De natura rerum* in British Museum MS Roy. 12. E. XVII, fol. 73–74.

25. See Odon Lottin, *Psychologie et morale aux XII' et XIII' siècles* (6 vols. in 8, Louvain and Gembloux: Abbaye du Mont César, 1942–1960), especially I, 220–221, 393–424; II, 493–496, 588–589.

Afterword: 1979

Reading this ten years after it was written, I don't find it as much of a period piece as I might have expected. Then there was the Vietnam war and campus "unrest." Then people still thought the supply of new Ph. D.'s would never meet the demand. But all one can divine from this essay is that people at John Hopkins, where I had gone in 1967, were talking about phenomenology and structuralism, reading Foucault and Lacan. I think some actually did believe that language and consciousness are identical. Of course a medievalist is not expected to be concerned about such matters, but anyway what I ended up doing was describing what Chaucer himself thought. One could read the essay as an experiment in writing biography.

That the paper was written for a volume honoring Francis Lee Utley dictated some of its concerns. The *Festschrift*, one of the more pompous and ineffectual traditions of the academic subculture, bestows dubious homage; Utley would have been more honored by a collection of his scattered writings (some of his reviews are classics). The volume didn't contain the traditional bibliography of his own writings; one was made after his death by Mark Amsler and published in the journal *Names*. But Utley in his generous way was greatly pleased by the volume. He was one of those incredible polymaths who can keep abreast of several fields where the rest of us can barely keep our heads above water in one. His specialties were medieval literature, folklore, and linguistics. In my essay I wanted to touch on points that would interest him. This was the genesis of the passage about "knightlore," a coinage he had complimented me on. And it is why the article contains a reminiscence of a discussion with him. When the essay was published he told me I hadn't got the story right. After he had persuaded me to change my ideas about folklore, he had changed his and subsequently backed down in print about the term having to be restricted to purely oral tradition.

If I were to write this article again, I would say more about Pandarus' philosophy (as I did later in the introduction to the Signet paperback edition, done in collaboration with James Dean). And I would say more about Criseyde's innocence. She never does anything wrong until she has left Troy. Until then she has demonstrably been lied to and badgered, by her uncle and by Troilus or with his consent. Those who find guile in her in the early books of the poem must presuppose it — Chaucer makes it possible for one to do so — but it is not there in black and white like the two men's lies and scheming. One of the reasons why the *Troilus* has such power is that it cannot, or can just barely, be read without some touch of sexist bias. It would not be so gripping a poem if it didn't invite us to take sides. And there is no right side.

D. R. H.

The Heart and the Chain
by John Leyerle

Several of Chaucer's major poems have as a poetic nucleus either the heart or the chain. As such, the heart represents both love and its mutability; the chain represents order and its confinement. The word "nucleus" here is not italicized because the English word, first recorded in the *Oxford English Dictionary* in 1704, is meant, not the Latin. I use the word in two senses: the first is kernel, or seed, the latent beginning of growth or development; the second is the center around which other parts or things are grouped. As a critical term, nucleus means both seed, implying origin and growth, and center, implying a surrounding structure. The term is not difficult or new, but it provides a means to approach to Chaucer's narrative poetry not often taken.[1] In this paper I propose to show how a number of /114/ Chaucer's poems are developed around such a nucleus lying at the core of the text that focuses the surrounding elements of the whole composition. In these poems the organizing effectiveness and centripetal force of each nucleus vary, but a strong nucleus controls the main narrative and thematic development of its work. Not all of Chaucer's poems have a nucleus, but those that do range from his early work to that of his poetic maturity.

His earliest long poem, *The Book of the Duchess*, ends as the man in black, usually taken to be John of Gaunt, and the dreamer emerge from the dark forest in which most of the poem is set.

They gan to strake forth; al was doon,

Reprinted with the kind permission of the author and the English Department, Harvard University, from *The Learned and the Lewed, Harvard English Studies* 5 (1974): 113-145. The volume is subtitled "Studies in Chaucer and Medieval Literature," and was written for Bartlett Jere Whiting. Mr. Leyerle wrote, "This paper was written for Jere Whiting, a man of gret auctorite." The original pagination is indicated between slashes in the text.

181

For that tyme, the hert-huntyng.   (1312-12)[2]

The nucleus of the poem is *hert-huntyng*. The deer, a hart, cannot be
found by the hunters in their chase, nor can Gaunt recover his lady,
usually taken to be his first wife Blaunch, who, he reports, had long
possessed his heart; the two hunts proceed together and show how the
nucleus has a literal and a metaphoric sense. The hunters pursue the
deer, but lose their quarry.

> and so at the laste
> This hert rused, and staal away
> Fro alle the houndes a privy way.   (380-382)

The dreamer follows one of these hounds into a parklike forest and sees
there "many an hert and many an hynde" (427). The dark wood, a refuge
for harts and hinds that are beyond the hunt, is a medieval *topos* familiar
from the opening of Dante's *Inferno*; the dress of the man in black, his
manner, and his words all reinforce the associations of the ominous place
with death.[3] The dreamer overhears Gaunt reciting a lament (lines
475-486) /115/ about the death of Blaunch and then describes his state.

> Hys sorwful hert gan faste faynte,
> And his spirites wexen dede;
> The blood was fled for pure drede
> Doun to hys herte, to make hym warm —
> For wel hyt feled the herte had harm —
> To wite eke why hyt was adrad
> By kynde, and for to make hyt glad;
> For hit ys membre principal
> Of the body.   (488-496)

Following the specific statement about the death of Blaunch in Gaunt's
lament, this passage shows how the loss has affected his heart, the *membre
principal of the body*. The relevance of the story of Seys and Alcyone
which the dreamer read before he fell asleep becomes apparent here, for it
indicates the risk that Gaunt, who has lost Blaunch to death, may die of
grief as Alcyone had died of grief over the loss of Seys. The dreamer has
just left the literal hunt in which the hart *staal away*, overhears the
lament, and utters what must be a calculated ambiguity.

> "Sir," quod I, "this game is doon.
> I holde that this hert be goon;
> These huntes konne hym nowher see."   (539–541)

Gaunt's reply, "Y do no fors therof," (542) elicits from the dreamer an explicit offer of help.

> For, by my trouthe, to make yow hool
> I wol do al my power hool.
> And telleth me of your sorwes smerte;
> Paraunter hyt may ese youre herte,
> That semeth ful sek under your syde.   (553–557)

/116/ The balance of the poem is the working out of this offer to ease the heart sickness of Gaunt by getting him to articulate his sorrows; the cure is thus to have him talk about his loss. At this point the dreamer starts a metaphoric game of *hert-huntyng*.[4] Contrary to a critical commonplace about the poem, Gaunt is the one who does not comprehend what is afoot, not the dreamer who sets about to make him whole. The dreamer is concerned about the risk that Gaunt's heart, which he gave to Blaunch, *staal away* at her death to the dark forest, as the hart had done in the literal hunt, there to remain. In less metaphoric language, the dreamer fears that Gaunt, like Alcyone, will die of grief. Whatever may have been the truth about Gaunt's actual reactions to the death of his wife in 1369, Chaucer attributes to his patron a profound grief with lightness of touch by presenting his loss in metaphoric language so delicate and graceful that its point is easy to miss; Chaucer's narrator is not obtuse.

In telling the dreamer of his *sorwes smerte* Gaunt makes four long speeches that show an interesting progression. The first, lines 560 to 709, reveals a self-pity evident in the fifty-two repetitions of the first-person pronouns, *I, me* and *my*, in the first sixty lines. The main point of this speech is a wish for death, showing that the diagnosis made by the dreamer about Gaunt's grief sickness is accurate. He then elaborates the metaphor of the chess game with fortune in which he lost his queen and was mated. The next move would be the final checkmate[5] when the king, Gaunt himself, would, as had happened to his *fers* Blaunch, /117/ be swept off the board by fortune. Gaunt concludes his first long speech with a question and his own answer to it:

> but yet, what to doone?

Be oure Lord, hyt ys to deye soone.   (689–690)

The dreamer makes a skillful reply, saying that no man would "for a fers make this woo" (741). By taking Gaunt's metaphor of the chess game literally, he leads Gaunt to praise Blaunch in an effort to show how great a loss he had indeed suffered. The difference in tone in Gaunt's second long speech, lines 758 to 1041, is important, because he moves from the self-pitying grief of his first long speech to the eloquent praise of his dead lady. Gaunt's preoccupation has shifted from himself to the dead duchess, and the curative process of consolation, the heart-hunting, is well under way. In his third long speech, lines 1052 to 1111, Gaunt compares her to riches of all sorts and decides that she was superior to them all. In the fourth long speech, lines 1144 to 1297, Gaunt answers the dreamer's specific questions and reverts to his courtship, the time when Blaunch first possessed his heart.

> She was lady
> Of the body: she had the herte.
> And who hath that, may not asterte.   (1152–54)[6]

He then repeats the first love song to Blaunch, one that he made his "herte to glade" (1172). This song is a sharp contrast to the earlier, self-pitying lament and shows how his mood has shifted. Gaunt then recalls how Blaunch took pity on his sorrowful heart and gave him "The noble yifte of hir mercy" (1270), which caused his heart to be joyous (1275–76). In his mind Blaunch /118/ has now returned in death to her first inaccessibility and he has resumed his attitude of courtship; then he was happy to love her at a distance, but now the distance is the permanent one of death. At the same time she is shown to be fixed in his memory; in medieval times the memory was commonly thought to be a thesaurus where treasures of the past would be safe. While Gaunt lives, Blaunch is wholly his own and her heart has been found within his heart. To the dreamer's insistent questioning, he replies, with a hint of impatience, that Blaunch is dead. At once the dark forest is left and the heart-hunting is over.

> And with that word ryght anoon
> They gan to strake forth; al was doon,
> For that tyme, the hert-huntyng.   (1311–13)

The word *hert* is used nearly forty times in the poem, and this frequency is significant. The word occurs so often and so naturally that one hardly notices its full importance, but once that importance is recognized and the nucleus is identified, the supporting evidence is found throughout the text. This point has an obverse; if there is no repeated, specific statement, a poetic nucleus, as defined here, does not exist in a work.

Another of Chaucer's treatments of courtship and death — a combined theme that he liked — is *The Knight's Tale*, which also has a nucleus, but one less apparent than the *hert* of *The Book of the Duchess*. This nucleus is bonds in the literal sense of confinement, the poem's *prisoun*, and in the metaphoric sense of order in the created world, the *faire cheyne of love*. The idea that love is a bond was a medieval commonplace;[7] the lofty speech of Theseus at the end of *The Knight's Tale* draws on the last meter of Book II of the *Consolation of Philosophy*, one of Chaucer's favorite passages in that text. Use of an actual prison may derive from the fact that Boethius wrote while in prison, and he uses his confinement metaphorically to stand for the human condition. Chaucer's contemporary, Thomas Usk, uses the same device in *The Testament of Love*, a work dating from /119/ 1385–1386, about the time when Chaucer was writing *The Knight's Tale* and *Troilus and Criseyde*.

Near the beginning of the tale Arcite and Palamon are found half dead in a pile of slain warriors outside Thebes and are carried to the tent of Theseus. He arbitrarily sends them to Athens "to dwellen in prisoun / Perpetuelly" (1023–24). From a window in their tower of confinement the two glimpse Emelye and suffer love sickness. Their argument over priority of claim to her threatens the bond of sworn brotherhood between them (1131–51 and 1604), an indication that the breaking of social bonds easily leads to anarchy. Through the arbitrary intervention of a certain Perotheus, Arcite is released and then protests that his figurative prison of exile away from Athens is worse than the actual prison of the tower (1224 and 1244–48). Palamon remains in the prison and complains to the cruel gods who control the world with "byndyng of youre word eterne" (1304). In his view man is little better than an animal cowering "in prison and arreest" (1310). Palamon is a prisoner, not only because of walls, but also because of the bonds that love has laid upon him, a metaphorical way of describing man's condition in the deterministic world of the poem where the actions of the characters are controlled by the gods, or the numinous Theseus.

> In derknesse and horrible and strong prisoun
> Thise seven yeer hath seten Palamoun
> Forpyned, what for wo and for distresse.
> Who feeleth double soor and hevynesse
> But Palamon, that love destreyneth so
> That wood out of his wit he goth for wo?
> And eek therto he is a prisoner
> Perpetuelly, noght oonly for a yer.   (1451-58)

Venus has caught him in her snare (1951), and that is harder to escape than the tower.

Palamon manages to break free from the prison after the seventh year of confinement and flees to a grove near Athens where he meets Arcite. They attempt to resolve their quarrel over Emelye with a duel, but Theseus interrupts their unsupervised battle; he imposes the elaborate rules and order of a tournament /120/ that is to end when either Arcite or Palamon is slain or driven from the lists. Just before the tournament a year later Theseus alters the rules so that the end will come when one or the other is caught and brought to the stake, another example of the way Theseus imposes order by placing those around him under bondage of one sort or another. This bondage is, in fact, a form of order and proceeds from the "Firste Moevere" (2987) through the planets to man on earth. The planetary gods take precedence according to their proximity to the *primum mobile* (Saturn, Jupiter, Mars, Sun, Venus, Mercury, and Moon). Saturn controls the outcome; Mars has his wish granted first and Arcite wins the tournament. Venus has her wish granted next and Palamon wins Emelye; this overrides the wish of Diana, the moon, goddess of maidenhood. Without order, the condition of the world and all the men in it would be anarchy; examples of such chaos in the poem are the absence of funeral rites at Thebes, the argument between Palamon and Arcite, the duel in the forest, and the strife among Diana, Venus, and Mars. In the poem this order takes the form of bonds — prison at the most extreme — and the rationale given by Theseus in his long, eloquent speech at the end of the tale is that order on earth is natural and is linked by a great chain with divine order above.

> The Firste Moevere of the cause above,
> Whan he first made the faire cheyne of love,
> Greet was th'effect, and heigh was his entente.
> Wel wiste he why, and what thereof he mente;

> For with that faire cheyne of love he bond
> The fyr, the eyr, the water, and the lond
> In certeyn boundes, that they may nat flee.   (2987-93)

He goes on to say that Arcite has departed "Out of this foule prisoun of this lyf" (3061) and ends by establishing the bond of wedlock between Palamon and Emelye, "the bond / That highte matrimoigne or mariage" (3094-95). The wedding at the end of the tale recalls the beginning when Theseus returned from the Scythian war in which he captured his enemy Ypolita, queen of the Amazons, and married her, thereby ending the chaos of war with the bond of marriage. As women were thought /121/ to have less capacity for reason than men, the women in the poem are forced to submit to the order decreed by men, Ypolita and Emelye to Theseus, Venus and Diana to Saturn. This submission of women, especially in marriage, is another example in *The Knight's Tale* of imposition of rational order. Clearly the knight gives the opening statement in *The Canterbury Tales* of two major themes of the whole poem, love and order.

Saturn and Theseus are the controlling figures of *The Knight's Tale*, and they impose on others an order associated with divine causation. Theseus before the tournament is described as being "at a wyndow set, / Arrayed right as he were a god in trone" (2528-29), and he presides over the poem with numinous presence imposing order, bonds, and captivity on those subject to him. Saturn also imposes order on those subject to him and says that he is patron of prisons, "Myn is the prison in the derke cote" (2457). One result is that the human condition portrayed in the poem has a dark side to it, because the choice seems to be between freedom and anarchy on the one hand and bondage and order on the other. Chaucer gives the knight a tale with a highly developed sense of order, as is appropriate for a professional soldier, and his tale has a markedly deterministic attitude toward events. As such, it is notably lacking in humour, one of Chaucer's special talents, an absence that reinforces its somber mood. As often, Chaucer's silences are significant, and the absence of laughter in *The Knight's Tale* compared to its presence in *The Miller's Tale* following it makes clear the close connection in Chaucer of comedy and disruption of order.

The word *prisoun* and equivalents such as *cage, cheyn, dongeon, fettre, laas,* and *tour* occur over fifty times in the tale. The specific and repeated statement of the nucleus is as pronounced here as in *The Book of the Duchess*. Actual or figurative bonds form the nucleus of *The Knight's Tale* and establish the theme for what follows. *The Canterbury Tales* are, in effect, a "faire cheyne of love" on the themes of love and order, especially the bond of marriage. When the bonds of order are most evident, as in *The Knight's Tale* or *The Clerk's Tale*, the mood is serious, even somber. Chaucer's comic touch is most evident where these bonds rest lightly and slip, as in *The Wife of Bath's Prologue* or *The Miller's Tale.* /122/

The Miller's Tale concerns *deerne love* (3200) set up by a wild story of chaos imminent in a second flood, and culminating in hilarious disorder. It has an appropriate nucleus: holes, both apertures and pits. The action of the tale involves two levels of *privitee; hende* Nicholas pretends to have knowledge of *Goddes privitee* on order to involve the superstitious carpenter in a far-fetched plot that will enable Nicholas to enjoy Alisoun's *privitee*. Some of the holes are in the carpenter's house, put there, no doubt, by his own gnarled hands. The carpenter's house-boy Robin uses a cat hole to spy on Nicholas whom he discovers gaping upward with open mouth. The carpenter is reminded of another clerk who fell into a *marle-pit* (3460) while star-gazing, yet sees no danger in listening to Nicholas who had, supposedly, been doing the same. He breaks open the door, another of the holes, with the help of Robin. Like the clerk who fell in the *marle-pit*, the old man has a tumble in the night, but his is more humiliating even than the clerk's, for he occupies a pit he has provided himself (cf. Psalm 7.16), the *tubbe* "hangynge in the balkes" (3626), and unintentionally provides a pit for Nicholas who has a somewhat different tumble in the night, finally satisfying his *queynte fantasye*. All this takes place on a Monday night inverting the rites due Diana, goddess of chastity, and mocking the careful astrological orderings of *The Knight's Tale*. Other holes in the tale are human: *yen, nether yen, towtes,* and *mouthes*. They all come together in yet another hole, the *shot-wyndow*, scene of the chaotic climax of the tale. Absolon, whose mouth "hath icched al this longe day" (3682), has his ardent passion quenched by its object, described in one of the many indecorous puns of the tale, "His hoote love was coold and al yqueynt" (3754). To gain revenge, Absolon offers Alisoun a ring, another of the holes in the tale, hoping that she will expose herself a second time so he can brand the offending part with the red-hot iron, but Nicholas incautiously decides that he will "amenden al the jape" (3799) and gets scalded by the glowing plowshare applied "amydde the ers" (3810). His wild cry for water causes the carpenter to axe the rope holding his *tubbe* thinking, "Allas, now comth Nowelis flood" (3818); the old man never gets a chance to use the axe on the gable end to make the one hole he planned for. In sum, *The Miller's Tale* /123/ has an apparent nucleus, holes and the chaotic license that results from their very complex connections. This nucleus is, like the tale itself, a parodying inversion of *The Knight's Tale*; bonds and decorous order of love are turned into holes and wild chaos of licence almost as if Chaucer noticed that every link in the "faire cheyne of love" had a hole in it and wrote two poems as a result, one on the links and the other on the holes. Wild laughter accompanies *The Miller's Tale* in contrast to the unsmiling seriousness of *The Knight's Tale*; order is a grave business.

In Chaucer's poetry order is also a subtle business, because his work resists simplification. *The Parliament of Fowls*, for example, presents a balance of attitudes to love and order without reaching any firm conclusion about the conflicting attitudes. Like much of what Chaucer wrote, this poem presents no single resolving doctrine, a situation too often ignored by the poem's critics.[8] *The Parliament of Fowls* has an appropriate nucleus; it is *place*. In the poem *place* has the senses of area and of degree, both controlled by

> Nature, the vicaire of the almyghty Lord,
> That hot, cold, hevy, lyght, moyst, and dreye
> Hath knyt by evene noumbres of acord.   (379–381)

The *sterry place* (43) in the passage drawn from Macrobius and the walled garden are *places*, "areas" where *place*, "degree," should prevail, although the mortal creatures in the poem do not always follow this order of divine intelligence because of the chaotic promptings of desire engendered by Venus, who also has her *place* in the poem. The word and its variants are repeated over twenty-five times in this short text. Nature can no more enforce degree and order on the classes of birds than the knight can do the same on the other pilgrims. The reverse is true; serious high-mindedness draws out the cries of the worm fowls just as it draws out the drunken Robin to "quite the Knyghtes tale" (3127). /124/

This tendency in Chaucer's poetry to leave conflicting viewpoints unresolved must be kept in mind in discussing any of the texts that are organized about a nucleus so as to avoid reductive interpretations. Indeed, the nucleus itself is usually ambiguous in significance. Each nucleus has a contradiction within itself: the hunting of the *hert* is accomplished when its loss is finally recognized: the *prisoun* of order imposes a restrictive captivity; and the holes of license produce a love that famishes the craving. A nucleus does not, of course, explain everything in a poem where it is found, but it does reinforce from the core the ambiguities present in the whole. Each nucleus has a literal sense, but as the poem develops, each also tends to become invested with metaphoric sense representing the main abstract ideas present.

Here one sees Chaucer as the poet of ideas; he was not a philosopher, and his ideas in abstract statement are commonplace, because so many of them are taken from *The Consolation of Philosophy*, a work of wide influence throughout the Middle Ages. In his imagination, however, these ideas produced a creative reflex in which abstract conceptions took specific form in the nucleus. Perhaps this formation was a carefully worked-out process; more likely, it was the way his imaginative perception instinctively worked. Either way, a nucleus, once identified, provides a very powerful tool for discovering the center and seed of a narrative poem and the way the poet perceived ideas. The nucleus is, of course, very different from the passages of versified ideas inserted into a poem, such as the soliloquy of Troilus on free will and foreknowledge, set down like a lump in Book IV of *Troilus and Criseyde*.

Troilus has an extremely simple and pervasive nucleus, the heart. It is the cause of love and its variable fortune in the poem, thus subsuming both of the main themes. There is a significant difference between the two lover's hearts, however. Troilus has a stable heart, and this steadfastness in love accounts, I think, for his ascent from the mutable love of the world to the stable love of the heavens. Criseyde, on the other hand, is "Tendre-herted, slydynge of corage" (V. 825) and moves to the arms of another man, the "sodeyn Diomede" (V. 1024). References to the heart abound in the poem and are prominent at every /125/ crucial development of the love affair. Owing to the length and complexity of this work, arguably the finest narrative poem in the language, there is need to trace the nucleus in some detail, for it is less obvious than the others discussed above.

In the temple of the Palladion Troilus scoffs at the men in his company whom he suspects of showing signs of love, conduct that betrays his ignorance of the strength of love and its application as a universal bond. He supposes that

> nothing hadde had swich myght
> Ayeyns his wille that shuld his herte stere,
> Yet with a look his herte wax a-fere.   (I. 227–229)

In falling in love he becomes one more example of the power that love has as the binding force of the world (I. 253–259). At the end of Book III Troilus acknowledges this bond in his song in praise of love and its binding force, a passage translated from meter 8 of Book II of *The Consolation of Philosophy* and already noted in connection with *The Knight's Tale*. Love in terms of a bond or knot is also present in *Troilus*, and the discussion of the nucleus of *The Knight's Tale* should be kept in mind here.[9] As Troilus looks about him, his glance penetrates the crowd and falls on Criseyde. "Therwith his herte gan to sprede and rise" (I. 278); a deep and fixed impression of her sticks "in his hertes botme" (I. 297). In Book II he uses the same expression of himself, saying

> so soore hath she me wounded,
> That stood in blak, with lokyng of hire eyen,
> That to myn hertes botme it is ysounded.   (II. 533–535)

The process follows the traditional pattern of "loveris maladye": the "subtile stremes" (I. 305) from Criseyde's eye enter the eye of Troilus, sink to the root of his heart, and cause love, which is regarded as a disease.[10] /126/

> hym thoughte he felte dyen,
> Right with hire look, the spirit in his herte.   (I. 306–307)

This is the first part of the "double sorwe" that Chaucer announces as his subject in the opening line of the poem. The connection between eye and heart is taken further when the narrator states that Troilus' "herte, which that is his brestes ye, / Was ay on hire" (I. 453–454).[11]

Criseyde, so far as the text indicates, is unaware in Book I of the effect she has produced and is not especially concerned with Troilus until Pandare informs her of his friend's love in Book II. The scene at the window follows this news, and Criseyde watches Troilus, who does not notice her, for his eyes are modestly cast down at the acclaim of the people, enthusiastic over his day's achievements against the Greeks in the field.

> Criseÿda gan al his chere aspien,
> And leet it so softe in hire herte synke,
> That to hireself she seyde, "Who yaf me drynke?"
>   (II. 649–651)

/127/ In her the process of love is slower (II. 673–679) than in Troilus, and she is deliberate and cautious before committing herself, unlike him

whose love is a headlong, final plunge from the first. Her measured
reaction may be due to the fact that his eyes with their streams from his
heart are not on hers, and she does not at once suffer lover's sickness as a
sudden onslaught. Her love is also wavering, "Now was hire herte warm,
now was it cold" (II. 698). Her mood shifts back and forth. In this
undecided state she leaves the window (II. 809–812). The vacillation here
is a hint of the variable nature of her heart which leads her, eventually, to
forego Troilus when the circumstances turn against their love.

She goes to her garden and hears Antigone singing a lyric vowing
service to love.

> But I with al myn herte and al my myght.
> As I have seyd, wol love unto my laste,
> My deere herte, and al myn owen knyght,
> In which myn herte growen is so faste.
> And his in me, that it shal evere laste.   (II. 869-873)

These lines make a strong impression on Criseyde; the suggestion of
exchange of hearts is probably what prompts Criseyde's subsequent
dream, for she is acute in picking up hints and then in acting on them. The
development of her awakening love for Troilus is summarized a few lines
later by the narrator.

> But every word which that she of hire herde,
> She gan to prenten in hire herte faste,
> And ay gan love hire lasse for t'agaste
> Than it dide erst, and synken in hire herte,
> That she wex somewhat able to converte.   (II. 899-903)

The dream of the eagle that changes hearts with her is a particularly vivid
and specific manifestation of the nucleus, and it further inclines her to
love Troilus.

> And as she slep, anonright tho hire mette
> How that an egle, fethered whit as bon,
> Under hire brest his longe clawes sette,   /128/
> And out hire herte he rente, and that anon,
> And dide his herte into hire brest to gon,
> Of which she nought agroos, ne nothyng smerte;
> And forth he fleigh, with herte left for herte. (II. 925-931)

Here the exchange of hearts happens in a dream in which the white eagle stands for Troilus. In Book III the exchange is carried out symbolically, a token of the deep love that has by then developed between the pair. A similar symbolic exchange accounts for the *hert-huntyng* of *The Book of the Duchess* and is so important to Chaucer's poetic treatment of love that some discussion of it is necessary here, but is best left to the end.

In Book II the development of Criseyde's love is described in terms of her heart; and we see how it arises, less from Pandare's urgings than from a series of chance circumstances: the glimpse of Troilus from her window, Antigone's song, and the dream of the eagle. One characteristic of this development is her wavering attitude, which is particularly clear as she debates with herself over sixteen stanzas beginning at II. 694. She balances a growing emotional involvement with Troilus against her own circumstances in Troy, the same process that afterward characterizes her waning love for Troilus and her growing involvement with Diomede in the Greek camp.

Book III begins with the meeting of Troilus and Criseyde at the house of Deiphebus. The first words that Troilus utters directly to Criseyde are "Ye, swete herte?" (III. 69), and this is the form of address he uses for her, with a few exceptions, throughout the poem.[12] He calls her *swete herte, dere herte,* or simply *herte* thirteen times and refers to her the same way, when she is absent, ten more times. Eight of these references or apostrophes to his absent lady are in Book V. The last time he addresses her is at the end of his letter, "And far now wel, myn owen swete herte" (V. 1421); his final words of address to her are thus the same as his first. Surprisingly enough, Criseyde uses the word *herte* in addressing Troilus, or referring to him, even /129/ more frequently. There are thirty-four instances, all of them in Books III and IV. The only example in Book V is at line 1189 where Troilus quotes Criseyde's promise to return, a promise that includes her words to him, "O deere herte swete." The fact that Criseyde in the Greek camp never refers to Troilus with the word *herte* bears out the change taking place in her love for him and reveals the deftness of Chaucer's control of dialogue; here, as elsewhere, his silences are significant.

After the evening at the house of Deiphebus, the love sickness of Troilus improves.

> His olde wo, that made his herte swelte,
> Gan tho for joie wasten and tomelte.   (III. 347-348)

He is compared by the narrator to "thise holtes and thise hayis" (III. 351) that are dead and dry in winter only to reclothe themselves in green when May returns. In the same way "wax sodeynliche his herte ful of joie" (III. 356).

In the consummation scene during the "smoky reyn" (III. 628) the two lovers refer to their hearts repeatedly. Pandare tells Criseyde that Troilus, who is supposedly out of Troy, has suddenly arrived because he has heard a report that Criseyde has taken a lover named Horaste. This unworthy device is ironic; what is here a complete fabrication becomes fact in the Greek camp afterward. Her gentle rebuke of Troilus for mistrusting her strikes home since he knows she is guiltless and he feels death's cramp creep "aboute his herte" (III. 1069). The lovers are soon accorded, and Criseyde opens "hire herte, and tolde hym hire entente" (III. 1239). Later she pins to his nightshirt a brooch of gold and azure in which a ruby "set was lik an herte" (III. 1371), a symbolic gift of her heart to Troilus and a gift he cherishes faithfully. The two lovers make their farewells as the day approaches. Troilus protests that he feels his heart break in two (III. 1475) and wishes that he were certain that he is as firmly set in her heart as she is in his (III. 1486-89). Her reply is one of the few places where she abandons her usual circumspection and says that natural order /130/ will be disrupted "er Troilus out of Criseydes herte" (III. 1498) will move, because he is "so depe in-with myn herte grave" (III. 1499).

The book ends with the two in a state of temporary joy. Criseyde is firmly knotted in the heart of Troilus (III. 1730-36); his subsequent song in praise of love as a universal bond has already been noted, but the last of the four stanzas of this song is worth quoting here.

> So wolde God, that auctour is of kynde,
> That with his bond Love of his vertu liste
> To cerclen hertes alle, and faste bynde,
> That from his bond no wight the wey out wiste;
> And hertes colde, hem wolde I that he twiste
> To make hem love, and that hem liste ay rewe
> On hertes sore, and kepe hem that ben trewe! (III. 1765-71)

The emphasis on *hertes* is Chaucer's addition to the original, which mentions *animos* but once.

> O felix hominum genus,

si uestros animos amor
quo caelum regitur regat![13]

In his *Boece* Chaucer is more literal with the passage and renders *uestros animos* as "yowr corages" (II, metrum 8, 26). The added emphasis on *herte* in the song indicates that Troilus regards his love as part of the ordering bond of universal love; the song also bears out the invocation in the Prologue of Book III to the planet Venus and her universal power in love. The third book ends quietly with the lovers together.

> And Troilus in lust and in quiete
> Is with Criseyde, his owen herte swete.   (III. 1819-20)

/131/ The ideas in the third book are related to those in *The Knight's Tale*, and comparison of the two is instructive, because the bond of love in *Troilus* also has a dark aspect; Troy is a besieged city, and the Trojans "alle and some/In prisoun ben," as Diomede in later days cruelly points out to Criseyde (V. 883-884), a situation brought about in the first instance by the love of Paris for Helen and the harsh consequences for all concerned.

Bondage in *Troilus* is the subject of an admirable paper by Stephen A. Barney,[14] who shows that there are three types of bondage evident throughout the poem. The first type is the bondage of the world controlled by fortune, who binds all creation to her mutable wheel; this category includes the Boethian ideas of order coming from the stars, "the faire cheyne of love" discussed as the nucleus of *The Knight's Tale*. Second is the bond of earthly love, in literal language, the attracive net of sexuality. Third is the snare of sin and, ultimately, of the devil. The heart is involved in all three types of bondage, for the heart is what is caught, whether by the world that leads it to the devil or by the woman who may do the same, although the woman may also lead the heart to God, as happens to Troilus.

Including three variant readings — which might well be accepted on the basis of the present discussion — there are ninety-six uses of the words *herte* or *hertes* in Book III alone. The concentration and substantial use of the term at each crucial stage of the action are here, as in Books I and II, significant. Although only a fraction of the instances in the first three books has been discussed, the evidence indicates that the nucleus of the poem is the heart.

Book IV adds further evidence, but it can be presented briefly. Here the second sorrow of Troilus begins when the Trojan parliament agrees to

exchange Criseyde for Antenor. Troilus is compared to a wild bull
"idarted to the herte" (IV. 240). His eye stream like wells "for piete of
herte" (IV. 246), and his heart is twisted and vexed with torment. He
beseeches his soul to "fle forth out of myn herte" (IV. 306) to follow
Criseyde, /132/ and he prays that she will receive it when "myn herte
dieth" (IV. 319).

On hearing the news of the exchange, Criseyde is, as usual with her,
afraid, but her heart remains firmly fixed on Troilus.

> As she that hadde hire herte and al hire mynde
> On Troilus iset so wonder faste,
> That al this world ne myghte hire love unbynde.
> Ne Troilus out of hire herte caste,
> She wol ben his, while that hire lif may laste. (IV. 673–677)

So long as she remains with Troilus she is steadfast. She ends her
soliloquizing complaint by wondering how the "tendre herte" (IV. 795)
of Troilus will sustain her departure.

Pandare comes to visit her and suggests (IV. 935) that she might be
able to return immediately after she has gone; from this hint she
formulates her plan to return in ten days. Pandare goes to Troilus and
says that she

> Hath somwhat in hire hertes privete,
> Wherwith she kan, if I shal right arede,
> Destourbe al this of which thow art in drede. (IV. 1111–13)

Her "hertes privete" does indeed bring Troilus out of his distress, but in a
way very different from what Pandare supposes as he speaks. Her heart
changes and leads to the death of Troilus. The narrator says that her plan
was made in good intent and that her heart was faithful (IV. 1417) when
she spoke. Troilus hears the plan "with herte and erys spradde" (IV.
1422), but is loath to let her go.

> His herte mysforyaf hym evere mo.
> But fynaly, he gan his herte wreste
> To trusten hire, and took it for the beste.   (IV. 1426–28)

He agrees to her plan, but continues to have misgivings in his heart (IV.
1518-19), which prompts him to steal away with her. /133/ The fourth

book ends as they make their last private farewell, very different from the joyous end of the third book. The difference, as might by now be expected, is specifically stated in terms of his heart.

> For whan he saugh that she ne myghte dwelle.
> Which that his soule out of his herte rente.
> Withouten more, out of the chaumbre he wente. (IV. 1699–1701)

In the fifth book Criseyde departs, escorted by Diomede, who woos her with practiced and cynical swiftness, the competitive urgency of an army-camp seduction. He does not suffer lover's malady; he merely sets about winning her with what seems like complete emotional detachment. His calculating smoothness is a complete contrast to the spontaneous blundering of Troilus in the first part of the poem. He speaks about his heart twice to Criseyde (V. 138 and 156), but there is little evidence that his words reflect any true bond of love in his heart. The only metaphoric knots he ties are to a fish hook or in a net to catch Criseyde.

> This Diomede, of whom yow telle I gan,
> Goth now withinne hymself ay arguynge
> With al the sleghte, and al that evere he kan,
> How he may best, with shortest taryinge,
> Into his net Criseydes herte brynge.
> To this entent he koude nevere fyne;
> To fisshen hire, he leyde out hook and lyne.   (V. 771–777)

For Diomede the bond of love is not the great chain of being, but merely a snare for catching delicacies.

Troilus, meanwhile, suffers real affliction at heart; the contrast between the two men is reinforced by this difference. After Criseyde's exchange, he returns to his palace "with a swollen herte" (V. 201) and turns on his bed like Ixion on the wheel. Although weeping assuages his heart a bit (V. 214–215), he laments that he is dying. /134/

> O herte myn, Criseyde, O swete fo!
> O lady myn, that I love and na mo!
> To whom for evermo myn herte I dowe,
> Se how I dey, ye nyl me nat rescowe!   (V. 228–231)

He suffers a tremor "about his herte" (V. 255) and is so full of despair that he gives Pandare instructions for his funeral pyre. He asks that the ashes of his heart be sent in a golden urn to Criseyde (V. 309–315); this gesture, if carried out, would actualize the metaphoric gift of his heart often alluded to earlier in the poem. His thoughts and love are all on her.

> For evere in oon his herte pietous
> Ful bisyly Criseyde, his lady, soughte.
> On hire was evere al that his herte thoughte. (V. 451–453)

He suffers continuing affliction in his heart; for example, when he visits the barred palace of Criseyde, "Hym thoughte his sorwful herte braste a-two" (V. 530) and "his herte gan to colde" (V. 535).

Although Criseyde worries about Troilus, her heart is so filled with fear that she is paralyzed, caught between desire to return to Troy and fear of exposing herself in the attempt. Her situation in the Greek camp is the reverse of what it was in Troy, and circumstances turn her away from Troilus, not toward him. Within two months her heart has let her love for Troilus slide away: "bothe Troilus and Troie town / Shal knotteles thorughout hire herte slide" (V. 768–769). This reference is to the bond of love which should be knit and tied in her heart. A few lines later she is described as "Tendre-herted, slydynge of corage" (V. 825); the sense is that her heart is too weak and soft to stand adverse circumstances and lets slip the bond of love. She is sliding of heart and does not keep the knot of love knit tight. The knot in the heart, without its sexual implications, was borrowed from *Troilus and Criseyde* by Thomas Usk and used in his *Testament of Love* as the central metaphor for stable, binding love. /135/

Diomede keeps up his insistence that she let her circumstances rule her heart. She yields to his influence and begins to adapt her emotions to her new situation. At lines 953–954 she is said to have "hire herte on Troilus / So faste, that ther may it non arace." Yet in the speech that follows she denies to Diomede ever having loved anyone but her husband, already dead when the poem starts.

> "I hadde a lord, to whom I wedded was,
> The whos myn herte al was, til that he deyde;
> And other love, as help me now Pallas,
> Ther in myn herte nys, ne nevere was."   (V. 975–978)

The narrator disclaims knowledge of whether or not she gave her heart to Diomede (V. 1050), but she does vow to be true to him, "To Diomede algate I wol be trewe" (V. 1071); this vow seems based on a more superficial love than she had for Troilus and is even less likely to be one she can keep. Certainly in the literary tradition subsequent to Chaucer she becomes regarded as a wavering woman, loose in the bonds of love, a view taken of her, for example, by Ulysses in Shakespeare's *Troilus and Cressida*.

> Fie, fie upon her!
> There's language in her eye, her cheek, her lip;
> Nay, her foot speaks. Her wanton spirits look out
> At every joint and motive of her body.[15]

On the last day of the period in which Criseyde promised to return to Troy she talks with Diomede and agrees to see him again the next day, the eleventh, thereby effectively abandoning any real plan to go back to Troy.

Throughout the period of waiting the faithful Troilus is torn between hope and dread. "Bitwixen hope and drede his herte lay" (V. 1207; cf. V. 1102 and 1118). His affliction grows worse when she does not keep her promise. /136/

> His hope al clene out of his herte fledde;
> He nath wheron now lenger for to honge;
> But for the peyne hym thoughte his herte bledde.
> (V. 1198–1200)

As time goes on he realizes that she will not return as she had promised. His disability is obvious to all, for he is thin, pale, and so feeble that he walks with a crutch; *loveris maladye* has beset him again. Whenever asked about his sickness, he says that "his harm was al aboute his herte" (V. 1225) and that "he felte a grevous maladie / Aboute his herte, and fayn he wolde dye" (V. 1231–32). His dream of the boar which embraces Criseyde makes him so fear that she has turned her heart elsewhere that he writes her a letter filled with references to their hearts. He ends the letter "And far now wel, myn owen swete herte" (V. 1421). As noted earlier, his last words of direct address to her are the same as his first in Book III. Cassandra interprets the dream correctly, adding a bit of information that the narrator claimed not to know, "This Diomede hire herte hath, and she his" (V. 1517).

Troilus returns vindictively to war, but his heart is firmly fixed on Criseyde (V. 1571). His remaining slight hope is finally dashed when he sees on a coat taken from Diomede in battle the same pin he had given Criseyde the morning she left Troy. This discovery convinces him at last of her "hertes variaunce" (V. 1670), and yet he remains true to her, exclaiming to the absent Criseyde that he cannot "withinne myn herte fynde / To unloven yow a quarter of a day" (V. 1697–98). He dies in battle, and his soul ascends into the heaven; he gets what he freely chose, enduring and stable love, but not where he looked for it with Criseyde. From on high his spirit laughs at those who weep at his death and, if I understand the difficult syntax correctly, urges that all ought "oure herte on heven caste" (V. 1825). The presence of the nucleus in the epilogue reinforces the now general view that it is an integral part of the poem, not a loosely attached palinode. The point is that the heart, as seat of love, should be fixed on Christ "For he nyl falsen no wight, dar I seye, / That wol his herte al holly on hym leye" (V. 1845–46). /137/ The same point is made in more poetic language in the famous stanza just before.

> O yonge, fresshe folkes, he or she,
> In which that love up groweth with youre age,
> Repeyreth hom fro worldly vanyte,
> And of youre herte up casteth the visage
> To thilke God that after his ymage
> Yow made, and thynketh al nys but a faire
> This world, that passeth soone as floures faire.
>
> (V. 1835–41)

The "visage" "of youre herte" recalls the reference in the first book to the heart as the "brestes ye."

There are repeated, specific textual references that show how the heart is the nucleus of *Troilus and Criseyde* and controls the main narrative development of the poem. The word is so ordinary that readers miss its pervasive force and frequency in the text; first reaction to the data, once they are presented and analyzed, tends to be surprise. The analysis here is incomplete, because less than half the more than 350 occurrences of the word are discussed. The significance of this nucleus is clear, nevertheless. The heart is source and seat of love and makes man subject to love's universal bond. Since earthly love is imperfect, love's bond may, for a time, be mocked, as Troilus mocks, or it may allow for some sliding, as Criseyde slides. The self-absorbed Troilus mocks what he does not understand, and for a time he suffers unrequited love for Criseyde; this is his first sorrow. She loves him for a time, but her sliding heart lets slip the bond. Again he suffers unrequited love for Criseyde; this is his second sorrow. He dies, and his soul ascends to the stable love of the heavens. In the process sorrow is revealed as a means to higher love, as the narrator observed, "sondry peynes bryngen folk to hevene" (III. 1204), both worldly and divine. The poem shows the continuity as well as the progression from worldly to divine love, a progression not unlike the one presented in *The Divine Comedy*, if less explicit and systematic in the English poem than in the Italian. /138/

Chaucer's use of the heart and chain as nucleus metaphors for love and order belongs to long-existing literary traditions. Lovejoy's classic study, already cited, is a systematic history of the idea of the chain as a metaphor for order and degree. There is no equivalent single work on the heart as the seat of love, but enough studies have been written to make clear the long history of the idea.[16] One aspect of this tradition does need some attention here, the tradition of the movable heart exchanged in love.

The exchange of hearts is implicit in the *hert-huntyng* of *The Book of the Duchess* and explicit in *Troilus and Criseyde*. Not surprisingly, the idea of a movable heart occurs in religious writing long before the rise of aristocratic love poetry. An example is a passage in a homily by Gregory the Great on the Ascension.

> Unde, fratres charissimi, oportet ut illuc sequamur corde, ubi
> eum corpore ascendisse credimus.[17] /139/

The actual exchange of hearts with Christ can be found in saints' lives, notably in that of Catherine of Siena, whose experience of 1370 is recounted in considerable detail by her contemporary biographer, Raymond of Capua. Christ appeared to her while she prayed, and he removed her heart; she reported the event to her confessor, who merely laughed. She maintained her story, however, and several days later as she finished praying and was emerging from an abstracted meditation, Christ reappeared to her, holding a radiant heart in his hands; he opened her left side again and inserted the heart, telling her that he had given her his own heart which she had prayed to have. Christ then healed her side, but an elongated scar remained as a visible token, afterward seen by many, of the exchange.[18] Exchanges of hearts recounted in medieval literature either have such miraculous aspects of divine intervention or else they are metaphors; there seems to be no indication in medical literature of the period that the heart, like the womb, could move.[19]

As so often happened in the Middle Ages, the religious tradition /140/

of the exchange of hearts in divine love has parallels in profane love. Sometimes the religious aspects are explicit, such as those evident in *Troilus and Criseyde*. In the first book Troilus prays to the god of love and remarks that he does not know whether Criseyde is a goddess or a woman, a confusion also apparent in Palamon's reactions to Emelye in *The Knight's Tale*; the religious vows that Troilus makes in the consummation scene (III. 1254ff.) and his apostrophe to Criseyde's empty palace as a "shryne, of which the seynt is oute" (V. 553) are other examples, and the list could be extended. Sometimes the religious aspects are only implied, and the exchange itself indicates a religious devotion in love and the deep bond existing between the man and the woman, especially when they are forced by circumstances to conceal their love or must spend much of the time apart. A familiar example occurs in Chrétien's *Lancelot* when the knight must leave Guenievere after spending the night with her in Meleagant's castle.

> Au lever fu il droiz martirs,
> tant li fu griés li departirs,
> car il i suefre grant martire.
> Ses cuers adés cele part tire
> ou la reïne se remaint.
> N'a pooir que il l'an remaint,
> que la reïne tant li plest
> qu'il n'a talant que il la lest:
> li cors s'an vet, li cuers sejorne.[20]

> It cost him such pain to leave her that he suffered a real martyr's agony. His heart now stays where the queen remains; he has not the power to lead it away, for it finds such pleasure in the queen /141/ that it has no desire to leave her: so his body goes and his heart remains.

An extended treatment of the motif of the exchange of hearts occurs in a work of the fifteenth century, *Le Livre du cueur d'amour espris*, written about 1457 by King René d'Anjou, an allegorical prose account of love interspersed with verse and written in the tradition of the first part of *Le Roman de la Rose*.[21] The exchange of hearts also occurs in more than one fabliau, an indication that the motif was well enough known to make its cynical employment an amusing parody.[22]

Chaucer's use of the heart as the nucleus of a poem about human love, its mutability, and its capacity to lead to divine love thus has historical probability. Both the narrative and the nucleus of *Troilus and Criseyde* are drawn from well-established literary traditions of great antiquity; Chaucer does not so much invent his material as reimagine it. With characteristic economy of means Chaucer put a traditional metaphor at the core of his poem and thereby transformed complex, abstract ideas about love and its relative stability into a nucleus that is so apt and simple that it has remained all but invisible to readers despite its appearance, often in repeated statement, at every crucial turn in the narrative.

In Chaucer's immediate source, *Il Filostrato*, the heart is mainly mentioned in casual references to inner thought or in connection with the affliction of love sickness. There are, however, three times where Troilo refers to Criseida as *cor del corpo mio*, "heart of my body," and two times where Criseida refers /142/ to him the same way.[23] This expression implies the exchange of hearts, a motif explicit only in Troilo's dream of Criseida and the boar.

> E poi appresso gli parve vedere
>   Sotto a'suoi piè Criseida, alla quale
>   Col grifo il cor traeva, ed al parere
>   Di lui, Criseida di così gran male
>   Non si curava, ma quasi piacere
>   Prendea di ciò che faces l'animale.   (VII. 24)

And then afterward it seemed to him that he saw
beneath its feet Cressida, whose heart it tore
forth with its snout. And as it seemed, little
cared Cressida for so great a hurt, but almost
did she take pleasure in what the beast was
doing.

In Chaucer's poem Troilus dreams that Criseyde lies with a boar, but no mention is made of losing her heart. Chaucer uses the motif in Criseyde's dream of the eagle, an episode which is not in *Il Filostrato*. This shift seems to indicate that the episode in *Il Filostrato* provided Chaucer with a hint for his treatment of the heart. Certainly, the shift from animal to bird is indicative of the delicacy of Chaucer's poem in contrast to the vivid sensuality of his source, evident here.

If the hint came from *Il Filostrato*, sustained use of the heart as the nucleus of *Troilus and Criseyde* may be explained by Geoffrey of Vinsauf's advice near the beginning of his *Poetria Nova* on how to start a poem, a passage Chaucer repeated at the end of Book I of *Troilus*. /143/

> For everi wight that hath an hous to founde
> Ne renneth naught the werk for to bygynne
> With rakel hond, but he wol bide a stounde,
> And sende his hertes line out fro withinne
> Aldirfirst his purpos for to wynne.
>
> (I. 1065–69)[24]

The Latin phrase translated in line 1068 is *intrinseca linea cordis*, which applies the heart and the bond to the initial act of writing poetry. The suggestion made earlier that *The Canterbury Tales* form a "faire cheyne of love" may have a basis in poetic theory known to Chaucer. If so, the links of *The Canterbury Tales* appear more aptly named than might be thought. The extent of this specific debt to the *Poetria Nova* must not be pressed, however. *The Consolation of Philosophy* has so many passages on order described in terms of bonds and *The Romance of the Rose* sufficient passages on love described in terms of the heart that one need look no further for Chaucer's source of the heart and the chain as organizing metaphors for love and order than in those two works which he translated, works that influenced him profoundly throughout his entire poetic career from first to last.

Chaucer's use of a poetic nucleus illustrates a medieval literary theory that is of more significance than the few lines from the *Poetria Nova*. The heart as nucleus of a poem about love and its variance and the chain as nucleus of a poem about order and its confinement are significant instances of a medieval attitude toward poetic language in which key metaphors such as these were apprehended as we would apprehend abstract statement; the metaphor of the chain would thus be thought to have the same literal truth about the organization of the cosmos that we would find in abstract statements about order and degree. This attitude toward poetic language is the subject of an important paper by Judson B. Allen. Using evidence from medieval /144/ *accessus*, especially those on hymn collections dating from Hilarius in the twelfth century to Johannes Baptista Cantalycius in the fifteenth, Allen presents evidence that in late medieval poetic theory, the transfer of meaning inherent in metaphor was thought of as the literal truth, because the cosmos "was already, in modern terms, so poetic that there was no need to claim for the poet greater powers than those of an honest reporter."[25] The chain of order and the heart of love were as real to the medieval mind as, for example, were the crystalline spheres of the Ptolemaic universe, which are only metaphoric to us. The analysis here presents independent support and illustration for Allen's analysis by showing that what he suggests about poetic theory can be documented with extensive citation from several works of one of the major philosophical poets of the late medieval period. Chaucer has long been recognized as a philosophical poet, but the centrality of philosophical thought in his poetry has not been grasped, because the essence of his thought has been expressed in the highly creative form of a poetic nucleus. The modern separation of poetic language into concrete and abstract vocabulary is misleading in Chaucer's poetry because of the way that the poetic nucleus is given abstract significance even as it continues to be concrete.

Use of a nucleus in a long text may be a fairly rare occurence and is difficult to detect in a poem of any considerable complexity.[26] Once found, however, a nucleus can provide a lucid /145/ perception "of a work's centre, the source of its life in all its parts, and response to its total movement" which is Helen Gardner's lucid definition of the purpose of critical actvity.[27] The molecular cohesion and focus of the work are, so to speak, apprehended from within, and the reader's basic experience of the text alters as a result. An apprehension of the functions of the heart and the chain in Chaucer's poetry provides a new perspective on familiar material as when the city dweller, long used to a night sky hazy with reflected artificial light, goes into the country and sees, as if with new eyes, the stars come out in the evening sky until the dark is full of light.

Notes

1. The English word nucleus has been used as a critical term before. John Press, writing of Valéry, says that he "once admitted that sometimes God give him a line of poetry and that this single line was enough, for, having been granted a nucleus, he could then proceed to construct his flawless architectural patterns" *The Fire and the Fountain* (London: Methuen, 1966). p. 3. I am indebted to my colleague, R. A. Greene, for this reference.

2. All quotations are from *The Works of Geoffrey Chaucer*, ed. F. N. Robinson, 2nd ed. (Boston: Houghton Mifflin, 1957). Line references are to this edition.

3. The black and white imagery of the poem develops from the death in September 1369 of Blaunch, or White, as she is called in the poem, as a result of black plague. This black and white contrast occurs several times in the poem, for example, in the dark forest and the white-walled castle at the end. The point is not to be pressed, however, because black death is a post-medieval term.

4. A similar interpretation is made by Joseph E. Grennen, *"Hert-huntyng* in the *Book of the Duchess," Modern Language Quarterly*, 25 (1964), 131–139. The game of hunting is one of several connected games in the poem, such as the game of chess with fortune, ll. 617ff., and, less evidently, the game of love itself. Similar interlocking games of love and hunting occur in *Sir Gawain and the Green Knight* in which various games, complexly related to each other, form the nucleus of the poem. See John Leyerle, "The Game and Play of the Hero," in *Concepts of the Hero in the Middle Ages and the Renaissance*, ed. Norman T. Burns and Christopher Reagan (Albany, N.Y.: State University of New York Press, 1975), pp.49–82.

5. The English word checkmate is derived, by way of Old French, from the Arabic, *al-shah mat*, "the king is dead." In Middle English usage, the word appears in collocations with death; see the relevant citations in the *Middle English Dictionary* under *chek-mat*, 2 (a).

6. The colon in l. 1153 here is my substitution for the semicolon printed by Robinson, because the second part of the expression explains the first as may be seen in the source for the passage: "Il est assez sires dou cors / Qui a le cuer en sa comande" (1996–97), Guillaume de Lorris, *Le Roman de la Rose*, ed. Ernest Langlois, Société des Anciens Textes Français (Paris: Firmin-Didot, 1914–1924), II, 103. Compare the *Romaunt* version: "For of the body he is full lord / That hath the herte in his tresor" (2084–85).

7. See Arthur O. Lovejoy, *The Great Chain of Being* (Cambridge, Mass.: Harvard University Press, 1936).

8. An important exception is the book by J. A. W. Bennett, *The Parlement of Foules* (Oxford: Clarendon Press, 1957), which presents the complex intellectual and literary traditions behind the poem, not one particular reading of it.

9. In *The Parliament of Fowls* love is twice described in terms of a knot, ll. 435-438 and 624-628.

10. The standard study remains John Livingston Lowes, "The Loveres Maladye of Hereos," *Modern Philology*, 11 (1913-14), 491-546. Lowes is mainly concerned with the medical doctrine behind the lines of *The Knight's Tale*, which, like so much else in the poem, is directly relevant to *Troilus*. A late, but clear, statement of the process occurs in Book III of Castiglione's *Il Libro del Cortegiano*. See *The Book of the Courtier*, trans. Sir Thomas Hoby, intro. W. H. D. Rouse (London: Dent, 1928), pp. 246-247.

11. The idea that the heart was the eye of the breast, or that the heart itself had eyes, is interesting because of the explicit connection of vision with the seat of love. The heart is often reported in Middle English texts to have eyes; see the relevant citations in the *MED* under *eie*. The usage is traditional and is common in the fathers. It occurs, for example, in Jerome's commentary on Isaiah: "Istos cordis oculos et sponsa habebat in Cantico canticorum, cui sponsus dixit: *Vulnerasti cor meum, soror mea sponsa, uno ex oculis tuis,"* S. *Hieronymi Presbyteri Opera*, Pars 2, *Commentariorum in Esaiam Libri I—XI*, Corpus Christianorum, Series Latina, vol. 73 (Turnholt: Brepols, 1963), Book I. 1, ll. 42-45, p. 6. The verse from the Song of Songs, 4:9, may be the most important single source for the idea of love as a wound in the heart inflicted by the eyes of the beloved. References to *oculi cordis* are common in Augustine; see, for example, *Sermo* 159 (Caput 3.3) *Patrologia Latina*, ed. J. P. Migne, 38, col. 869, *Sermo* 286 (Caput 8.6) *PL* 38, col. 1300, *Epistola* 147 (Caput 17.41), the famous *De Vivendo Deo, PL* 33, col. 615, and other references given in the index to Augustine in *PL* 46, cols. 469-470.

12. The constant address of Troilus by Criseyde as *herte* is noted by Sanford B. Meech,

Design in Chaucer's Troilus (Syracuse, N. Y.: Syracuse University Press, 1959), pp. 315-316.

13. *Philosophiae consolatio*, ed. Ludwig Bieler, Corpus Christianorum, Series Latina, 94 (Turnholt: Brepols, 1957), II, metrum 8, ll. 28-30, p. 36.

14. "Troilus Bound," *Speculum*, 47 (1972), 445-458. Relevant studies are cited there; of particular interest is Pierre Courcelle, "Tradition platonicienne et traditions chrétiennes du corps-prison (Phédon 62b; Cratyle 400c)," *Revue des Etudes Latines*, 43 (1966 for 1965), 406-443.

15. *The Complete Works of Shakespeare*, ed. George Lyman Kittredge (Boston: Ginn, [1936]), IV. v. 54-57, p. 911.

16. Of particular help are two long papers by Xenja von Ertzdorff, "Das Herz in der lateinisch-theologischen und frühen volkssprachigen religiösen Literatur." *Beiträge zur Geschichte der deutsche Sprache und Literatur*, 84 (1962), 249-301, and "Die Dame im Herzen und das Herz bei der Dame. Zur Verwendung des Begriffs, Herz in der höfischen Liebeslyrik des 11. und 12. Jahrhunderts," *Zeitschrift für deutsche Philologie*, 84 (1965), 6—46. Von Ertzdorff traces the literary use of the heart from the Bible through the fathers up to the high Middle Ages. The apparatus provides useful bibliographical information. I am indebted to Prof. James Rochester Shaw of the University of Rochester for these references and helpful advice on medieval medical views on the heart.

17. Sermon 29, In Ascensione Domini, *PL* 76, col. 1219. This passage is the source for Cynewulf's *Christ II*, lines 751-755:

	Is us þearf micel
þaet we mid heortan	hælo secen,
þaer we mid gaeste	georne gelyfaδ
þæt þaet hælobearn	heonan up stige
mid usse lichoman,	lifgende god.

The Exeter Book, ed. George Philip Krapp and Elliott van Kirk Dobbie (New York: Columbia University Press, 1936), p. 24. For a discussion of this connection, see Colin Chase, "God's Presence through grace as the theme of Cynewulf's *Christ II* and the relationship of this theme to *Christ I* and *Christ III*," *Anglo-Saxon England*, 3 (1974), 87–101.

18. The material is discussed by Pierre Debongnie, "Commencement et recommence-ments de la dévotion du coeur de Jesus," in *Le Coeur*, Les Etudes carmélitaines, 29 (1950), 147-192. For the text of the story, see *Acta Sanctorum Aprilis*, ed. J. Carnandet (Paris: Victor Palmé, 1866), III, 907. The feast day of St. Catherine is April 30; the account of her exchange of hearts with Christ is in Part II of her *Vita*, chap. 6, secs. 178-180. See also Jean Leclercq, O. S. B., "Le Sacré-Coeur dans la tradition bénédictine au moyen âge," in *Cor Jesu*, ed. Augustinus Bea, S. J., Hugo Rahner, S. J., Henri Rondet, S. J., and Friedrich Schwendemann, S. J. (Rome: Casa Editrice Herder, [1959]), II. 3-28. Other papers in this collection are also of interest to the subject here.

19. Alfredus Anglicus, for example, in his tract *De Motu Cordis*, written about 1210, reflects medical opinions then current and ultimately derived from Galen; he has nothing whatever about a shift or transfer of the heart; *Des Alfred von Sareshel (Alfredus Anglicus) Schrift De Motu Cordis*, ed. Clemens Baeumker, Beiträge zur Geschichte der Philosophie des Mittelalters, 23 (Münster: Verlag der aschendorffschen Verlagsbuchhandlung, 1923). See also James Otte, "The Life and Writings of Alfredus Anglicus," *Viator*, 3 (1972). Nor

does "the cursed monk, daun Constantyn" (*CT*, IV. 1810) allude to any exchange of hearts; see Paul Delany, "Constantinus Africanus' *De Coitu*: A Translation," *The Chaucer Review*, 4 (1969), 55-65. For medieval medical opinion on the movable womb, see Vern L. Bullough, "Medieval Medical and Scientific Views of Women," in *Marriage in the Middle Ages*, ed. John Leyerle, *Viator*, 4 (1973) pp. 485-501.

20. *Les Romans de Chrétien de Troyes*, vol. III: *Le Chevalier de la Charrete*, ed. Mario Roques, Les Classiques Français du Moyen Age, 86 (Paris: Honoré Champion, 1958), ll. 4689-97. The translation is from Chrétien de Troyes, *Arthurian Romances*, trans. W. W. Comfort (London: J. M. Dent, 1914), 329. The motif also occurs in Chrétien's *Yvain* (ll. 2635ff.) and, from there, in Hartmann von Aue's *Iwein*. For other examples of the exchange of hearts, see *La Mort le Roi Artu*, ed. Jean Frappier, 10th ed. (Geneva: Droz, 1956), p. 35, and Juan Ruiz, *Libro de Buen Amor*, ed. and trans. Raymond S. Willis (Princeton: Princeton Univ. Press, [1972]), stanzas 209ff.

21. For a miniature illustrating this text showing Amour entrusting the heart of the sleeping king to Vif-desir, see Germain Bazin. "En quête du sentiment courtois," in *Le Coeur*, Les Etudes carmélitaines, 29 (1950), 129-146, pl. 1 facing p. 138. Bazin also gives three other plates of late medieval/early renaissance illustrations of the exchange of hearts, or the offer to make such an exchange. In Jeanine Moulin, *Christine de Pisan* (Paris: Seghers, [1962]), the plate facing p. 113 shows Venus, in a circle of stars, collecting hearts in her skirt held up to form a lap; her votaries, both men and women, offer to her their hearts which they hold in the hand.

22. For example, see *Fabliaux: Ribald Tales from the Old French*, trans. Robert Hellman and Richard O'Gorman (New York: Thomas Y. Crowell, [1965]), pp. 137 and 148-149. One of these fabliaux is by Rutebeuf and the other by Gautier le Leu.

23. *The Filostrato of Giovanni Boccaccio: A Translation with Parallel Text*, Nathaniel Edward Griffin and Arthur Beckwith Myrick (Philadelphia: University of Pennsylvania Press, 1929); the expression occurs in the following stanzas: III. 50, IV. 90 and 145, V. 25 and 59. The *cor/corpus* trope in love poetry is found widely in romance languages and may be no more than an ornament arising from the verbal closeness of the words.

24. For the Latin text see Edmond Faral, *Les arts poétiques du XIIe et du XIIIe siècle* (Paris: E. Champion, 1924), 198: "Si quis habet fundare domum, non currit ad actum/Impetuosa manus: intrinseca linea cordis/Praemetitur opus . . . . " A useful English version is *Poetria Nova of Goeffrey of Vinsauf*, trans. Margaret F. Nims (Toronto: Pontifical Institute of Mediaeval Studies, 1967).

25. "Commentary as Criticism: Formal Cause, Discursive Form, and the Late Medieval Accessus," in *Acta Conventus Neo-Latini Lovaniensis: Proceedings of the First International Congress of Neo-Latin Studies Louvain 23-28 August 1971*, ed. J. IJsewijn and E. Kessler (Munich: Wilhelm Fink Verlag, 1973), p. 39. The present paper was in substantially finished form when Allen's work first came to my attention as a conference lecture.

26. *The Shipman's Tale* has *dette* as a nucleus, but the poem's relative lack of the usual Chaucerian complexity makes its existence very clear. In this tale *dette* operates at both a commercial and sexual level; the reckoning of the *dette* is another pun with *tailles* referring to tallies, tails, and, perhaps, tales. The point has been discussed before; see Albert H. Silverman, "Sex and Money in Chaucer's *Shipman's Tale*," *Philological Quarterly*, 32 (1953), 329-336. Janette Richardson, *Blameth Nat Me: A Study of Imagery in Chaucer's Fabliaux* (The Hague: Mouton, 1970), pp. 100-122, discusses image clusters in the tale including those pertaining to *dette*.

27. *The Business of Criticism* (Oxford: Clarendon Press, 1959), p. 23.

In a rather different form this paper was read at the annual meeting of the Mediaeval Academy of America in April 1967. Thanks are due three of my Toronto students, Ms. Linda Marshall, Ms. Anne Quick, and Mr. Gernot Wieland, who have provided me with assistance in the research on the heart in medieval medical and religious writing.

Addenda: 1979

1. In Book III of *Troilus* the lovers exchange rings and Criseyde gives Troilus

> a broche, gold and asure,
> In which a ruby set was lik an herte.   (III, 1371)

For an interesting account of heart-shaped pins in late medieval England, see J. Cherry, "The Medieval Jewellry from the Fishpool, Nottinghamshire, Hoard, "*Archælogia*, 104 (1974), 307–21. The heart-shaped pin from the hoard found at the village of Fishpool is shown in Plate 86a; also shown is a pin of similar design now in the Victoria and Albert Museum. On the back of the Fishpool brooch is the inscription *Ie suy vostre sans de partier*. Appendix I of the article (p. 319) lists six rings with inscriptions including the heart symbol and Appendix II (p. 320) lists eight heart-shaped brooches. Cherry points out (p. 320) that Hugh, earl of Stafford, left a heart-shaped brooch to his daughter Joan in his will of 1383. Chaucer's Criseyde had fashionable taste in jewelry.

2. John Gower alludes to the idea of the movable heart in his *Confessio Amantis*.

> Into hire bedd myn herte goth,
> And softly takth hire in his arm
> And fieleth hou that sche is warm,
> And wissheth that his body were
> To fiele that he fieleth there.   (IV, 2884–88)

The passage is quoted from *The English Works of John Gower*, ed. G. C. Macaulay, 2 vols., E.E.T.S., E.S., 81–82 (London: Oxford University Press, 1900; reprint ed., 1957). Compare the refrain of Gower's "Balade XXXIIII", "U li coers est, le corps falt obeir." The refrain is quoted from *The Works of John Gower: The French Works*, ed. G.C. Macaulay (Oxford: Oxford University Press, 1899), p. 360.

3. The movable heart is represented in a tapestry of about 1400 to 1410 now in the Cluny Museum, Paris. A seated lady in a park-like space is approached by a man who holds a small heart in his right hand. See Roger–A. d'Hulst, *Flemish Tapestries from the Fifteenth to the Eighteenth Century*, trans. Frances J. Stillman (Brussels: Editions Arcade, 1967), chapter 4, 'The Gift of the Heart', pp. 25-32 and 296; a plate in color appears on p. 27, and one in black and white on pp. 30-31.

J.L.

The Audience of Chaucer's "Troilus and Criseyde"

by Dieter Mehl

When we talk about Chaucer's audience we can mean very different things. We usually think of the poet reading his latest tale to a courtly circle of aristocratic men and women, including, perhaps, the king himself, as on the charming *Troilus* frontispiece of the Corpus Christi Manuscript.[1] Many recent critics have rightly insisted on the fact that Chaucer's poetry was written for a live performance, not for the study, and that this must have very definite consequences for our way of understanding these poems. There is no doubt that Chaucer belongs to a tradition of oral poetry, that he is essentially pre-Gutenberg, and that serious critical distortions result if we read him with the kind of expectation that the European novel from Richardson to James Joyce has helped to create. But it has also been observed that this particular audience at the court of Richard II is, for us, only a piece of historical fiction.[2] Whatever reality it may have had for Chaucer, for us it can never be more than an abstract reconstruction which does not really affect our experience when we read Chaucer.

There is, however, another, less specific kind of audience: Chaucer himself often mentions the more solitary and bookish reader who, like the Clerk of Oxenford, has a few manuscripts "at his beddes heed," and at the outset of *The Book of the Duchess* he pictures himself as a person who, troubled by insomnia, picks up a book, which then promptly sends him to sleep. I do not suggest that the poet wrote his works for that particular

Reprinted by permission of the author and George Allen & Unwin, Ltd., from *Chaucer and Middle English Studies in Honour of Rossell Hope Robbins*, ed. Beryl Rowland (London: Allen & Unwin, 1974), pp. 173–89. The original pagination is indicated between slashes. The Afterword was written for this anthology.

211

purpose, but I am sure that we take too limited a view of the kind of poetry he intended if we think of his audience only in terms of a well-defined group on one or two particular occasions. Chaucer, as is evident from every one of his major works, was deeply concerned with the function of literature within our experience of reality and our desire for wisdom and reliable authority. The ending of *Troilus* suggests very strongly that he saw himself, among other things, as a potential classic or at least as an author whose appeal would reach beyond the limits of his immediate /174/ surroundings and — more importantly — beyond the sphere of his personal control. When, in the Prologue to the *Canterbury Tales*, he warns the reader of what is to come and asks him to skip a story if he does not approve of it, he is obviously not talking to the courtiers listening at his feet, but rather to the anonymous reader of one of the many manuscripts that were soon to circulate. It is this audience he has in mind when at the end of *Troilus* he expresses his anxiety about the formal integrity of his book and its transmission for the benefit of future generations. It is an audience that is, almost by definition, undefinable, unpredictable and independent of time and place; but it is not necessarily out of the author's reach. On the contrary — Chaucer seems to have been well aware of the challenge presented to his poetry by his consideration for such a wider appeal and he must have wondered, as many poets did before and after him, how he could extend his own influence beyond the personal recital. One of the obvious and traditional means of doing this is to incorporate into the text the idea of a close relationship between the author and his public, a relationship that would thus not depend on the actual presence of the author.

In a simpler form this problem applies to many of the so-called "popular" romances, many of which are, as Richard L. Greene once said of carols, only "popular by destination," not "by origin." The thirteenth-century romance of *Havelok the Dane* provides a good example. It is told by a lively entertainer who is evidently anxious to establish a friendly and sociable contact with his audience. Before launching into his tale he wants to make sure of a relaxed atmosphere and, like Chaucer's Pardoner, asks for a drink:

> At the beginning of ure tale
> Fil me cuppe of ful god ale;
> And y wile drinken, er y spelle,
> That Crist us shilde alle fro helle![3]

The usual interpretation of these lines is that the poem was composed by a minstrel who would often recite it in some public place. This may of course be true of the first performances, but the work as we have it is a carefully constructed, highly rhetorical poem, neatly copied into a manuscript that could hardly be called a minstrel's book. It is a distinctly literary product and this means that the social occasion has become, as it were, fossilized; it has been turned into a literary motif designed to give to the poem an air of convivial spontaneity which survives even when we read *Havelok* in the study, far from any available "cuppe of ful good ale."

Spontaneity, as many modern theatre productions designed in /175/ the name of spontaneity have proved, is as a rule unique and not repeatable; but poetry, as Keats knew and demonstrated, can preserve this spontaneity and give an impression of fresh and transitory uniqueness at every reading. Every time we read *Havelok* we are included in an audience that is independent of the particular occasion and we are, at least to a certain point, persuaded to react to the poem in the same way as its first audience. In this sense, what Geoffrey Shepherd says of *Troilus* is true of *Havelok* and many less sophisticated poems as well: "Chaucer has convincingly stylized in permanent form the ephemeralness of a living entertainment and the mobility of actual delivery."[4] This is a very good description of one important aspect of poetry that is at the same time oral and literary, composed for a live performance, but also meant to be preserved for an unlimited number of future performances.

More sophisticated poets have used subtler and less conspicuous means of controlling the reader's response, often in a way that openly admits the artificial and contrived character of such a relationship. In this respect, the English novelists of the eighteenth century are not as original as is sometimes assumed: Fielding's officious, patronizing and yet deferential concern for the good will of his reader can, I believe, teach us a good deal about the practice of earlier writers like Chaucer. Sterne is perhaps an even better example because his grotesque exaggerations of some of the traditional formulas adopted by sociable narrators can startle even the most innocent reader into an awareness of the author's method: "How could you, Madam," exclaims the author at the beginning of a new chapter, "be so inattentive in reading the last chapter?"[5] Why "Madam"? Surely, the novel is not just addressed to ladies? In fact, there are several places in the book where exactly the opposite is implied; but at this particular point, it is obviously the ladies' attention that is more important or more likely, and when we realize the extremely delicate nature of the question at issue, the author's comic intention becomes very clear.

Chaucer, in his rather more subdued way, achieves very similar effects. Like Sterne and like Gottfried von Strassburg with his insistence on the "*edele herzen*" before him, he does not treat his imaginary audience as an amorphous assembly of identical minds, but he makes pointed discriminations when it suits his purpose. He creates the illusion of a lively and mutual relationship between the fictional narrator, who has been singled out so often and so out of proportion in recent criticism, and the fictional audience with which we are asked to identify ourselves.

That this fictional audience has its own very definite kind of reality will be felt by most readers because as we follow the poet /176/ through his narrative there emerges a clear picture of the sort of listeners this story is addressed to and of the reponse that is expected of them. It is not a static picture and it is by its very nature not to be confused with the actual court circle to which the poem was perhaps first read. Even if we did not know anything at all about Chaucer's real audience, the poem would still give us a very lively and precise idea of the quality of mind it wants to appeal to and of a personal relationship it seeks to establish between narrator and listener or reader. The poem, as it were, creates its own audience and it implies a set of expectations which it partly fulfils and partly disappoints. Taken in this sense, the term "fictional audience" describes a very important aspect of the poem's rhetoric and can be useful in approaching many problems of interpretation.[6]

At the outset of *Troilus*, Chaucer, developing a hint from Boccaccio, addresses himself to the lovers among his audience, but not, as Boccaccio did, to ask for their personal sympathy and pity, but to appeal to their superior experience. Only they can really appreciate what is to come and only they can therefore react in the right way, which is, not to judge, but feel sympathetic compassion for the characters in the story and for all who are in similar pain. To move his audience to such pity is the poet's chief object:

> For so hope I my sowle best avaunce,
> To prey for hem that Loves servauntz be,
> And write hir wo, and lyve in charite,
> And for to have of hem compassioun,
> As though I were hire owne brother dere. (47–51)

By suggesting this distinction among his audience, the poet sets up a standard by which we are to judge ourselves and our response to the

story. There is a challenge in the poet's claim that only certain members
of his audience can really understand his poem. Again *Tristram Shandy*
can illustrate this technique in its more extreme form: "I told the
Christian reader — I say Christian — hoping he is one — and if he is not,
I am sorry for it — and only beg he will consider the matter with himself,
and lay not the blame entirely upon this book, — I told him, Sir — " (VI,
33). Chaucer does not, of course, carry the trick as far as Sterne, but the
effect is not entirely different. He forces us into a reflection on how far we
ourselves qualify for inclusion in his audience. The point is not so much
that, as one critic says, "the poem is addressed to lovers, not to
theologians,"[7] but that there is a provocative tension between the ideal
audience the poet seems to envisage and our own particular and
necessarily limited reading. Once alerted to the poet's claims, /177/ the
reader will become more self-conscious and more aware of the variety of
possible responses.

In the course of the poem the lovers among the audience are several
times singled out as the only people whose understanding and experience
can make up for the shortcomings of the poet. This is, of course, a fairly
conventional rhetorical device, but Chaucer often elaborates it in a way
that makes us more conscious of the fact that we are part of an audience
and that more than passive submission to the poet's spell is expected of
us. Both the conventional and the more personal touch come out in the
appeal to the experienced lovers to imagine the intensity of Troilus'
experience:

> Of hire delit, or joies oon the leeste,
> Were impossible to my wit to seye;
> But juggeth ye that han ben at the feste
> Of swich gladnesse, if that hem liste pleye!
> I kan namore, but thus thise ilke tweye,
> That nyght, bitwixen drede and sikernesse,
> Felten in love the grete worthynesse. (III, 1310–16)

Boccaccio is far more conventional at this point.

At other points in the poem, however, it is not the lovers to whom the
story is specifically addressed. Troilus' conversion to love in the first
book is presented as a warning to "Ye wise, proude, and worthi folkes
alle," (I, 233) and at the end of the poem it is the "yonge, fresshe folkes,
he or she" (V, 1835) who are the particular object of the poet's concern.
The function of these varying appeals is again a sharpening of our

awareness of the poem's different levels of meaning and our active response.

More interesting and provocative is the poet's appeal to the audience's judgement in questions concerning the characters of the story. We are sometimes told by historically-minded critics that medieval poets, including Chaucer, were not interested in drawing psychologically consistent characters. This is true to a point, but only to a point, because at certain stages of the story Chaucer does invite us to form our own judgement of a character in terms that go beyond the stereotyped situation and can only be defined by the psychology of human behaviour. The most elaborate instance is Chaucer's ambiguous statement about Criseyde's complicity in the lover's meeting arranged so resourcefully by Pandarus. When he asks her to dinner at his house it is, in view of his previous strategy, only natural that she suspects a plot:

> Soone after this, she gan to hym to rowne,
> And axed hym if Troilus were there. /178/
> He swor hire nay, for he was out of towne,
> And seyde, "Nece, I pose that he were;
> Yow thurste nevere han the more fere;
> For rather than men myghte hym ther aspie,
> Me were levere a thousand fold to dye." (III, 568–74)

This is not completely reassuring and Criseyde has every reason to remain unconvinced, but Chaucer, in one of his most brilliant auctorial interventions, leaves the situation open:

> Nought list myn auctour fully to declare
> What that she thoughte whan he seyde so,
> That Troilus was out of towne yfare,
> As if he seyde therof soth or no;
> But that, withowten await, with hym to go,
> She graunted hym, sith he hire that bisoughte,
> And, as his nece, obeyed as hire oughte. (III, 575–81)

That Criseyde is not, in fact, reassured becomes clear from the following stanza where she asks him to be discreet whatever he may do with her.

In view of this deliberately unexplicit treatment of Criseyde's state of mind, the attempt of some critics to leap to her defence and prove her complete ignorance of Pandarus' scheme seems to me rather touching and, at any rate, to miss the point, because it is obvious that the audience

is not given a piece of precise information, but an incomplete and
therefore ambiguous statement that demands an active effort of
imagination and judgement.[8] Each reader has to make up his own mind
about Criseyde at this point, as at many other points of the story, and
attempts by critics to make up his mind for him or to prove that Chaucer
does, in fact, suggest a clear-cut answer to his question, should be
regarded with suspicion. What the poet asks, as Fielding does so
frequently in *Tom Jones*, is simply this: "What would you think if a living
person into whose mind you cannot penetrate behaved like Criseyde?"
The poet wants to present us with the same kind of uncertainty, pleasure
and provocation that we meet in our daily relationship with complex and
unpredictable human beings. He makes us aware that a poetic
characterization is but an outline that has to be filled in by every member
of the audience according to his own experience and knowledge of human
nature.

Chaucer's use of direct intervention by the narrator to draw the
reader's attention to the artificial nature of his narrative can be seen in
two other places in the second book, where two possible objections of the
readers are answered before they even occur to most readers. /179/

The first is the famous passage describing historical changes and their
influence on our attitude towards stories of the past. There may be, says
Chaucer, among his audience a lover who, while listening, thinks to
himself that he would have gone about love-making in a very different
way. Nowhere else in Middle English literature — as far as I know — do
we find this acute consciousness of the problems of historical fiction. At
first sight we may feel that what Chaucer says here does not really apply
to his treatment of Troilus and Criseyde because in many ways he has
made his characters contemporaries of his audience. At least it can hardly
be said that he has deliberately removed them from the manners and the
sensibility of the fourteenth century. This is obviously not an example of
historical pastiche, like the Waverley novels, for Chaucer does not intend
that: he wants to make clear that these differences between periods are
not more surprising and no more relevant than differences between
individual human beings. His intervention here is obviously an appeal to
his audience to distinguish between the ephemeral literary form and the
genuine matter that cannot be made obsolete by linguistic and cultural
changes. The responsibility for a true appreciation of the story is thus
again returned to the audience and any potential criticism of the poem's
style on the grounds of simple realism is refuted in advance.

Later on in the book an even more surprising kind of objection is

singled out and crushed, "with a fine show of indignation."[9] Again some
particular members of the audience are separated from the rest and we are
warned not to identify ourselves with them:

> Now might som envious jangle thus:
> "This was a sodeyn love; how might it be
> That she so lightly loved Troilus,
> Right for the firste syghte, ye, parde?"
> Now whoso seith so, mote he nevere ythe! (II, 666-70)

To reproach Criseyde for falling in love too hastily would be far more
appropriate in the case of *Il Filostrato* where things do indeed develop
rather rapidly. Chaucer, however, goes out of his way to avoid any
impression of undue hurry so that his intervention at first sight seems
humorously pointless. In fact, it is another effective appeal for the mental
cooperation of the audience. Once more we are reminded that literary
fiction and reality are two very different things. Reality, as a rule, has no
structure and no clearly recognizable transitions, but the poet has to
select and to confine himself to a limited number of crucial moments.
This is a commonplace of literary theory, but it is anything but a
commonplace to be explicit reminded of it in the /180/ midst of a most
engrossing part of the story. Chaucer obviously does not care to have his
audience too much engrossed by the story alone and therefore ignorant of
the problems of its presentation. He also seems to urge his listeners, as at
the outset and at the end of the poem, not to judge the characters by
standards that are — in view of the fictional nature of his narrative —
totally irrelevant.

Chaucer, it has been said, thought he was reporting a story that had
actually happened. Even if this is true, it does not alter the fact that for
him, the distinction between any historical Criseyde that may once have
enjoyed and betrayed the love of a Trojan prince and his stylized portrait
of her mattered far more than any kind of supposed accuracy. The reader
is not simply encouraged to picture Criseyde as a human being of flesh
and blood, although Chaucer's ambiguous rhetoric makes him do so most
effectively, but he is also invited to help the poet recreate a particular
emotional experience that cannot be adequately defined by literary
means. By suggesting an objection which many readers might never have
thought of he makes us wonder whether there are not many other
possible responses to this story, whether we have, in fact, been
sufficiently attentive to the text. And this constant awareness of our

duties as an intelligent audience seems to me far more important than any specific interpretation we would like to elicit from the narrative.

Several critics have claimed that Chaucer's professed refraining from judgement is, in truth, his most effective means of judging his characters. This is, I think, one of the errors that result from too simple and anachronistic a conception of Chaucer's narrator. Nothing is gained, but a good deal is lost by putting Chaucer's tale into the mouth of a naive narrator who does not understand the meaning of his own story or commits serious errors of judgement, a "narrator" who "would have been unhappy if he had realized the effect he was producing."[10] It seems to me far more appropriate to see him as a poet who assumes different parts in the course of the narrative, who intentionally withholds information to sharpen our critical awareness or who pronounces simple judgements in order to suggest to us how inadequate such judgements are.

The most uncomfortable character problem in *Troilus and Criseyde*, and one that still baffles critics, is, of course, Criseyde's sudden moral collapse in the fifth book. Even a very recent introduction to the works of Chaucer repeats the traditional opinion that Chaucer "minimizes Criseyde's guilt in every way possible."[11] In fact, he does no such thing, but it would not be true to say that he does the opposite. I am convinced that all attempts to discover in the earlier books character-traits that would provide sufficient motives for her /181/ behaviour are beside the point. What can be proved, however, with some cogency is that Chaucer, despite all his declarations of sympathy for Criseyde, altered the story in such a way as to make her betrayal much harder to explain. Although the contrast between Troilus and the "sodeyn" Diomede is heightened to the point of comedy, Criseyde is more easily persuaded to transfer her favours to Diomede than Boccaccio's Criseida. "Why," a critic asks, "has Chaucer created unnecessary difficulties for himself by stressing at the same time the sincerity and beauty of her love and the suddennes and meanness of her betrayal. It would have been easy enough for him to make Criseyde's behaviour more consistent either by portraying her as an untrustworthy character from the start, as Shakespeare did 200 years later, or by softening her betrayal and making her appear less guilty (as he is claimed to have done by many critics). In fact, both alternatives have been seriously advanced in many interpretations and this genuine difference of opinion points to a real problem in the text. Perhaps this much discussed question becomes a little clearer if we see it as an aspect of Chaucer's treatment of his audience.

The poet (or, if you like, the narrator), as Chaucer presents him, is faced with the problem of having to tell a story he does not like and he cannot even find consistent. His solution is to pass the problem on to the reader and to incorporate into his work the difficulties of its composition. In this part of the book, more than in any other, we are constantly reminded of the fact that this is not a faithful image of reality, but an attempt to recapture events that have long passed out of existence, with insufficient information and the limited means of the poet's craft. We are made to distinguish between the bare story-material, the efforts of the poet and the full truth that lies somewhere behind all this and can never be recovered. It can only be tentatively approached by the groping gestures of the poet and the reader's active imagination they try to stimulate. From other parts of the poem we know perfectly well that Chaucer did not, in principle, hesitate to alter his material by inventing new details or providing motives for his characters where it suited his purpose. This makes it fairly certain that his scrupulous adherence to his source at this particular point is a calculated attitude to ensure the cooperation of the audience. Giving the stark facts of the story, he claims to have added nothing because he does not want to appear to blame Criseyde. Whether we read into this an even more devastating condemnation of the heroine or take the narrator's innocent apologies at their face value, is our own responsibility, but any interpretation that simplifies /182/ the issue or denies the need for the audience's own effort reduces the haunting provocation of the text to the level of plain statement. This is not so much a case of poetic ambiguity, but a supreme example of the way good narrative can involve the reader in the process of deciding, inferring and evaluating. And it is precisely this quality that gives us such a strong sense of the reality of Chaucer's characters.[13]

At this point, the poet no longer appeals to the lovers alone. Every member of the audience is included and no particular knowledge is required to appreciate the pathos of Troilus' disillusion and Criseyde's guilt, but at the same time the poet keeps us at a rational distance from his characters by constantly reminding us of the limitations of the poetic medium and his own deficiencies.

His appeal to the audience is not, however, confined to our evaluation of the characters, but applies to nearly all aspects of the poem's structure. One of the most interesting examples is the poet's treatment of time at the end of Book II. Troilus, whose pretended illness has by now almost turned into a genuine disorder, is waiting in his sickchamber while Pandarus is about to lead Criseyde to him. In the final stanza the poet makes another appeal to the lovers' sympathy and creates a moment of intensely dramatic suspense:

> But now to yow, ye loveres that ben here,
> Was Troilus nought in a kankedort,
> That lay, and myghte whisprynge of hem here,
> And thoughte, "O Lord, right now renneth my sort
> Fully to deye, or han anon comfort!"
> And was the firste tyme he shulde hire preye
> Of love; O myghty God, what shal he seye? (II, 1751–57)

The last line takes us right into Troilus' mind; it could be described as an early example of interior monologue or reported thought which hardly reappears in English fiction before Jane Austen. But at the same time the poem breaks off abruptly (*"Explicit Secundus Liber"*). "In performance" this might even have meant the end of a sitting. There is, at any rate, a lengthy invocation at the beginning of the following book before we hear again from Troilus. After forty-nine lines the story is resumed:

> Lay al this mene while Troilus
> Recordying his lesson . . . .(III, 50–1)

"Al this mene while" obviously means the time it has taken us to read the invocation. This deliberate confusion of two time levels is /183/ again very like Sterne's "It is about an hour and a half's tolerable good reading since my Uncle Toby rung the bell. . . ." (II, 8). It makes us conscious of the poem's careful artistry and again encourages us to dissociate the story from the way it is told. Yet at the same time we are persuaded to identify ourselves with Troilus and to enter imaginatively into his state of mind. It is a very personal and surprising version of the traditional topos which asks the audience to make up the deficiencies of the poet's art by an effort of good will and imagination, to "piece out our imperfections with your thoughts."

Modern literary criticism often draws attention to the fact that a work of fiction has no complete existence of its own, but depends on contact with a reader's mind to be brought to life. It is, to use Saussure's almost suspiciously useful terms, on the level of *langue*, not *parole*, that is to say, it is not a complete, self-sufficient statement, but a kind of abstract matrix, suggesting and allowing for an indefinite number of potential statements.[14] Every narrative asks us, implicitly or explicitly, to read between the lines, to supply by our own experience, intelligence and imagination what the text has left out. Some poets, not usually the best ones, try to disguise this fact by being as explicit as possible on all important points of the story, thus leaving us very little room for independent mental co-operation; but it is in the very nature of fictional narrative that it must omit large portions of the story and it is most important for a critical understanding to recognize where these blanks occur and how the author makes use of them. What many lesser writers seem to be unaware of or try to pass over as an unavoidable failing, Chaucer deliberately exploits as a chief means of his narrative rhetoric. By directing the attention of the audience to gaps in his account at the most crucial points in the story, he makes sure that our imagination becomes active in the right direction. The simplest way of doing this is a demonstrative withholding of precise information. In some cases this may be a merely playful fussing over minor points, as in the question of Criseyde's age or the possible existence or non-existence of her children; but it becomes more disturbing when the poet confesses ignorance on such an important point as the time it took for Criseyde to give her heart (or at least the appearance of it) to Diomede. It is a very characteristic example of Chaucer's relationship with his audience:

> But trewely, how longe it was bytwene
> That she forsok hym for this Diomede.
> There is non auctour telleth it, I wene,
> Take every man now to his bokes heede;
> He shal no terme fynden, out of drede. (V, 1086–90)

/184/ Again, this is obviously a calculated effect. If we take up the author's suggestion to do some independent source-study we shall find that it would have been easy enough for Chaucer to get some idea of a possible time-scheme from his sources, especially from Benoit, or to make up his own time-scheme; but, like Jane Austen at the end of *Mansfield Park*, he "purposely abstain[s] from dates on this occasion, that everyone may be at liberty to fix their own, aware that the cure of unconquerable passions and the transfer of unchanging attachments, must vary very much as to time in different people." This auctorial statement seems to fit Criseyde hardly less well than Edmund Bertram, and the function of the author's reticence is very much the same in each case.

Chaucer does not withhold this information in order to excuse Criseyde, but to make us aware of the very imperfections of the story, of

its many blank spaces, and this applies to all the other instances of the
poet's appeals to his audience I have quoted. No narrative can give all the
information any reader might require, but to deny us even information
that most readers would consider essential and, in addition, draw our
attention to this refusal, throws us back on our own mental resources,
and this is precisely what Chaucer's poetry does.

Of course we also have to recognize the limits of this freedom the poet
allows to his audience or, rather, to define the areas in which we are
meant to exercise it. Most critics, without giving much thought to the
problem, take for granted this lack of explicitness in Chaucer's poetry by
expecting or persuading us to read between his lines to a considerable
extent. But an important distinction has to be made here, for although
Chaucer does leave a good many decisions to the reader, he is, as a rule,
very clear about where these decisions lie and he does not encourage us to
ask the wrong sort of question. Probably no two readers would quite agree
on this, but I think it is important to keep in mind the difference between
questions the poem really provokes and those it ignores.

To give a well-known example: one question which, I feel, we are not
meant to ask, but many readers seem to like to ask, concerns the problem
of marriage. From time to time it is claimed, even very recently, that this
is, in fact, the crucial moral issue in the poem.[15] If this were so, Chaucer
would indeed expect a great deal of mental co-operation from his reader,
but to me, at least, the only thing the text suggests very strongly is that we
are not invited to pursue this point any further than the poem does. The
concept of marriage is only mentioned in a very few places and mostly in
very conventional terms; it is never made a real issue. Criseyde, in her
first soliloquy, /185/ refers to marriage in passing rather like the Wife of
Bath as a form of power-game: "Shal noon housbonde seyn to me 'chek
mat!'" (II, 754) and, in their last interview, Troilus expresses his fear
that she might be conveniently married off to some Greek by her father.

The most important reference to marriage in the poem is, however, a
non-reference, to be read by the learned reader between the lines of
Troilus' ecstatic praise of love towards the end of the third book where he
gives a fairly close paraphrase of Boece (II, Metrum 8). Several critics
have noted that whereas Boece speaks of the "sacrement of mariages of
chaste loves," Troilus means his own union with Criseyde. But does this
really imply a criticism of Troilus's love? The argument that is used to
support such an interpretation is one that turns precisely on the problem
of the audience's participation: Chaucer's readers or listeners, it is said,
would have noticed Troilus' misapplication of Boece. But would they

really? Chaucer's way of handling his audience suggests, on the contrary, that his readers should not notice the discrepancy or else if they noticed, nothing should be made of it. There is nothing to alert us to the presence of a real problem here, nothing to draw our attention to any basic flaw in Troilus' attitude at this particular point or to a significant silence on the part of the poet.[16]

It is, of course, perfectly possible for a modern or medieval reader, taking a sinister view of any extra-marital affair and of courtly love in general, to raise the question Chaucer has left alone, but this is a different kind of literary criticism from the one I am concerned with here.

Chaucer's rhetorical involvement of his audience is not arbitrary and it does not include all aspects of his story, but it concentrates on a number of important points where central questions of interpreting the story are at stake. Moreover, the poet does not leave us without any help or at least a precise idea of how we are to exercise our critical faculties. The first lines of the poem set the tone and describe very clearly the spirit in which all the following story should be read. This spirit underlies all the poem's rhetoric and its provocative silences, and as most readers feel — unless they are obsessed by a very naive and narrow idea of medieval Christianity — it is a spirit of sympathy and compassion for the sufferings and shortcomings of others. Although the poem continually appeals to our judgement and imagination it does all along give indications as to the direction our own appraisal should take. In this sense, the poet was perfectly right and sincere when he claimed in the Prologue to the *Legend of Good Women* that — whatever the spirit of his source may have been — his own intention was to further truth and to teach people to avoid falseness and vice. /186/

The most interesting thing about this passage to me is the emphasis it puts on the effect of Chaucer's poetry on his audience. This is not a question of didactic poetry. Chaucer does not portray himself as a straightforward moral teacher, but he is evidently worried about the reception of his poetry and the whole debate in the *Prologue* concerns not so much the subjects of Chaucer's actual writing, but the audience and its response. If Chaucer had any more specific or topical reason for writing this apology for his poetry it may well be that he felt his courtly audience had mistaken his intentions and he had to be more explicit about the impression he wished to create.

The theme of the poet's effect on his audience recurs again and again in Chaucer's poetry, especially, of course, in the *Canterbury Tales* where it is implied in the very structure of the work. The way the pilgrims react to the individual stories is sometimes nearly as interesting as the stories themselves and tells us a lot about Chaucer's poetic intentions.

The problem of the audience and the way it is affected by poetry also lies at the heart of Chaucer's much discussed retraction at the end of the *Canterbury Tales* and, we may gather, of his poetic career. I am sure it is not a sudden impulse of humourless puritanism or a righteous rejection of all art and his own poetic achievement, but an expression of a deep concern for the effect of his poetry on the reader and, perhaps, a last effort to guide our response. Chaucer does, of course, explicitly revoke *Troilus and Criseyde* in its entirety, but "revoke" in this context can only mean that he does not wish to be responsible for any unedifying influence his poem might have and that he deeply regrets the fact that this poem and the others he mentions could ever have encouraged the wrong kind of response on the part of the reader. The *Retraction*, if it is not just a private confession of faith, is surely a last earnest appeal to the reader to believe in the good intentions of the poet and to read all the poems in this spirit. In this, the *Retraction* is not unlike the ending of *Troilus* where, though perhaps more ambiguously, the audience is also forced to reconsider the implications of the story and its presentation.

Middle English narrative literature before Chaucer was for the most part written with the expressed aim of entertaining and educating a public unable to read French or Latin. Often the audience is addressed as the recipient of a particular favour and of wholesome instruction. That is, the relationship between poet and audience is strictly a one-way communication. The only kind of co-operation expected of the listeners is attention and belief. Chaucer's attitude to his reader, as we have seen, is completely different. Even where his purpose is purely educational as in the treatise on the Astrolabe, /187/ written for the benefit of a ten-year-old boy whose Latin is not yet up to the original texts, he presents himself as the unworthy transmitter of his material: "I n'am but a lewd compilator of the labour of olde astrologiens." He goes far beyond the traditional humility formula in disclaiming any merit his work might have, and he thus draws the reader's attention to the author in a way quite unprecedented in Middle English literature; and this is not a particular cunning and subtle method of self-praise, but rather an intentional *Verfremdungseffekt* to make us a self-conscious and critical audience. The colourful diversity of Chaucer criticism shows that his poetry still achieves that aim, at least among a certain section of his audience.

To claim, as I have done, that Chaucer leaves many of the crucial questions raised by his story for the audience to decide, is not to confuse

the poetry with our personal reaction to it or to return to a simple form of
New Criticism, but merely to state that Chaucer's poetry consciously
presupposes and depends on an intelligent and co-operative reader, more,
perhaps, than any other Middle English poetry. To be one of his audience
does not mean just to listen to what he tells us, but to encounter a
fictional reality that is full of questions and provocative blanks and to be
in mental contact with an author who makes us aware of the truly sociable
character of narrative poetry. In a general sense this is, of course, true of
most good poetry, but it is often forgotten or ignored by less interesting
authors and not often exploited in such a deliberate way as in Chaucer's
text. To pronounce on the "meaning" of his stories is nearly always the
wrong kind of critical approach. It is not our business as readers and
critics to discover what Chaucer "really meant," how he himself judges
his characters or what he thought about courtly love, but to respond to
his appeal and participate in the dialogue his poetry wants to provoke.

Again, a classic statement of this kind of relationship occurs in *Tristram
Shandy*, and though the critical vocabulary is clearly dated, due to
"chaunge in forme of speche," it describes a fundamental quality of
Chaucer's writing:

> Writing, when properly managed, (as you may be sure I think
> mine is) is but a different name for conversation: As no one,
> who knows what he is about in good company, would venture
> to talk all; — so no author, who understands the just
> boundaries of decorum and good breeding, would presume to
> think all: The truest respect which you can pay to the reader's
> understanding, is to halve this matter amicably and leave him
> something to imagine, in his turn, as well as yourself. (II, 11)

In using the words of an eighteenth-century practitioner of the art
/188/ of fiction I will not, I hope, appear to be blurring basic historical
differences. It hardly needs saying that Sterne activates the reader's mind
in a completely different direction and to completely different ends and
that the audience Chaucer has in mind is very unlike the eighteenth-
century reading public. And yet, the explicit appeal to its imagination and
judgement, the teasing omission of information and unambiguous
guidance reveal the same awareness of the limits and potentialities of
poetic fiction. To say that "no author, who understands the just
boundaries of decorum and good breeding, would presume to think all"
seems to me a very Chaucerian statement — although Chaucer would

have seen the problem as one of rhetoric and "curteisie" rather than of decorum and good breeding. Consciously or not, Chaucer seems to have realized that to engage the readers' minds in a process of imaginative exploration and sympathetic evaluation can be a more effective means of instruction than anything that can be achieved by over-explicit and unquestioning didactic poetry.

Notes

1. On the significance of the frontispiece see the interesting but highly speculative article by Margaret Galway, "The 'Troilus' Frontispiece," *MLR*, 44 (1949), pp. 162-77.

2. "Geoffrey Chaucer reading aloud to certain groups in the late fourteenth century is for us a fiction; what remains is Geoffrey Chaucer addressing us from the printed page." Paull F. Baum, *Chaucer: a Critical Appreciation* (Durham, N.C.: Duke Univ. Press, 1958), p. 204. A similar suggestion with regard to the *Troilus* frontispiece is made by Derek S. Brewer in his excellent interpretation of the poem in W. F. Bolton (ed.), *Sphere History of Literature in the English Language*, I, *The Middle Ages* (London: Sphere Books, 1970), pp. 195-223: "It (i.e. the frontispiece) might itself even be a product of the poem's power to create the sense of a listening group" (p. 196). Brewer's interpretation agrees with mine in a number of important points.

3. I have slightly modernized the text by W. W. Skeat, 2nd edn, rev. by K. Sisam (Oxford: 1915). On the artistry of the poem see Judith Weiss, "Structure and Characterization in *Havelok the Dane*," *Spec.*, 44 (1969), pp. 247-57, and my *The Middle English Romances of the Thirteenth and Fourteenth Centuries* (London: Routledge, 1968), pp. 161-72.

4. G. T. Shepherd, "Troilus and Criseyde," in *Chaucer and Chaucerians: Critical Studies in Middle English Literature* (London: Nelson, 1966), p. 72.

5. *Tristram Shandy*, I, p. 20. I quote from the edition by Ian Watt (Boston: Houghton Mifflin, 1965).

6. I am here, of course, indebted to a number of recent works on narrative theory. One of the most interesting accounts of *Troilus and Criseyde* from this point of view is to be found in Robert M. Durling, *The Figure of the Poet in Renaissance Epic* (Cambridge, Mass.: Harvard Univ. Press, 1965), pp. 44-66. There are also some very interesting observations on the audience of *Troilus* in Robert O. Payne, *The Key of Remembrance: A Study of Chaucer's Poetics* (New Haven: Yale Univ. Press, 1963), pp. 228-32.

7. See Durling, op. cit., p. 48.

8. See the rather one-sided interpretation by Robert P. apRoberts, "The Central Episode in Chaucer's *Troilus*," *PMLA*, 77 (1962), pp. 373-85.

9. See E. Talbot Donaldson, *Chaucer's Poetry: An Anthology for the Modern Reader* (New York: Ronald Press, 1958), p. 970.

10. See E. Talbot Donaldson, "Criseide and Her Narrator," in *Speaking of Chaucer*

(London: Athlone Press, 1970), pp. 65–83; the quotation occurs p. 77.

11. See S. S. Hussey, *Chaucer: An Introduction* (London: Methuen, 1971), p. 76.

12. See Hans Käsmann, " 'I wolde excuse hire yit for routhe.' *Chaucers Einstellung zu Criseyde*," in Arno Esch (ed.), *Chaucer und seine Zeit: Symposium für Walter F. Schirmer* (Tübingen: Max Niemeyer, 1968), pp. 97–122; the quotation occurs p. 110. Käsmann's essay gives a particularly clear and thorough account of the difficulties of interpretation.

13. See Payne, op. cit., p. 182: " a fair share of the illusion of reality comes not from the actual processes of characterization, but from the affective immediacy of the moral and emotional problems within which the existences of the characters are defined."

14. See the interesting discussion of these problems in **Hans Robert Jauss**, *Literatur geschichte als Provokation* (Frankfurt: Suhrkamp, 1970), pp. 144–207.

15. I am largely in agreement with Derek S. Brewer on this point; see his "Love and Marriage in Chaucer's Poetry," *MLR*, 49 (1954), pp. 461–4. The question has been re-opened by Käsmann whose interpretation is rather different on this point than the one suggested here.

16. See T. P. Dunning, "God and Man in *Troilus and Criseyde*," in Norman Davis and C. L. Wrenn (eds), *English and Medieval Studies Presented to J.R.R. Tolkien on the Occasion of his Seventieth Birthday* (London: Allen & Unwin, 1962), pp. 164–82, especially pp. 175–6, and H. Käsmann, p. 118.

Afterword: 1979

Since this article was written, it has become almost a critical fashion to direct as much attention at the reader and his response as at the text itself. The danger of this approach is that it tends to put the individual reader's psychological disposition in the place of the author's voice and makes our subjective impressions the chief guide.

This is not, however, what I tried to do here. My main concern was with the reader implied in the narrative itself, and I still feel that Chaucer's poetry involves the audience in the process of seeing, understanding and judging to a degree quite unusual in Middle English literature. It would be foolish to deny, however, that the poet has a definite point of view of his own and that he is far from indifferent. In the case of Criseyde, for instance, he insistently emphasizes the difficulties of judging a person whose real motives we can only infer from a distance of many centuries, but he is by no means uncertain about his standards and far from simply exonerating his heroine. What he wants is to prevent the reader from enjoying his own moral superiority. Pity and an awareness of human frailty are to be our final reactions. In reading Chaucer we have an exhilarating sense of being in the company of a particularly wise, tolerant and kind human being and it is this imaginative companionship that makes each new reading of *Troilus and Criseyde* a challenge and a pleasure.

A more detailed and comprehensive account of Chaucer's narrative art and its relationship to its audience may be found in my book *Geoffrey Chaucer: Eine Einführung in seine erzählenden Dichtungen*, Grundlagen der Anglistik und Amerikanistik, 7 (Berlin, 1973); I have used some of the material again in my article, "Chaucer's Audience," *Leeds Studies in English* New Series, X (1978) 58-73.

D.M.

The Terms of Love: A Study of Troilus's Style
by Davis Taylor

IN CHAUCERIAN CRITICISM it is now a truism to say that Troilus speaks like a courtly lover or, more exactly, like a great number of lovers in medieval poems, but although it is a truism, or perhaps because it is a truism, no one has closely described those conventions in medieval poetry which form the basis of Troilus's style. Charles Muscatine comes closest in his book *Chaucer and the French Tradition*. He is helpful in the early chapters where he surveys in some detail the courtly idiom of French poetry, and he is also convincing when he looks at the ironic oppositions in Chaucer's long poem, but his actual description of Troilus's style is disappointing, partly because he fails to use specific terms, mentioning only such things as Troilus's "fine, lyric expression," the "courtly choiceness of [his] idiom," and the "patterned, symbolic business of the high style," and partly because he fails to correlate specific features of Troilus's speech with his behavior, saying only that Troilus's speech is conventional and his behavior equally conventional, impractical, and idealistic.[1] By a more detailed study of Troilus's style, I hope to show how Chaucer uses specific medieval conventions to create Troilus's speech and how an understanding of them can sharpen one's evaluation of some central issues in the poem.

Other than Muscatine's early chapters on the French tradition, two articles, one by Leo Spitzer and the other by Paul Zumthor, provide a helpful survey of stylistic conventions in medieval love poetry.[2] Using their work as a point of departure, I have centered on three recurrent

Reprinted with the kind permission of the author and the editor of *Speculum* from *Speculum* 51 (1976): 69–90. The author has revised the essay for this anthology.

conventions which distinguish medieval love poetry. The first of these is the use of superlatives to characterize the speaker and his beloved.

In Spitzer's analysis of the English lyric "Blow, Northerne Wynde," he shows how superlatives and a range of constructions which have the force of superlatives are used to characterize the lady as the best of all women, the summation of all value, and the man as the most sorrowful of all lovers, just as unworthy as the mud which drops from the lady's boot.[3] This extreme relationship is, of course, typical of medieval love lyrics, and therein lies a problem, at least to the logically minded reader, for if every woman is most worthy, every man most unworthy, how is any one of them distinguishable, much less superlative? Fortunately, this problem exists more on a logical than experiential plane. As Spitzer notes, when we read the best lyrics, we are swayed by the cumulative power of the superlatives and by the details of the poem to grant lover and beloved a unique individuality. We are convinced by the convention. Another dilemma, however, also arises from the superlatives: no matter how eloquently the man pleads, his cruel mistress cannot yield, for if she does, she ceases to be perfectly virtuous (the basis of her identity) and he to be utterly unworthy (the basis of his identity). Any progress toward sexual consummation thus undermines the poem's characterization as well as its pathos and morality. The solution, clearly, is to put the demands of convention over those of nature and to celebrate as sacred the very distance between lover and beloved. As Joseph Bédier affirms of *amour courtois*: "Ce qui lui est propre, c'est d'avoir conçu l'amour comme un culte qui s'adresse à un objet excellent et se fonde, comme l'amour chrétien, sur l'infinie disproportion du merite au désir."[4] Medieval love lyrics, in much the same way as Keats's "Ode on a Grecian Urn," thus offer a suspended realm where perfection depends on immobility and incompletion, a world far more appropriate for lyric than narrative poetry.

A second stylistic trait, which is also discussed by Spitzer, is the frequent occurrence of quantitative terms, like *al*, *ful*, and *hele*, in the lover's statements of commitment to his lady — he will love her best of *all*, for *all* time, and with *all* his heart. Such absolute commitments are traditionally demanded by the god of love. In "Blow, Northerne Wynde," for example, the god of love bids the lover to offer the "hord of [his] huerte hele," with the implication that only such a treasure might satisfy the lady, and in the *Roman de la Rose*, Amors makes the command:

Vueil je e comant que tu aies

En un seul leu tot ton cuer mis,
Si qu'il n'i soit mie demis,
Mais toz entiers, senz tricherie,
Car je n'aim pas moiteierie.[5]   (2240-44)

In these and other poems, the lover seeks his lady's approval and his own
salvation through his total commitment, although by the fourteenth
century, at least in French court poetry, the lady's approval, or, more
exactly, the extent of her approval and any moral implications which
might thereby be raised, are far less important than the pathetic tone of
the poems. What is emphasized is not the possibility but the impossibility
of love, not the joy of the lovers but their martyrdom.

A third stylistic characteristic of medieval love poetry is the recurrence
of long internal monologues filled with invocations and complaints.
These were immensely popular in French literature, and from the time of
Jean de Meun onwards they tended to dwarf the narrative. In Machaut's
Remede de Fortune, for example, a young man attacks love for seizing his
will and placing him at the mercy of his lady and of fortune. His attack
takes up half the poem, for Machaut is less interested in the outcome of
the man's love than in his psychology, how he changes from the naïve
bliss of innocence to the painful recognition that his love might not be
returned. Stylistically, these monologues are characterized by repeated
elements and by balanced as well as extended phrasing. The poet is in no
hurry to reach a conclusion, even the conclusion of a sentence. He wants
to keep the emotion suspended, which is the rhythm of both pathos and
romance.

One can find other stylistic traits which characterize medieval love
poems, but the three noted above — recurrent superlatives, absolute
commitments, and extended monologues — occur frequently throughout
medieval poetry and form the rhetorical basis for Chaucer's elevated love
poems, including the complaints as well as portions of *The Book of the
Duchess* and *Anelida and Arcite*. Chaucer knew how to combine these
characteristics to achieve the greatest degree of pathos. When he came to
writing *Troilus and Criseyde*, he changed Boccaccio's *Filostrato* — as C. S.
Lewis has said so aptly, he "medievalized" it[6] — not only by making
Troilus a more innocent lover, which is Lewis's point, but also by giving
him a more characteristically medieval style.

The extent to which he medievalized Troilus's style can be seen by
comparing Troilus's use of these traits with Troiolo's. To look first at
superlatives, one can find ten subjects defined by unqualified superlatives

in Troiolo's speech in the *Filostrato*, eight in the narrator's speech, seven in Pandaro's, and three in Criseida's[7]; but since Troiolo has almost twice as many lines as Pandaro and three times as many as Criseida, their proportional use of superlatives is just about equal. In Chaucer's poem, on the other hand, Troilus describes twenty-one subjects by unqualified superlatives, the narrator twenty-two, Pandarus nine, and Criseyde four[8]; and if one thinks of them all speaking the same number of lines as Pandarus, the proportional figures are Troilus twenty-six, the narrator eleven, Pandarus nine, and Criseyde six. Nineteen of Troilus's twenty-one superlatives, moreover, Chaucer has added in his reworking of Boccaccio's poem, partly because a considerable number of Troiolo's superlatives occur in passages which Chaucer has not translated or has given to the narrator in the Prohemium to Book III.

Not only does Troilus use more superlatives than Troiolo or his fellow characters in Chaucer's poem, he uses them in particularly medieval ways. Boccaccio's Troiolo, for example, praises Criseida's beauty and good manners in superlative terms but not her goodness or virtue. The closest he comes to such general praise is in his defense of Criseida before Cassandra, where he begins by denying his love (since he is embarrassed to admit it before Cassandra and her companions) and then qualifies his praise with conditionals, like the following:

> Ed elle sono in lei tutte vedute
> Se dall'opra l'effetto s'argomenta.   (VII, 94)

> Se non m'inganna forte la veduta,
> E quel ch'altri ne dice, più onesta
> Di costei nulla ne fia o è suta.   (VII, 95)

In this context, his conditional praise betrays his worldly bitterness and duplicity. Troilus, on the other hand, does not hesitate to praise both Criseyde's beauty and her virtue, finding her the fairest and the best (III, 1280, IV, 449); and when he answers Cassandra, he praises Criseyde without qualification, comparing her to Alceste. One might argue that this comparison cannot be considered truthful since Troilus, by this point in the poem, clearly suspects that Criseyde is false, but if there is a lie in this comparison, it is a subconscious lie which Troilus says not to fool others but to fool himself.

Troilus's praise of Criseyde, moreover, contrasts markedly with her praise of him. On one occasion, she starts to think of him as the worthiest, but then she checks herself: "For out and out he is the worthieste, / Save only Ector, which that is the beste" (II, 739–40). Twenty lines later, she calls Troilus, "this knyght, that is the worthieste," but that rhyme between "worthieste" and "Ector . . . the beste" lingers in the reader's ear as it probably does in hers. By placing Troilus second to Hector among Trojan knights, she shows the same guarded as well as traditional appraisal which one finds in both Pandarus and the narrator (II, 178, IV, 1565). The narrator is particularly careful in his praise. Christ is best, then Hector, then Troilus, whom he praises for distinct qualities, like his desire for worthiness and his friendly behavior (I, 566, 1079). He sees Pandarus not as, "O frend of frendes the alderbeste / That evere was" (III, 1597–98), which is Troilus's appraisal, but as he who is best at doing those services needed by a friend, a statement which might be taken ironically (III, 489). Chaucer thus establishes a definite hierarchy among the knights, with Christ firmly placed at the top, although explicitly placed there only at the end of the poem, and by this hierarchy, he calls into question Troilus's less realistic praise.

Troilus can also be distinguished from Troiolo by his use of superlatives to characterize himself. While Troiolo uses only two, and both of these early in the poem, Troilus uses eight. Some are self-deprecatory; others express his overwhelming sense of love or sorrow. More significantly, Troilus is the only character in Chaucer's poem to individualize himself in this conventional, medieval way.

Similar patterns can be found in the characters' statements of absolute commitment — that is, to love someone best of *all*, for *all* time, or with *all* one's heart. Chaucer's Troilus makes twenty-nine such statements, Boccaccio's Troiolo only seven, [9] and while Troilus's final statement of love is made in absolute terms (V, 1696–1701), Troiolo's is hedged with qualifications. He says that he no longer wants to love but has no choice since Criseida's image has not left his heart (VIII, 15). In these statements, Chaucer again contrasts Troilus's style with Criseyde's. Criseyde makes only three absolute commitments and these on only two occasions, just before and after making love, when her commitments are obviously influenced by her passion (III, 999, 1494, 1499). Normally, she prefers conditional commitments, in which the love of one of them depends on that of the other. In her first conversation with Troilus, she asks Pandarus to beseech Troilus: "for Goddes love, that he / Wolde, in honour of trouthe and gentilesse, / As I wel mene, eke menen wel to me" (III, 162–64); after making love, she says that since she is true to him, he should be true to her (III, 1511–12). In these conditional statements, she suggests that she sees love not as an absolute and eternal state but as one that depends on a particular person and time.

Finally, Troilus's style is conventional because of his frequent long monologues. Troilus's monologues extend for 477 lines, Criseyde's for 248 lines, and Pandarus's for sixteen lines. While Troilus tends to consider philosophic subjects, like love and destiny, Criseyde considers practical ones, like the consequences of loving Troilus or Diomede. In these monologues, Troilus frequently invokes classical gods, personified objects, and absent persons in expressions which are more extended and formal than common oaths. To show the comparative prevalence of these invocations in his speech, I counted after formal apostrophes all imperative and interrogative verbs. I counted only imperatives and interrogatives to limit the examples to the most emphatic, and I counted the verbs inflected rather than the nouns apostrophized because to invoke or question one god several times normally represents a more sustained effort than to invoke or question several gods one time. Troilus uses ninety-six such verbs, Criseyde sixteen, and Pandarus three, and all the verbs in Pandarus's speech occur when he gives Criseyde an example of how well Troilus can speak on love.[10] Pandarus obviously associates these expressions with the conventional language of love. Monologues and invocations are also prevalent in Troiolo's speech in the *Filostrato*, but Chaucer has increased the philosophic and medieval cast of Troilus's monologues by giving him two long passages from *The Consolation of Philosophy*, the hymn to love and the discourse on destiny. Through such passages, Chaucer raises central questions about the value of love and the existence of freedom with an insistence which Boccaccio avoids, perhaps because Boccaccio is far more interested in appealing to his mistress than in questioning love.

Chaucer thus uses conventional traits — superlatives, commitments, and monologues — to fashion Troilus's style. He reworks Boccaccio's poem to emphasize these traits; he distinguishes Troilus's style from that of the other characters by them. He thus portrays a conventional lover but not, we must add, in a lyric poem. Rather, he puts Troilus in the midst of a narrative with the result that the very action of the narrative challenges the static ideals of the lyric. How well Troilus survives, first from a moral, then from a realistic perspective, is the next focus of this paper.

Troilus tends, as we have noted, to use absolute statements, both in his superlative praise of Criseyde and in his total commitment to her. The narrative clearly shows that his praise is neither a helpful nor an accurate judgment, for Criseyde proves unfaithful. It also calls into question his commitment, for although his commitment may bring him one moment of bliss, it later intensifies his suffering. The narrative suggests, in brief, that anyone who puts his trust in this world will be disappointed since this world and all within it are changeable, mortal, and imperfect. This suggestion is made explicit at the poem's end where the narrator calls on young lovers to love Christ, since He is "best" to love.

Chaucer's criticism of Troilus's love, however, is not completely condemning. Even when one emphasizes the narrative, one can find patterns which reaffirm the moral values underlying Troilus's conventional language. One of these values is truth, the keeping of a commitment, and Troilus's truth to Criseyde seems all the more valuable if one notes that the major action in the poem, both political and personal, turns on the faithfulness or lack of faithfulness of the characters. In the political action, the poem opens when Calkas steals privily out of Troy to the Greek host. Since he is a Trojan, he should, as Troilus later points out, be truthful to Troy, but Calkas lacks Troilus's courage to be faithful when he can foresee that such faithfulness may lead to death. The next breach of faith occurs when the parliament supervenes Hector's promise to Criseyde and treats her not as a citizen but as a prisoner of war to be traded for Antenor. By this breach of faith, the people of Troy bring about their own destruction since Antenor later opens the gates to the wooden horse. Chaucer's argument is that a civilization's existence depends on the faithfulness of its citizens.[11]

If one turns from the political to the personal sphere, one finds much the same point, a linking of truth with existence. E. Talbot Donaldson in his commentary on the poem notes this linking when he praises Troilus's truth:

> [His] integrity, the quality that he will not surrender even to keep Criseyde with him, is the one human value the poem leaves entirely unquestioned: it is because of it that Troilus is granted his ultimate vision. It places him, of course, in sharp contrast with Criseyde and her *untrouthe*, and since one of the meanings of *trouthe* is reality, he emerges as more real than she.[12]

In fact, we question Troilus's reality only at those moments when he is not perfectly truthful — for example, when Criseyde asks Troilus how he came to be jealous and the narrator tells us:

> Withouten more, shortly for to seyne,
> He most obeye unto his lady heste;
> And for the lasse harm, he moste feyne.
> He seyde hire, whan she was at swich a feste,
> She myght on hym han loked at the leste, —
> Noot I nought what, al deere ynough a rysshe,
> As he that nedes most a cause fisshe.   (III, 1156–62)

Here, Troilus slips out of focus, for neither the narrator nor the reader can imagine exactly what he would say; but such moments are rare, and Troilus, because he remains essentially true to Criseyde, remains at the center of the narrative, the action following him even beyond his death to his ascension, where he is associated with the truth and reality of heaven. Criseyde, on the other hand, grows increasingly unfaithful, and as she does so, the action slips away from her. Her ultimate reality, as she recognizes, will be associated only with fiction: "O, rolled shal I ben on many a tonge! / Thorughout the world my belle shal be ronge!" (V, 1061–62). She becomes the subject of our judgment, not, like Troilus, judging us from heaven.

Several readers do not accept this emphasis on faithfulness as an important virtue in the poem. Although they would agree that Troilus is faithful, they discount his faithfulness by claiming that Troilus is faithful to an evil passion, that is, to cupidinous love. Taking this line of reasoning, D. W. Robertson finds Troilus the most culpable of all the characters in the poem:

> Neither Criseyde nor Diomede, both of whom seek momentary footholds on the slippery way of the world, is capable of the idolatry of which Troilus is guilty, or of the depths to which he descends.[13]

I certainly agree with Robertson that Troilus's love is misplaced, but I cannot accept his extreme condemnation of either Troilus or of secular love.

Although Troilus and Criseyde's love ends far from happily, the narrative still suggests that love itself is a positive, natural force, for it is love which takes Troilus out of his original self-absorption and changes him from an arrogant, mocking adolescent into a much more mature person, one who sees in a moment of bliss that love controls the world and one who later learns, when Criseyde must leave, that human love depends on personal choice, that all earthly love is transitory, and that Criseyde, far from being the best, is unfaithful. I do not wish to argue that Troilus's love is rational or perfect, for it is far too centered on Criseyde and far too dependent on her physical presence for such praise, but it is still the one force which connects him with the outer world. In fact, Troilus's behavior is most foolish and destructive when he is farthest from love's influence. One can point to the first two books where, before he really knows Criseyde or anything about love, his passion is primarily a self-construction, or to the first half of the fifth book, where his attention again spins back on himself and, caught between hope and dread, he can even mistake a "fare-carte" for Criseyde herself. The end of the narrative would be totally bleak if it did not show Troilus, once more moved by love, turning outwards, first to praise Criseyde before Cassandra, then to reassert his love for her to Pandarus. Since love is the one force which connects Troilus with the outer world, one can further argue that it together with his faithfulness is responsible for his final ascension and vision. Not until then, because he is a pagan, can Troilus see the truth. Perfected by his love, he is finally like the good soul in Boethius "that hath in itself science of gode werkes" and "beynge in hevene rejoyseth that it is exempt fro alle erthly thynges" (*Consolation*, Bk. II, prose 7, 151–57).

From a moral point of view, the narrative thus affirms the central values of secular love poetry: first, its emphasis on total commitment and faithfulness, without which a lover is hopelessly lost, even ceases to be; second, its promise of perfection, for although the lady may not herself be perfect, her association with perfection is fitting because love takes the individual beyond himself even to God. The poem's affirmation of these conventional values can be further illustrated by looking at some stylistic features in the characters' speech and at some general patterns in the imagery.

Although the following stylistic features may seem rather trivial, some important statements can be drawn from them. For example, Troilus never uses common idioms like *ich mente wel* or *I non yvel mene* while Pandarus and Criseyde use these expressions frequently, especially when they want to conceal the moral significance of a statement by avowing their good intentions.[14] A shocking example occurs at the end of Criseyde's letter where she says, "Th'entente is al, and nat the lettres space" (V, 1630), an avowal which reduces all the truth of language to the intention behind it. Troilus's avoidance of these idioms suggests that he has faith in his truthfulness and therefore does not think to distinguish between his meaning and intention. His inherent truthfulness can also be seen by his infrequent use of the oath, *by my trouthe*, which is one of Pandarus's favorites.[15] Pandarus probably uses this oath so frequently because he feels a continuing need to affirm as true what he suspects is false. Troilus, furthermore, does not pun, he does not mix terms of highly varied qualitative force to blur the moral implications of his statements, and he does not change his definition of various abstracts, like fortune or love, to fit the occasion.[16] For him, love cannot slide, as it does for Pandarus, from a gift of grace (I, 896) to a casual pleasure (IV, 419). By these small traits, one can see that Troilus is an absolutist not only in his commitment to Criseyde but also in his sense of language. He accepts the meaning of words, their integrity, just as he accepts the integrity of other people. These details show that Chaucer is concerned with the moral implications of everyday speech — that is, with the relation between habitual language patterns and habitual behavior. On this level, Troilus is not, as Robertson states, the lowest character in the poem; rather, he is the most praiseworthy.

The imagery of the poem, moreover, works against Robertson's polar distinctions between cupidity and charity, for it suggests that all love is part of God's love, that sexuality and charity are in one continuum.[17] In the Prohemium to Book III, for example, Venus is described both as the divine force of life itself, the "vapour eterne" which is normally associated with the Holy Spirit, and immediately afterwards as the sexual force behind the amorous exploits of Jove. Because Chaucer adds to Boccaccio the explicitly sexual reference to Jove, his intention is clear: he wants to include the sacred and physical under the influence of Venus. He thus sets up a pattern continued throughout Book III.

After Troilus and Criseyde first make love, Troilus praises love in the following stanza:

> "Benigne Love, thow holy bond of thynges,
> Whoso wol grace, and list the nought honouren,
> Lo, his desir wol fle withouten wynges.
> For noldestow of bownte hem socouren
> That serven best and most alwey labouren,
> Yet were al lost, that dar I wel seyn certes,
> But if thi grace passed oure desertes."   (III, 1261–67)

The passage is surprising, for Troilus, although he has just experienced the physical delight of love, emphasizes not the physical but the spiritual.

He invokes love as "thow holy bond of thynges," a phrase which recalls
Boethius, and then uses an image taken from Dante's final Canto in the
Paradiso, where Dante praises the Blessed Virgin Mary for so ennobling
human nature that God, man's Creator, did not disdain to become His
creation. The parallel is significant because Mary is the mortal link which
joins God and man and because Mary, throughout the *Divina Comedia*,
represents woman's pity and love. She first urges Beatrice to have pity on
Dante (*Inferno* II, 94–99). What Chaucer has done in this stanza and the
one preceding it, where Troilus praises the planet Venus as "O Love, O
Charite," is to bring together a wide range of references traditionally
associated with love. These references give a spiritual significance to
Troilus and Criseyde's love.

One can sense this same combination of physical and spiritual love in a
stanza at the end of the poem. The narrator is admonishing young lovers
to return home from worldly vanity and love Christ:

> the which that right for love
> Upon a crois, oure soules for to beye,
> First starf, and roos, and sit in hevene above;
> For he nyl falsen no wight, dar I seye,
> That wol his herte al holly on hym leye.
> And syn he best to love is, and most meke,
> What nedeth feynede loves for to seke?   (V, 1842–48)

Although the main purpose of this stanza is not to remind us of Troilus,
the narrator's superlative to describe Christ, "syn he best to love is," and
his quantitative intensifiers to describe the perfect lover, who "wol his
herte al holly on hym leye," do recall Troilus and his conventional
language. The language of secular love, "the olde clerkis spech / In
poetrie," is thus shifted to describe the perfect Christian love, a shift
suggesting that the old speech is not ultimately opposed to the God of
love, just as the Old Law is not ultimately opposed to the New.[18] The Old
is imperfect but it promises the New. Troilus's love is imperfect,
particularly because it is misplaced, but in his faithfulness and
commitment he represents an essentially heroic and worthy lover.

One can make similar moral evaluations without all the work of
stylistic criticism, but the stylistic criticism does show Chaucer's explicit
concern for the language patterns of lyric poetry and for the values
inherent in them. An attention to Troilus's style can also lead into
another area of criticism, one concerned less with an evaluation of moral

issues than with an understanding of Troilus's believability as a character. At the turn of the century, many critics were delighted with *Troilus and Criseyde* because they found it like a novel, calling it, in fact, "the first novel in the modern sense," and they praised in particular the realism of the character motivation.[19] More modern critics have backed away from this interpretation by arguing that Troilus, in any case, could not be considered as a realistic character. Instead, they have viewed him as the type of the idolator or the conventional lover. My emphasis up to now has been on Troilus as a conventional lover, and I do not want to transform him into a purely realistic character who can be understood by the rules of the nineteenth-century novel or Freudian psychology. I do want, however, to change my emphasis and consider him from a more realistic point of view. From this point of view, Troilus often looks helpless or absurd.[20] He is the static, lyric protagonist who is incapable of action and therefore the butt of many jokes. It is important to recognize Troilus's absurdity, for Chaucer questions not only the moral but also the practical implications of his language and behavior. I think Troilus's stature survives all the irony and jokes, but before coming to his defense, let me again clarify the extent to which Chaucer challenges him.

Irony occurs particularly when the realistic demands of the narrative call into question Troilus's idealism. For example, early in the poem Troilus pictures Criseyde as the cruel lady of traditional poetry:

"But also cold in love towardes the
Thi lady is, as frost in wynter moone,
And thow fordon, as snow in fire is soone."   (I, 523–25)

Although the poetry may be effective, this description of Criseyde is ridiculously inaccurate, partly because Troilus has never spoken with her. The narrator, however, does not raise this objection so that he can raise an even more obvious one:

All was for nought: she herde nat his pleynte;
And whan that he bythought on that folie,
A thousand fold his wo gan multiplie.

(I, 544–46)

One has the distinct impression that if it were not for Pandarus, Troilus would wear out his life in woeful verses.

Once Pandarus comes into the poem, he takes up the ironic role. He particularly deflates Troilus's long invocations. Before the meeting with

Criseyde at Pandarus's house, Troilus appeals to all the gods of Olympus, much to the frustration of Pandarus who wants to bring him and Criseyde together. Pandarus finally interrupts, "Thow wrecched mouses herte, / Artow agast so that she wol the bite?" (III, 736–37). Pandarus shows the same frustration at the end of Troilus's monologue on predestination where he mocks Troilus's invocation, "Almyghty Jove in trone, / That woost of al this thyng the sothfastnesse . . .," with his own, "O myghty God . . . in trone, / I! who say evere a wis man faren so?" (IV, 1079–80, 86–87). His reply is brilliant because he radically changes the perspective from the heavens to the earth. Pandarus sees Troilus's logical errors clearly. Troilus has forgotten that he lives in time, that time gives man freedom, and that Criseyde, quite simply, has not yet gone. In effect, he has confused his foresight with God's foresight.

Through Pandarus's and the narrator's comments, Chaucer keeps in the foreground the impracticality of Troilus's speech and action. Troilus's long monologues and invocations are dismissed as retreats; his conventional praise of Criseyde is undercut by his ignorance. Chaucer particularly questions Troilus's absolute commitments and the meaning of his repeated adverbial intensifiers. When Pandarus says to Criseyde,

> "Ther were nevere two so wel ymet,
> Whan ye ben his al hool, as he is youre . . ."

Criseyde understands all the sexual implications,

> "Nay, therof spak I nought, ha, ha!" quod she;
> "As helpe me God, ye shenden every deel!"   (II, 586–90)

But when Troilus uses similar intensifiers in his vows of service,

> "God woot, for I have,
> As ferforthly as I have had konnynge,
> Ben youres al, God so my soule save . . ."

Criseyde is understandably confused,

> "Now thanne thus," quod she, "I wolde hym preye
> To telle me the fyn of his entente.
> Yet wist I nevere wel what that he mente."
>   (III, 100–102, 124–26)

By such comparisons, Chaucer is obviously poking fun at conventional language. What *does* it mean to commit oneself totally to another person, to say, I am all yours? The speaker in a lyric poem does not need to worry about the realistic implications of such commitments — he exists outside of time and the statement is all — but Troilus does have to worry because his statements about love, unless realized in action, will not satisfy his desire. His problem is that of all conventional lovers: he wants Criseyde to remain an idealized object whom he can worship in a thousand selfless and acceptable acts, but he also wants her as a woman in bed, and this problem is only resolved when Pandarus hefts him into Criseyde's bed. Troilus, I think, seems most foolish in the first three books, since it is in these that Chaucer particularly makes fun of the impractical idealism inherent in the traditional love poetry.

If one stresses only the irony, then Troilus begins to look like a caricature of a lover. Such an interpretation, however, misses his strength. Troilus is a far more convincing character partly, as has been suggested, because he remains faithful but also because his speech implies a coherent sense of the world and has a peculiar force and energy.

When the conventional traits in Troilus's speech are considered together, the emerging patterns are surprisingly consistent. For example, Troilus is the one character who uses unqualified superlatives to describe himself. In these he separates himself from others either as someone who is unique in all time, "For nevere man was to yow goddes holde / As I, which ye han brought fro cares colde" (III, 1259-60), or as someone who is unique in a group of people, "O Troilus, what may men now the calle / But wrecche of wrecches, out of honour falle" (IV, 270-71). In the second example, he increases his feelings of separateness by worrying what the world will say. He has the same fear just after he falls in love:

> "What wol now every lovere seyn of the,
> If this be wist? but evere in thin absence
> Laughen in scorn, and seyn, 'Loo, ther goth he
> That held us loveres leest in reverence.'"   (I, 512-16)

Later, when he thinks about disobeying his father's decree, he fears the "blame of every wight" (IV, 551), and, in Book V, he believes that he has become so woe-begone that "every wight" looks on him as they pass him by (V, 625). Even when he is happy, he thinks that he is being watched and thus accuses the sun: "For every bore hath oon of thi bryghte yën!" (III, 1453). In these expressions, he shows an unusual degree of self-consciousness, which one does not find in the other characters, not even in Criseyde. She also fears the blame of others and even, at the end of the poem, worries that her name will be rolled on every tongue, but she does not think of herself as unique, for she finds consolation in the thought that she is not the first to do amiss (V, 1061–67). Others may place her in a separate category; she refuses to do so herself.

Troilus's tendency to think of himself as unique is also clear in another conventional feature of his language, his infrequent use of proverbs.[21] One might dismiss this infrequency as an accident of style — courtly lovers do not tend to use proverbs — but Chaucer has made it an obvious part of Troilus's personality by showing how Troilus, early in the poem, consciously rejects Pandarus's proverbial wisdom:

> ". . . Now pees, and crye namore,
> For I have herd thi wordes and thi lore;
> But suffre me my meschief to bywaille,
> For thi proverbes may me naught availle."   (I, 753–56)

In effect, Troilus does not want to be consoled with proverbs. On other occasions, he used them only to mock Pandarus's and Criseyde's own proverbial statements or to single out a highly specific feature of some person or event. He implicitly rejects their basic assumption: that he and everyone else are always alike. Reta Anderson Madsen, in an unpublished dissertation on rhetorical figures in Chaucer, does not discuss Troilus's tendency to isolate himself, but she does draw an important conclusion from his rejection of proverbs:

> He confronts reality much more nakedly than Pandarus or even Criseyde. Neither his emotions nor his reactions are dulled by the recognition that others have felt and reacted in the same way and with predictable results. . . . Paradoxically, he is a basically conventional character who cannot be comforted by conventions, while the more realistic characters of the poem draw much of their strength from their recognition of and use of the power of convention.[22]

In stressing the conventionality of Troilus's language, I have implied that he is similar to most medieval lovers. It is true that he is similar, but not true that he is exactly the same, for he is far more insistent about his unique and special fate than most lovers. Typically, lovers in Machaut and Froissart commit themselves, then draw back to think about love and fortune. In their monologues on these subjects, they compare themselves with others. Mars in Chaucer's *Compleynt of Mars* goes through the same pattern. After an early commitment, he thinks of his hopeless fate, ironically questions love, and then finds some consolation in the recognition: "So fareth hyt by lovers and by me." Similar statements can be found in Anelida's complaints from *Anelida and Arcite* and in Criseyde's complaints. Only after doubts and comparisons do the above lovers recommit themselves to love. Troilus also has his doubts about love, especially before he commits himself to Criseyde, and about fortune, especially in Books IV and V, but once he commits himself, he does not equate his experience with that of others. Even in his three long complaints about fortune, he always thinks of himself as unique. In the first, he calls himself the most wretched person who has ever lived (IV, 270-71); in the second, he appeals to lovers who are at the top of Fortune's wheel to come and look down at his sepulture (IV, 323-39); in the third, he carries on a running argument between what some clerks would say and what he would say (IV, 958-1078).

Troilus's instinctive tendency to separate himself from others, to think of himself as unique, and to think of his destiny as determined helps to explain why he experiences life with such a singular intensity. In the context, his extreme language, including his superlative praise, his total commitments, even his highly rhetorical complaints, becomes more realistic and believable, since only this language has sufficient intensity to fit his sense of himself and his destiny. In fashioning the character of Troilus, Chaucer thus uses conventional rhetoric, but he increases its moral significance and its realism by giving it to a lover whose behavior and self-consciousness are consistent.

Troilus's strength and intelligence are also implied by the rhythm and energy of his syntax. When reading the poem, one tends to think of Troilus's style as opposed to Pandarus's style. Troilus's style is courtly and lyric and therefore, one assumes, artificial, while Pandarus's style is naturalistic and life-like and therefore convincing, but one has to guard against too easy an acceptance of this distinction because, in fact, all the characters share basically the same language and can use a wide range of styles from the most courtly to the most naturalistic. When Troilus loses his temper with Pandarus, he can sound just as colloquial as Pandarus (I, 621-24, 752-56); when Pandarus must beg a favor of Deiphebus, he employs all the conditional verbs and balanced phrases which one expects when Troilus is addressing Criseyde (II, 1430-42). One has to recognize

that Pandarus and Troilus are flexible in their speech, that they are not
caricatures locked into a single idiom. To make this reservation, however,
is not to deny that Pandarus tends to speak one way, Troilus another, as
can be shown by a comparison of two passages. In the first, Pandarus is
telling Troilus to accept the wisdom of his experience, even if he,
Pandarus, has not been all that successful in love:

> "A wheston is no kervyng instrument,
> But yet it maketh sharppe kervyng tolis.
> And there thow woost that I have aught myswent,
> Eschuw thow that, for swich thing to the scole is;
> Thus often wise men ben war by foolys.
> If thow do so, thi wit is wel bewared;
> By his contrarie is every thyng declared.
>
> "For how myghte evere swetnesse han ben knowe
> To him that nevere tasted bitternesse?
> Ne no man may ben inly glad, I trowe,
> That nevere was in sorwe or som destresse.
> Eke whit by blak, by shame ek worthinesse,
> Ech set by other, more for other semeth,
> As men may se, and so the wyse it demeth."   (I, 631–44)

The overall impression of these two stanzas is that one pithy phrase is
added to the next with the meaning of each statement contained within a
line or a couplet. The number of t-units (independent clauses plus their
modifiers) is high, nine for fourteen lines, and the co-ordination from one
clause to the next is either done by parataxis or by co-ordinating
conjunction. The movement is one of addition, not of subordination.
There is some verb suspension for rhetorical emphasis, as in the last two
lines where the suspension is neatly parallel. There is also some padding
with conversational tags, like "I trowe" and "as men may see." Finally,
there are nineteen finite verbs in a total of 113 words for a finite verb
percentage of 16.8%. The percentage of finite verbs in a passage can be an
indication both of the level of style (that is, the more finite verbs, the
more informal the style), and of the argumentative forcefulness of the
language (the more finite verbs, the more forceful).[23] Pandarus's average
finite verb percentage is 14.7%. Troilus's is 13.5%, which is not
remarkably lower but an indication of his tendency on a serious or
uncomfortable occasion to use a more periodic and formal style. Troilus
particularly uses this more formal style with Criseyde. With her, his

finite verb percentage is 11.7%.

The following passage is spoken by Troilus when he promises that he shall never reveal his love for Criseyde:

> "Thow woost how longe ich it [Criseyde's name] forbar to seye
> To the, that art the man that I best triste;
> And peril non was it to the bywreye,
> That wist I wel, but telle me, if the liste,
> Sith I so loth was that thiself it wiste,
> How dorst I mo tellen of this matere,
> That quake now, and no wight may us here?
>
> "But natheles, by that God I the swere,
> That, as hym list, may al this world governe, —
> And, if I lye, Achilles with his spere
> Myn herte cleve, al were my lif eterne,
> As I am mortal, if I late or yerne
> Wolde it bewreye, or dorst, or sholde konne,
> For al the good that God made under sonne —
>
> "That rather deye I wolde, and determyne,
> As thynketh me, now stokked in prisoun,
> In wrecchidnesse, in filthe, and in vermyne,
> Caytif to cruel kyng Agamenoun:
> And this in all the temples of this town
> Upon the goddes alle, I wol the swere
> To-morwe day, if that it like the here."   (III. 365–85)

The syntax of the first stanza is relatively simple, but it contains two examples of a construction which occurs frequently in Troilus's speech. These are the embedded clauses, "If the liste" and "Sith I so loth was that thiself it wiste," which come between the imperative, "telle," and its complement, "How dorst I mo tellen. . . ."

The syntax of the next two stanzas is far more complex, primarily because of such embedded clauses. The stanzas can be simplified by omissions and re-arrangements and the change of an *if* to a *than* to read in Modern English: I swear by God, I would rather die and come to an end in prison [than] reveal your secret, and if I lie, let Achilles end my life, even if my life were as eternal as it is mortal. I have changed the *if* to *than* since *rather* in both Middle and Modern English calls for the latter conjunction.[24] A major difference between the original and my rearrangement is that in the original one can feel Troilus's energy as he works through all kinds of contingent materials, like God's creation of the world, to his emphatic conclusion, his readiness to die in prison. The passage shows his habit of exploring all sides and possibilities, even though his explorations seldom, if ever, change his original feelings. One can indicate the syntactic involutions in the passage by pointing out that the number of t-units is fairly low, six in twenty-one lines, and the number of embedded clauses extremely high, ten for the same number of lines. (There were nine t-units and two embedded clauses in Pandarus's passage of fourteen lines.)[25] Given this syntactic involvement, one might expect that the finite verb percentage would also be low, indicating a high degree of nominal elements; but, in fact, the percentage is rather high, 16.2%, and in the first two stanzas, extremely high, 19.7%, for here Troilus's thought is most active and complex. In the last stanza, where he is moving to a rhetorical conclusion, the percentage drops to 8%, and the syntax also becomes more additive and balanced, as shown by the repeated prepositional phrases. These two extremes, either of syntactical complexity or of rhetorical balance, are frequent in Troilus's verse and sometimes occur together, as in this passage. He either puzzles over an argument or seeks a rhetorically balanced statement. To gain this balance in other passages, he uses such figures as anaphora (the repetition of opening words or phrases) and *similiter cadens* (the repetition of concluding sounds in one part of speech), or he repeats larger sentence units, like introductory dependent clauses or short independent and interrogative clauses.[26]

Although it is dangerous to make general statements about a character merely by looking at his syntax, I think one can use syntactic evidence to reinforce and re-evaluate statements based on other criteria. For example, one can argue that the involved movement in Troilus's argumentative passages and the heavy repetition in his rhetorical conclusions — his tendency to twist, turn, and repeat before he concludes a sentence — that these interruptions suggest a desire for stasis, a desire to stop the movement of time in order to understand. The syntactic evidence thus reinforces what we have already observed: namely, that Troilus, a lyric protagonist, constantly wants to withdraw from the narrative. This evidence, however, can also lead to a re-evaluation. I think we tend to assume that a character who constantly withdraws must be yielding and passive, but after noting the energy in Troilus's syntax, one must qualify this assumption. Troilus may decide that an action is impossible — for example, in the predestination speech where he begins with the wrong premises — but his decision is marked by the most vigorous argument. Throughout the poem, he struggles with words, seeking the best expression for his ideas and feelings. In this struggle, he is quite unlike Boccaccio's Troiolo, whose language tends to have an almost slick self-assurance as well as an evenness of pace which Troilus's language almost never assumes.[27]

An examination of syntax can likewise lead to both a reinforcement and a re-evaluation of our observations on Pandarus. If we tend to think of Troilus as passive, we also tend to think of Pandarus as active. He is always busy, jumping and leaping, and his language, with its colloquial diction and pat phrases, bustles with life. The syntactic evidence — Pandarus's use of an accumulative, open, and co-ordinate style — reinforces these basic impressions. Pandarus's language flows along as Pandarus flows along, with an easy and assured acceptance of time. Perhaps, however, the very easiness of his language can lead to a re-evaluation of our original impressions, and even if we cannot deny his *bysynesse,* we can question its quality, especially when recognizing that his language and thoughts, although often perceptive, tend to be lazy. Unlike Troilus, he does not seek an original expression for his thoughts or feelings. Instead, he relies on the most convenient idioms or proverbs and seldom varies his syntax. In brief, Pandarus accepts language as it comes, and it comes easily to him, while Troilus, although he uses many conventional images, never gives the impression that such language is automatic or natural. He is always examining, always thinking or feeling as shown by his dense syntax. The energy of his expression as much as anything else convinces the reader that he must not be dismissed merely as a caricature of a lover.

In this paper, I have concentrated on Troilus's style, not because it is the most distinctive in the poem, but because it leads to the poem's central issues. One responds to the moral issues as one responds to Troilus. If one finds Troilus foolish, then I think one tends to find the whole poem and all the praise of love foolish (or perhaps ironic); but if one finds Troilus heroic, even in a limited way, then the poem also has a serious stature and Troilus's values seem worthy of respect. In his conclusion, Chaucer bids his poem to be subject to all great poetry and to "kis the steppes, where as thow seest pace / Virgile, Ovide, Omer, Lucan, and Stace" (V, 1791–92). For all his humility in this prayer, Chaucer is still placing his poem in the most esteemed poetic company of his time and thereby asking us to consider it as a highly serious work. The irony in the poem is there, but Troilus is also there — stubborn, consistent, and faithful. About Troilus's style, one can say that it is conventional but not that it is artificially conventional, since it is perfectly consistent with his character even to the extent of revealing some subtle aspects of his motivation. One can also say that his style is sometimes foolish but not foolish for the same reasons that Pandarus's and Criseyde's styles are foolish, not because he is shifting vaguely from one issue to the next or swearing profusely by his good intentions. His arguments may be unconvincing but his energy is convincing. Finally, although the poem questions all the values of Troilus's style, the narrator at the end uses the same style to describe the perfect Christian love. Chaucer does not renounce the traditional values of the "olde clerkis speche." Instead, he embodies them in Troilus, who is second only to Hector in all Troy.

APPENDIX: FINITE VERB PERCENTAGES IN CHAUCER

Finite verb percentages provide an accurate indication for the level of speech, from formal to colloquial, throughout Chaucer's poetry, and fairly small differences in percentage can show appreciable difference in style. The sensitivity of F-V percentages as an indicator derives from Chaucer's decasyllabic line. In passages which are neutral in level of formality, Chaucer uses about one finite verb per line, and since the number of words per line averages out at 7.8, the F-V percentage is just over 12.5%. Chaucer's normal narrative, in fact, shows a slightly lower F-V percentage since about one line in four or five will not have a finite verb. Chaucer gains variety by using either a series of infinitives which have been introduced by a modal verb, a series of present particles, or even a few lines without verbal elements. In conversational passages, the F-V percentage rises above 12.5% since the speakers use more short clauses and more common idioms. The following F-V percentages for Chaucerian narrators in *The Canterbury Tales* have been computed on passages totalling at least 1,000 words, except for the Summoner and Friar, where the base is 500 words. The percentages indicate the general levels of formality and clearly distinguish between the fairly formal narrators, like the Friar and the Clerk, and the clearly informal ones, like the Canon's Yeoman and the Wife of Bath: Friar 11.0%, Clerk 11.3%, Nun's Priest 11.3%, Knight 11.6%, Pardoner 11.7%, narrator of General Prologue 11.8%, Miller 12.4%, Summoner 12.8%, Canon's Yeoman 13.2%, Wife of Bath 14.4%.

The following percentages for various characters in the tales themselves are based on passages of 500 words or more: in The Knight's Tale, Arcita 12.4%, Palamon 12.4%, Theseus (in the Chain of Love speech) 12.4%, Theseus (at the end of Book II) 13.6%; in The Nun's Priest's Tale, Chauntecleer 14.2%; in The Friar's Tale, the Summoner and the Fiend 14.2%; in the Miller's Tale, Nicholas 14.8%.

The following percentages for *Troilus and Criseyde* are from passages totalling 6,000 words or more: the narrator 12.2%, Criseyde 13.2%, Troilus 13.5%, and Pandarus 14.7%. It is interesting to note that Pandarus's percentages do not vary with auditor, an indication that his level of style remains pretty much the same. He averages 14.7% when speaking with·Troilus and 14.6% with Criseyde, while Troilus's F-V percentages show considerable variation, 14.1% with Pandarus, 14.0% in monologues, and 11.7% with Criseyde. Criseyde's percentages also vary. She is most colloquial, perhaps because she is most at ease, in her monologues where the F-V percentage is 14.1%. With Pandarus, it is 13.5% and with Troilus, 12.6%.

Notes

1. Charles Muscatine, *Chaucer and the French Tradition* (Berkeley, 1964), pp. 124–65, quotations from pp. 134, 135, 148.

2. Leo Spitzer, *Essays in English and American Literature*, ed. Anna Hatcher (Princeton, 1962), pp. 192–247; Paul Zumthor, "Style and Expressive Register in Medieval Poetry," in *Literary Style, A Symposium*, ed. Seymour Chatman (New York, 1971), pp. 263–84. These articles helped me focus on certain stylistic traits, but my indebtedness by no means ends with them. My greatest debt is to my dissertation adviser at Yale University, Marie Borroff, who helped me develop the methods of stylistic analysis used in this paper. Stephen Barney read my dissertation and encouraged me to continue my work. His article, "Troilus Bound," SPECULUM 48 (1972), 445–58, complements mine and is one of several important studies which emphasize Troilus's imagery. These include: Sanford B. Meech, *Design in Chaucer's Troilus* (Syracuse, 1959); Peter Dronke, "L'Amor che move il sole e l'altre stelle," *Studi Medievali* 6 (1965), 389–422, and "The Conclusion of *Troilus and Criseyde*," *Medium Aevum* 33 (1964), 47–52; P.M. Kean, *Chaucer and the Making of English Poetry*, 1 (London, 1972), 112–178; D.W. Robertson, Jr., *A Preface to Chaucer* (Princeton, 1963); Ida Gordon, *The Double Sorrow of Troilus* (Oxford, 1970). I have not particularly emphasized the figures in Troilus's speech because the above authors have covered this field with considerable thoroughness even though they often disagree in their conclusions.

3. These medieval constructions include negative comparisons which exclude the possibility of any equal in time or space. "For nevere man was to yow goddes holde/As I" (III, 1259–60), and metaphoric identifications with an object representing a superlative degree of excellence, "O swerd of knyghthod" (V, 1591). Spitzer mentions other

superlative phrases which do not occur in Chaucer's *Troilus* (*Essays*, pp. 198–99), and to his list, one can add a particular genitive construction which occurs twice in Troilus's speech, first when he thinks of himself as, "wrecche of wrecches" (IV, 271), and second when he calls Criseyde's house, "O hous of houses" (V, 541). This construction is probably modeled on Latin genitives, like *servus servorum* and *sanctus sanctorum*, which themselves are modeled on Hebrew partitive genitives. For a further description of this construction, the reader can refer to my dissertation, "Style and Character in Chaucer's *Troilus*," Yale University, 1969, pp. 25–26. Throughout this article, I have referred to the above constructions simply as superlatives, not as superlative phrases.

4. "Les Fêtes de mai et les commencements de la poesie lyrique au Moyen Age," *Revue des deux mondes* (mai, 1897), p. 172.

5. Guillaume de Lorris and Jean de Meun, *Le Roman de la Rose*, ed. Ernest Langlois, 5 vols., SATF (Paris, 1914–24), 2:115.

6. "What Chaucer Really Did to *Il Filostrato*," *Essays and Studies by Members of the English Association* 17 (1932), 56 [above, p.37].

7. The term "unqualified superlative" refers to superlatives which are not qualified in one of the following ways: by the specification of a limited place or time, by the indication of a clearly subjective opinion, or by the use of a conditional, future, or interrogative verb that calls into doubt the firmness of the statement. The stanza references given below are to Vittore Branca, *Tutte le opere di Giovanni Boccaccio*, 2 (Verona, 1967), and those in italics designate superlatives where the character is referring to himself: Troiolo: I, *50, 55*; III, 58, 81, 81, 84; IV, 50, 164; V, 62; VII, 93. Narrator: I, 17, 19, 25; III, 90; IV, 86; V, 1, 41; VIII, 28. Pandaro: II, 22, 23, 41, 42, 44, 54; IV, 64. Criseida: III, *66*; IV, *128, 162*.

8. Quotations and references for Chaucer are to the second edition of F. N. Robinson, *The Works of Geoffrey Chaucer* (Boston, 1957). Each line reference below indicates a subject which, in one or more aspects, is designated as superlative without limiting qualification, and the italics are used as in note 8. Troilus: I, 331, 339, *514, 534*, 603; III, 417, *1259, 1268*, 1271, *1279*, 1280, 1597, 1604; IV, *270*, 288, *304*, 449, *516*; V, 541, 547, 1527. Narrator: I, 152, 171, 174, 230, 241, 243, 247, 248, 283, 566, 1079; II, 450; III, 488; V, 20, 198, 247, 439, 447, 808, 821, 1565, 1847. Pandarus: I, 1002; II, 177, 204, 293, 348, 1030, 1150; III, 781, 1626. Criseyde: II, 729, 740, 761; V, 1591.

9. Citations for Chaucer are to the first line of each minimal terminal unit (t-unit) containing a commitment. A t-unit is an independent clause with its modifying dependent clauses and phrases, and in modern punctuation, a t-unit might properly be separated from other t-units by periods. Troilus: I, 427, 535, 1053, 1055; III, 100, 131, 141, 390, 417, 712, 1297, 1604, 1611; IV, 320, 442, 447, 472, 1654; V, 229, 573, 586, 593, 1317, 1364, 1412, 1414, 1417, 1696, 1699. Criseyde: III, 999, 1494, 1499. Pandarus: I, 593, 988; IV, 624. Citations for Boccacio are to stanzas in Branca's text. Troiolo: I, 38; III, 36, 59; IV, 50, 54; VII, 47, 52. Criseida: III, 49, 50. Pandaro: none. Narrator: I, 4.

10. For line references, see Taylor, "Style and Character," pp. 287–88.

11. See, e.g., W. F. Bolton, "Treason in *Troilus*," *Archiv* 203 (1967), 255–62.

12. E. Talbot Donaldson, *Chaucer's Poetry, An Anthology for the Modern Reader* (New York, 1958), p. 974.

13. D. W. Robertson, Jr., *A Preface to Chaucer: Studies in Medieval Perspectives* (Princeton, 1962), p. 499.

14. Expressions with the verb, *menen*, like *Ich mente wel*: Pandarus, II, 364, 438, 581, 592, 721; III, 337; Criseyde, III, 164, 1164; V, 1004. Expressions with the nouns, *entente* and *entencioun*, like *And sith I speke of good entencioun*: Pandarus, I, 683; II, 295, 363, 580; Criseyde, III, 1166; V, 1630.

15. This expression occurs thirteen times in Pandarus's speech and twice in Troilus's speech.

16. For Pandarus's puns, see II, 1238-39, 1319-20, 1638. Troilus's word play consists of a rhetorical repetition of sounds, in which the meaning of the words is not changed. See his letter to Criseyde (V, 1354-55). For passages where Pandarus mixes terms of highly varied qualitative strength, see II, 430-35, III, 913, IV, 596-97. For Pandarus's conflicting comments on Fortune, see I, 848-49, where he emphasizes the turning of the wheel, and III, 1630-31, where he suggests that if one sits very still, the wheel will stop.

17. See Kean's and Dronke's works cited above for a more complete treatment of this subject.

18. In *Troilus and Criseyde*, what has often been called courtly love is set in a pagan world, and Christian ideas, like sin and forgiveness, are associated with pagan gods, like Venus, Cupid, Jove, Mars, and Fortune. Chaucer is thus bringing together two worlds, the medieval courtly and the classical pagan, or, more exactly, he is associating the courtly with the pagan. When he refers to the "olde clerkis" in the phrase, "olde clerkis speche," he is probably continuing this association of pagan and courtly and may thus be referring to both classical writers, like Statius, Lucan, and Ovid, and to medieval Christian writers in the French tradition. The "olde clerkis speche" would thus include the secular love language which has been described in this paper. The relationships between Christian and pagan worlds are treated at greater length by Donald R. Howard, *The Three Temptations, Medieval Man in Search of the World* (Princeton, 1966), pp. 111-18.

19. For examples of this criticism, see Thomas R. Price, *"Troilus and Criseyde*: A Study in Chaucer's Method of Narration," *PMLA* 11 (1896), 307-22, and George Lyman Kittredge, *Chaucer and his Poetry* (Cambridge, Mass., 1960), especially p. 112 [above, p. 3], from which I have quoted above. A list of articles treating *T&C* as a novel is given by Karl Young, "Chaucer's *Troilus and Criseyde* as Romance," *PMLA* 53 (1938), 38-39. For a survey of more recent criticism, see Alfred David, "The Hero of Troilus," SPECULUM 37 (1962), 566-69.

20. R. K. Root emphasizes his helplessness, Charles Muscatine his absurdity, although Muscatine also feels that Troilus keeps his dignity even in comic situations. My own position is close to Muscatine's. See R. K. Root, *The Poetry of Chaucer*, 2nd ed. (Boston, 1922), p. 117, and Muscatine, *Chaucer*, pp. 136-39, 150-53.

21. A full discussion of proverbial statements in Chaucer is given by Bartlett Jere Whiting, *Chaucer's Use of Proverbs*, Harvard Studies in Comparative Literature 11 (Cambridge, Mass., 1934). Using his references, I have considered all proverbial statements which give or support instruction, thus implying a standard behavior for everyone, and all those which make comparisons between someone and a proverbial person or animal, thus implying that everyone is alike. Troilus makes ten such comments, but four of these occur on two occasions when he is obviously impatient with Pandarus's and Criseyde's proverbs (IV, 463-69, 1450-59). Of the other six, two occur in his early and rather adolescent pronouncements on love (I, 202, 509), and three stress the singularity of some quality in himself or another (II, 985, IV, 1459, V, 426). On one occasion, he uses a proverbial statement to generalize about life, but on that occasion, he makes from his experience a proverb. He does not use a pre-existent proverb to understand his experience (III, 1282).

Pandarus uses sixty-one proverbial comments that fall into the above categories, Criseyde twenty-eight, and the narrator twenty-five, seventeen of which occur in Book I and the Prohemium to Book II. As Troilus's experience in love deepens, the narrator seems to feel less and less confident that life can be understood or directed from a proverbial point of view.

22. "Some Functions of Medieval Rhetoric in Chaucer's Verse Narratives," Diss. Yale University, 1967, p. 207. The dissertation is listed at Yale University under her maiden name, Reta Margaret Anderson, and it is quoted with the permission of the author.

23. Professor Marie Borroff first directed my attention to both t-units and finite verb percentages as significant measures of syntactic complexity. For a fuller discussion of F-V percentages in Chaucer, please see Appendix.

24. Troilus could follow the clause, "If I reveal it," with a main clause, "let me die." He uses instead the clause, "I would rather die," a change which suggests that he has somewhat lost his original train of thought, but the sentence does not radically break apart, as in an anacoluthon where a new construction takes over before an old one is completed. I have found only one anacoluthon in Troilus's speech (III, 361) but ten in Pandarus's speech (I, 659-62, 806-09; II, 337-43, 379-80, 1279-81; III, 771-77; IV, 397-99, 1086-87; V, 324-26, 337-41). While Troilus's sentences often show emotional strain, they do not fall apart from casual thoughtlessness. His syntax is more strict and formal, while Pandarus's syntax is more open and colloquial. For a full discussion of colloquial traits in Chaucer's verse, see Margaret Schlauch, "Chaucer's Colloquial English: its Structural Traits," *PMLA* 67 (1952), 1103-16, and for a fuller application of her criteria to *Troilus and Criseyde*, see Taylor, "Style and Character," pp. 78-88.

25. To provide further statistical support, I have chosen in a random though even distribution several passages, which add up to at least 700 lines for each speaker, and counted within them both t-units and embedded clauses. I have defined an embedded clause as a clause which occurs somewhere between the subject, verb, and complement of another clause, regardless of the order of those elements. In the following passage,

> "Love, ayeins the which whoso defendeth
> Hymselven most, hym alderlest avaylleth,
> With disespeyr so sorwfulli me offendeth,
> That streight unto the deth myn herte sailleth,   (I, 603-06)

the entire clause, "ayeins the which whoso defendeth / Hymselven most, hym alderlest avaylleth," is considered an embedded clause because it occurs between the subject of the main clause, "Love," and the complement of that clause, "With disespeyr so sorwfulli me offendeth." The noun clause, "Whoso defendeth / Hymselven most," is not counted as a separate embedded clause since it is the subject of its clause and not a separate interruption. The final clause in the passage is not self-embedded but right-branching and therefore not counted. Finally, I have excepted those embedded clauses which are common idioms and do not add new information but merely enforce what has already been said, idioms like the oath, "God helpe me so," and the tag, "that is to seyn." I made this exception since Pandarus frequently uses such idioms, and if they were counted as equal to the interruptions in Troilus's speech, they would have blurred the statistics.

Occurrence / 1,000 lines

	Troilus	Pandarus
Embedded phrases:	140	45
t-units	435	526

26. For examples of anaphora, see III, 1744–64; IV, 1206–10; V, 565–81, 610–16. For *similiter cadens*, see I, 603–09. For repeated sentence units, see III, 328–47, 1454–63; IV, 260–66; V, 39–50, 218–45, 1254–68, 1674–76.

27. The differences in the syntax and style of Troilus's and Troiolo's speech can most easily be seen by comparing their letters to Criseyde, especially the two stanzas which begin, "If any servant dorste or oughte of right" (V. 1345), and, "Se 'l serviodore in caso alcun potesse" (VII, 54). For a full discussion of these passages, see Taylor, "Style and Character," pp. 52–57.

"Feynede Loves," Feigned Lore, and Faith in Trouthe

by Barbara Newman

Near the end of Book I of *Troilus*, when Pandarus has learned the first of his friend's two sorrows, he consoles him in terms of a well-worn distinction:

> Was nevere man or womman yet bigete
> That was unapt to suffren loves hete,
> Celestial, or elles love of kynde. (I. 977–79)[1]

It is the latter which Troilus pursues, so "love celestial" is soon dispatched, with due respect, until Book III. There, in the narrator's exultant Proem and the lover's Dantesque and Boethian hymns, the two loves are found to be at one. But love of kynde again dominates until the epilogue, when it is finally ousted by its celestial counterpart. By this time the contraries, once so tidily reconciled, have leapt asunder. What had passed for love of kynde now appears, to Troilus's disembodied vision, as blind lust and vanity. To the narrator it qualifies as "feigned" love based on this wretched world's appetites, as opposed to the love of the "sothefast Crist" who will falsen no wight.[2] But no amount of fudging can obscure the fact that Troilus — despite his false gods and the old clerk Boccaccio — receives the reward owing to trouthe, not to vanity.[3] Herein lies a dilemma. Though the last twelve stanzas have already yielded all that can be reasonably asked of them, the "problem of the epilogue" remains.[4] If the progress from a simple alternative through *concordia discors* to *contemptus mundi* does not make sense of Troilus's love, or of his much-touted trouthe, we are entitled to ask what in the poem *is* trouthe — or better, how is love true? how feigned? how kind?

The first action in the poem — Calkas's defection to the Greeks — is, like Criseyde's after him, an obvious violation of trouthe. But it is also, though less frequently noted, a prophecy of truth. Because the devious divine is both traitor and soothsayer, his actions compel us to recognize from the start that trouthe (fidelity) and truth (actuality) need not coincide.[5] The dichotomy is borne out by other characters as well. Throughout the poem Pandarus busily swears by his trouthe to the sheerest falsehoods;[6] yet his fidelity to his friend's cause, as he conceives it, does not falter. Criseyde bases a plan to hold her trouthe on the false hope that Calkas had construed the oracles of Troy's destruction falsely (IV. 1405–10); she does not herself become false until the treacherous Diomede persuades her of her treasonous father's truth (V. 883–910).[7] Meanwhile, back in the city, Troilus is attacking Cassandra and her "false goost of prophecye" because she has told the truth about Criseyde's untrouthe (V. 1516–26). And on the largest scale, Criseyde's falseness confirms her (true) opinion that this world affords but "fals felicitee," while Troilus grounds his trouthe on the (false) assumption that "al the world be trewe" (V. 651). These are not gratuitous ironies, but indices to a fundamental Chaucerian theme: moral trouthe and factual truth in this world diverge. "False worldes brotelnesse" precedes the love of Troilus and Criseyde, and would frame it even were the lady true; as she is false, her faithlessness reinforces the moral of Vanity Fair. But given the background of "this false world", the middle ground of the Trojan War, fought over a faithless woman and lost by manifold treason, and the foreground of a milieu where "honor" in love means concealment, even the truest of loves could scarcely exist without feigning.[8]

As the social context requires, Troilus may be "trewe as stiel" but he, no less than Pandarus, can and must feign — from the first assault of Love in the temple (I. 326, 354) to his half-real, half-bogus, and wholly conventional malaise at Deiphebus's house (II. 1527–33). When he dissembles even to the point of lying to Criseyde, there is a hint of censure — "And for the lasse harm, he moste feyne" (III. 1158) — but at the height of erotic suspense, the moral note is scarcely heard. Criseyde, who already doth protest too much, tells Pandarus she will not feign when she yields Troilus her love (III. 167). But later, as she plans an elaborate feint

to beguile her father, Troilus fears her wiles will not be as deceptive as
they ought to be.

> Ye shal nat blende hym for youre wommanhede,
> Ne feyne aright; and that is al my drede.
>
> (IV. 1462–63)

Trouthe seems to be of no import where a traitor is concerned, although
Troilus's fears prove truthful. It is in fact Diomede, not Criseyde, who
feigns successfully before Calkas (V. 846), so that Troilus need no longer
feign sick (V. 413) but sickens in earnest. Pandarus, as usual, sums up the
course of these feigned loves in a proverb: "While folk is blent, lo, al the
tyme is wonne" (II. 1743). More naively, the narrator lists his hero's
talent for feigning among the many virtues of his love:

> But in hymself with manhod gan restreyne
> Ech racle dede and ech unbridled cheere,
> That alle tho that lyven, soth to seyne,
> Ne sholde han wist, by word or by manere,
> What that he mente, as touchyng this matere.
> From every wight as fer as is the cloude
> He was, so wel dissimulen he koude.   (III. 428–34)

The point is not that Troilus is a fraud. By his own standard of trouthe
(the highest in the poem, excluding the epilogue), he is impeccably and
even painfully sincere. But the standard itself is contradictory because,
after fidelity itself, the first virtue of these Trojan lovers is to "kepe
tonge" (III. 294). A liar and an "avauntour" — the man who would kiss
and tell — are one in the world's eyes (III. 309), as Pandarus sophistically
proves; a "true" lover keeps silent. So for the lesser harm, Troilus must
feign. Dissimulation is not the contrary but the condition of his trouthe
in love.

One of Criseyde's ends, amid all the feigning and feinting of Book III,
is to learn from Troilus "the fyn of his entente" (III. 125). When at last
she trusts that it is "clene" (III. 1229), she yields her love in return for
his trouthe. Yet this consummation belies his earlier promise not to break
her defense on pain of death (III. 138). While allowing for the double
entendres,[9] we cannot fail to see a discrepancy between the sworn
intention and the end, between what the lovers "mente" and what they
are about to do. Criseyde had suspected as much from her first interview
with Pandarus, who gave himself away with a bawdy jest but claimed he

"mente naught but wel" even when he spoke ill (II. 580–95). At any rate, whatever the intent that Pandarus fully has for his niece at the end of Book III (1582), it is more than a little sinister.[10] Like Chaucer himself, he has concealed his own ends beneath the feigned simplicity of a smooth, ingratiating surface, as Troilus conceals his beneath a thick veneer of convention. On this deeper level, the game of love demands that its players conceal their objectives not only from polite society but from each other, and above all, from themselves.[11] When Criseyde leaves Troy with a trail of promises behind her, her old assurance speaks so loudly that even the prescient narrator is tempted to believe her, although the still unwitting Troilus demurs (IV. 1415–28). Surely she believes herself; with the fine irony of projection, it is her lover she doubts.

> For in this world ther lyveth lady non,
> If that ye were untrewe (as God defende!),
> That so bitraised were or wo-bigon
> As I, that alle trouthe in yow entende.   (IV. 1646–49)

"I, who place all my trust in you . . . I, who expect perfect fidelity from you . . . I, who mean to be wholly faithful to you" — Criseyde may intend all of these, but she performs none. Has she lied then? Trouthe has but slipped through her fingers: she has a heart tender enough to mourn, but too slippery to hold it. For what she truly loves is the image of herself as true (V. 1054–64) — and that image, alas, is feigned.

Throughout the poem, the lady has followed a path of least resistance well-paved with pity, much of it self-pity, and the fact that she "means well" does not alter her tragic course. One of the few proverbs Pandarus does not cite, about the common fate of good intentions, applies perfectly to Criseyde. Two of Chaucer's favorite rhyme words, *trouthe* and *routhe*, are frequently on her lips,[12] but as the story proceeds they chime uneasily off-key. It is small wonder: Langland found it hard to reconcile Mercy and Truth even as Daughters of God. For the daughter of Calkas, trouthe as often as not rests in some ineffectual oath, and routhe is revealed chiefly in sexual surrender. The pity which runs too soon in gentle hearts undoes her.[13] Criseyde's routhe continually undercuts her trouthe, as when she promises Diomede:

> If that I sholde of any Grek han routhe,
> It sholde be youreselven, by my trouthe!   (V. 1000–01)

In the end, the narrator's apology for Criseyde is disturbing because he so nearly succumbs to her ethic, as the new coupling of routhe with untrouthe suggests.

> And if I myghte excuse hire any wise,
> For she so sory was for hire untrouthe,
> Iwis, I wolde excuse hire yet for routhe.   (V. 1097-99)

When the original rhyme pair returns in V. 1586-87, the traits stand in full opposition. Now that Criseyde has undeniably betrayed her trouthe, the narrator can only ascribe her faithless and unkind letter to routhe. In fact she shows no mercy for Troilus, only sentimental regret which feeds upon the ruins of her trouthe. But this is the same emotion which the narrator feels for Criseyde and, if we still trust him, conveys to us.

Midway between trouthe and routhe, the lovers appeal to a third and more elusive virtue, "kyndenesse." Any temptation to read the poem backwards from the epilogue, identifying love of kynde with false or feigned love, is countered by the persistent linkage of two key epithets, "trewe" and "kynde." The narrator uses "unkynde" as a euphemism for "untrue" in the Proem to Book IV:

> For how Criseyde Troilus forsook,
> Or at the leeste, how that she was unkynde,
> Moot hennesforth ben matere of my book.   (IV. 15-17)

Troilus often employs the same usage (IV. 1439-40, V. 1441), at last recognizing that false Criseyde "nas nought so kynde as that hire oughte be" (V. 1643). A kynde love, it appears, is both faithful and merciful — or perhaps each of these in turn, an ambiguity which Diomede exploits when he is making his case for the Greeks.

> But wolde nevere God but if as trewe
> A Grek ye sholde among us alle fynde
> As any Troian is, and ek as kynde.   (V. 124-26)

Criseyde accepts his terms; she can resist only by claiming, pitifully enough, that the Trojans are as kynde as the Greeks (V. 970). By this point kindness is so bound up, in Criseyde's mind, with her equivocal routhe that it too becomes the contrary of its erstwhile synonym, trouthe.

The third and most common sense of kynde, "natural," is submerged to the point of absurdity when Troilus complains, apostrophizing Fortune:

> Allas! how maistow in thyn herte fynde
> To ben to me thus cruwel and unkynde?   (IV. 265–66)

Even Troilus would recognize, if he stopped to think, that Fortune has acted after her kind in toppling him from her wheel. But he so far identifies kindness with trouthe, as befits one who seeks to love truly in the sphere of kynde, that he does not realize his mistake. Criseyde is subjected to a similar confusion when the Trojan ladies, seeing her grief at their farewell party, "thoughte it kyndenesse" (IV. 719). No doubt they thought her tears "only natural," and thought too that she wept for routhe at their parting. But there is no truth in this kindness, for Criseyde cannot tell her friends what she feels and must feign a love she does not feel for them. The lovers' expectation that a kind heart will be a true heart beguiles them, for trouthe can rarely survive in the world of kynde — whether that world is represented symbolically as Fortune, or concretely as the realm of wars, parliaments, and polite society.[14]

On every level in the poem — psychological, social, political, moral, metaphysical — trouthe in love is compromised by feigning. But *Troilus and Criseyde* is a tragedy, not an indictment; it evokes tragic pity as well as celestial laughter. Much of its poignancy springs from the lovers' betrayed and misplaced trust, in a social climate where trouthe is thwarted by naïveté as well as by treason (III. 326). One prominent aspect of trouthe, much stressed by Pandarus, is trust; and an essential component of the lover's "worthynesse" is his trustworthiness.[15]

> For for to trusten som wight is a preve
> Of trouth, and forthi wold I fayn remeve
> Thi wronge conseyte, and do the som wyght triste.
>
> > (I. 690–92)

> But who may bet bigile, yf hym lyste,
> Than he on whom men weneth best to triste? (V. 1266–67)

Pandarus spends a good part of Book I persuading his friend to trust him, and in Book II he does the same for his niece.[16] The consummation in Book III is preceded by a mutual exchange of trust (the "trouthe-plight").[17] In Book IV, Criseyde begs the reluctant Troilus to trust her before she goes, while in Book V Diomede sues for her trust with disarming ease. In fact almost all the action in the poem turns on the winning or betraying of some trust, a pattern which extends beyond the story to include the relation between narrator and reader.

By stressing his own ineptitude in love and in poetry, the narrator encourages his audience to be more skeptical than he himself is. Yet the more spellbound we are by his story, the more trust we place in him *faute de mieux*, and conversely the more he reminds us that he does not deserve it. At times, we who think ourselves wise in the ways of love — for such is the role in which the raconteur casts us — can almost wink behind his back at his limited insight. Yet we cannot alter one word of his equivocal making, and we are as impotent as he to change the course of events. For this reason, we are in no position to feel superior when the unsuspecting Troilus yields his trust to Pandarus who, like the narrator, freely admits his lameness in love's dance.[18] In the quantum leap from Troilus's initial skepticism:

> Thow koudest nevere in love thiselven wisse:
> How devel maistow brynge me to blisse?   (I. 622–23)

to his unlimited surrender:

> Now, Pandare, I kan na more seye,
> But, thow wis, thow woost, thow maist, thow art al!
> My lif, my deth, hol in thyn hond I leye.   (I. 1051–53)

we see a paradigm of our half-conscious response to the narrator in the first three books. Our trust in his authority, compromised as it is, enables us to participate by analogy in the predicament of Troilus. Thus both the tragic action and its power to move us depend on trust: the hero's in Pandarus and his niece, the narrator's in his "olde bokes" and in blissful Venus, and ours in the narrator. If, *per impossibile*, Troilus were less trusting or Pandarus and Criseyde more trustworthy, the tragedy would be averted. On the other hand, if the narrator were less sympathetic or the reader more suspicious, it would be as trivial as the Monk's Tale.

Troilus ostensibly proves his trouthe and wins Criseyde's love "by proces and by good servyse" (II. 678). Though the narrator's anxiety on this point awakens doubts, he clearly wants us to believe that Criseyde's trust is won by solid evidence. With Troilus it is otherwise. Pandarus, first appealing to friendship and to all he knows of rhetoric and dialectic, finally asks Troilus to accept his counsel on faith:

> Bileve it, and she shal han on the routhe:
> Thow shalt be saved by thi feyth in trouthe.   (II. 1502–03)

The rich ambiguity of this verse, with its Biblical echo, suggests both the nobility and the naïveté of Troilus's "feyth in trouthe." In the immediate context, Pandarus is outlining a complicated plan of "sleyghte" to fool Deiphebus and all his friends, and urges Troilus to feign as well as he can. The faith he asks is faith in his own devices, which are meant to move Criseyde to mercy. Troilus does take Pandarus's advice and he does gain Criseyde's routhe, so in a sense the promise comes true: Troilus is saved by his faith in guile. But insofar as he is finally "saved," wherever Mercury sorts him to dwell,[19] it is surely his faith in trouthe which redeems him. Vis-à-vis Pandarus and the means of love, Troilus's faith is credulity and his trouthe mere impudence. But vis-à-vis Criseyde and the end of love, his faith is fidelity, and trouthe his object. The accent can fall on either side, and Troilus's love will accordingly seem true or feigned, his "salvation" real or ironic.

Pandarus's art of persuasion — and to a lesser degree, the narrator's — leans heavily on that most versatile of *auctours*, the proverb.[20] One reason proverbs occur so often in the *Troilus* is that they raise essential questions about the manipulation of trust and the relation of trouthe to truism. As R. W. Frank has observed, "The monitory matter creates a world of 'wisdom' which at times supports and guides the lovers, at times deflates or misleads them."[21] Within this world, feigned love takes its place in a context of what we might call feigned lore: "feigned" because proverbs, while purporting to convey the truth of experience, can be twisted by the less truthful to dupe the less experienced.[22] Application alone marks them as trite or profound, and a misapplied proverb is like the "yerde / With which the maker is hymself ybeten" (I. 740–41). Homely folk wisdom, like Scripture, can be turned to any purpose whatsoever. Its easy familiarity lulls the consumer to suppose he is only repeating the obvious, when he is actually making some crucial decision. Look before you leap? Yes, but he who hesitates is lost. Great oaks from little acorns grow (II. 1335); yet "that erst was nothing, into nought it torneth" (II. 798). Even the pithy and concrete language of proverbs can be misleading, for it gives an illusion of specificity which disguises their abstract character.

The equivocal nature of proverbs is most apparent in the cluster dealing with wisdom and folly or, to use the familiar Chaucerian terms, the authority of experience. Troilus, archenemy of proverbs, first states the theme as he struts through the temple jeering at Love's fools: "Ther nys nat oon kan war by other be" (I. 203). Lacking experience himself, he too refuses to trust the experience of others and even presumes to deride it, like the scoffers of Antigone's song who speak ill of Cupid but never bent his bow (II. 861), or the blind man who would set himself up as a judge of colors (II. 21). Young and callow, he is a classic rebel against authority, telling his older and presumably wiser friend, "thi proverbes may me naught availle" (I. 756). But Pandarus outwits him. Although he too is "blind," a self-confessed failure in love, he avers that a blind man can sometimes walk where a sighted one stumbles, and a fool can be a wise man's guide (I. 628–30). While Troilus is an innocent fool, Pandarus is a wise fool who can turn his folly to advantage. When he finally wrests Troilus's secret from him, we know the blind will henceforth be leading the blind. From one point of view, Troilus's submission is yet another proof of his blindness. But from the narrator's vantage point, it is an aspect of his well-deserved nemesis: "Kaught is proud, and kaught is debonaire" (I. 214). Troilus has not fully submitted to love until he has submitted to lore, and if there is any feigning in the one, the other will of course be affected.

An even subtler treachery is at work in Pandarus's counsel, for his proverbs are slyly betrayed by their context. According to his lore of contraries, a fool's folly should warn the truly wise man to go and do otherwise. Pandarus later remarks, recalling Troilus in his pre-Criseyde days, "wyse ben by foles *harm* chastised" (III. 329). The gist of his advice, however, is that Troilus should commit exactly the same folly he does and worship "Seynt Idyot, lord of thise foles alle" (I. 910). Flattery comes to his aid, for in casting himself as the fool, he automatically casts Troilus (and Criseyde) as wise — provided, of course, that they do what he tells them. Whenever he proposes some unusually daring or dubious act — for example, when he urges Criseyde to admit Troilus to her bedchamber — he flatters their vanity with "but ye ben wis," or some such appeal. On several occasions the narrator uses similar wiles, in the same breath deprecating his own insight and appealing to the reader to confirm it.[23] Thus the criterion of "wisdom" becomes trust in the self-styled fool and, by the same token, the "fool's" authority is confirmed.

"Wisdom" in Criseyde's world means discretion, and discretion means hedging her bets. She is a lady who "kan hire good" (V. 1149), Troilus thinks, and Pandarus says much the same when he calls her wise "in short avysement" (IV. 936). Love for her is not a question of destiny and Cupid's arrows, but a matter of choice, to be decided at least partly on prudential grounds. Even Antigone's rosy-hued lyric warns that the game is a dangerous one:

> And forthi, who that hath an hed of verre,
> Fro cast of stones war hym in the werre!
>
> (II. 867–68)

But Criseyde, fearful wight that she is, wants the excitement without the anxiety. Troilus risks himself by trusting Pandarus, but Criseyde protects herself by trusting Troilus (III. 477–83), and her trust will last only as long as her safety. Her own proverbs convince her that she cannot survive out of her element, like a fish out of water or a plant torn from its roots (IV. 765–70). But Criseyde's element is present, sheltering love — the substance *amor*, not the accident Troilus. From the standpoint of self-preservation, her untrouthe is the wise choice and Troilus's fidelity the fool's choice. "He is a fool," says Diomede, "that wole foryete hymselve" (V. 98). Thus wisdom and folly, like pity and kindness, prove two-faced with respect to trouthe. Likewise, whenever a truism sounds too self-evident, we can be sure that an amphibology lurks somewhere behind it.

Many proverbs in the *Troilus* seem sophistic in their context, but turn out to be true in an unsuspected sense which appears only in retrospect. First cited to justify some course of action, they can later serve to gloss the action when it fails, showing once more how the end belies the intention. A notable instance is the narrator's homily advising the audience to trust in the god of Love:

> The yerde is bet that bowen wole and wynde
> Than that that brest; and therfore I yow rede
> To folowen hym that so wel kan yow lede.
>
> (I. 257–59)

In this figure, the man who will not give himself to Love is presumably the rod that breaks, and the lover is the one that bends. Pandarus uses a comparable image to reassure Troilus that Criseyde will eventually yield. Although she has bowed to his initial pressure, he remarks, she still seems as firmly rooted as an oak. Yet when the oak finally falls, it will never rise again, unlike the inconstant reed which easily yields and easily returns to its place (II. 1377–93). Since the great oak takes longer to fell than the "lighte" reed, it is of proportionately greater worth. Thus while both proverbs recommend submission to Love, the first commends pliancy and the second persistence. In the former Troilus (or the reader who imitates him) is compared to the bending rod; in the latter, Criseyde is likened to the oak. Both Pandarus and the narrator are deceived, however. When the storm winds blow a second time, Troilus proves to be the oak and Criseyde the reed.[24] Her own proverb — "Cesse cause, ay cesseth maladie" (II. 483) — illumines both her own untrouthe and the truth of Pandarus's misapplied byword:

> And reed that boweth down for every blast,
> Ful lightly, cesse wynd, it wol aryse.
>
> (II. 1387–88).

If the narrator's standards were consistent, he would have to approve of Criseyde's pliant behavior, which he does not. Conversely, Pandarus has given his praise to the oak, but once Criseyde is lost he counsels Troilus too to become a reed. New loves often chase out the old, he says,[25] and new situations call for new opinions (IV. 415–16). Absence should not make the heart grow fonder, for out of sight is out of mind (IV. 427). All these proverbs, taken together, abound in contradictions which perversely confirm their sense. Pandarus, Criseyde, and the narrator all prove inconsistent with one another and with their own language, and the rules of love which supposedly govern them amount, in the end, to near anarchy. This massive assault on trouthe gives force to yet another truism, "Thorugh love is broken al day every lawe" (IV. 618).

Time and again the law of the shifting context betrays Criseyde, as her proverbs expose her inconstancy. "He which that nothing undertaketh,/ Nothyng n'acheveth" (II. 807–08), she says, concluding her first deliberation on love. This is an omen of things to come, but not in the way Criseyde expects, for she unwittingly anticipates the suit of Diomede. Three books and more than five thousand lines later he also muses, "He that naught n'asaieth, naught n'acheveth" (V. 784).[26] Again, Criseyde avows her intent to leave the Greek camp with the proverb, "Who may holde a thing that wol awey?" (IV. 1628). Yet she will away, not from the traitor Calkas as she thinks, but from her true and faithful servant. Her own faithlessness certifies the truth of a proverb the narrator has applied to Fortune, who "semeth trewest whan she wol bygyle" (IV. 3).[27] A similar transposition lends irony to the lore of Pandarus, which fits Criseyde's predicament better than Troilus's:

The wise seith, 'Wo hym that is allone,
For, and he falle, he hath non helpe to ryse.'

(I. 694-95)

This proverb is actually a quotation from Scripture (Eccles. 4:10), and
Criseyde, who twice finds herself alone and friendless, exemplifies its
point.[28] If she could have studied her Bible, she might have excused her
untrouthe in light of the following verse: "If two lie together, they are
warm; but how can one be warm alone?"

Chaucer's prophetic and ironic use of proverbs also contributes to his
theme of historical truth as against poetic feigning. The narrator cites
proverbs to increase his credibility (II. 36-37), to reveal Troilus's
thoughts (I. 384-85, 740-41), and to gloss the proverbs of Pandarus (II.
21, III. 1060-64); but their most important function is to "predestine"
future events. Insofar as proverbs reveal habits of thought, they enable
the reader to predict, within limits, their speakers' probable choices. In
this way they meet the artistic demand for consistent characterization
and at the same time serve the narrator's apologetic needs. By revealing
his plot at the outset and foreshadowing events by means of proverbs, the
narrator absolves himself from blame when his story goes awry.[29]
Everything that exists must begin at *some* time, he says in defense of
Criseyde's love (II. 671), thus protecting her from the charge of "sodeyn
love" which would otherwise not arise until Book V. Nervously aware of
the story's outcome, he sees the end already implied in the beginning. In
the same vein he introduces Troilus and Criseyde's first night of love with
the inauspicious proverb, apropos of Pandarus's dinner party, that
"every thyng hath ende" (III. 615).

Pandarus and Criseyde share this concern with predicting the end
before they begin, but in their case, proverbs reflect character as well as
the fated conclusion. Criseyde's lore prophesies and in a sense justifies
her defection. While all the characters say a great deal about Fortune,
Criseyde speaks primarily of the downward turns of her wheel. "Ful sharp
bygynnyng breketh ofte at ende" (II. 791), she notes, and "the ende of
blisse ay sorwe it occupieth" (IV. 836). *Ex nihilo nihil fit* (II. 798). Where
love did not always exist, love will not always endure — or at any rate,
hers will not. Her notorious "fear," largely a fear that others will behave
as she will, leads her to a resignation that rivals even the passivity of
Troilus.[30] Since she habitually expects the worst, she sees little use in
crying over spilt milk.

> Harm ydoon is doon, whoso it rewe.   (II. 789)
>
> Tyme ylost may nought recovered be.   (IV. 1283)
>
> Whoso wol han lief, he lief moot lete.   (IV. 1585)
>
> But al to late comth the letuarie,
> Whan men the cors unto the grave carie.
>   (V. 741–42)

Hers is the Chaucerian "vertu of necessite" (IV. 1586), the pliancy of soul which stands at the furthest remove from that "moral vertu, grounded upon trouthe" (IV. 1672) which she claims (wrongly) to have first admired in Troilus.[31] False to her vows and her true love, she is true to her fears and her proverbs. From Troilus's point of view, her love may be feigned but her lore is all too truthful.

Pandarus, on the other hand, defines his trouthe solely as fidelity to Troilus, right or wrong (I. 593–94); all the rest is feigning. His lore is "for the nones alle" and his Fortune, untroubled by Boethian scruples, helps those who help themselves (IV. 600–02). As Alan Gaylord points out, this "consolation" is quite the opposite of Lady Philosophy's.[32] While Boethius reconciles fate and free will at the highest level, Pandarus reconciles them at the lowest, blending theoretical fatalism with practical opportunism. But despite his disregard for the truth of logic, his wisdom carries conviction, for it is by and large that of the average man. *Carpe diem*, he urges: there is a time for everything (II. 989, III. 855) and no time to lose (II. 1739, III. 896). Opportunity knocks but once:

> For to every wight som goodly aventure
> Som tyme is shape, if he it kan receyven;
> But if that he wol take of it no cure,
> Whan than it commeth, but wilfully it weyven,
> Lo, neyther cas ne fortune hym deceyven,
> But ryght his verray slouthe and wrecchednesse.
>   (II. 281–86)

This, perhaps the most forceful argument for free will in the poem, triumphantly asserts the priority of action over principle. Pandarus himself is one to strike while the iron is hot (II. 1276), and advises his niece to gather her rosebuds while she may.

'To late ywar, quod beaute, whan it paste';
And elde daunteth daunger at the laste.   (II. 398-99)

As Criseyde sees only the dark face of Fortune, Pandarus has eyes only
for the bright — or so he feigns, meeting Troilus's jejune sorrow with his
own facile optimism. The same ground that brings forth noxious weeds
will also nourish sweet herbs, dark night gives way to glad morning, and
so forth (I. 946-52). The narrator, too, takes comfort in the thought that
"sondry peynes bryngen folk to hevene" (III. 1204), and April showers
bring May flowers (III. 1060-64). But by the same logic, after rich
harvests blow winter winds. If Fortune is the sole arbiter of affairs,
Troilus notes, life is but a senseless play: "Nettle in, dok out, now this,
now that, Pandare" (IV. 461). Pandarus tries to keep his eye on the wheel
and beat Fortune at her own game, but his comic lore proves inadequate
to comprehend either moral trouthe or the truth of events. "Th'ende is
every tales strengthe" (II.260), as he foretells, and he himself meets the
same fate as many an artist — including the narrator of *Troilus and
Criseyde*. His characters escape his control, and when Criseyde takes the
role he assigned her beyond the plot she was meant to enact, all he can do
is hate her evermore (V. 1733). She, as an exemplar of "false worldes
brotelnesse," is at least prepared for it. He, for all his expertise in
feigning, is not.

Troilus, as several critics have remarked, prefers to uphold his trouthe
by resisting truisms.[33] Significantly, the few proverbs he does cite cluster
around a single theme, the futility of feigning. To be sure, he is willing to
go to any length to preserve secrecy, for "love to wide yblowe / Yelt bittre
fruyt" (I. 384-85). Yet he objects to Criseyde's stratagems, not because
they offend his moral virtue, but because he does not trust her to carry
them out. Seeing that she cannot have her cake and eat it too — "Hard it
is / The wolf ful, and the wether hool to have" (IV. 1373-74) — Criseyde
accepts the necessity of compromise, and makes a virtue of it. But Troilus
knows this guilor will be beguiled, and lets loose a salvo of proverbs to
prove it.

For thus men seyth, 'that on thenketh the beere,
But al another thenketh his ledere.'
Youre syre is wys; and seyd is, out of drede,
'Men may the wise atrenne, and naught atrede.'

It is ful hard to halten unespied

Byfore a crepel, for he kan the craft.   (IV. 1453–58)

Once again, this lore is verified by the event, for when Criseyde fails to achieve one deceit she falls into another. It may be cold comfort but Troilus and Criseyde are both, Cassandra-like, true prophets of the untrouthe they dread. While their trouthe is betrayed by falsehood, their truisms eventually yield the truth.

The last three proverbs in *Troilus*, all spoken by the narrator, express a resignation which begins to close the gap between conventional wisdom and a faith unfeigned.

> But Troilus, thow maist now, est or west,
> Pipe in an ivy lef, if that the lest!
> Thus goth the world. God shilde us fro meschaunce,
> And every wight that meneth trouthe avaunce!
>
>   (V. 1432–35)

> But natheles, men seyen that at the laste,
> For any thyng, men shal the soothe se.   (V. 1639–40)

> . . . thynketh al nys but a faire
> This world, that passeth soone as floures faire.
>
>   (V. 1840–41)

The narrator, disillusioned at last with the feigned loves of Troilus and Criseyde and the feigned lore of Pandarus, arrives at his own version of faith in trouthe. But the soothfast Christ, who finally enables him to "fordon the lawe of kynde" (I. 238) and embrace love celestial, could not help his Trojan forebears. Hence our initial question returns: is the trouthe of Troilus, pagan that he is, wisdom or foolishness in the end? Pandarus and Criseyde disappoint us because they trust little and can be trusted less. On the other hand, irony warns us and the epilogue all but tells us that Troilus is a fool to trust in earthly love and worldly wisdom. From their representatives, Criseyde and Pandarus, he gets only the betrayal he asked for — or does he? Despite all feigning, Troilus keeps his trouthe for the love of a faithless creature even to death, and thereby wins more affinity with the soothfast Christ than his cursed old rites would permit. Ingeniously, Chaucer interpolates his "pleyn felicite" stanzas before "Swich fyn hath, lo, this Troilus for love!" and so grants him a celestial reward for fidelity in love of kynde.[34] The narrator henceforth speaks only of *contemptus mundi*, but the poet satisfies both his craving for trouthe and his ever-present routhe.[35] He insists on having the wolf full and the wether whole — faithfulness blessed, feigning accursed — and by the sheer force of his good intentions, emerges almost unscathed by his ironies.

Notes

1. All quotations are from the text of F. N. Robinson, 2nd ed. (Boston, 1957).

2. The fullest treatment of the two loves, with an optimistic view of *kynde*, can be found in Donald W. Rowe, *O Love, O Charite! Contraries Harmonized in Chaucer's* Troilus (Carbondale: Southern Illinois University Press, 1976).

3. A rare dissenting voice is that of Edmund Reiss ("Troilus and the Failure of Understanding," *Modern Language Quarterly*, 29 [1968]: 131-44), who contends that Troilus in his final scorn and bitterness is morally if not technically damned. Yet we are explicitly told that his soul ascends through the spheres "ful blisfully."

4. Literature on the epilogue is vast, but the more stimulating recent discussions include Alfred L. Kellogg, "On the Tradition of Troilus's Vision of the Little Earth," *Mediaeval Studies*, 22 (1960): 204-13; Peter Dronke, "The Conclusion of *Troilus and Criseyde*," *Medium Ævum*, 33 (1964): 47-52; Anthony E. Farnham, "Chaucerian Irony and the Ending of the *Troilus*," *Chaucer Review*, 1 (1967): 207-16; E. Talbot Donaldson, "The Ending of *Troilus*," in *Speaking of Chaucer* (New York: Norton, 1970), 84-101 [above, pp. 115-130]; Murray F. Markland, "*Troilus and Criseyde:* The Inviolability of the Ending," *Modern Language Quarterly*, 31 (1970): 147-59; John M. Steadman, *Disembodied Laughter: Troilus and the Apotheosis Tradition* (Berkeley, 1972); and John W. Conlee, "The Meaning of Troilus' Ascension to the Eighth Sphere," *Chaucer Review*, 7 (1972): 27-36.

5. The two senses of *trouthe*, and their gradual disintegration, are discussed in Adrienne R. Lockhart, "Semantic, Moral, and Aesthetic Degeneration in *Troilus and Criseyde*," *Chaucer Review*, 8 (1973): 100-18.

6. Cf. Lockhart, p. 113, and Davis Taylor ("The Terms of Love: A Study of Troilus's Style," *Speculum* 51 [1976]: 69-90) [above, pp.231-256], who notes that Pandarus uses this oath thirteen times, as against Troilus's twice (p. 254, n. 15).

7. This is the thesis of Robert apRoberts, "Criseyde's Infidelity and the Moral of the *Troilus*," *Speculum*, 44 (1969): 383-402.

8. Robert W. Frank, Jr. comments on the position of love in society: "However hypothetical the courtly code may be, as a convention it operates simultaneously to deify love and to outlaw it." See *"Troilus and Criseyde: The Art of Amplification,"* in *Medieval Literature and Folklore Studies: Essays in Honor of Francis Lee Utley*, ed. Jerome Mandel and Bruce Rosenberg (Rutgers, 1970), p. 164.

9. "Defence" means primarily secrecy, but can also have a sexual meaning. For the familiar pun on "deth" see Haldeen Braddy, "Chaucer's Playful Pandarus," *Southern*

Folklore Quarterly, 34 (1970): 71-81.

10. Cf. Braddy and Beryl Rowland, "Pandarus and the Fate of Tantalus," *Orbis Litterarum*, 24 (1969): 3-15.

11. Self-deception is treated by Farnham, "Chaucerian Irony," in terms of original sin; Sheila Delany approaches it from a Brechtian viewpoint in "Techniques of Alienation in *Troilus and Criseyde*," in *The Uses of Criticism*, ed. A.P. Foulkes (Bern and Frankfort: Lang, 1976), 77-95.

12. See II. 489-90, 664-65, 1138-39, 1280-81; III. 120-22, 1511-12; IV. 1609-10, 1672-73; V. 1000-01, 1070-71.

13. Peter Elbow observes that Criseyde "will always give in to a certain amount of importunity and shrewdness — the qualities of Troilus and Pandarus which Diomede so happily combines. This is not a random characteristic in her; Chaucer identifies it as 'pite' (V, 824), one of the highest courtly virtues." See "Two Boethian Speeches in *Troilus and Criseyde* and Chaucerian Irony," in *Literary Criticism and Historical Understanding: Selected Papers from the English Institute*, ed. Phillip Damon (New York: Columbia, 1967), p. 94.

14. For a perceptive discussion of Kynde and the limits of idealism, see Rose A. Zimbardo, "Creator and Created: The Generic Perspective of Chaucer's *Troilus and Criseyde*," *Chaucer Review*, 11 (1977): 283-98.

15. Cf. W.F. Bolton, "Treason in *Troilus*," *Archiv für das Studium der neueren Sprachen und Literaturen*, 203 (1966): p. 261.

16. This theme is treated more fully, in light of traditional doctrines of friendship, by Alan T. Gaylord ("Friendship in Chaucer's *Troilus*," *Chaucer Review*, 3 [1969]: 239-64) and Leah R. Freiwald ("Swych Love of Frendes: Pandarus and Troilus," *Chaucer Review*, 6 [1971]: 120-29).

17. John B. Maguire ("The Clandestine Marriage of Troilus and Criseyde," *Chaucer Review*, 8 [1974]: 262-78) presents evidence that the lovers' trothplight would, in Chaucer's England, be sufficient to constitute a valid marriage, legitimate although disapproved by canon law.

18. Analogies between the roles of Pandarus and the narrator have been persuasively developed by Morton W. Bloomfield ("Distance and Predestination in *Troilus and Criseyde*," *PMLA*, 72 [1957]: 14-26) [above, pp. 75-89]; E. Talbot Donaldson ("Chaucer's Three 'P's': Pandarus, Pardoner, and Poet," *Michigan Quarterly Review*, 14 [1975]: 282-301); and Zimbardo ("Creator and Created"), among others.

19. His possible destinations are reviewed by Gertrude C. Drake in "The Moon and Venus: Troilus's Havens in Eternity," *Papers on Language and Literature*, 11 (1975): 3-17.

20. The two fullest studies of proverbs in the *Troilus* are B.J. Whiting, *Chaucer's Use of Proverbs*, Harvard Studies in Comparative Literature, 11 (1934), and R.M. Lumiansky, "The Function of the Proverbial Monitory Elements in Chaucer's *Troilus and Criseyde*," *Tulane Studies in English*, 2 (1950): 5-48.

21. "*Troilus and Criseyde*: The Art of Amplification," p. 160. Frank's brief discussion of the "prudential context" of love is illuminating.

22. Robert O. Payne defines proverbs as "the formulae of a wisdom they do not contain" (*The Key of Remembrance: A Study of Chaucer's Poetics* [New Haven: Yale University

Press, 1963], p. 226), and Charles Rutherford makes a similar observation: "Aphorism is public wisdom, tested by time and rhetorically formalized, wisdom that evokes a conditioned and calculated response with a minimum of personal involvement by the speaker" ("Pandarus as Lover: 'A Joly Wo' or 'Loves Shotes Keene'?" *Annuale Mediœvale*, 13 [1972]: 5).

23. Pandarus uses the stratagem in I. 991; II. 584, 1023; III. 266, 324, 937, 947, 1189; IV. 936, 1087. The narrator adopts it in the first Proem and in I. 233, II. 917 and especially III. 1328–36.

24. Cf. Alfred David, *The Strumpet Muse: Art and Morals in Chaucer's Poetry* (Bloomington: Indiana University Press, 1976), pp. 34–35.

25. This proverb, which Pandarus credits to "Zanzis," appears as Rule XVII in Andreas Capellanus, *De arte honeste amandi* (Book II, Ch. VIII).

26. The parallel has been noted by H. R. Patch, *On Rereading Chaucer* (Cambridge, Mass., 1959), p. 76, and Gerry Brenner, "Narrative Structure in Chaucer's *Troilus and Criseyde*," *Annuale Mediœvale*, 6 (1965): 10 [above, p. 135].

27. Charles Berryman remarks on the assimilation of Criseyde and Fortune in "The Ironic Design of Fortune in *Troilus and Criseide*," *Chaucer Review*, 2 (1967): 5. Cf. E. Talbot Donaldson, "Criseide and Her Narrator," in *Speaking of Chaucer*, p. 69.

28. Robert G. Cook ("Chaucer's Pandarus and the Medieval Ideal of Friendship," *Journal of English and Germanic Philology*, 69 [1970]: 412–13) notes that the same verse is cited as an argument for friendship in the *De spirituali amicitia* of Aelred of Rievaulx (PL 195, 671A).

29. For the problem of history as destiny and the narrator's attitude toward it, see Bloomfield, "Distance and Predestination," and Donaldson, "Criseide and Her Narrator."

30. Georgia R. Crampton discusses this aspect of Criseyde's character, finding her "at once diffusely alarmed and specifically inattentive," in "Action and Passion in Chaucer's *Troilus*," *Medium Ævum*, 43 (1974): 34–35.

31. "Moral vertu" is mentioned in II. 167, but the qualities to which Criseyde feigns indifference in IV. 1667–73 are very like her reasons for loving set forth in II.659–65. Cf. Ida L. Gordon, *The Double Sorrow of Troilus, A Study of the Ambiguities in* "Troilus and Criseyde" (Oxford, 1970), pp. 107–8, and Donald Rowe, *O Love, O Charite!*, p. 129.

32. "Uncle Pandarus as Lady Philosophy," *Papers of the Michigan Academy of Science, Arts, and Letters*, 46 (1960): 571–95.

33. Cf. Charles Muscatine, *Chaucer and the French Tradition: A Study in Style and Meaning* (Berkeley, 1957), pp. 132–53, for the contrast between courtly and "bourgeois" conventions; Richard A. Lanham, "Opaque Style and Its Uses in *Troilus and Criseyde*," *Studies in Medieval Culture*, 3 (1970): 169–76; and Davis Taylor, "The Terms of Love."

34. Gertrude Drake ("The Moon and Venus," p. 15) calls this effect "downright double-dealing." For evidence of the interpolation see Robert K. Root, *The Textual Tradition of Chaucer's Troilus* (London: Chaucer Society, 1916), pp. 245–48.

35. Similar views are expressed by Markland, who attributes the narrator's rejection of love to "moral timidity" ("Inviolability," p. 154), and Rowe, who remarks, "Chaucer makes the narrator's 'for the nones' rejection of this world demonstrate that we cannot

and ought not to reject it" (*O Love, O Charite!*, p. 168). Dorothy Bethurum ("Chaucer's Point of View as Narrator in the Love Poems," *PMLA*, 74 [1959]: 518) compares the total effect of the *Troilus* to that of the *Inferno*. The tale itself expresses *trouthe* but the teller adds his *routhe*, thus making the agony bearable.

Proverbs and the Authentication of Convention in "Troilus and Criseyde"
by Karla Taylor

Writers have long found it natural to associate poets and lovers. Socrates links them in the *Phaedrus*, as does Theseus in *A Midsummer Night's Dream*. Petrarch's *rime* intertwine poetics and love and exhaust the implications of their relationship through the elusive figure of Laura. In his dream visions, Chaucer more often contrasts the two through the oft-noted duality of books and experience, as when *The House of Fame's* eagle chides him for being too "daswed" from reading to know anything about the world of love outside his library. In *The Parlement of Foules*, he again appears to separate books and love, the garden of love unfolding only after the book falls closed. Despite structural juxtaposition of the two spheres of concern, however, Chaucer on a subtler level conflates love and poetics from the opening line, which describes love with an aphorism generally applied to the craft of poetry. The dream results directly from his reading,

> For out of olde feldes, as men seyth,
> Cometh al this newe corn from yer to yere,
> And out of olde bokes, in good feyth,
> Cometh al this newe science that men lere[1]

and the theme of poetics thus also invades the garden of love. In the debate, the cacaphony of avian perspectives raises questions *The Parlement* chooses not to answer, ultimately creating a disjunction between artistic and thematic resolution when the final roundel imposes an artificial veneer of harmony over the birds' dissension. This unsettling thematic irresolution, at odds with satisfying artistic closure, has led Robert Payne to note that Chaucer turns "the form and the substance of a poem into a mutual critique . . . consequently making of the whole an essay in poetics as well as a poem about its subject."[2]

The theme of poetics similarly pervades Chaucer's great love poem, *Troilus and Criseyde*. The poet often intrudes into his text to direct our attention to the process of composition ("translation"). Less overtly, he also weaves poetics into the fabric of the love story, as when Pandarus conceives the nascent love affair in words from Geoffrey of Vinsauf's *Poetria Nova*,[3] or advises Troilus in the craft of writing love epistles. There is a vast difference in tone, but none at all in premeditated rhetorical design, between "Biblotte it with thi teris ek a lite" (II. 1027) and "Thise woful vers, that wepen as I write" (I. 7). So many of the lines which refer most immediately to the love affair also comment on the poem itself that this conflation of love and poetics constitutes an important aspect of the "idea" of *Troilus and Criseyde*.

The disjunction between artistic and thematic resolution we find in *The Parlement* is, if anything, more powerfully present and unsettling here. The poem's ending especially requires an act of faith so rigorously that it breaks the illusion, forcing us to reexamine the entire poem. My own search for resolution has led me to explore *Troilus and Criseyde*'s attitude toward language and the manner in which its self-conscious poetic informs and comments upon its treatment of love.

Mutability is the name of *Troilus and Criseyde*; hence, I will concentrate on matters of change and stability in its language. As in *The Parlement of Foules* — as well as in romance generally[4] — Chaucer moves to fix his poem in the continuous literary tradition embodied in his revered "olde bokes." He invokes the passage of time in order to lend history's authenticity to his story, and simultaneously attempts to overcome time by renewing Lollius's old book for his present audience. In *Troilus and Criseyde* more than anywhere else,[5] Chaucer also employs the country cousins of literary tradition, proverbs, which ordinarily reach us through the *Volksmund* rather than through transmission in written form. Conventional modes of oral expression can provide the same kind of stay against time and change as can written texts, and because proverbs represent an extreme form of convention, so petrified in form that they seem immutable, their treatment in the poem can illuminate the use of other traditional modes as well.

Past studies of *Troilus and Criseyde*'s proverbs, which concentrate on them as means of characterization, define the term so broadly as to include nearly any *sententia*.[6] Such breadth of definition, however, obscures the special linguistic phenomenon I wish to single out. Following more recent attempts to define *proverb*, I will focus not on the whole range of traditional sententious utterances, but on a narrower class, those *sententiae* involving metaphor, enabling them to comment by analogy on their contexts.[7]

Proverbs are crystallized statements of traditional wisdom which posit a logical relationship "mediating between two aspects of reality, two levels of classification."[8] They possess a peculiar linguistic status derived from the fact that, although they are syntagms whose content appears specific and unambiguous, they cannot be treated as such without comic effect or reduced meaning. Each term in a proverb — for example, *leopard* in "the leopard cannot change his spots" — is stable with respect to the rest of the sequence, and cannot be substituted for by any ordinarily available lexical alternative. The equally possible syntagm "the Holstein cow cannot change her spots" communicates a good deal less, in part because it lacks the weight of traditional use.[9] A proverb must be treated as a single significant unit, frozen and selected whole from the lexicon of all complete proverbial statements, rather than as an ordinary syntagm produced by the combinative freedom of the speaker. As a stereotypically fixed articulation, the proverb thus wavers on the threshold between speech and language, syntagm and system,[10] and its comforting authoritativeness stems from this ambiguous linguistic character. Because it is a syntagm, individual speakers "invent" a proverb each time they articulate it; but because the same articulation recurs frequently, it appears to describe a universal truth of nature which many have observed and remarked upon. Once selected, a proverb issues automatically, and hence seems outside human influence and more objective than ordinary sentences.

Nonetheless, proverbs do allow a certain amount of combinative freedom. Because they belong to the language system independent of their articulation in any specific instance, a speaker can allude to them in the same way he "alludes" to a noun with a pronoun. Thus he might say, "You know about the leopard's spots," and although he does not state the proverb in its complete form, this does not inhibit its "automatic issue" as an essential underlying element. The full significance of his statement depends on a double mediation, for although he refers directly only to the proverb, the proverb in turn supplies the metaphoric analogy he wishes to make. Even the statement "the Holstein cow . . ." can acquire a significance beyond the literal, if speaker and listener understand it as an allusion to the traditional proverb whose structure is so similar. A proverb's form can change within certain limits as long as both parties understand it as the realization of a shared concept. The immutability in a proverb's form resides at the level of deep structure, a systemic concept which individual "performances" more or less realize — if less, then the speaker invokes the proverb by way of allusion, or as a proverbial phrase.

Despite a proverb's immutability at the level of deep structure, its meaning is not immutable. This results from its character as a specific, metaphoric statement describing another situation by analogy, a character distinguished from that of a maxim, which is a general, literal *sententia*. Both maxims and proverbs can comment on the same situation, as in the following example from Nigel Barley: Albert Smith, previously convicted of theft, has been caught stealing again. We can either invoke the general maxim "once a thief, always a thief," dispensing with metaphoric mediation, or we can comment, "The leopard cannot change his spots." The logical relationship the proverb posits is: leopard is to Albert Smith as spots are to criminality.[11] It acquires its authority by inviting us to derive, from two examples, a general law of nature. Proverb and maxim demand different responses; if we accord both formulations the same treatment, we react to the proverb as Judy Holliday did in *Born Yesterday*: "Of course not — they're right there, in his fur!" This comic failure to acknowledge the analogy disrupts the proverb's power, reducing it to a literal, purely syntagmatic statement which is not only too obvious for words, but also irrelevant.

In this example, both maxim and proverb apply equally well to the recidivist thief Albert Smith. However, if we take the case of Kate Thomas, an unregenerate slob who has once again failed in her New Year's resolution to reform her slovenly habits, we can no longer say, "Once a thief, always a thief." The maxim's general statement refers only to those it describes literally — thieves. But we can still shake our heads and say, "The leopard cannot change his spots;" the same proverb easily encompasses both situations, even with the change in gender. This is possible because, although we can manipulate a proverb's form only within limits, its meaning depends on the context which evokes it.

Conversely, a proverb may create as well as describe a situation, since it exists in the language prior to any particular articulation. Albert Smith may relapse into thievery because he has already identified himself as the leopard incapable of changing his spots. Or if he is in fact innocent, falsely accused on the basis of incriminating circumstantial evidence, the proverb offers a convenient, familiar — and prejudicial — framework conditioning the observer's perceptions. Though Smith is innocent, belief in the proverb may cause justice to light upon him as the likely suspect, and his subsequent conviction circularly confirms the authority of the old saying which influenced it. The proverb thus becomes a self-fulfilling expectation.

Since a proverb varies its meaning according to context, it betrays slightly the stability promised by its fixed form. Because, then, a sort of treachery inheres in proverbs, when we find them — as we do in *Troilus and Criseyde* — "as 'slydyng of corage' as ever Criseyde was,"[12] it is not Chaucer's peculiar invention. Proverbs by their nature betray the expectations of stability they arouse, and the regularity with which they do so here bespeaks the poet's perception and exploitation of proverbial language's semantic slippage in order to comment on language in general. In transmitting traditional forms of expression, Chaucer seeks not only to validate "truth by finding it in the past and making it live in the present,"[13] but also to warn us of the limitations of this endeavor.

Chaucer exploits this semantic slippage most clearly in the variations on a single proverb, and on a set of catalogues expressed in proverbial language. My first example appears at I. 257–258: "The yerde is bet that bowen wole and wynde / Than that that brest." These words, or allusions to the proverb they represent, recur so frequently that they become a *Leitmotif* in the poem. Here the poet, considering the inescapable power of Love, offers two possible descriptions of the shortly to be smitten Troilus. He can be either the wood that breaks, if he tries to withstand Love's inexorable attack, or the flexible wood that survives by bending, if he succumbs. The second alternative is clearly more desirable, and because Troilus does indeed succumb, he defines himself here as the wood that bends.

The next reference to the proverb changes the image slightly, but not the fundamental structure or concept:

> And reed that boweth down for every blast,
> Ful lightly, cesse wynd, it wol aryse;
> But so nyl nought an ook, whan it is cast . . .
>   (II. 1387–1389)

The comparison between a flexible survivor and a stiff victim remains, although a reed and an oak tree replace the two "yerdes." More important, however, the contextual reference has shifted as well as the desirable alternative, for the image offers two descriptions of Criseyde. She can either bend but never break, never yielding to Troilus' advances; or she can seem unbending until she finally gives way altogether, becoming Troilus's mistress. Up to this point Troilus has met with little success in breeching the lady's defenses, and Pandarus wants the second alternative to assure his friend that, if he perseveres, Criseyde will eventually capitulate. Combining this with the first realization of the proverb, we can see a developing distinction: Troilus is the reed (or "yerde") that bends and Criseyde is the oak that falls.

Thus Pandarus. But the poet begins to have other ideas which complicate the facile distinction I have just made. Shortly before Pandarus defines Criseyde in such comforting — and wishful — terms, the poet describes the growth of Troilus's desire with several proverbial analogies, including:

> Or as an ook comth of a litel spir,
> So thorugh this lettre, which that she hym sente,
> Encressen gan desir, of which he brente.   (II. 1335–1337)

This is our familiar "Great oaks from little acorns grow," modulated slightly to sustain the basic opposition between a great stiff stick and a small flexible one. But here Troilus is an oak grown out of his former sapling state, and through the juxtaposition of "Thorugh more wode or col, the more fir" (II. 1332), he is an oak threatened with conflagration. Chaucer thus qualifies the optimistic reference to Criseyde as an oak ripe for the axe before Pandarus makes it.

As one would expect of a central image, our opposed pair reappears at the consummation in Book III:

> And as aboute a tree, with many a twiste,
> Bytrent and writh the swote wodebynde,
> Gan ech of hem in armes other wynde.   (III. 1230–1232)

Though this is not precisely an allusion to the original proverb, the diction — tree, wode-, -bynde, wynde — forces us to connect it to the other related images I have cited. Here at the moment of stasis, the zenith before the poem's declining action, the image also reaches a state of equilibrium. Unlike earlier instances, it makes no opposed identifications.

Instead it is a picture of mutuality, sustaining the ambiguity which arose when Troilus grew into an oak, not sixty lines before Criseyde became one too.

The final transformation of the proverb occurs in Book IV. When Troilus returns from the parliamentary decision to exchange Criseyde for Antenor, the poet describes him with an image from Dante:[14]

> And as in wynter leves ben biraft,
> Ech after other, til the tree be bare,
> So that ther nys but bark and braunche ilaft,
> Lith Troilus, byraft of ech welfare,
> Ibounden in the blake bark of care . . .
>
> (IV. 225–229)

Again, the image alludes to rather than states the proverb, but when Troilus is thus clearly bound in a tree, it supplies a new reference for the matrix of language originally invoked by "The yerde is bet that bowen wole and wynde/Than that that brest." If Troilus has finally put down roots, then Criseyde, although the poem does not state it in so many words, finally becomes the bending reed, surviving each storm because of her lack of firmness. But what are we to do with the proverb, which seemed so clear and authoritative when it first appeared? Its clarity depends on isolating a moment in the narrative, but we cannot choose to see the analogy as the characters do, in terms of action in time. For us, as for the poet, the entire cumulative text — beginning, middle, and end — exists simultaneously, transcending the gradual unfolding of meaning. The transformations in reference the proverb undergoes cause us to distrust it, wherever it appears, as a figure pretending to stability, calling upon a venerable tradition which crystallizes its structure — but not its meaning. It is an example of a failed attempt to secure stability through traditional language.

Both the attempt to secure stability through traditional language and the failure of that attempt are aspects of a deliberate poetic strategy in *Troilus and Criseyde*. When Chaucer bids his poem farewell, he includes a plea for the preservation of his text: "So prey I God that non myswrite the,/Ne the mysmetre for defaute of tonge" (V. 1795–1796). Exact transmission and order of a poetic text are crucial to its meaning, but the act of making such a plea implies a recognition that change and instability in language are likely.[15] The poet demonstrates the importance of order to meaning with a set of catalogues, once again expressed in proverbial

language, which seek to establish in metaphor a relationship between
fixed natural phenomena and the course of the love affair. Each catalogue
comments optimistically on the ascending action, but Chaucer realizes its
potential for reversal when he transposes the order of terms or shifts the
context in the descending action of the last two books. In the midst of
Troilus's first sorrow, his lovesickness for Criseyde, Pandarus attempts
to exorcise despair with;

> "For thilke grownd that bereth the wedes wikke
> Bereth ek thise holsom herbes, as ful ofte
> Next the foule netle, rough and thikke,
> The rose waxeth swoote and smothe and softe;
> And next the valeye is the hil o-lofte;
> And next the derke nyght the glade morwe;
> And also joie is next the fyn of sorwe."   (I. 946–952)

Immediately before Troilus faints in Book III, the poet anticipates the
imminent transformation of abject failure into success with a similar list:

> But now help God to quenchen al this sorwe!
> So hope I that he shal, for he best may.
> For I have seyn, of a ful misty morwe
> Folowen ful ofte a myrie someris day;
> And after wynter foloweth grene May.
> Men sen alday, and reden ek in stories,
> That after sharpe shoures ben victories.   (III. 1058–1064)

By offering the cycles of nature as metaphors for the course of the love
affair, this string of proverbs makes the reversal of fortune seem
inevitable. A low point is but a prelude to a high one. But once again,
proverbial language proves treacherous; by invoking cycles as analogues
to the story, the words also imply their own inversion. It is equally true
that after day comes night, winter follows summer, and victories often
evaporate in the renewal of strife. What transpires later in *Troilus and
Criseyde* serves only to emphasize the double potential of these proverbs.
Their apparent fixity of meaning is compromised in Book IV, when
Pandarus, offering his ineffectual consolations "for the nones alle" (IV.
428), uses the same words to convey precisely the opposite advice:

> "For also seur as day comth after nyght,

The newe love, labour, or oother wo,
Or elles selde seynge of a wight,
Don olde affecciouns alle over-go."

(IV. 421–425)

Proverbs cannot transfer the stability of fixed natural cycles to the love
affair — a metaphorical analogy is after all nothing more than a verbal act
— but they succeed in arousing Troilus's expectation of the immutability
they seem to promise. Promising so much, they must inevitably
disappoint, and when Chaucer puts an end to the illusion he himself
perpetrated, its unreality is starkly evident:

The day goth faste, and after that com eve,
And yet com nought to Troilus Criseyde.   (V. 1142–1143)

After these lines, we can no longer deny that analogies first proposed by
verbal fiat can be disposed of in the same manner. Proverbs are apt not to
describe reality as it is, but only as we wish it to be. They operate in the
optative mode, for the relationship Chaucer reveals in them, taking with
one hand what he gives with the other, is not that between love and
nature, but that between love and the element of desire implicit in the
language we use to formulate reality.

    In this context, let us return for a moment to the point at which
Criseyde becomes an oak, a passage extraordinary for the conspicuous-
ness of its rhetoric:

"Peraunter thynkestow: though it be so,
That Kynde wolde don hire to bygynne
To have a manere routhe upon my woo,
Seyth Daunger, 'Nay, thow shalt me nevere wynne!'
So reulith hire hir hertes gost withinne,
That though she bende, yeet she stant on roote;
What in effect is this unto my boote?

"Thenk here-ayeins: whan that the stordy ook,
On which men hakketh ofte, for the nones,
Receyved hath the happy fallyng strook,
The greete sweigh doth it come al at ones,
As don thise rokkes or thise milnestones;
For swifter course comth thyng that is of wighte,

Whan it descendeth, than doth don thynges lighte.

"And reed that boweth down for every blast,
Ful lightly, cesse wynd, it wol aryse;
But so nyl nought an ook, whan it is cast;
It nedeth me nought the longe to forbise." (II. 1373–1390)

By introducing the first half of the proverbial comparison with
"peraunter," Pandarus identifies it as a rhetorical "opposite" to be
discarded when he proposes the second half. This kind of rhetorical
structure arouses strong expectations; as soon as we read "peraunter,"
we know that "thenk here-ayeins" will eventually follow. When Cicero
writes "*non solo*," one can rest assured that "*sed etiam*" will complete his
thought, and when a sonneteer begins his octave with "when," one
expects the sestet to begin with "then." A poet can play with these
expectations. An excellent example is Shakespeare's Sonnet 29, in which
he postpones "then" until a line and a half into the sestet, thus bringing
the reader's desire for rhetorical fulfillment to such a pitch that when it
finally comes, his spirit, out of pure relief, soars "like to the lark at break
of day arising." Here, Pandarus arouses the same expectations in Troilus,
and strengthens his rhetorical structure with proverbial language, which
itself contains a strong element of desire. What prevents the argument
from convincing absolutely is its purely verbal nature. In addition to the
emphatic rhetorical structure, Pandarus adorns the argument with
personifications. And curiously, amidst all the words, Criseyde disappears. The bending-reed-opposite clearly refers to her, but thereafter, not
even a pronoun connects her to rhetorical fulfillment. Formally,
structure and proverb mime arousal and fulfillment of desire, but this
verbal process can be extended to reality outside words only by an act of
faith. Pandarus does not say, "Criseyde *is* an oak," he merely suggests,
"Think of it rather this way." Troilus believes because he wants to, but
Chaucer, by stressing the fictive, rhetorical nature of the passage, asks us
to consider whether its formal fulfillment can be extended beyond words.
And in an act parallel to his retraction of a relationship between natural
cycles and the love affair, he shows that there is no necessary connection
when he makes Criseyde ultimately more similar to a bending reed than a
sturdy oak.

To summarize: the stability proverbial language promises is doubly
deceptive, because the same words can mean various things in various
contexts, and because the relationship to reality they propose is not

direct, but mediated by desire. Chaucer stresses the same elements in
other conventional manners of speaking, especially the poetic words of
love, which seek to fix experience by supplying a stable context of verbal
tradition. These traditions constitute a lexicon like that of proverbs, and
the inherent mutability of proverbs also marks the conventions which
appropriate the language of religion and the hunt to describe the love
affair between Troilus and Criseyde.

Pandarus, who knows the "olde daunce," teaches Troilus the words
which portray love as a religious experience. But he finds himself
suddenly out of control just as his schemes verge on success. As Troilus
waits in the secret stew, Pandarus bids him make ready, "For thow shalt
in to hevene blisse wende" (III. 704), then adding, "this nyght shal I
make it weel,/Or casten al the gruwel in the fire" (III. 710–711).
Troilus's response, a prayer for "hevene blisse," shows how thoroughly
the parodic language of religion has shaped his conception of love. In
Troilus's eyes, Criseyde is a goddess who bestows grace, and whose
presence defines the meaning of his entire world. Love becomes the
Beatific Vision in his hymn at III. 1261ff., a passage imitated from
Bernard's prayer in the *Paradiso* (Canto xxxiii). Pandarus understands
the nature of *amour courtois*: its conventions are fiction, or literally lies.[16]
Only figuratively can a mortal woman be a goddess, and when a lover
expresses his feelings in such terms, he refracts objective reality through
the prism of his desire. But Troilus does not use the conventions merely
in a manner of speaking; believing, as it appears, in a natural link between
res and *verbum*, he treats the two as commutative terms. However, he is a
character in a poem where this relationship is problematic, where
language as convention rather than ideal is a theme.[17] In his desire for
transcendence, he reifies the fiction and confounds words with the reality
they only indirectly represent.

Attempting to create a reality to match the verbal image, Troilus
creates instead a burden too heavy for any mortal love to bear. His
religious language is a convention abstracted from its original context,
and as we know from proverbs, contextual shift signals mutability.
Although Troilus tries thereby to make his love transcendent of time and
place, to seize the day and fix it eternally, the unfixed nature of his
language — along with his blind trust — betrays him. In a sense, this
traditional form of love discourse causes the tragic end of the story by
arousing expectations it cannot fulfill. Through his language Troilus
seeks to achieve the stability of the ideal; instead, he makes the
comparative inadequacy of the real stand out the more sharply.

The same reversal — poetic description confounded with the thing described — is also at work in another convention, love as the hunt. By shaping action and response after its own image, this convention creates rather than describes the course of events. Troilus is a bird of prey, a noble falcon who catches his victim; and "What myghte or may the sely larke seye,/Whan that the sperhauk hath it in his foot?" (III. 1191-1192). Much of what goes wrong in the love affair can be traced to this attitude toward love, arising out of the conventions of artistic language. Hunt imagery determines that the men pursue Criseyde without much regard for her desires and fears, and she responds like a chased animal, postponing the inevitable for as long as possible.

In Criseyde's second courtship, Chaucer again exploits the duplicity of conventional language by reusing the same elements in a different context. We are alerted to the lexical similarities by repetition of a maxim, previously uttered by Pandarus: "Unknowe, unkist, and lost, that is unsought" (I. 809), and by Criseyde: "He which that nothing undertaketh,/Nothyng n'acheveth" (II. 807-808). Diomede's version echoes Criseyde's: "For he that naught n'assaieth, naught n'acheveth" (V. 784). The poet recalls the convention of love as hunt when Diomede considers

> How he may best, with shortest taryinge,
> Into his net Criseydes herte brynge.
> To this entent he koude nevere fyne;
> To fisshen hire, he leyde out hook and line.   (V. 774-777)

The hunt seems embedded in the prehistory of the poem, enabling Cassandra to interpret Troilus's dream correctly by establishing Diomede's descent from Meleager, the mythological slayer of the Calydonian boar. Diomede's promises resemble Troilus's previous oath of service, and in this relationship as well, the lovers exchange (the same) jewelry. Language and action are essentially the same, if speedier, as when Troilus woos Criseyde — but for all the similarity, most readers find the two courtships very different. This results from a paradox of conventional language; when Troilus expresses himself with the time-honored words of *amour courtois*, we would gladly believe in the permanence he seeks to achieve by linking his love with tradition. Yet when Diomede uses the same words, precisely because they are conventional, he casts a shadow of mutability on the stability Troilus thought to guarantee. At this point in the poem, many readers pore back over the development of Criseyde's character, searching for clues of the emotional instability that would make her infidelity comprehensible. It is unlikely, however, that Chaucer intends full psychological realism here. Criseyde's betrayal was in the story as he found it; to this he adds a second betrayal, that of the conventional languge of love. In giving Troilus and Diomede the same words to express their feelings, Chaucer confronts us with the impossibility of Troilus's idealist treatment of language. The words of love are conventions which mean only what we can agree that they mean; just as with proverbs, their significance is relative to context — speaker, listener, the worsening political circumstances in Troy — and their fixed form derives not so much from true semantic stability as from our desire for such an absolute relationship to reality: *ut nomina consequentia rerum sint.*

Troilus and Criseyde thus expresses a profoundly ambivalent attitude toward conventional love language. On one hand, religious parody exalts the love affair, embellishing it with the lovely poetic fiction of *amour courtois*: the use of convention in general, because of its history of repetition, mimes timelessness. Troilus seeks connection to the ideal and the timeless through convention, but his attempt imperils an inevitably imperfect human love, for the formative power of conventional language consists only in constituting his sights of what is possible. Mistaking the flexible reed of poetry for a sturdy oak, he expects the affair to take its nature from the words of love. But conventions derive their meaning from cumulative usage, and the meaning of love in this poem resides in the *relation* of convention to the new context supplied here. Criseyde recognizes the change her history works on tradition when she laments, "O, rolled shal I ben on many a tonge!" (V. 1061) — she becomes a new *topos* embodying not the correspondence between convention and context Troilus expected, but the difference. On this level, *Troilus and Criseyde* is about both the desire to fix an inherently mortal, transitory love permanently, and the impossibility of fulfilling that desire. When the poet proclaims as his purpose to help lovers to "pleyne," he refers to information not only about the steps of the "olde daunce," but also about the traps which await us if we begin to believe literally that love is the same thing as conventional love language.

It is now time to turn the tables and see what Chaucer's treatment of the love affair reveals about his poetic, for I think it a matter of reciprocal illumination. One of the most interesting recent articles on *Troilus and Criseyde* traces the parallels between Pandarus and the poet himself.[18] Just as Chaucer poses as an unsuccessful lover and servant to love's servants, so Pandarus, likewise unsuccessful, becomes such a servant by mediating between Troilus and Criseyde. In order to join potential lovers, Chaucer forges a link between his English audience and Lollius's old Latin history, and in general Pandarus's use of oral wisdom parallels the poet's use of written authority, "olde bokes." Chaucer constructs a poem to accomplish his historical and amatory mediations in which he follows the precepts of rhetorical theory, just as Pandarus, taking his cue from the same text — the *Poetria Nova* — constructs his own poem, the love affair. Given the analogous roles played by the two artists, it is not surprising that when Pandarus describes his part in furthering love, his words often have a double reference. They pertain not only to the immediate narrative context, but also to the poem as a whole. For example, leaping in to discover Troilus suffering in the throes of terminal lovesickness, Pandarus unleashes a barrage of proverbs, including: "I have myself ek seyn a blynd man goo/Ther as he fel that couthe loken wyde" (I. 628–629). This not only advertises Pandarus's skills as advisor to the lovesick, but also validates the poet's mediation. When Chaucer uses the same idea to rationalize his own inadequacies as a redactor ("A blynd man kan nat juggen wel in hewis," II. 21), he modifies it to include a pun on the colors of rhetoric, and so reinforces the analogies between Pandarus and poet, love affair and poem.

Why would Chaucer wish to incorporate into the text a poet-surrogate whose similarity comes at precisely the points where he ultimately fails, the furtherance of love and the attempt to fix experience in a stable context of authority? Through Pandarus, proverb-wielder and poet whose text is a love affair, Chaucer extends the instability clinging to the shifting reference of proverbs, and to the love affair itself, to his own artistic endeavor. Significantly, the poet participates fully in the conventional modes of expression whose equivocation he exploits. The loss of control Pandarus experiences in the latter portion of the poem is analogous to Chaucer's role as a translator who has no control over the text, who must tell the story of "how that Criseyde Troilus forsook,/Or at the leeste, how that she was unkynde" (IV. 15–16).[19] The poet describes his ambivalent relationship to his own poem most succinctly in his comment on Troilus's refusal to divulge the name of his beloved:

> For it is seyd, "man maketh ofte a yerde
> With which the maker is hymself ybeten
> In sondry manere . . ."
>
> (I. 740–742)

Chaucer is a maker, his poem the "yerde" (remember the flexible reed, or "yerde," of poetry) by which he is himself beaten. What so peculiarly disturbs us about Criseyde's second courtship is the betrayal of the conventional language with which Troilus had thought to secure permanence, and Chaucer's problem is the same. The instability which troubles him most deeply is not simply that of a mortal love affair, but that of his poetic language, his medium for drawing together the past tradition of "olde bokes," the present, and, he hopes, the future of that tradition. His solution is to go between the horns of the dilemma — dependence on his poetic language and simultaneous recognition of its mutability — by incorporating into the text a metalanguage in which the image of Troilus's and Criseyde's love refers to *Troilus and Criseyde* itself. Writing both sides of the dilemma into his text as a matter of thematic concern may not guarantee resolution, but Chaucer in a sense exorcises his devil by exposing it.

The mutual mutability of love and language conditions *Troilus and Criseyde's* relationship to literary tradition. Chaucer's exhortation to his poem to "kis the steppes, where as thow seest pace/Virgile, Ovide, Omer, Lucan and Stace" (V. 1791-1792) is analogous to the lovers' desire to fix their love permanently through conventional language. Throughout the poem (as indeed elsewhere in his writings), Chaucer seeks extratextual authentication, both in Lollius's old history and in the more recent literary tradition of Dante and Petrarch. Both elements inform the central passage on authentication, Book II's proem, which opens:

> Owt of this blake wawes for to saylle,
> O wynd, o wynd, the weder gynneth clere;
> For in this see the boot hath swych travaylle;
> Of my connyng, that unneth I it steere.
>
> (II. 1-4)

The conceit refers to the monumental effort required to write the poem (particularly for the inept poet Chaucer claims to be), but by postponing "of my connyng" to 1.4, the poet allows us to think at first that it refers to the love affair. Although he imitated these lines from Dante (*Purgatorio* i. 1-3), Chaucer would have found the *topos* in Petrarch as well, and in fact the *rime* give him a precedent for using conventional love language to talk about poetry. Typically, the Petrarchan poet/lover seeks union with Laura, who among other things is the laurel, a symbol for poetic immortality. By locating his poem in this particular tradition, Chaucer tells us why he needs its support: he too desires poetic immortality.

But he cannot rest easy with joining *Troilus and Criseyde* to a tradition which will help preserve it; seeking the poetic laurel does not guarantee that one will find it. In the rest of the proem, Chaucer discusses the problems he faces in saving ancient written tradition from time's oblivion — his own ignorance and changes in language and custom generally which might interfere with his mediation:

> Ye knowe ek that in form of speche is chaunge
> Withinne a thousand yeer, and wordes tho
> That hadden pris, now wonder nyce and straunge
> Us thinketh hem, and yet thei spake hem so,
> And spedde as wel in love as men now do . . .
>
> (II. 22–26)

Primarily, these lines ask his audience's indulgence for Lollius's old-fashionedness, but they also have a more proleptic significance. Chaucer's real concern is the same one implicit in his plea for the future of his own text, the fear that mutability in language will preclude Troilus and Criseyde's participation in the immortality of literary tradition.

If it weren't for the ambiguous figure of Lollius, we could consider this merely a modesty *topos*, the apology an inverted assertion of authenticity. Chaucer appeals to Clio, the muse of history, and even problems in transmission imply that transmission takes place. But the proem touches on a problem of deep concern: survival of a text is possible only by anchoring it in tradition, and Chaucer sees every word he writes qualifying that tradition, thus prefiguring the fate of his own text. Perhaps the failure to admit *Il Filostrato* as a source is "anxiety of influence," but I think a more distinct artistic purpose conditions the choice. While insisting on the need for authenticity, Chaucer quite deliberately pulls the rug out from under himself by basing his authentication on a fiction. To transmit old history is to assert the permanence of literary tradition through repetition. Of course, since Lollius never wrote a history, none could have survived for Chaucer to translate. If he believed that there once had been such a text, however, it would be the perfect example of the transience of language. His redaction would then constitute mediation between present and not only things past, but something passed entirely out of existence and mediating memory. The fiction of Lollius embodies the problematic authenticating endeavor more resonantly than admission of a newer, surviving source could have done. On this level, *Troilus and Criseyde* is about the poet's desire for permanence and stability in the medium he depends on, and the impossibility of fulfilling that desire because of the fundamental mutability of language.

I am dissatisfied with this essay because its dispassionate analysis cannot convey the sadness and poignancy of the situation it attempts to describe, that of a poet who has recognized the final and inescapable limitations of his language. I can try once more by extending the analogy between poem and love affair. Chaucer's attitude toward his poem is much the same as his attitude toward Criseyde: both affairs must eventually disappoint because of the "slydyng corage" of their participants. Chaucer loves Criseyde, the "hevenyssh perfit creature" (I. 104), but he must finally and reluctantly admit that she is neither heavenly nor perfect, only extraordinarily lovely and lovable. Moreover, Chaucer's bittersweet relationship to poetry resembles the attitudes of both Troilus and Pandarus toward Criseyde. Pandarus, clearly a poet, plays on Criseyde as Chaucer does with the words he gives his stand-in, taking obvious joy in prodding her into conformity with his will. Yet at the end, no longer able to manipulate her, he can say, "I hate, ywys, Cryseyde" (V. 1732). Here Chaucer follows instead his second poet-figure, Troilus, who makes poetry through the mediation of Petrarch, whose words he speaks in his first lyric. As a Petrarchan lover, Troilus dons the mask of the poet who desires immortality of love and language. Just before the consummation, he prays to (among others) Apollo, the god of poetry, for aid:

> O Phebus, thynk whan Dane hireselven shette
> Under the bark, and laurer wax for drede,
> Yet for hire love, O help now at this nede!
>
> (III. 726–728)

The story of Apollo and Daphne constitutes a summation of the process of pursuit embedded in *Troilus and Criseyde*. Troilus's use of myth, like the use of proverbs and conventional language throughout the poem, stems from the desire to capture experience in the timeless repetition of traditional words. But by building this particular myth so integrally into his text, Chaucer shows the equivocation of formal, verbal stability. In the poem as a whole, he uses apparently stable conventions to talk about mutability, just as this myth disjoins its acquired fixity of form from its content — metamorphosis. The story does indeed immortalize Apollo's love, but in the form of a pursuit which can never succeed. Like Troilus's other attempts to fix Criseyde in the safe confines of tree-ness, it describes his desire rather than her essence; it is Troilus who later becomes "Ibounden in the blake bark of care." The myth also represents the desire for the poetic laurel which Petrarch embodied in Laura, and, I believe, Chaucer in Criseyde.[20] By analogies of this sort, Chaucer too becomes a crashing oak, failing always to fix the bending reed of his poetry. Troilus's helpless sorrow when he can no longer deny Criseyde's metamorphosis also represents Chaucer's final attitude toward his own faithless bride of poetry:

> . . . and I ne kan nor may,
> For al this world, withinne myn herte fynde
> To unloven yow a quarter of a day!
> In corsed tyme I born was, weilaway,
> That yow, that doon me al this wo endure,
> Yet love I best of any creature!   (V. 1696–1701)

I am reminded of George Herbert's palinode, "The Forerunners," which describes his relationship to poetry as a marriage of equivocal worth. His rejection notwithstanding, however, what speaks most strongly in that poem, as here, is Herbert's love of the words which fail him:

> Farewell sweet phrases, lovely metaphors,
> But will ye leave me thus?
> . . .
> Lovely enchanting language, sugar-cane,
> Hony of roses, whither wilt thou flie?[21]

Chaucer offers two escapes from this impasse at the end of *Troilus and Criseyde*. The first is silence, the route taken by his two surrogates. When Pandarus leaves the stage, his last words are "I kan namore seye" (V. 1743), and when Troilus's soul is translated out of "this litel spot of erthe" (V. 1815), he leaves behind not only love but also language. He says nothing, and his final destination is not recorded in words. The second solution Chaucer offers is to ground language in the only power capable of transcending all change and referential shifts, the Christian Word so markedly absent from the pagan world of the rest of the poem. Following the same impulse that motivates the Retraction at the end of the *Canterbury Tales*, Chaucer chooses this second course, ending the poem with a prayer to the Trinity. In both cases the poet dissociates himself from the equivocal language of mortals, because the fundamental nature of human love and human poetry is tied to this sublunary world. The flowers of rhetoric are as any other worldly flowers, of which Chaucer writes: "Al nys but a faire,/This world, that passeth soone as floures faire" (V. 1840–1841). They cannot transcend their own limitations, and I think it is for this reason that the concluding prayer describes the Trinity as "uncircumscript." Its nature, resolving all change in an all-encompassing unity, is beyond the scope of this poet to write about, and as the poem ends, he too falls silent.

Notes

1. *Parlement of Foules*, ll. 22–25. References are to *The Complete Works of Geoffrey Chaucer*, ed. F. N. Robinson, 2nd ed. (Boston: Houghton Mifflin, 1957).

2. Robert Payne, *The Key of Remembrance* (New Haven: Yale University Press, 1963), p. 144.

3. Robinson, notes, p. 818.

4. See Larry Benson's discussion of romance authentication in *Art and Tradition in Sir Gawain and the Green Knight* (New Brunswick, N.J.: Rutgers University Press, 1965), pp. 1–10.

5. B. J. Whiting, *Chaucer's Use of Proverbs*, Harvard Studies in Comparative Literature, Vol. XI (Cambridge, Mass.: Harvard University Press, 1934), p. 49.

6. Whiting, pp. 48–75, and Robert M. Lumiansky, "The Function of Proverbial Monitory Elements in Chaucer's *Troilus and Criseyde*," *Tulane Studies in English*, 2 (1950): 5–48.

7. Barbara Kirshenblatt-Gimblett, "Toward a Theory of Proverb Meaning," *Proverbium*, 22 (1973), 821.

8. Nigel Barley, "A Structural Approach to the Proverb and Maxim, With Special Reference to the Anglo-Saxon Corpus," *Proverbium*, 20 (1972): 737.

9. Barley, p. 741, suggests that the entire proverb can be translated onto another level of diction, as for example, "birds of a feather flock together," or "fowl of similar plumage congregate together." Nonetheless, it seems to me that such a change considerably weakens the proverb's power, here by eliminating the poetic, pointed language of the original. See, however, below in this essay.

10. Roland Barthes, *Elements of Semiology*, trans. Annette Lavers and Colin Smith (New York: Hill and Wang, 1967, reprint ed., 1977), p. 19.

11. Barley, pp. 739–740.

12. Payne, p. 211.

13. Payne, p. 175.

14. Robinson, in his note to these lines, p. 828, cites the first three as an allusion to the *Inferno*, iii.12 ff. But the last two lines also recall the Pier della Vigne episode in xiii, where the Emperor's councillor is metamorphosed into a tree because of his despair.

15. Perhaps we can divide the conflicting impulses and attribute the attempt to fix language to Chaucer in his pose as the redactor of Lollius, and the sober recognition of futility to Chaucer *in propria persona*; but I think such a distinction would be too facile. What are we to do with passages such as this one in which both impulses are simultaneously present, one implying the other, and indeed so intertwined that it is impossible to separate them? The difficulty of making such a distinction has led me in this argument to equate poet and narrator; although I am in general agreement with the now traditional separation between Chaucer and his narrative *personae*, it does not seem pertinent here.

16. Norman E. Eliason, *The Language of Chaucer's Poetry: An Appraisal of the Verse, Style and Structure, Anglistica* 17 (Copenhagen: Rosenhild and Bagger, 1972), pp. 126-134.

17. Susan Schibanoff, in "Argus and Argive: Etymology and Characterization in Chaucer's *Troilus*," *Speculum*, 51 (1976): 657, says: "In his *Troilus*, a poem which consists much more of words than of action, Chaucer seems preoccupied with the conventional aspects of language, and with the attempts of the two lovers to probe the realities behind the words which had, by common usage and agreement, become the highly codified language of love. That words fail miserably to communicate realities, or that the people of *Troilus* fail miserably to detect the truths they represent, is poignantly symbolized in the lover's realization that Criseyde's absence will be permanent: Troilus accepts the fact that Criseyde's 'name of trouthe/Is now fordon' (V. 1686-1687) not because of Cassandra's words, but because of the undeniable implications of a material object — Criseyde's brooch torn from Diomede's cloak."

18. E. T. Donaldson, "Chaucer's Three 'P's': Pandarus, Pardoner, and Poet," *Michigan Quarterly Review*, 14 (1975): 282-301.

19. Again, Donaldson is best on the narrator's growing pain and helplessness in the last two books; see "The Ending of Troilus," in *Speaking of Chaucer* (London: Athlone Press, 1970), pp. 84-101 [above, pp. 115-130].

20. Schibanoff (note 17 above) states that, in contrast to her parents' names, Criseyde's name plays no role in determining her character, destiny, or symbolic value. This bit of Greek may not have been available to Chaucer, but it is an interesting coincidence, if nothing more, that Criseyde's name means "daughter of gold," linking her to one of the puns Petrarch makes on Laura: *l'oro*.

21. George Herbert, "The Forerunners," ll. 12-13, 19-20, in *The Works of George Herbert*, ed. F. E. Hutchinson (Oxford at the Clarendon Press, 1941, reprint ed., 1970), p. 176.

The Descent from Bliss: *"Troilus" III. 1310-1582*

by Winthrop Wetherbee

"O deere herte, may it be
That this be soth, that ye ben in this place?"
"Ye, herte myn, god thanke I of his grace."

The "place" which Troilus and Criseyde occupy during the hundred or
so lines which follow the physical consummation of their love is the still
center of their experience in the poem. Between line 1309, in which
Criseyde, grown finally impatient, "welcomes" Troilus, and the cockcrow
of 1415-16, which reminds us again of the passage of time, the lovers are
"floating," suspended "bitwixen drede and sikernesse," and we are invited
to consider the implications of their reactions, and the narrator's, to this
state of suspension. To do so is to discover that the tranquillity of the scene
is deceptive and that it is charged, from the very moment of the
consummation, with hints of the finite, transitory and self-betraying
nature of the lovers' bliss. Throughout this portion of the poem Chaucer is
concerned to show the consequences of the materialization of their love.
The consummation is more than a translation of love into physical terms,
and its betrayal of Troilus's idealism has implications which Chaucer
points up by means of an elaborate pattern of allusion, bringing the
experience of Troilus into juxtaposition with that of the pilgrim of Dante's
Commedia, and setting off the moral and spiritual significance of his

betrayal with surrealistic intensity. It will be the purpose of this paper to trace the process by which Chaucer provides us with a gradually broadening perspective on the aftermath of the consummation, confirming and developing a series of hints which first appear in the form of a certain nameless anxiety in the mind of the narrator.

The narrator, indeed, plays a highly active role in this scene. While the lovers are coming gradually to terms with their new intimacy he is bothered by a need to justify his presence in some way. Again and again he claims that his language cannot do justice to this sublime moment, but he insists on defending the lovers and the supreme quality of their love against the potentially demoralizing forces of fear, detraction and the insensitivity of "wrecches." He says nothing which cannot be construed as in some sense affirmative of the lovers' bliss, but he seems incapable of affirming it in a wholly unequivocal way. Like Troilus, the narrator has felt intense anxiety in looking forward to this moment; unlike Troilus he is left deeply unsatisfied by the consummation of their common desire.

I think we may understand the narrator's difficulty as a failure to discover in himself the note of feeling appropriate to the celebration of the union he has described. In a curiously anticlimactic conclusion to the praise of love in the Proem to Book Three he had appealed to Venus for "sentement," a capacity to appreciate the "swetnesse" of love, and then summoned Calliope to help him describe it in a worthy way:[1]

> For now is nede; sestow nat my destresse,
> How I mot telle anon right the gladness
> Of Troilus, to Venus heryinge?   (III. 46–48)

This same "distress" appears in the narrator's behavior in the present scene. The moment has arrived toward which all his faithful service in the cause of love has been directed, and he *must* respond in a way which shows that his faith and hope have been rewarded. Given the desperate, obsessive nature of his commitment, anything less than total affirmation is unthinkable, but he cannot, it seems, bring forth such a response.

A hint of the difficulty appears in the final couplet of the stanza in which the narrator first responds to the consummation:

> That nyght, bitwixen drede and sikernesse,
> They felte in love the grete worthynesse. (III. 1315–16)

There is surely something blunt and vaguely unsatisfying about "the grete worthynesse," whether we hear behind it the more resonant "ultimo valore" of the corresponding line in the *Filostrato* (3. 32. 8), or are simply led by the movement of the stanza itself to expect in the concluding phrase a suggestion of something unique and supreme. Harder to assess, but again not so positive as we might expect in its implications, is the placing of the lovers "bitwixen drede and sikernesse." On the one hand this phrase reminds us of Troilus's long journey from fatalism and self-doubt to his present happiness; on the other it hints at the element of tension, a combination of hope and fear, that is both part of the emotional pleasure of erotic love and a symptom of its instability. From the perspective of the anxious narrator, the words hint at a falling short, a failure to attain a sure hold on happiness.

The lovers of course show no conscious awareness of any such misgivings and the narrator is left to cope with his own hopes and fears in solitude, wilfully denying the "drede" which continues to haunt him. It is the effect of this conflict that flaws the attempt at affirmation in the following stanza, which includes the narrator's wish to have sold his soul for one night, for the least part of such joy as he imagines the lovers to share. The spiritual emptiness of this quasi-prayer reminds us of the "derknesse," cut off from any hope of love's joy, in which the narrator had languished at the opening of Book One;[2] and when he turns immediately to fend off "thow foule daunger and thow feere," we can see him beset by the devils of his own self-doubt.

The impasse at which the narrator has arrived is illustrated more clearly by his second major intrusion into the scene, an attack on those whose materialism disqualifies them to appreciate love's *vertu*. Two of the three stanzas of this diatribe are closely imitated from the *Filostrato* (3. 38–39); they constitute an effective rhetorical unit in themselves, and end resoundingly with the wish that God may bring these "wrecches" to grief and advance all true lovers (1371–72). Their effect is to make the third stanza, which is wholly Chaucer's, seem like an unpremeditated outburst on the part of the narrator. It merely repeats thoughts already expressed in the Boccaccian passage, and does so with what seems an uncalled-for vehemence:

> As wolde god, thise wrecches that dispise
> Servise of love, hadde erys also longe
> As hadde Mida, ful of coveytise,
> And therto dronken hadde as hoot and stronge
> As Crassus dide for his affectis wronge,

To techen hem that coveytise is vice,
And love is vertu, though men holde it nyce. (III. 1373-79)

That Midas and Crassus are emblems of the sort of punishment
appropriate to covetousness might be sufficient to account for their
appearance here; but the vividness of their evocation in an otherwise
gratuitous passage calls attention to itself and invites us to consider their
possible relevance to the narrator's own situation. Midas, we should
recall, was given his long ears, not because of his greed, but because of the
insensitivity which led him to prefer the song of Pan to that of Apollo.[3] He
was also greedy, of course, and for this was punished in a way which,
though not fatal, resembled the punishment of Crassus.[4] The common
element in his two-fold exemplary role is a sensibility so denatured as to
be incapable of distinguishing among the things which attract it: the ass's
ears merely confirm the insensitivity symbolized by his golden touch and
by the fate of Crassus, which reduces all pleasure to a common,
chronically unsatisfying materialism.

Chaucer's narrator, though one may cite inexperience in extenuation
of his fault, is guilty of a similar failure of sensibility. Alienated by his
chronic "unlikeliness" from a direct experience of love, he has tried to
appropriate to his own needs the love of Troilus and Criseyde, only to find
himself excluded from the feast, unable to buy the smallest part of their
pleasure. The imagery of food and commerce suggests the source of his
difficulty, the "coveytise" that flaws his idealistic view of love as
paradise. Because of this he has failed to appreciate the deeper
implications of his own quasi-religious rhetoric or the truly religious
attitude of Troilus. At the same time he is blind to the way in which the
materialization of the love itself has betrayed his idealism and exposed the
materialism which contaminates it in the very process of granting
fulfillment to his hopes. As a result he is suspended in an emotional and
rhetorical vacuum, and expresses his frustration at his inability to
participate imaginatively in the love he beholds by attacking Midas and
Crassus, whose punishments constitute a perverted image of their
materialism and his own.[5]

Though at first sight it is difficult to see a connection between the
narrator's experience and that of the lovers, the complex effects of love's
becoming physical serve to link them. The lovers feel no misgivings about
the security or value of what they have attained, and the emphasis in their
description is on joy throughout the scene, but Chaucer makes us
continually aware that the experience which has proven so strangely

unrewarding for the narrator has entailed as well an inevitable diminishment of the meaning which love can now hold for Troilus. In the five stanzas which intervene between the narrator's apology for his language and his outburst against the covetous, we may see Chaucer unobtrusively but clearly defining the boundaries which will henceforth contain his hero. In the first of these both lovers seek to reassure themselves, fearful "lest al this thyng but nyce dremes were" (1328). In the second Troilus, able now to gaze unfalteringly at Criseyde, is brought to the realization that all he had dreamed of is now present "in this place." In confirmation of this, Criseyde kisses him, with the result that "where his spirit was, for joie he nyste" (1337).

The contrast in this stanza between Criseyde's confident assertiveness and Troilus's continuing wonder, and the fact that he experiences a sense of *dis*location as his state is localized, point to the lingering effect of his earlier vision of Criseyde. The "aungelik" aspect of her beauty, the Paradise which men might behold in her eyes have been incarnated once and for all in an object of physical desire: like Jay Gatsby, Troilus has "wed his unutterable visions to her perishable breath." But the spiritual element in his fascination with her is still active, and expresses itself in a vague puzzlement about his situation which complements the lurking anxiety of the narrator. The pattern of recognition followed by wonder is repeated in the next stanza, where Troilus kisses the eyes of Criseyde and acknowledges that his woe was caused by nothing more than the power of their "humble nettes" to ensnare him,[6] only to be drawn into reflection again by the complex effect of her beauty:

> Though ther be mercy writen in youre cheere,
> God woot the text ful hard is, soth, to fynde;
> How koude ye withouten bond me bynde?
>
> (III. 1342-44)

Two partial answers to the question of line 1344 are provided by the next two stanzas: in the first Troilus embraces Criseyde again and sighs with pleasure;[7] in the second he and Criseyde act out a mock betrothal, as symbolically appropriate to Troilus's fidelity as it is ironically predictive of the failure of Criseyde's. But the more serious question raised in the passage just quoted, and one to which the present scene cannot provide an answer, is that of the nature of the "mercy" promised by Criseyde's beauty, and how its message is conveyed by that beauty. The face that Troilus sees, the eyes he has just kissed, both are and are not the "text" in which he has seemed to read so much. Just before the moment of consummation he had kissed Criseyde and felt himself borne aloft by a "mercy" beyond his power to deserve (1282–83), a feeling essentially continuous with the soaring ecstasy of his prayer to "Benigne love." Now kissing her confirms for him the granting of a mercy somehow different, less uplifting, more palpable, just as the curious sense of being "bound" here implies a constraint not present in his earlier intuition of love as the "holy bond of thynges."[8]

What Troilus has encountered without realizing it is the finitude of an experience of love in which the impulse to physical consummation has become dominant, so that its emotional intensity is now subject to a desire which ebbs and flows. The final three stanzas of this section of Book Three bring Troilus's experience into conjunction with that of the narrator by showing both the effects on the lovers of a love now made physical, and also the problems of expression it poses. Two of these stanzas are in effect two versions of a single stanza of the *Filostrato* (3. 40); in each the lovers review the history of "wo and feere" that has led to the present happiness. At the end of the first the narrator comments:

> . . . but al that hevynesse,
> I thanke it god, was torned to gladnesse. (III. 1385–86)

The second ends with the lovers uniting their efforts

> For to recoveren blisse and ben at eise,
> And passed wo with joie countrepeise. (III. 1392–93)

The nearly exact repetition in the movement of the two stanzas illustrates the closed circle within which the lovers' emotions now operate. And in the next stanza, which concludes the scene, the narrator can say no more of the night as a whole than that

> It was byset in joie and besynesse
> Of al that souneth into gentilesse. (III. 1399–1400)

As with "the grete worthinesse" a hundred lines earlier, there is a vagueness about the concluding abstract "gentilesse," a diffusion of potential energy in euphemism and generality which sums up in itself the problem that has bedevilled the narrator throughout the scene. At every point where a strong affirmative phrase has been called for he has undergone a momentary inability to focus clearly on the lovers' experience, and a consequent failure of rhetoric. It all happened, he assures us, yet somehow he "kan nat tellen al," and we may see in the contrast between his suspension in abstractions and the lovers' concrete engagement with one another a parodic resemblance to the way in which Troilus's scrupulous courtliness had insulated him from the realities of sexual intrigue earlier in Book Three. Formerly disqualified by his insensitivity from doing justice to the lovers' initial raptures, the narrator now appears incapable of reexalting by his powers of idealization a love which has subsided naturally into the rhythm of physical desire.

At this point the narrator steps forward to deliver a two stanza apology for his role.[9] He has, he declares, presented the gist of his author's meaning, and anything he may have added "at loves reverence" (1405) is subject to correction by those more fortunate than he, who "felyng han in loves art" (1410) and who will thus know how to edit and interpret for themselves what he has written. The phrases I have quoted suggest the two separate levels on which the passage may be understood: it is at once a rueful confession of the narrator's inadequacy to his task and at the same time a reminder that the poem has expressed a reverence for love, and an astuteness about the art that love involves, of which the narrator is almost wholly unaware.[10] What he has added to Boccaccio's narrative "at loves reverence" ranges from the invocation of *divinus amor* in the Proem of Book Three to the ingenuity with which the blissful night is prepared by Pandarus; it includes the elaboration of Troilus's visionary experience and his own less successful attempts at sublimity. In all of these areas what he has told us goes far beyond his conscious purposes, and it is his dim awareness of this that leads him to bid his audience accept his good intentions and "doth therwithal right as youre selven leste" (1407).[11] The openness with which he acknowledges his incapacity resembles the diffidence of Troilus, who has at one moment "putte al in goddes hond," and at another urged Criseyde to guide him lest he do her "displeasaunce" through his ignorance. But while Troilus is only confused as to the relation of the sensual and the visionary in his experience, the narrator, as we have seen, has failed to make contact with either.

What is hardest to detect in the passage, though it is finally of the utmost importance for the poem's meaning, is the sense in which it marks a stage in the evolution of the narrator's experience of his story. By pointing to the coexistence in the poem of widely diverging attitudes toward love and by its appeal to the reader's "felyng" it recalls the

narrator's wholly unconscious shifts of emphasis in the Proem to Book
One and his misgivings about "sentement" at the opening of Book Two,
and shows him concerned to deal with the inconsistencies he senses. And
while his extraordinary abrogation of responsibility at this crucial
moment shows how far he has yet to go, it is worth noting that the very
lines in which the abrogation takes place (1411–14) contain a clear
allusion forward to the moment at the poem's close when his attitude
toward the language of the poem, and his responsibility for it, will
undergo a complete reversal.

For the moment, of course, the narrator will continue to be deluded in
his view of love. Before going on to the complex aftermath of the
consummation scene I would like to look briefly ahead to the final, and
perhaps the most striking, juxtaposition of the narrator's experience with
that of the lovers in Book Three. This occurs in the course of his account
of their second night together, which gave them a thousand times more
pleasure than the first:

> And bothe, ywys, they hadde, and so they wende,
> As much joie as herte may comprende.
>
> This is no litel thyng of for to seye;
> This passeth every wit for to devyse;
> For eche of hem gam otheres lust obeye;
> Felicite, which that thise clerkes wise
> Comenden so, ne may nat here suffise.
> This joie may nat writen be with inke;
> This passeth al that herte may bythynke. (III. 1686–94)

This is the narrator's final attempt in the poem to speak of the love as
such, and we may note that the stanza just quoted contains four separate
declarations of the impossibility of doing so. Indeed the protestation of
inadequacy is so overwhelming as almost to obscure the reference to the
lovers themselves, which appears rather unclimactically in the third line
of the stanza, and which defines what is in fact the high point of their
love, the point at which their capacity for emotional fulfillment is
precisely circumscribed (and, for the moment, satisfied) by the limits of
physical pleasure.[12] It is a moment of considerable importance for later
developments in the story, but its significance is all but ignored by the
narrator at this point. Nothing in the poem better illustrates his
"unlikely" relation to love than the remarkable disjunction between the

"joie" of the lovers, which is satisfyingly commensurate with their hearts' desire (1686-87), and the narrator's insistence that this joy exceeds the heart's power to conceive (1694). As the lovers' pleasure approaches its peak the narrator is excluded from the sphere of their communion to the point at which his rhetoric ceases to bear any relation to their experience. While they have passed from an initial awe and uncertainty to an increasing appreciation of physical "suffisaunce," he has moved away from his initial desperate attempts to grasp some sense of their pleasure to the point at which he now celebrates a "felicity" that is wholly of his own imagining.

* * * * * * * * * * * *

The crowing of the cock (1415-16) introduces the elaborate *alba* or dawn-song sequence which organizes the lovers' leave-taking. The series of formal song-speeches in which they condemn departing night and oncoming day, and exchange protestations of dependence and fidelity, has several functions. Most obviously its slow ritual progress withdraws us in a gradual way from the sphere of lyric "joie" which is the literal and imaginative center of the poem. It also enables us to experience the lovers' anxious awareness of the tenuousness of their hold on joy, as the inexorable movement of departing night threatens them with exposure, and danger and fear are projected in the image of the sun's innumerable bright eyes.[13] An inevitable moral tension is present as well: we see Troilus, like John Donne, repudiating all claims of enterprise or responsibility in favor of a clandestine love which he identifies with life itself.

Chaucer's introduction of the *alba* sequence as a source of perspective at this point has rightly been recognized as the fulfillment of the capacities of this poetic genre, an important achievement in itself,[14] but his insight into the potential implications of the form is no more striking than the freedom with which he adapts it to his purposes. As I will suggest further on, the full meaning of the scene appears only when it is viewed as bracketed by the image of *Fortuna maior* which introduces it (1419-20) and by the following scene between Criseyde and Pandarus (1548-82), but Chaucer has also made a number of significant adjustments within the scene itself. Throughout it is the lady, Criseyde, who maintains the initiative, accepting the necessity for parting and ministering to the feeling of Troilus, whose role resembles that commonly assigned to the lady in *alba* tradition.[15] It is he who feels most strongly and expresses most vividly the pain of separation, and who inveighs most recklessly against the encroachment of reality; and it is his feeling which provides a source of continuity between this scene and the remainder of Book Three.

Chaucer's special purpose is clear from the opening stanza of the sequence, spoken by Criseyde. This introduces a denunciation of departing night which is fully in keeping with the demands of the genre (1427–42), but contains one couplet which is pure Criseyde:

> For tyme it is to ryse and hennes go,
> Or ellis I am lost for evere mo.[16] (III. 1425–26)

Though there are no more such nuggets of pragmatism in the scene, these lines are enough to revive our sense of Criseyde's practical and self-protective instincts, and to show her continual awareness of an outside world which Troilus, by contrast, wilfully ignores. He senses the note of finality in her song, and it is her words that make him feel "the blody teris from his herte melte" (1445), eliciting his song against the sun and its light. The stress on Criseyde's role, and on her words in particular, in inaugurating the sequence and catalyzing Troilus's response is important, for it shows us the extent to which his sense of reality is subject to her influence. With no further prompting Troilus passes from invective to reflections on his own hapless condition, cut off as he soon will be from "al the lyf ich have" (1477), and finally appeals to Crideyde for confirmation of her love for him. Her long protestation of fidelity, prefaced by " a sigh" and heavily freighted with appeals to God to witness her sincerity, forces upon us the sense that we, and Troilus, have nothing to rely on but her words, and their assurance

> That erst shal Phebus fallen fro his spere,
> And everich egle ben the haukes feere,
> And every roche out of his place sterte,
> Or Troilus out of Criseydes herte. (III. 1495–98)

The imagery of this promise is charged with irony: it hints ominously at the destruction of the city, and perhaps looks forward as well to the disappearance of Phoebus which will introduce the moment in Book Five when Criseyde resolves to accept the love of Diomede (V. 1016–17), who is, in the end, the eagle foreshadowed by her dream.[17] On this larger pattern of events depends the survival of Troilus's image, "grave" in

Criseyde's heart (1499) as though by one of those engravers of "smale selys" mentioned a moment earlier by Troilus himself, as having some use for that daylight which is so hateful to lovers (1461–62). The image is almost certainly taken from *Ecclesiasticus*,[18] where such engravers appear in a catalogue of artisans whose work absorbs all their attention: they work "by night as well as by day" and their work is skilful, but their absorption in it disqualifies them for the pursuit of wisdom and the exercise of political leadership.

The image of Troilus in Criseyde's heart is aptly represented by such a seal — unique and beautiful, but finally negotiable, like the brooch which she will give to Diomede. I think we may see this small hard image at the center as pointing up the significance of the *alba* sequence as a whole, an intricate ritual with no permanent meaning. By a further extension the two images of engraving may be seen as an implicit comment on the whole elaborate enterprise that has come to fulfillment in Book Three. Troilus and the narrator alike have committed themselves wholly to a union which, once realized in physical terms, becomes a mere *signaculum*, a material image of their hopes and ideals. It mocks the narrator's desire like Midas's golden food; and it repays Troilus's genuine "trouthe" with a promise of fidelity which will prove as meaningless as the rings and jewelry with which the lovers have ratified it when larger forces and events — the proper concern of wise men and governors of cities — conspire to dissolve it.

* * * * * * * * * * * *

In a brief coda to the *alba* scene Chaucer, following Boccaccio, shows us the lovers reacting in isolation to their experience. Troilus returns home and goes to bed, seeking in vain "to slepe longe, as he was wont to doone" (1536). This detail, inevitably anticlimactic after the intensity of his involvement in the scene just concluded, seems intended to suggest something of the adolescent innocence which still lingers about him as he enters the world of adult passion. If it carries a hint of mockery it also reminds us of the idealism which sustains that innocence, and it is this which dominates his feelings as he lies awake,

Thynkyng how she, for whom desir hym brende,
A thousand fold was worth more than he wende. (III. 1539–40)

"Desir" is a constant element in his feelings now (1531, 1539, 1546), but as he reflects on his memory of Criseyde's words and presence (1541–46) the contemplative element in his love is renewed, and we recall his feelings on first beholding Criseyde in Book One (295–98, 361–71). The desire he feels is reinforced by a newly aroused lust, but in his contemplative mood he does not notice it (1546–47).

Criseyde too finds herself "wel bisette," but characteristically she is better able to isolate the components of her satisfaction with Troilus, which include his "lust" along with his "gentilesse" (1551), and which bring her "desir" to focus on the specific object of a second meeting. Throughout this brief section Chaucer makes relatively few alterations in Boccaccio's account of the lovers' feelings,[19] but those he does make are quietly telling. In itself the single stanza devoted to Criseyde would scarcely interrupt the sustained emphasis on Troilus's exaltation to which Chaucer, following Boccaccio, devotes most of the remainder of Book Three; but when it is followed immediately by the wholly Chaucerian scene of her interview with Pandarus, its unobtrusive emphasis on the relatively more concrete nature of her pleasure in love becomes more suggestive.

Pandarus appears the next morning while Criseyde is still in bed, and by his bantering quickly reduces her from indignation to a kind of coquettishness. He then proceeds to thrust himself upon her with increasing urgency, rummaging under the bedclothes, proffering his "sword" and finally kissing her, before the narrator steps in to divert our attention:

> I passe al that which nedeth nought to seye,
> What! god foryaf his deth, and she also
> Foryaf, and with hire uncle gan to pleye,
> For oother cause was ther non than so.
> But of this thing right to theffect to go,
> Whan tyme was, hom to hire hous she wente,
> And Pandarus hath hoolly his entente. (III. 1576–82)

As always, we may take the narrator's tone of hearty reassurance here as a sign that he has missed the point: phrases like "I passe al that," and "right to theffect to go," which had earlier expressed his eagerness to hasten on the sexual climax, are now used in an attempt to gloss over what is taking place between Criseyde and her uncle. The high good humor of "What! god foryaf his deth" fails to obscure the glaring ambiguity and potential blasphemy of the phrase in this context, and the conclusiveness of the final line obviously raises more questions than it answers. But there is no sure way to determine the object of Pandarus' "entente" here; we cannot tell just what takes place between uncle and niece and we do not need to: the real meaning of the scene is in the utter betrayal of Troilus which it represents, the travesty of his pure devotion in its combination of blatant innuendo with suggestions of blasphemy.

Whatever we make of this final triumph of Pandarus's "entente," [20] the bald suggestiveness of the scene is clearly unique in the poem, a departure from the prevailing courtly decorum fully as striking as Troilus's earlier appropriation of the climactic prayer of Dante's *Paradiso* to express his ecstacy just before the consummation of his love (III. 1262-67). I think we may see the two moments as balancing one another, and as defining the terms within which Troilus's precarious destiny is enacted. It is also possible, I think, to see the opposition between them as itself defined by a complex structure of allusions to Dante, a sustained ironic parallelling of Troilus's experience with that of Dante in the central portions of the *Commedia*. This continual allusion is never allowed to dominate the surface action of the *Troilus*, but serves to expand the implications of that action, and invites us to see a deeper meaning in moments which we might have tended to view as simply comic or sentimental. I am aware that the analysis offered in the following pages will appear to some as an exercise in overreading, and I must ask the reader's indulgence for linkages between Chaucer and Dante which may at first seem farfetched, in the hope that they will appear more plausible when viewed as part of a larger pattern.

Within its immediate context as part of the aftermath of the consummation scene the Pandarus-Criseyde episode carries forward an allusion to Dante's *Purgatorio* which had been initiated by the reference to *Fortuna maior* at the opening of the *alba* sequence. The source of this reference is *Purgatorio* 19, where it introduces Dante's dream of the Siren, a female figure who is grotesquely malformed and inarticulate until endowed with beauty and eloquence by the effect of fleshly desire on Dante's imaginative perception of her (Purg. 19. 10-15). She sings seductively to him until the sudden appearance of a *donna santa*, at whose admonition Vergil seizes her and tears away her garments to expose the foulness within. Dante awakes at the shock of this and finds himself in broad daylight.

The sequence of events provides a broad parallel to those which follow the consummation scene in the *Troilus*. The image of *Fortuna maior* is

followed immediately by Criseyde's singing of an *alba* or dawn-song
which corresponds to the Siren's song of enticement in Dante. Over the
next hundred lines we see Troilus gradually coming to terms with the
physical presence and appearance of Criseyde, and allowing his vision of
divine love to be subverted by desire, which keeps him suspended in the
bonds of his attraction to her and cuts him off from an awareness of other
cares and duties. Finally Pandarus's grossly sexual address to Criseyde
and his "prying" at her body beneath the bedclothes correspond to
Vergil's baring of the Siren's corruption, with the significant difference
that his episode takes place wholly outside the sphere of Troilus's
consciousness and exposes his deluded sense of Criseyde's worth without
in any way disabusing him of it. Pandarus's own situation, of course, is
also set in ironic contrast to Vergil's: where Vergil, awakening Dante with
a brisk "surgi e vieni," had urged him toward the terrace where avarice
and prodigality are purged (35–36), Pandarus is here acting out his own
covetous design on the lovers' bliss, mirroring a greed and materialism
which the narrator had already dimly sensed as a potential contaminant
of his own participation in their happiness.[21]

But reference to the Siren episode defines only one of the levels on
which allusion to Dante is operative here. The fuller significance of the
scene lies in its function as part of an extended parody which sets the
central portion of Book Three of the *Troilus* in contrast to the cantos
which describe Dante's experience at the summit of Purgatory. This
section of the *Commedia*, centering on the appearance of Beatrice and
constituting what Charles Singleton has called "the pattern at the
center,"[22] may be said to begin with Dante's emergence from the fire
which purges lust, guided and drawn forward by Vergil's assurance that
Beatrice awaits him beyond. Its climax is the vision of Beatrice herself,
followed by the harsh catechizing which precedes Dante's reunion with
her, and it concludes for our purposes with the pageant of the history of
the Church which prepares for Beatrice's prophecy of deliverance.

The parody begins with the prelude to the consummation scene, when
Pandarus, having seen to the bedding down of his guests, comes to
summon Troilus to the "hevene blisse" that awaits him in Criseyde's
chamber. The comic exchange which follows, in which Pandarus is forced
to cope with Troilus's unanticipated misgivings, corresponds very
broadly to Dante's account of the final speech of Vergil in *Purgatorio* 27
and his own reaction to it. Vergil's words, a summary of Dante's moral
progress up to this point, confirm the stability and right orientation of his
reason and will, his readiness for spiritual experience and the uselessness

of any further guidance from Vergil himself. Pandarus, by contrast, can only exclaim at the helplessness of his recalcitrant pupil, who lapses perversely from action into contemplation as he draws closer to the promised bliss, and who is incapable of self-determination.

Like Pandarus, Vergil begins with a promise of bliss and the satisfaction of all longing. At his words Dante is overcome by "desire upon desire" and feels himself on the point of taking wing (121–23). Troilus's response to Pandarus's equivalent announcement of bliss and his promise that "it shal be right as thow wolt desire" (709) is one of near panic: in place of Dante's sense of undergoing a metamorphosis of desire (123) we have Troilus's catalogue of hapless mortals pursued in love by gods, centering around the transformation of Daphne, who "laurer wax for drede" (727). And where Vergil concludes by commending Dante's reconstituted will, "libero, dritto e sano," bids him take his own *piacere* as his guide and bestows upon him the "crown and mitre" of self-command (131, 140–42) Pandarus is compelled to rebuke the "wrecched mouses herte" of his disciple, throw a fur robe over his shirt and literally drag him into Criseyde's presence (736–42).

The difference between the two lovers' relations with their guides is pointed up again when Troilus is brought face to face with his lady and finds that he can no longer depend on his mentor for reassurance. Where Vergil had withdrawn his support only after rendering Dante psychologically capable of enduring the agony of self-recognition he must undergo as Beatrice chastizes him, Pandarus has prepared for this confrontation by inventing the story that Troilus suspects Criseyde of having given her love to "Horaste" (792–98). Faced with Criseyde's elaborate display of grief at his suspicion, Troilus is utterly demoralized. In place of Dante's powerful expression of sorrow and love in response to Vergil's sudden disappearance (*Purg.* 30. 49–54) we see Troilus forced to the inescapable recognition that through his involvement with Pandarus he is guilty of complicity in a plot both dishonest and, worse, unsuccessful:

> "O Pandarus," thoughte he, "allas, thi wile
> Serveth of nought, so weylaway the while." (III. 1077–78)

And where Dante finally comes to terms with the history of his pursuit of *false imagini* and is made to confess a guilt of which his whole previous experience in the *Commedia* conditions his awareness, Troilus, whose moral awareness has systematically subverted, can only disclaim responsibility for his role in the "game" that Pandarus has played (1084–85). Thus when he, like Dante, swoons under the pressure of his feelings, it is owing to a confused and inarticulate remorse, a conflict of feelings only dimly recognized, rather than the vivid *riconoscenza* of Dante (*Purg.* 31.88). His moral dislocation is made worse by the fact that Criseyde is much less concerned with proving Troilus's character and submitting him to penance than with defending herself from suspicion, and when she miscalculates the effect of her tears, causing Troilus to swoon, she too becomes desperate. Thus, instead of the stern but all-confirming "ben son, ben son Beatrice," we are shown Criseyde bending over Troilus's inert body and promising him "in his ear"

> "Iwys, my dere herte, I am nat wroth,
> Have here my trouthe, and many another ooth;
> Now speke to me, for it am I Criseyde."
> But al for nought . . .   (III. 1110–13)

Where Beatrice rebukes Dante's moral childishness and admonishes him to live up to the manhood seemingly implied by his beard (*Purg.* 31. 61–69), confident that the shame will ultimately strengthen him, Criseyde's chiding of Troilus ("is this a mannes game?" 1126) merely exposes the hapless innocence in which he had been led to play the "childissh jalous" (1168).

But the swoon, for Troilus as for Dante, is a *rite de passage:* Dante revives to see the face of Matelda moving above him as she bears him through the absolving stream (31. 91–96), Troilus to find himself in bed, with Criseyde doing "al hir peyne" to bring him around (1118–20). Dante's absolution from his old error is symbolized by his emergence from the stream into the dance of the Cardinal Virtues, who "cover him with their arms" as they dance about him (31. 103–5); that of Troilus, more simply, by the gesture of Criseyde herself:

> hire arm over hym she leyde,
> And al foryaf . . .[23]   (III. 1128–29)

Though Troilus will require some further assurance of his forgiveness, his emergence from Purgatory to a state of readiness to receive the promised bliss is essentially complete at this point. It is easy enough to trace the arc of his *paradiso*, the intensity of feeling which rises to issue in his beautiful prayer to divine love before descending into physical lovemaking. Here I wish only to suggest how the scene between Pandarus and Criseyde completes the pattern of allusion to the *Purgatorio*, exposing both Pandarus and Criseyde as utterly incapable of living up to Troilus's lofty conception of what they have given him.

In *Purgatorio* 32, after a second loss of consciousness, Dante awakens to see again Matelda, who points out Beatrice, transformed from her earlier almost unendurable splendor to reappear as the reflected glory of truth revealed, the guiding wisdom of the Church in the world, seated on the bare ground and guarding the chariot which is the image of the Church. She grants Dante a vision of the earthly history of the Church, represented as a series of violations visited upon the chariot itself (*Purg.* 32. 109–60). A diving eagle strikes the chariot, causing it to roll like a ship in a storm; a ravenous fox tries to enter it but is repelled by Beatrice; the eagle reappears and enters, leaving the car adorned with his plumage; a dragon comes out of the earth and breaks open the bottom of the car. Then the chariot itself is transformed into a monster; a harlot appears seated on its back, attended by a giant who kisses her repeatedly until, when she looks lustfully at Dante, he beats her from head to foot and finally drags both monster and harlot away into the forest.

Such densely symbolic panoramas are a temptation for the medievalist, who tends to see in them what he most wants to see. And it would be an arbitrary exercise at best to seek any too precise relation between this vision and the events of the *Troilus*. Nonetheless I would suggest a broad parallel between Dante's imagery and that which the *Troilus*, by various means, concentrates around the person and bed of Criseyde. As the repeated violations of the Church lead to its corruption and finally the Babylonian captivity of the Avignon papacy, so the equivalent images in the *Troilus* trace the effects of the encroachments of Pandarus, Troilus, Diomede and history itself on the freedom and integrity of Criseyde.

Like the chariot of Dante's vision, Criseyde is first "violated" by the eagle of her dream,[24] then with increasing importunity by Pandarus and at last by Troilus. Criseyde's union with Troilus, I would suggest, corresponds to the second descent of Dante's eagle upon the chariot. Representative originally of the endowment of the Church with temporal goods, it is equivalent in Chaucer's scheme to the materialization of love; without in itself involving any base motive (Dante himself concedes that the "feathering" of the chariot had been done "perhaps with sincere and kind intent" 138) the union nonetheless marks a stage in a process of corruption by material things which leads to eventual harlotry.

Pandarus's role is easily enough related to that of the heretics and false counsellors who corrupt the Church from within by claiming to speak with true authority, and whom Dante represents by the fox, "starved of all good food" (120), who seeks to enter the chariot. It is this scene, I think, that Chaucer is recalling as he describes Pandarus's dealing with Criseyde on the morning after the consummation. Like Beatrice, Criseyde recognizes Pandarus for what he is — "fox that ye ben" she calls him (1565) — and recognizes the danger of his "wordes white" (1567); but she has already acquiesced in his design on her, and the scene in which he reveals the effects of his "starvation" by seeking to act out that design in his own person, literally or symbolically, merely confirms its corrupting effect.

The remaining events of Dante's vision, the dragon's damaging of the chariot, its metamorphosis, and the final scene of harlot and giant, may be loosely correlated with the disruptive events of the war and Criseyde's later, far more compromising submission to the aggressive and cynical Diomede. These specific matters are less important than the broad Dantean pattern of which they form a part, which enables us to gauge the dimensions of Troilus's experience of love and recognize the seriousness with which Chaucer views both the love and its betrayal. The point of this elaborate borrowing from the *Commedia*, the casting of Pandarus as arch-heretic, Criseyde as Siren and harlot and her bed as a mock-church, is not simply to condemn their moral and spiritual blindness, though we should certainly be warned by it not to let sentimentality obscure our awareness of these failings. Its primary function is to provide a setting in which to consider the love of Troilus for itself, and the identification of these lesser characters with evil archetypes becomes meaningful only to the extent that we see Troilus's vision of love as comparable to Dante's. Chaucer has appropriated the resources of the greatest Christian poet to show us through Troilus's experience what human love is in itself and what, being only human, it cannot be; what rich spiritual capacities are implied by its aspirations and how inevitable it is that any worldly attachment, taken too seriously, will betray these aspirations. The scene between Pandarus and Criseyde completes the pattern at the center of the *Troilus* both by giving us a powerful image of the violation of Troilus's devotion and by setting this violation in an allusive context which makes it not simply a human betrayal but the desecration of something at least potentially divine. It exposes in the most forceful way the emptiness at the heart of Troilus's love, the failure of that love to integrate the spiritual and physical elements in his experience. There is no meaningful connection between the Criseyde of Troilus's vision and the Criseyde who incarnates that vision: the pattern at the center of the *Troilus* has no true center, no transforming event to offset the steady descent from vision into materiality. The Dantean parallel makes us aware of this absence where Chaucer's hapless and self-deceived narrator could not have done so, and by forcing us to view Troilus's betrayal in a context which emphasizes its enormity, provides an intimation of what we and the narrator will finally come to realize as the true spiritual dimensions of the poem. But this final discovery will take place only after Troilus himself his lived through the consequences of his betrayal and come to his own posthumous realization that "felicite," whatever it may be, is something different from the love of Criseyde.

Notes

1. The text for all quotations from the *Troilus* is that of R.K. Root (Princeton, 1926).

2. The effect of the narrator's prayer is very different from that of the passage which may have suggested it, *Fil.* 2. 88. 7-8, where Troiolo, apostrophizing the absent Criseida in a speech to Pandaro, declares "or stess'io teco una notte d'inverno,/ cento cinquanta poi stessi in inferno" ("might I stay one winter night with thee, I would then stay one hundred and fifty in hell").

3. Ovid, *Metamorphoses* 11. 146-79.

4. See Ovid's account of the aurification of Midas' food and drink, *Metamorphoses* 11. 119-30.

5. Cp. the use of the story of Midas in *Canterbury Tales* D 952-82, where the Wyf of Bath, seeking to derive a different exemplum from it, ends by exposing the chronic materialism which has motivated her own sexual career.

   Midas and Crassus are both named in the song of the souls being purged of avarice in *Purgatorio* 20. 106, 116-17. We are told that the zeal (*affezion*) of each soul against its own greed determines how loudly it sings (118-20). It is perhaps the *Troilus* narrator's lurking sense of being somehow implicated in his own reference to the "affectis wronge" of Crassus (1391) that makes him speak with such *affezion* in denouncing him.

6. Earlier Criseyde's "eyen clere" (1353) had been invoked in an almost religious way: see 3. 128-30 and cp. the invocation of Venus's "bemes clere" in the opening line of Book Three.

7. It is, however, worth noting the difference between Troilus's sighs, which "shewed his affeccioun withinne," and the "pious" sighs of Boccaccio's lovers (3.37.6), which also purport to show "the affection which dwelt in their breasts," but which in fact are just a prelude to the renewal of intercourse. Chaucer plays down the inward quality of Troilus's feeling and at the same time suspends overt sexual activity, and so conveys more convincingly the impression of a balance between internal and merely physical feeling.

8. On the different levels at which the imagery of bondage operates in the poem and the

interplay between them, see the fine discussion of Stephen A. Barney, "Troilus Bound," *Speculum* 47 (1972): 451–58. Barney, however, does not consider the striking suggestions of a transcendent, contemplative experience of love in Troilus's prayer at III. 1254–74, and sees the reference there to the "holy bond of thynges" only as anticipating the prayer in his later Boethian hymn (III. 1765–71; Barney, p. 454). But the point of the later hymn is largely to show how Troilus's earlier vision of divine love has been combined (and confused) with his subsequent experience of bondage.

9. The placement of these stanzas at this point is a distinguishing feature of the "Beta" text of the poem, which Root considered the most nearly authoritative; editors since Robinson have printed them in a slightly altered form as 1324–37. Charles A. Owen, Jr. defends the "B" reading, largely on the grounds of dramatic propriety, in "Mimetic Form in the Central Love Scene of *Troilus and Criseyde*," *Modern Philology* 67 (1969–70): 132; on the linguistic and metrical superiority of the "B" text generally see his "Minor Changes in Chaucer's *Troilus and Criseyde*," in *Chaucer and Middle English Studies in Honor of Rossell Hope Robbins*, ed. Beryl Rowland (London, 1974), pp. 302–19 (on the passage under discussion, pp. 314–18); also Daniel Cook, "The Revision of Chaucer's *Troilus*: the *Beta* Text," *Chaucer Review* 9 (1974–75): 51–62.

10. See Ida L. Gordon, *The Double Sorrow of Troilus*, (Oxford, 1970), pp. 78–80.

11. The line may recall the earlier apology of Pandarus for his role in preparing that night when, as he assures Troilus, "al shal ben right as thi selven liste" (III. 259); his misreading of Troilus's intentions exposes the limitations of his "felyng" as plainly as the present passage exposes those of the narrator's.

12. The negative implications of this depiction of fulfillment within strict limits are conveyed also by its context, an account of the lovers' second night together which presents it as largely a reenactment of the first, and which seems intended to expose the love itself as bound to the repetition of a single emotional cycle.

13. I am surely not the first to have sensed in these lines (1450–56), which show the lovers seeking to "wrye" or conceal their joy from a "spy," a power which relentlessly seeks it out, a subliminal awareness of the presence of Pandarus just offstage. Cp. 1555–82 and especially 1569–71, where Criseyde seeks to "wrye" herself under the bedclothes while Pandarus's hands "pry" at her.

14. See Jonathan Saville, *The Medieval Erotic Alba* (New York, 1972), pp. 213–14.

15. On this and other incongruities in Chaucer's use of the alba see Robert E. Kaske, "The Aube in Chaucer's *Troilus*," in *Chaucer Criticism*, ed. R. J. Schoeck and Jerome Taylor, 2 vols., (Notre Dame, 1960), 2: 167–79. On the conventional sexual roles which Chaucer adjusts, see Saville, *The Medieval Erotic Alba*, pp. 153–55.

16. As Kaske notes, "The Aube in Chaucer's Troilus," pp. 171–72, these lines are strikingly at variance with their counterparts in *Filostrato* 3.43 as well as with the *alba* convention, and Criseyda's request for further embraces in the same stanza of Boccaccio has no equivalent in *Troilus*.

17. The eagle-hawk imagery is perhaps recalled by the comparison of Criseyde to a falcon at III.1784. On the irony of the passage as a whole see Susan Schibanoff, "Criseyde's 'Impossible' Aubes," *JEGP* 76 (1977): 326–28; she suggests that the impossibilia cited by Criseyde to affirm her constancy would have reminded a medieval listener of the popular anti-feminist "lying-song," in which such formulae were used to illustrate the impossibility of a trustworthy woman.

18. See Kaske, "The Aube," p. 177, and *Ecclesiasticus* 38.28.

19. Lines 1534–40 follow closely *Fil.* 3.53, but Chaucer has omitted line 6, in which Troiolo recalls "il lasciato diletto." In *Fil.* 3.54 Troiolo by recalling "ciascuno atto" of the night just past arouses "amor forte" in himself, whereas "desire" and "lust" come over Troilus as he recalls, more broadly, Criseyde's "wordes alle, and every contenance" (1542). In *Filostrato* 3.55.3 the phrase "si fatto amante" sums up what in Chaucer becomes "his worthynesse, his lust, his dedes wise, /His gentilesse, and how she with hym mette" (1550–51). Chaucer seems clearly concerned to render Troilus's experience in more general terms than Troiolo's, and to emphasize the particularizing and analytical in Criseyde's response.

20. As P.F. Baum suggested, there is a sense in which line 1582 constitutes the climax of the poem: "After this," he observes, "there is no more laughter." See *Chaucer: A Critical Appreciation* (Durham, N.C., 1958), p. 147.

21. In a sense, of course, the narrator had commended Pandarus's enterprise by invoking "Janus, god of entre" on his behalf (II. 77), a line which is worth setting against Vergil's words on awakening Dante from his siren-dream: "troviam l'aperta per la qual tu entre" ("let us find the opening by which you may enter," *Purg.* 19.36).

22. *Commedia: Elements of Structure, (Dante Studies* 1, Cambridge, Mass., 1957), pp. 45–60.

23. John Gardner, *The Poetry of Chaucer* (Carbondale, Ill., 1977), p. 106, points out the importance of forgiveness in this portion of the poem (cp. III. 1106, 1178, 1182, and finally 1577–78), and suggests the parallel of the forgiveness of God, but does not seem to me to allow for the extent to which forgiveness serves as a way of easing Pandarus and the lovers over the moral hurdles.

24. Mario Praz, *The Flaming Heart* (New York, 1958), pp. 39–40, suggests a number of correspondences between the imagery of Criseyde's dream and that of the pageant of *Purg.* 32.

Index